# Living and dying at Auldhame, East Lothian

# Living and dying at Auldhame, East Lothian

*The excavation of an Anglian monastic settlement and medieval parish church*

ANNE CRONE and ERLEND HINDMARCH
*with Alex Woolf*

Jacket photography: engraving of Tantallon Castle by W H Lizars *c* 1849
(© Courtesy of RCAHMS. Licensor www.rcahms.gov.uk).
Back: artefact: © Trustees of National Museums Scotland

Published in 2016 in Great Britain by the Society of Antiquaries of Scotland

Society of Antiquaries of Scotland
National Museum of Scotland
Chambers Street
Edinburgh EH1 1JF
Tel: 0131 247 4115
Fax: 0131 247 4163
Email: administration@socantscot.org
Website: www.socantscot.org

The Society of Antiquaries of Scotland is a registered Scottish charity No. SC010440.

ISBN 978 1 90833 201 1

*British Library Cataloguing-in-Publication Data*
A catalogue record for this book is available from the British Library.

Copyright © contributors 2016

All rights reserved.

The authors and the Society of Antiquaries of Scotland gratefully acknowledge funding towards the publication of this volume from Historic Scotland and AOC Archaeology.

Design and production by Lawrie Law and Alison Rae
Typesetting by Waverley Typesetters, Warham, Norfolk
Manufactured in Serbia by Štamparija Grafostil

# CONTENTS

*Acknowledgements* ix

*List of Figures* xi

*List of Tables* xv

1 INTRODUCTION 1
   1.1 Structure of the monograph 1
   1.2 Geographical setting 1
   1.3 Archaeological discoveries around Auldhame 2
      1.3.1 Hamilton's excavations on the headland in 1949 6
   1.4 Fieldwork 2005 and 2008 7
      1.4.1 Introduction 7
      1.4.2 Walkover survey 9
      1.4.3 Evaluation 9
      1.4.4 Excavation 9
      1.4.5 Walkover survey 2008 10

2 THE EXCAVATED FEATURES 11
   2.1 Introduction 11
   2.2 The graveyard 11
      2.2.1 The extent of the graveyard 11
      2.2.2 Soils 13
   2.3 The chapel complex 14
      2.3.1 Introduction 14
      2.3.2 Building 1 16
      2.3.3 Building 2 16
      2.3.4 Building 3 16
      2.3.5 Building 4 17
   2.4 Burials 18
      2.4.1 Introduction 18
      2.4.2 Grave alignment 18
      2.4.3 Body position 20
      2.4.4 Grave type 20
      2.4.5 Grave markers 31
      2.4.6 Grave goods 31
      2.4.7 Gender and age 31

|  |  |  |  |
|---|---|---|---|
| | 2.5 | Other features | 31 |
| | | 2.5.1 Ditch 1 | 31 |
| | | 2.5.2 Zone 1 | 34 |
| | | 2.5.3 Zone 2 | 35 |
| | | 2.5.4 Zone 3 | 35 |
| | | 2.5.5 Zone 4 | 35 |
| | | 2.5.6 Zone 5 | 37 |
| 3 | CHRONOLOGY | | 41 |
| | 3.1 | Aims and objectives | 41 |
| | | 3.1.1 Constraints on the evidence and analytical approach  *John Barber* | 41 |
| | 3.2 | Results | 43 |
| | | 3.2.1 Phase 1: AD 650–1000 | 44 |
| | | 3.2.2 Phase 2: AD 1000–1200 | 49 |
| | | 3.2.3 Phase 3: AD 1200–1400 | 49 |
| | | 3.2.4 Phase 4: AD 1500–1700 | 49 |
| | | 3.2.5 The date of the buildings | 49 |
| | 3.3 | Summary | 50 |
| | | 3.3.1 Age and gender over time  *Melissa Melikian* | 51 |
| 4 | THE ARTEFACT ASSEMBLAGE | | 53 |
| | 4.1 | Anglo-Saxon | 53 |
| | | 4.1.1 Copper alloy  *Alice Blackwell* | 53 |
| | | 4.1.2 Glass  *Ewan Campbell* | 58 |
| | 4.2 | Viking | 61 |
| | | 4.2.1 The copper alloy belt set and associated organic materials  *Penelope Walton Rogers* | 61 |
| | | 4.2.2 The iron artefacts  *Andrew Heald and Caroline Paterson* | 64 |
| | 4.3 | Medieval and post-medieval | 68 |
| | | 4.3.1 Pottery  *Derek Hall* | 68 |
| | | 4.3.2 Copper alloy  *Dawn McLaren and Fraser Hunter* | 70 |
| | | 4.3.3 Silver  *Nicholas M McQ Holmes* | 74 |
| | | 4.3.4 Iron  *Dawn McLaren and Fraser Hunter* | 75 |
| | | 4.3.5 Lead  *Dawn McLaren and Fraser Hunter* | 84 |
| | | 4.3.6 Vitrified material  *Dawn McLaren* | 85 |
| | | 4.3.7 Bone  *Dawn McLaren* | 86 |
| | | 4.3.8 Stone  *Dawn McLaren and Andrew Heald* | 86 |
| | | 4.3.9 Building materials  *Dawn McLaren* | 90 |
| | 4.4 | Miscellaneous date | 90 |
| | | 4.4.1 Pottery  *Ann MacSween* | 90 |
| | | 4.4.2 Fired clay  *Rob Engl* | 90 |
| | | 4.4.3 Chipped stone and quartz pebbles  *Rob Engl* | 90 |
| | | 4.4.4 Coarse stone  *Rob Engl* | 91 |
| | 4.5 | Summary of the artefactual evidence  *Andrew Heald* | 91 |
| | | 4.5.1 Chronology | 91 |
| | | 4.5.2 People and place | 92 |

| | | |
|---|---|---|
| 5 | OSTEOARCHAEOLOGICAL STUDIES  *Melissa Melikian* | 93 |
| 5.1 | Introduction | 93 |
| 5.2 | Results | 94 |
| | 5.2.1 Preservation and completeness | 94 |
| | 5.2.2 Demographic results | 94 |
| | 5.2.3 Sex determination | 94 |
| | 5.2.4 Metric data | 96 |
| | 5.2.5 Non-metric traits | 96 |
| | 5.2.6 Dental health | 96 |
| | 5.2.7 Pathology | 98 |
| 5.3 | Isotope analysis  *Jane Evans* | 105 |
| | 5.3.1 Introduction | 105 |
| | 5.3.2 Results | 107 |
| 5.4 | Discussion of the human remains from Auldhame  *Melissa Melikian* | 111 |
| | 5.4.1 The assemblage | 111 |
| | 5.4.2 Population origins and demographic composition | 111 |
| | 5.4.3 Skeletal pathology | 113 |
| 5.5 | Conclusions | 119 |
| 6 | THE ECOFACT ASSEMBLAGE | 121 |
| 6.1 | The faunal remains  *Jackaline Robertson* | 121 |
| | 6.1.1 Introduction | 121 |
| | 6.1.2 Discussion | 121 |
| | 6.1.3 Summary | 122 |
| 6.2 | The charred macroplant remains  *Jackaline Robertson* | 122 |
| | 6.2.1 Introduction | 122 |
| | 6.2.2 Results | 122 |
| | 6.2.3 Summary | 123 |
| 6.3 | Marine molluscs  *Ruby Ceron-Carrasco* | 123 |
| | 6.3.1 Introduction | 123 |
| | 6.3.2 Results | 123 |
| 6.4 | Micromorphological analysis of the buried soil [002]  *Lynne Roy* | 125 |
| | 6.4.1 Introduction | 125 |
| | 6.4.2 Summary description | 125 |
| | 6.4.3 Discussion and interpretation | 126 |
| 6.5 | Summary of the ecofactual evidence | 126 |
| 7 | LIVING AND DYING AT AULDHAME | 129 |
| 7.1 | Introduction | 129 |
| | 7.1.1 Later prehistoric activity | 129 |
| 7.2 | Episode 1: The monastic settlement AD 650–1000 | 129 |
| | 7.2.1 Anglian Lothian: the historical and archaeological context | 129 |
| | 7.2.2 Phase 1a: an Anglian monastic settlement | 135 |
| | 7.2.3 Phase 1b: Viking activity: contacts, conversion and the end of the monastic settlement?  *Andrew Heald* | 142 |

|      |        |                                                                                          |     |
|------|--------|------------------------------------------------------------------------------------------|-----|
| 7.3  |        | Episode 2: The parish church and graveyard AD 1000–1650                                 | 145 |
|      | 7.3.1  | A documentary history of Auldhame from AD 1000 to *c* AD 1830   *Morag Cross*           | 145 |
|      | 7.3.2  | Phase 2: AD 1000–1200                                                                    | 159 |
|      | 7.3.3  | Phase 3: AD 1200–1500                                                                    | 161 |
|      | 7.3.4  | Phase 4: AD 1500–1700                                                                    | 163 |
| 7.4  |        | A historian's view of the evidence from Auldhame   *Alex Woolf*                          | 166 |
|      | 7.4.1  | Auldhame and Tyninghame                                                                  | 166 |
|      | 7.4.2  | The 'Viking' burial                                                                      | 170 |
| 7.5  |        | Summary                                                                                  | 170 |

*Bibliography*    173

*Appendices*    187
- Appendix 1   The Hamilton archive    187
- Appendix 2   Burial data    190
- Appendix 3   Osteoarchaeological studies: methodology    198
- Appendix 4   Osteoarchaeological studies: tables    202
- Appendix 5   Isotope analysis: methodology    221
- Appendix 6   Micromorphological analyses: thin-section descriptions    225

*Index*    228

# ACKNOWLEDGEMENTS

Erlend Hindmarch managed the fieldwork and Anne Crone managed the post-excavation programme through to publication. In the course of our various roles we would jointly like to thank the following people.

First and foremost, thanks are due to Dougie Dale and his family for allowing access to the site and for their patience during the excavation. The fieldwork and post-excavation programme were funded by Historic Scotland under their Human Remains Call-off contract which was managed at that time by Patrick Ashmore and subsequently by Rod McCullagh; both are thanked for their advice and support.

The AOC Archaeology excavation team was managed from his desk by John Gooder. Erlend would like to thank him for his guidance but, above all, for having the faith to let him get on with it! The excavation team consisted of Vicky Clements (site supervisor), Len Anderson, Edward Bailey, Richard Haywood, Helen MacQuarry, Gemma Maitland, Melissa Melikian, Roddie Regan, Helen Robertson, Laura Scott and Ralph Troup, all of whom are thanked for their effort. It is not possible to name all the volunteers who participated in the community excavation phase but particular mention should be made of Ben Fairgrieve, Ian Hawkins, Dianne Laing, Bill Maclennan, Bill Patterson, Kenny Roland and Irene Taylor, as well as Steve Hackenberger and his students from the Central Washington University, USA, all of whom formed the core group of volunteers. We would also like to thank the Scottish Detector Club, who proved that archaeologists and metal detectors can work together.

Over and above their published contributions to the monograph, we are grateful to many other AOC colleagues for helpful discussion and advice; these include John Barber, Andy Heald and Mike Roy. We would not have had the confidence to pursue our particular interpretation of the evidence were it not for the support of Barbara Crawford, who organised a stimulating and enjoyable meeting in June 2010, hosted by Simon Taylor and attended by Alex Woolf, Gilbert Markus, Bill Patterson, Andy Heald and the authors; their comments and advice have helped to shape this work. We are also immensely grateful to Dr James Marple for his dogged pursuit of the Hamilton archive in the National Archives of Scotland.

All illustrations are by Graeme Carruthers and Stefan Sagrott, except for those of the prick spurs and their reconstruction, which were drawn by Alan Braby. Finally, we are grateful to Chris Lowe for his useful comments and thorough review of the draft; these have helped to shape the final version presented in this volume.

*Morag Cross* would like to express her gratitude to the following for their support, help and advice during this project: Bill Patterson, East Linton, and Dr Simon Taylor, University of Glasgow; Sheila Millar, East Lothian Local History Centre; Sheila Asante and Biddy Simpson, of East Lothian Council Museums Service; Rod McCullagh, Historic Scotland; Lis Smith and Rachel Hart, St Andrews University Archives and Special Collections; Edwina Proudfoot, St Andrews; Mr T and Mr D Dale, Scoughall Estate; Tom Addyman; Pam Graves, University of Durham; Julie Franklin, Headland Archaeology.

*Jane Evans* would like to thank Angela Lamb and Carolyn Chenery for advice and supervision of the stable isotopes analysis.

*Dawn McLaren and Fraser Hunter* would like to thank Stuart Campbell for his advice on the medieval copper alloy objects.

*Melissa Melikian* would like to thank Rachel Ives for useful discussions during the osteoarchaeological study.

# LIST OF FIGURES

| | | |
|---|---|---|
| 1 | The environs of Auldhame, showing parish boundaries and places mentioned in the text | 2 |
| 2 | Excavation in progress with Tantallon Castle in the background | 3 |
| 3 | Aerial photograph of Auldhame promontory showing cropmark NT68SW 30 and the excavation area (AP © RCAHMS) | 3 |
| 4 | Auldhame environs. Locations of previous archaeological excavations: (1) St Baldred's Cave; (2) midden; (3) later prehistoric roundhouses?; (4) Roman Iron Age structure?; (5) cist burials; (6) medieval kitchen midden | 4 |
| 5 | Top: extract from Blaeu's Atlas of Scotland, *Lothian and Linlitquo/Joh. Et Cornelius Blaeu* exc. Amsterdam 1654 (National Library of Scotland); Bottom: extract from Roy's *Military Survey of Scotland*, 1747–55 (National Library of Scotland) | 5 |
| 6 | Top: extract from Forrest's *Map of Haddingtonshire* 1802 (National Library of Scotland); Bottom: extract from Sharp, T, Greenwood, C and Fowler, W *Map of the county of Haddington*, 1844 (National Library of Scotland) | 5 |
| 7 | Extract taken from Ordnance Survey 1854 Six inch 1st Edition, Scotland Sheet 3, *Whitekirk and Tynninghame* (National Library of Scotland) | 6 |
| 8 | Hamilton's sketch map of his initial works at Auldhame (see Appendix 1) | 7 |
| 9 | General site plan showing all excavated features and the position of excavated area on the headland. Features from Hamilton's sketch plan have been superimposed in red | 8 |
| 10 | Plan of Buildings 1–4. Section A–B through Ditch 6. Section C–D through Building 1 | 14 |
| 11 | View of the building complex looking east, Building 2 in the foreground. Burials SK714 and SK641 are also visible in the foreground | 15 |
| 12 | The relationship between SK641 and Building 2 | 15 |
| 13 | The relationship between SK843 and Building 3 | 16 |
| 14 | View of building complex looking west, Building 4 in the foreground. The socket stone, SF 1287, is visible between Buildings 4 and 2 | 17 |
| 15 | Plough damage to SK148. Note plough scars | 18 |
| 16 | Plan showing location of different grave types. Only those graves mentioned in the text are numbered | 19 |
| 17 | Flexed burial SK745 | 20 |
| 18 | Plan of G161 with capstones in situ and after removal | 20 |
| 19 | SK190 within G161 | 21 |
| 20 | G276 | 21 |
| 21 | G276 | 22 |
| 22 | SK724 lying on the stone base of G723 | 22 |
| 23 | Wooden coffins: (a) G529; (b) G468; (c) G851; (d) G584 | 23 |
| 24 | SK410 in G411 in which pillow stones have been used on either side of the head | 24 |
| 25 | Graves marked by pebbles and shells? [946] (in the foreground) and [952] | 25 |

| | | |
|---|---|---|
| 26 | The Viking burial SK752 | 26 |
| 27 | Distribution of males and females in the graveyard | 27 |
| 28 | Age of adults in the graveyard | 28 |
| 29 | Distribution of juvenile and neonate remains | 29 |
| 30 | Zones 1–5 | 30 |
| 31 | Zone 1 | 32 |
| 32 | Sections across Ditch 1 | 32 |
| 33 | Ditch 1 during excavation, with revetment [442] in the foreground | 33 |
| 34 | Zone 200 | 34 |
| 35 | Zone 300 | 35 |
| 36 | Zone 4. Hearth/oven [920] looking south | 36 |
| 37 | Zone 500 | 37 |
| 38 | Walls [944] and [945]00 | 38 |
| 39 | The radiocarbon dates (graph produced using OxCal v4 1.7 Bronk Ramsey 2010; r:5 Atmospheric data from Reimer et al 2009) | 42 |
| 40 | Radiocarbon dated burials and burials provisionally dated by stratigraphic relationships | 44 |
| 41 | Radiocarbon dates from animal bone and shell | 45 |
| 42 | Grave alignment by phase | 46 |
| 43 | Age and gender by phase | 47 |
| 44 | Burial type by phase | 48 |
| 45 | SF 300 – the cloisonné stud | 53 |
| 46 | (a) the front of the cloisonné stud (© Trustees of National Museums Scotland); (b) the back of the cloisonné stud (© Trustees of National Museums Scotland) | 54 |
| 47 | Anglo-Saxon pins | 56 |
| 48 | Pin SF 356 (© Trustees of National Museums Scotland) | 57 |
| 49 | The Anglo-Saxon inkwell, SF 748 | 58 |
| 50 | Anglo-Saxon inkwells from Lurk Lane, Beverley (a) and Brandon, Suffolk (b and c) | 59 |
| 51 | The Viking belt set: the buckle SF 1130 and the strap end SF 1131 | 60 |
| 52 | The buckle SF 1130 (© Trustees of National Museums Scotland) | 61 |
| 53 | Fragment of the leather strap behind the roundel of the buckle-plate. The tooled lattice pattern on the grain is visible | 62 |
| 54 | The Viking spurs, SF 1272a | 63 |
| 55. | The Viking spurs, SF 1272b | 63 |
| 56 | (a) strap guide, SF 1272c; (b and c) buckles and strap-end mount, SF 1272d and e | 65 |
| 57 | Reconstruction of the spurs | 66 |
| 58 | The spearhead SF 1271 | 66 |
| 59 | Medieval and post-medieval pottery | 69 |
| 60 | Medieval buckles and brooches (© Trustees of National Museums Scotland) | 71 |
| 61 | Brooches SF 305 and SF 1004 | 72 |
| 62 | Decorative mounts and fittings SF 757 and SF 1022b. Lead vessel fragments SF 306, SF 310 and SF 1022a | 73 |
| 63 | Coins | 75 |
| 64 | Miscellaneous iron objects | 76 |
| 65 | Looped hinges | 77 |
| 66 | Range of features from which nails were recovered | 79 |
| 67 | Iron tools | 80 |

| | | |
|---|---|---|
| 68 | Contexts of iron objects recovered (excluding nails) | 81 |
| 69 | Lead | 85 |
| 70 | Quantity of material by context | 86 |
| 71 | (a) The cross-incised stone [953] in situ; (b) The cross-incised stone, SF 270 | 87 |
| 72 | The socket stone SF 1280 | 88 |
| 73 | The decorated spindle whorl, BE618 | 89 |
| 74 | Preservation of the Auldhame skeletons | 93 |
| 75. | Completeness of the Auldhame skeletons | 94 |
| 76. | Mortality profile of the Auldhame skeletons | 95 |
| 77 | Number of adults (18+ years) in each sex category from Auldhame | 95 |
| 78 | Evidence of sharp blade cuts that passed straight through the left parietal of the skull (arrowed) with residual radiating fractures. There is no evidence of new bone formation on the bone margins, indicating the injury was fatal. (SK216, a 46+ years male) | 100 |
| 79 | Evidence of sharp force trauma to the frontal, parietals and occipital bones, and which also involved the left zygomatic arch. The injuries are from a sharp blade, which cut through the bone. There is no evidence of bone healing, indicating the injuries were fatal. (SK868, a 18–25 years male) | 100 |
| 80 | A left adult humerus with a well-healed fracture at the mid-shaft visible with ossified fracture callus on the lateral aspect towards the top of the image (SK520, a 46+ years probable male) | 101 |
| 81 | An adult left tibia and fibula with evidence of swelling and bone formation over the entire shaft of the tibia. The changes are indicative of a non-specific infection | 102 |
| 82 | A right adult pelvis with post-mortem damage having separated the anterior pubis. Remnants of a large, rounded bone covered swelling or cyst are evident on the medial or internal aspect of the ilium, as indicated by black arrows. There is some post-mortem damage to the bone covering the cyst. The internal surface is smooth with no bone formation and is likely to have been fluid-filled | 103 |
| 83 | $^{87}Sr/^{86}Sr$ plotted against strontium concentration for samples from Auldhame. The predicted isotope composition for digenetic fluids is highlighted, and is based on the values derived from a soil leach and dentine values (see Appendix 5) | 106 |
| 84 | Histogram of $\delta^{18}O_{SMOW}$ values for enamel samples from Auldhame | 107 |
| 85 | Average drinking water values for the UK (compiled by Carolyn Chenery) | 108 |
| 86 | The field of Auldhame data in $^{87}Sr/^{86}Sr$ vs $\delta^{18}O_{SMOW}$ highlighting the two main outlying samples SK158 and SK327 | 109 |
| 87 | $\delta^{13}C_{PDB}$ vs $\delta^{15}N_{AIR}$ of the Auldhame samples compared with data from northern English medieval population, a multi-age Orkney assemblage, Iron Age human populations and various faunal data (data from Müldner & Richards 2005, 2007a, 2007b; Richards et al 2002; Richards et al 2006; Jay & Richards 2007) | 110 |
| 88 | Phase 1 features and burials | 135 |
| 89 | Excavation in progress at Auldhame with the Bass Rock in the background. The Isle of May is visible on the horizon | 141 |
| 90 | Engraving of the Bass Rock, by George Cooke *c* 1825 (© Hulton Archive, Getty Images). Note the prominent ruins of a tower on the headland opposite the Bass | 164 |
| 91 | Engraving of Tantallon Castle by W H Lizars *c* 1849 (© Courtesy of RCAHMS. Licensor www.rcahms.gov.uk ). Note the ruins of buildings on the headland at Auldhame including a tower-like structure | 165 |

# LIST OF TABLES

| | | |
|---|---|---|
| 1 | Radiocarbon dates listed in order of age | 12 |
| 2 | Graves phased by stratigraphic association with dated burials | 43 |
| 3 | Types of medieval copper alloy objects present | 74 |
| 4 | Range of iron objects present | 82 |
| 5 | Iron objects and fittings recovered from graves | 83 |
| 6 | Dated graves containing iron objects. Displayed in order of date, earliest to latest | 84 |
| 7 | Range of lead objects recovered by context | 84 |
| 8 | Vitrified material classification | 86 |
| 9 | Summary catalogue of mortar fragments | 90 |
| 10 | The faunal assemblage; species and minimum number of individuals present | 121 |
| 11 | The charred macroplant assemblage | 122 |
| 12 | Quantification of the marine molluscs recovered at Auldhame | 124 |

## APPENDIX 3

| | | |
|---|---|---|
| Table A3.1 | Age categories | 200 |
| Table A3.2 | Sex categories | 200 |
| Table A3.3 | Metric data recorded | 201 |
| Table A3.4 | Dental codes | 201 |
| Table A3.5 | Dental caries codes | 201 |

## APPENDIX 4

| | | |
|---|---|---|
| Table A4.1 | Demographic profile of the assemblage of Auldhame skeletons | 202 |
| Table A4.2 | Summary of stature for the sexed adults from Auldhame | 202 |
| Table A4.3 | Summary of indices for the Auldhame adults | 202 |
| Table A4.4 | Frequency of cranial and mandibular non-metric traits | 202 |
| Table A4.5 | Frequency of post-cranial non-metric traits | 202 |
| Table A4.6 | Calculus presence and severity in individuals with one or more teeth by age from Auldhame | 203 |
| Table A4.7 | Calculus presence and severity on one or more teeth by sex in individuals from Auldhame | 203 |
| Table A4.8 | Alveolar disease scores from the Auldhame skeletons by age | 203 |
| Table A4.9 | Alveolar disease score of the Auldhame skeletons by sex | 204 |
| Table A4.10 | Ante-mortem tooth loss in the adults | 204 |
| Table A4.11 | Ante-mortem tooth loss in the maxilla by adult age category | 205 |
| Table A4.12 | Adult ante-mortem tooth loss in the mandible by age category | 206 |
| Table A4.13 | Prevalence of ante-mortem tooth loss of the adults by age category | 206 |
| Table A4.14 | Ante-mortem tooth loss of the maxilla in the adults by sex | 207 |
| Table A4.15 | Ante-mortem tooth loss of the mandible in the adults by sex | 207 |

| | | |
|---|---|---|
| Table A4.16 | Dental abscesses in the adults | 208 |
| Table A4.17 | Dental abscesses in the maxilla by age category | 208 |
| Table A4.18 | Dental abscesses in the mandible by age category | 209 |
| Table A4.19 | Prevalence of dental abscesses of the adults by age category | 209 |
| Table A4.20 | Dental abscesses in maxilla in the adults by sex | 210 |
| Table A4.21 | Dental abscesses in mandible in the adults by sex | 210 |
| Table A4.22 | Dental caries in the adults | 211 |
| Table A4.23 | Caries initiation site for the adults | 211 |
| Table A4.24 | Prevalence of dental caries of the adults by age category | 211 |
| Table A4.25 | Dental caries in the maxilla by age category | 212 |
| Table A4.26 | Dental caries in the mandible by age category | 212 |
| Table A4.27 | Dental caries in maxilla in the adults by sex | 213 |
| Table A4.28 | Dental caries in mandible in the adults by sex | 213 |
| Table A4.29 | Osteoarthritis in the adult skeletons from Auldhame | 214 |
| Table A4.30 | Prevalence of osteoarthritis by age category | 215 |
| Table A4.31 | Osteoarthritis by sex | 216 |
| Table A4.32 | Osteoarthritis of the vertebrae in the adults | 217 |
| Table A4.33 | Prevalence of osteoarthritis of the vertebrae for the adults by sex | 218 |
| Table A4.34 | Prevalence of IVD and Schmorl's nodes in the adults | 219 |
| Table A4.35 | Prevalence of IVD by age | 219 |
| Table A4.36 | Prevalence of IVD by sex | 220 |
| Table A4.37 | Prevalence of Schmorl's nodes by age | 220 |
| Table A4.38 | Prevalence of Schmorl's nodes by sex | 220 |
| Table A4.39 | Comparison of adult stature of Auldhame with other medieval sites | 220 |

## APPENDIX 5

| | | |
|---|---|---|
| Table A5.1 | Isotope results | 222 |
| Table A5.2 | Environmental samples | 224 |
| Table A5.3 | Summary of isotope results | 224 |

# CHAPTER 1

# INTRODUCTION

## 1.1 STRUCTURE OF THE MONOGRAPH

The site on the headland at Auldhame, East Lothian, the subject of this monograph, was initially interpreted simply as a church and associated graveyard when it was excavated in 2005. When Anglo-Saxon artefacts were recovered from the ploughsoil during the excavation, the likely connection with the local saint, Baldred (or Balthere as he shall be more correctly referred to throughout this volume) and his Anglian background was duly noted (Hindmarch & Melikian 2006). However, it was not until the post-excavation programme was well under way that the probable nature of this connection became apparent. Analysis of the radiocarbon dates, in conjunction with other excavated features that would be anomalous within a parish church and graveyard, has prompted the interpretation that there was a monastic settlement on the headland, which flourished between the mid-7th and mid-9th centuries AD. The local importance of St Balthere, together with contemporary descriptions of his life, makes it likely that he was associated with the monastic community at Auldhame, if not its founder. Although the monastic settlement ceased to exist some time towards the end of the 9th century AD, the site eventually became the church and graveyard for the parish of Auldhame and continued to function as such for the next seven centuries, albeit with periods of disuse. Thus, the headland has at least two distinct biographies, one as an Anglian monastic settlement and the other as a medieval parish church. There was also a brief Viking presence, which resulted in the burial of a richly dressed person.

This chapter presents the context for the 2005 excavations, the geographical setting and archaeological discoveries in the immediate environs of the headland. In Chapters 2 to 6 are presented the material evidence on which our interpretations are based, the excavated remains and the chronological framework, followed by the artefactual, osteological and ecofactual evidence. In Chapter 7 the discussion is split in two. In Chapter 7.2 the evidence for the Anglian monastery is summarised and its significance evaluated against the backdrop of its historical and archaeological context. The significance of the Viking presence is also evaluated. In Chapter 7.3 the site in its subsequent role as parish church and graveyard is discussed and the nature of the later buildings on the headland evaluated. As neither of the authors is a historian of Anglo-Saxon Scotland, Dr Alex Woolf was asked for his views on the evidence from Auldhame and his more nuanced, informed interpretation is presented in Chapter 7.4. This has been written independently of the rest of the discussion so there is necessarily some repetition of documentary evidence presented in the earlier sections of the chapter.

NB. Throughout the text, archaeological contexts are referred to in square brackets, as in [002], graves are prefixed by G, as in G563, and skeletons are prefixed by SK, as in SK474.

## 1.2 GEOGRAPHICAL SETTING

The site of Auldhame (NGR NT 6016 8476) is located in the county of East Lothian in south-east Scotland, 3.5km to the east of North Berwick (Figure 1). The site is reached by a track from the A198 which runs to the hamlet of Seacliff and its beach. The site itself is located on a coastal promontory with steep cliffs to the north and east, which stands at a height of 28m OD overlooking the Firth of Forth and the Bass Rock. The northern edge of the site overlooks a small bay, on the opposite side of which are the remains of Tantallon Castle, which was built in the mid-14th century (Figure 2). To the east of the promontory is the wide sweep of Seacliff Beach, which provides the first readily accessible landing place east along the rocky coast from North Berwick.

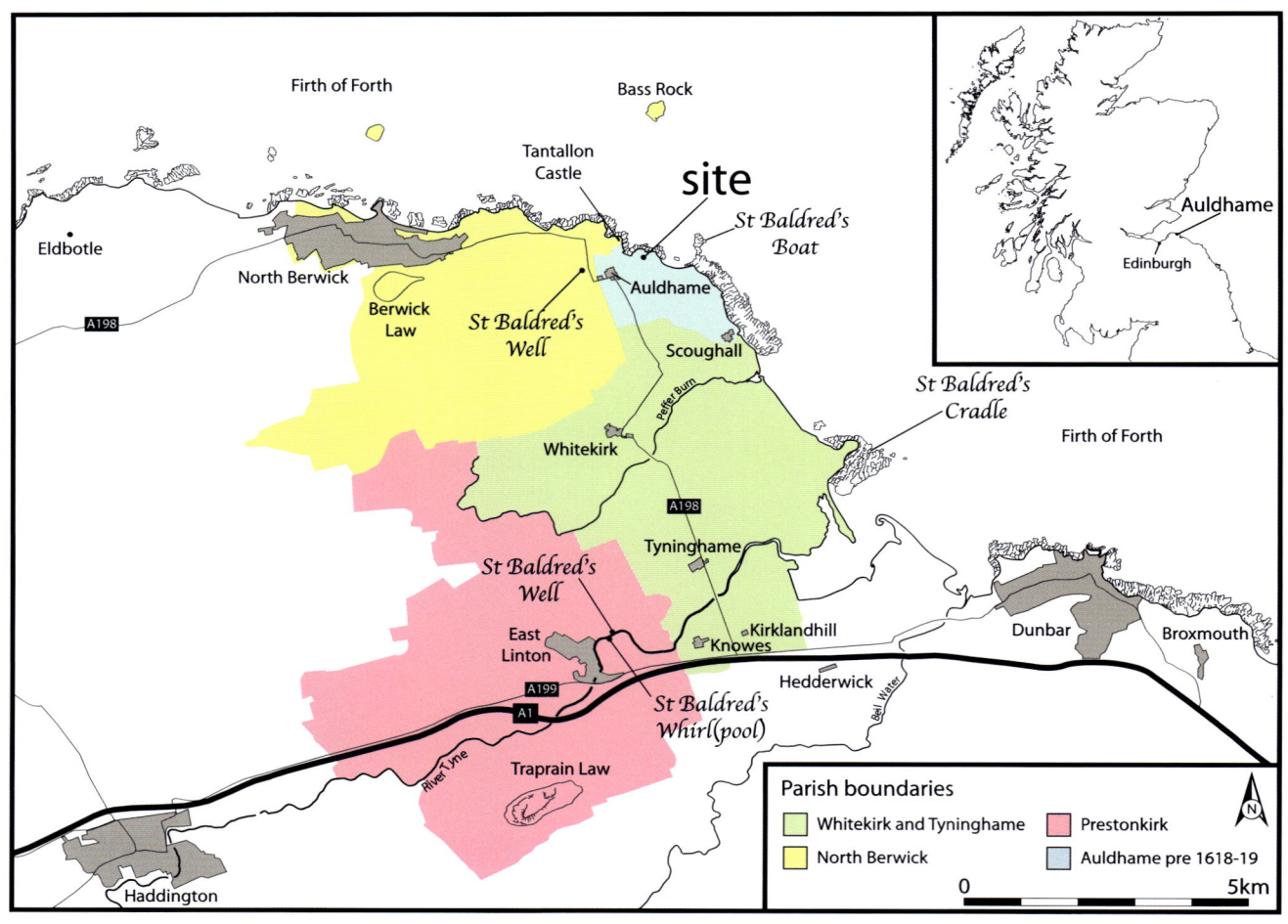

*Figure 1*
The environs of Auldhame, showing parish boundaries and places mentioned in the text

Auldhame sits on the coastal plain of the Midland Valley (Lothian Plain) of Scotland on soils of the Kilmarnock Association, which consist of thick brownish clay loams and clay tills derived from the underlying igneous rocks, mainly basalts, and sedimentary sandstones of Carboniferous age (Brown & Shipley 1982). In terms of Land Use Capability the soils are Class 2, soils that have minor limitations (Ordnance Survey of Scotland 1976). In recent years, the site has been under rotating root crop and arable cultivation. Prior to the excavations the site had been ploughed in readiness for the planting of potatoes.

## 1.3 ARCHAEOLOGICAL DISCOVERIES AROUND AULDHAME

The headland at Auldhame has long been thought to be the site of an Iron Age promontory fort. In 1989 a wide cropmark curving across the neck of the promontory from north-west to south-east was identified by aerial photography (NMRS No. NT68SW 30; NGR NT 6016 8473; Figure 3) and was interpreted as a probable ditch forming the defensive perimeter of the fort, although it did not extend across the full width of the headland. The ditch was seen in section in the cliff face during a Coastal Assessment Survey (James 1996; NMRS No. NT68SW 65) and was described as a U-shaped ditch, 2m in depth and 2m wide at the top narrowing to 1m at the bottom. This ditch is a significant feature of the recent excavations at Auldhame.

A number of early archaeological investigations were carried out within the vicinity of Auldhame by G Sligo, the owner of Auldhame during the 19th century. Sand-clearing works in 1831 led to the discovery of Baldred's Cave (NMRS No. NT68SW 7;

# INTRODUCTION

*Figure 2*
Excavation in progress with Tantallon Castle in the background

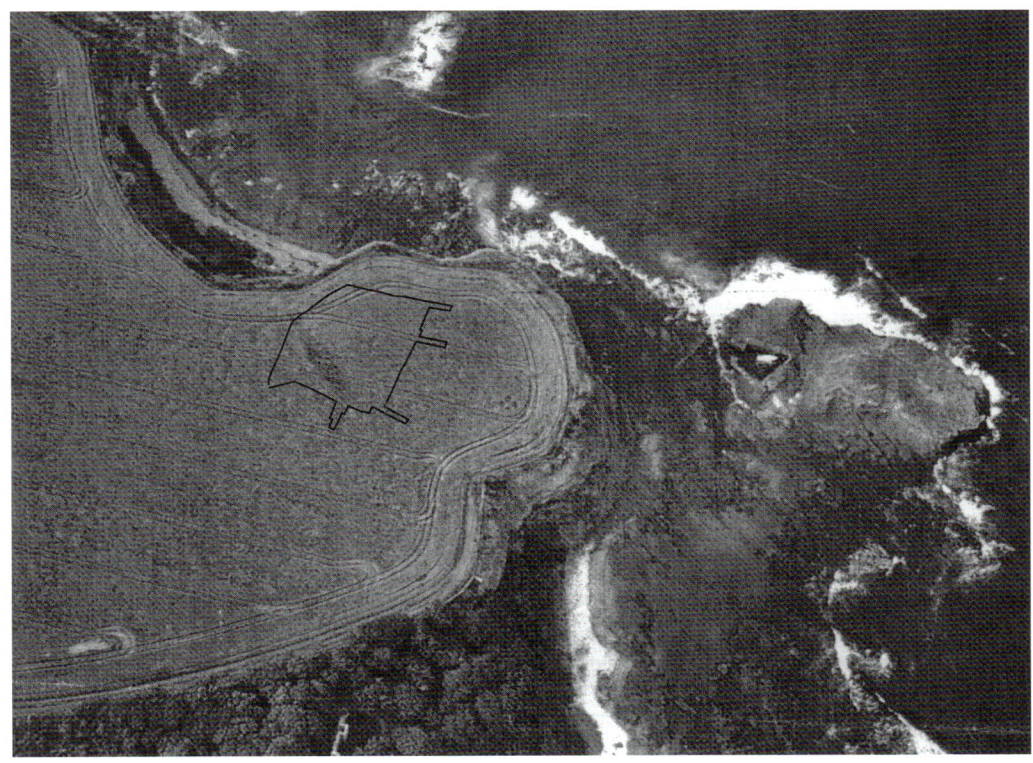

*Figure 3*
Aerial photograph of Auldhame promontory showing cropmark NT68SW 30 and the excavation area (AP © RCAHMS)

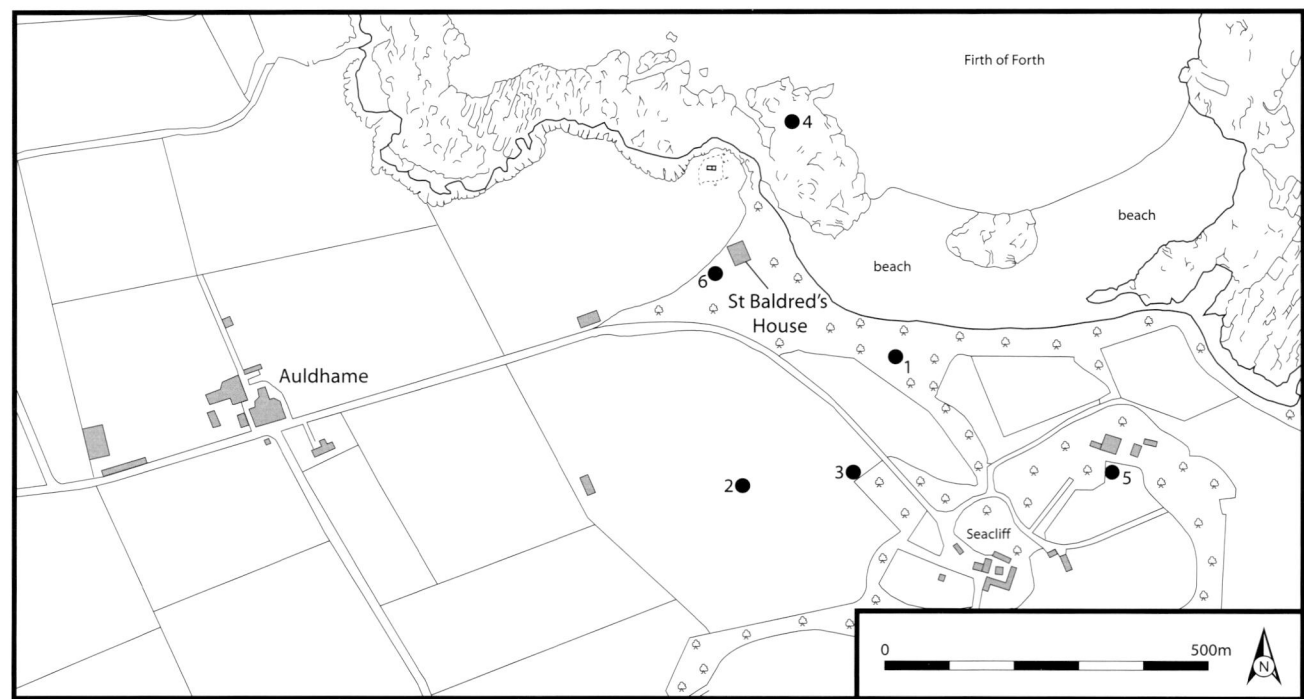

*Figure 4*
Auldhame environs: Locations of previous archaeological excavations. (1) St Baldred's Cave; (2) midden; (3) later prehistoric roundhouses?;
(4) Roman Iron Age structure?; (5) cist burials; (6) medieval kitchen midden

NGR NT 6045 8448; Figure 4, Site 1). Within the mouth of the cave was what Sligo described as an altar, consisting of a large pear-shaped stone with the flattened surface of the widest part uppermost. This stone rested on a section of elevated bedrock and had been secured in place by packing stones. In an attempt to consolidate this mound and prevent inquisitive people from toppling the altar, Sligo removed a loose stone, revealing the remains of a child's skeleton. The remains of a second child were discovered on the opposite side, close to the altar. Further animal and human bones were found as the cave was excavated, together with a bone knife handle and fragments of 'rude red ware'.

From the evidence gathered, Sligo (1857, 356) concluded that during the early Iron Age a pagan cult practised human sacrifice here. While the concept of 'sacrificial sites' has fallen out of favour, some forms of ritual associated with the burial of young people have been encountered (see, for example, Barber 2003, 140–1). Thus, the significance of the human bones and their context, their probable prehistoric date and their proximity to the recent excavations, should not go unnoticed.

Sligo also located a midden deposit near Seacliff, consisting of black earth mixed with animal bone, charred wood, limpet shells and pottery of the same type as that found within the cave. This deposit was found in conjunction with two vertical lines cut into a projecting rock (Sligo 1857, 357–8; NMRS No. NT68SW 8; NGR NT 6123 8428; Figure 4, Site 2). No evidence of this deposit, or of the stone cut feature, was found when OS visited the site in 1962.

Sligo also excavated some features that he called 'pavements' (NMRS No. NT68SW 9; NGR NT 604 843, Figure 4, Site 3) on the top of the cliffs south of Baldred's Cave. He described them as double pavements of flat sea stones set closely together, one of which measured 3.5m in diameter. A thin layer of charcoal and ashes lay over the upper pavement of stones, and below these stones he found a 0.3m thick deposit of animal bone, charcoal and ashes mixed with sand overlying a lower pavement of stone, which in turn rested on the natural clay (Sligo 1857, 358). Stuart (1867) later described them as floors of huts and they are almost certainly paved roundhouses of later prehistoric date, of the type found at Broxmouth hillfort and other sites in East Lothian (Hill 1982).

# INTRODUCTION

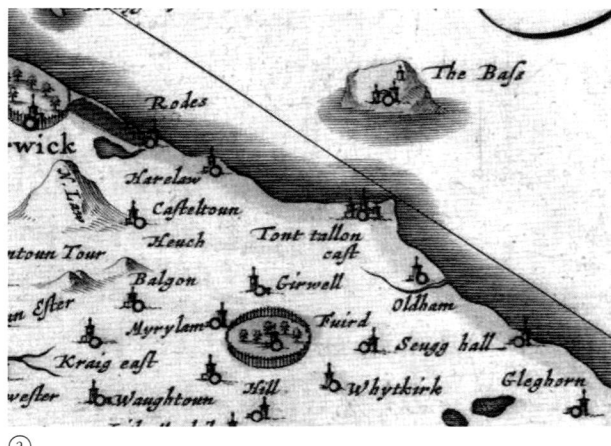

*Figure 5*
(a) extract from Blaeu's Atlas of Scotland, *Lothian and Linlitquo/Joh. Et Cornelius Blaeu exc. Amsterdam 1654* (*National Library of Scotland*); (b) extract from Roy's *Military Survey of Scotland, 1747_55* (*National Library of Scotland*)

A second possible settlement was excavated in 1871 on the Ghegan Rock, an outcrop which lies directly beneath the Auldhame promontory (NMRS No. NT68SW 3; NGR NT 6030 8483; Figure 4, Site 4). Here the remains of a building were found with an associated midden deposit (Laidlaw 1871). The building, which had been constructed with clay bonded stones, was rectangular, and measured about 11m east to west and 8.0m north to south. Within the structure was a well-made drain. Finds included large amounts of bone, of which a few were of human origin. The bones were dominated by cattle and sheep bone but goat, deer, pig, horse and dog were also present. Finds also included bone needles, awls, combs and several pot-boiler stones. The ceramic assemblage consisted of fragments of crude pottery together with better quality sherds, possibly of Roman origin. Roman artefacts included a carved piece of serpentine representing a human and an amphora fragment dated to the 1st or 2nd century AD (Robertson 1970). The comb from the site is one of the few bone objects from Scotland decorated in the La Tene style (MacGregor 1976, No. 274).

Numerous cist burials have also been found in the vicinity. What appears to be a large cist containing seven or eight human skeletons was found at Seacliff (NMRS No. NT68SW 10; NGR NT 608 843, Figure 4, Site 5) in 1867, and during the 20th century coastal erosion continued to expose human remains in cist-like structures in the same area (NMRS No. NT68SW 8; NGR NT 6123 8428; Nisbet 1975; Carter 1990).

The sites described above relate to human activity of probable later prehistoric and Roman Iron Age date. Later activity within the immediate vicinity of the site includes the discovery of a kitchen midden, 'on the eastern side of the wall separating the plantation from the field' (NMRS No. NT68SW 2; NGR NT 6019 8461; Figure 4, Site 6). The midden deposit

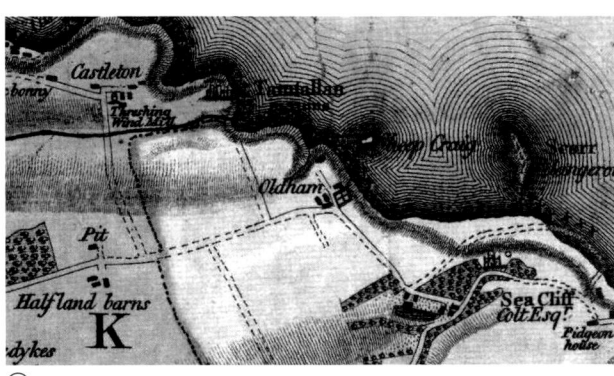

*Figure 6*
(a) extract from Forrest's *Map of Haddingtonshire* 1802 (*National Library of Scotland*); (b) extract from Sharp, T, Greenwood, C & Fowler, W *Map of the county of Haddington*, 1844 (*National Library of Scotland*)

contained a large amount of limpet and whelk shells and fragments of green glazed pottery indicating its medieval date (RCAHMS 1924). The midden may well relate to 'the kirk-town of Aldham' (NMRS No. NT68SW 18) and indicate its antiquity, predating St Baldred's House, a 16th-century laird's house (NMRS No. NT68SW 1; Figure 4). The heavily overgrown remains of this structure survive on the southern edge of the field in which the site is situated.

Nothing now survives of the kirk-town. The settlement appears as 'Oldham' in Blaeu's Atlas of Scotland (Figure 5a) and is represented by a symbol for a large building, presumably St Baldred's House. The settlement is represented in the same way on Adair's maps of 1682 and 1736. On Roy's Military Survey of Scotland (Figure 5b) Oldham is still marked but there are no details of buildings. Instead the plan of St Baldred's House is represented in great detail and there is a small square building to the north, which could represent a church (see Chapter 7.3.4).

On Forrest's map of 1802 (Figure 6a) 'Oldham' is located on both sides of a road that runs south to the Sea Cliff Estate and north to a small building that may be that represented on Roy's map. Thomson's map of 1820 shows the same layout but the settlement is not named, perhaps indicating that it was largely unoccupied at this time. On Ainslie's map of the following year the name 'Oldham' appears accompanied by a location symbol but with no detailed plan of the buildings (Ainslie 1821). Sharp's map of 1825 once again shows detail of buildings close to the location of St Baldred's House but the isolated building noted on previous maps does not appear (Sharp et al 1825). No alterations appear to have been made when this map was redrawn in 1844 (Sharp et al 1844; Figure 6b). By the mid-19th century, commentators described the village as completely ruinous (NSA 1845, Vol. 2, 29) and only one building at 'Old Auldhame' is depicted on the 1st edition Ordnance Survey map (Figure 7). '*Site of Grave Yard*' is recorded on this map just to the north of what is probably St Baldred's House, but this lies too far south of the graveyard reported in this volume.

### 1.3.1 Hamilton's excavations on the headland in 1949

In 1948 the Admiralty began the installation of a new radar system at various sites along this stretch of coast. One of these sites, the 'Cliff Hut site' is located on the Auldhame promontory. During the development human remains were found within pits that had been dug for the foundations of concrete posts, which formed a fence along the edge of the installation (NMRS No. NT68SW 17). Dr Richardson, an Inspector of Ancient Monuments with the Office of Works, recognised the significance of these remains and a programme of archaeological works was implemented. Until recently all records pertaining to these works had been lost

*Figure 7*
Extract taken from Ordnance Survey 1854 Six inch 1st Edition, Scotland Sheet 3, *Whitekirk and Tynninghame* (*National Library of Scotland*)

but thanks to the diligence of Dr James Marple, a few documents including a sketch map have now come to light (Appendix 1).

An evaluation was initially carried out in 1949 by J R C Hamilton, then an Assistant Inspector of Ancient Monuments, who examined the post pits and confirmed the presence of burials. He also located a cist burial within a cable trench dug along the line of the new fence and the remains of a wall, assumed to represent the remains of a medieval chapel. He illustrated his findings with a rough sketch plan (Figure 8).

# INTRODUCTION

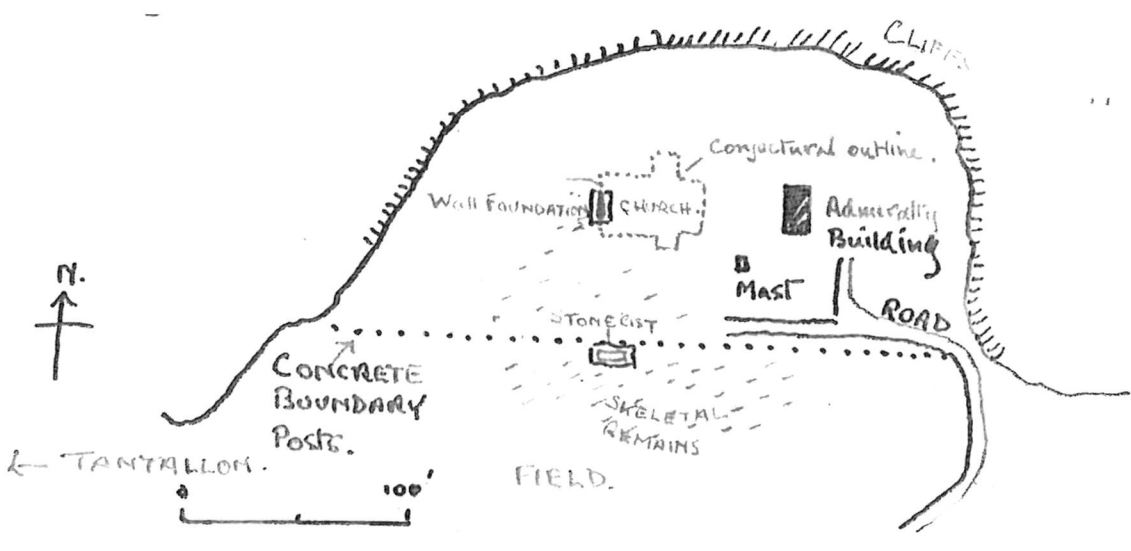

*Figure 8*
Hamilton's sketch map of his initial works at Auldhame (see Appendix 1)

Subsequently, a series of trial trenches was dug across the promontory to find the extent of the burials. It was also considered important to trace the walls of the supposed chapel and excavate its interior. Unfortunately, the location or contents of these trenches are not included within the archive, and neither is any detailed information as to what was found while investigating the building remains. In a brief note written some five years after the excavations, Hamilton confirmed the presence of a medieval graveyard, which he surmised was 13th–14th century in date on the basis of pottery found on the site. He described the building as drystone, built 'as would have been expected in the case of a medieval church' but thought that the building was probably domestic in nature because midden debris and a stone spindle whorl had been found on the paved path surrounding the structure. The human remains and pottery were sent to the Office of Works technical laboratory, then at Castle Terrace, Edinburgh, but their whereabouts is now unknown. The spindle whorl ended up in the National Museum of Scotland and is reported on in this volume (Chapter 4.3.8)

The information contained in this incomplete archive is an important component of the evidence from the site but the only locational information we have is that in Hamilton's sketch plan (Figure 8). As this includes a scale, we might assume a degree of accuracy but trying to reconcile the features that the sketch plan and the recent survey have in common is problematic. These are the cliff edge and the concrete boundary posts, which have survived as a series of concrete-filled post-holes surveyed during the AOC excavations (Figure 9). Aligning either of these features causes conflicts of evidence, the most critical being that in both alignments the area of skeletal remains indicated by Hamilton spreads far to the east of the actual extent revealed by plough and the subsequent walkover survey (see below), while his gable wall lies well to the north and east of the buildings uncovered during the recent excavations. To illustrate the conflict of evidence, Hamilton's sketch plan has been superimposed on the plan of the recent excavation using the post-holes as a common reference point and matching the scale (Figure 9). The best approach may be simply to accept the general disposition of features on Hamilton's sketch plan (ie building to north of boundary posts and somewhat to west of centre on the headland) rather than having to argue for another building for which we found no evidence. However, the implications of Hamilton's evidence are discussed in more detail in the relevant sections.

## 1.4 FIELDWORK 2005 AND 2008

### 1.4.1 Introduction

In February 2005, ploughing in preparation for the planting of potatoes uncovered human bone

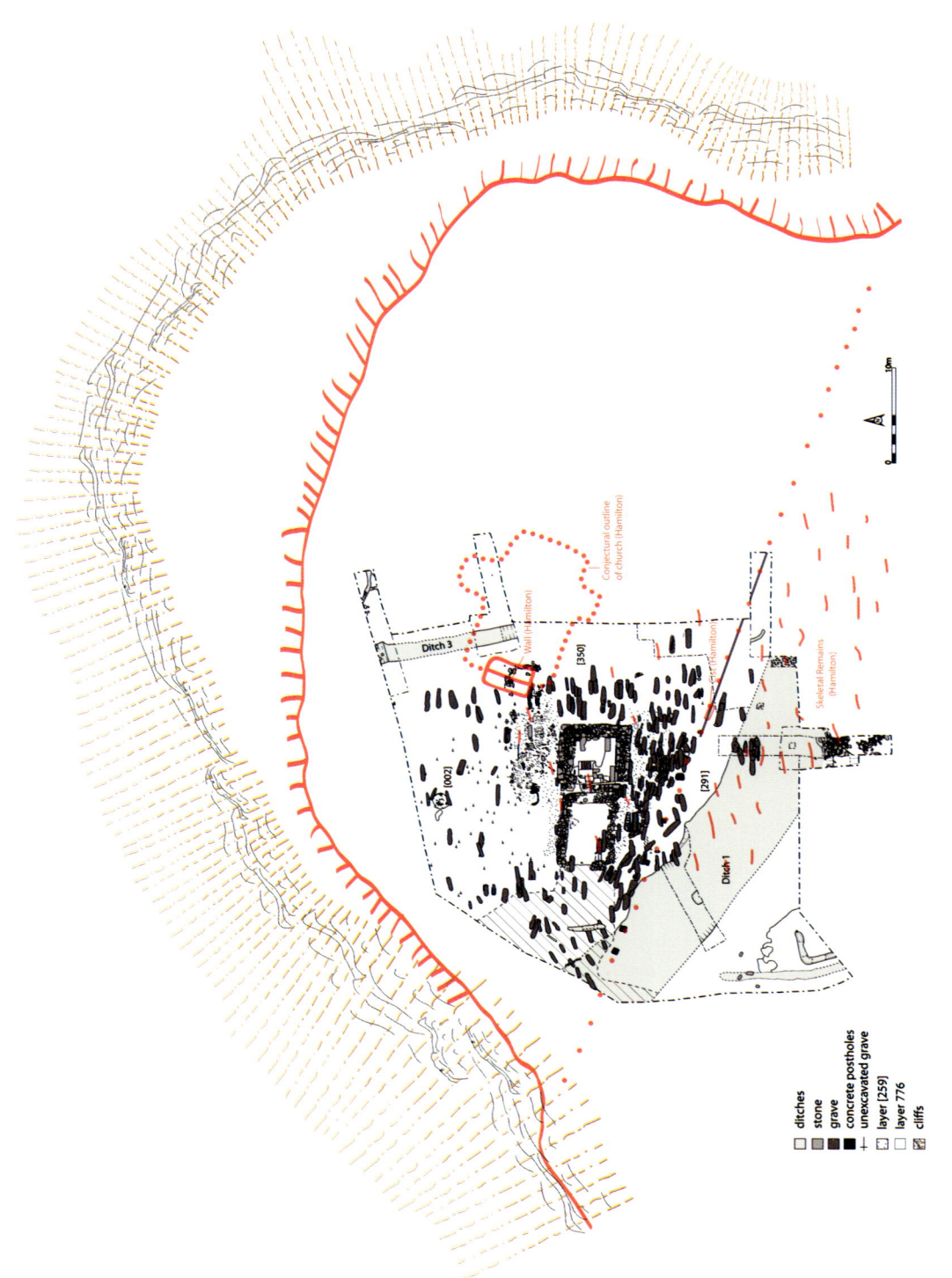

*Figure 9*
General site plan showing all excavated features and the position of excavated area on the headland. Features from Hamilton's sketch plan have been superimposed in red

along with a significant amount of stone. AOC Archaeology Group (AOC) was commissioned by Historic Scotland (HS) to investigate the discovery as part of their Human Remains Call-off contract.

AOC undertook a two-stage exploratory phase of work, comprising a walkover survey followed by a site evaluation and a scheme of test pitting. These exploratory works revealed the clear presence of a graveyard and other features including ditches and a possible structure. An excavation programme was designed, in collaboration with HS, which focused on those deposits that were at immediate risk of damage or destruction from the deep ploughing then practised on the site.

### 1.4.2 Walkover survey

The remit of the walkover survey was to recover the disturbed disarticulated bone from the surface of the plough soil and to survey the position of any articulated bone so that the extent of the archaeologically significant deposits, which had been disturbed, could be defined.

### 1.4.3 Evaluation

The recovery of disarticulated bone from the surface of the plough soil did identify the extent of the disturbed area, but not the extent of the in situ archaeological remains. An attempt was made to define the latter by means of test pitting. The remit of the test-pitting exercise was:

(i) to determine the significance, character, condition, extent, quality and date of the full suite of archaeological remains within the promontory
(ii) to determine the geographical limits of the area likely to be further disturbed by ploughing
(iii) to assess future possible threats to the site by relating current plough damage to the position of remains within the soil profile.

Ultimately, the test pitting was a risk assessment exercise that tried to zone the promontory into areas of greater or lesser archaeological significance, current condition and perceptible threat. Once obtained, this information informed decision-making in collaboration with HS on the range and scope of any further work that was immediately necessary to stabilise the archaeology of the site and to prevent further loss of archaeologically sensitive information. Following best practice in conservation management planning (CMP) the ultimate aim was to acquire the information necessary to enable us to conserve the cultural value of the site.

Following consultation with HS an excavation followed immediately after the evaluation. As there was significant local interest in the works at Auldhame it was agreed that interested members of the community could participate in the excavation. Volunteers subsequently played a significant role in the on-site works.

### 1.4.4 Excavation

The walkover survey and evaluation had demonstrated that most archaeological activity was confined to the western corner of the headland (Figure 3) and consequently an irregular area of 1510m$^2$ was excavated.

*Ground reduction phase*

An initial phase involved the rapid reduction of the ground surface by removal of the ploughsoil, further collection of disarticulated remains, and definition of the in situ features surviving on site. The ground reduction was carried out using a 360° type tracked excavator under constant supervision so that any significant remains would not be damaged. Further reduction was carried out using hand tools and proceded to the depth at which human burials and other archaeology could be clearly identified. The use of heavy plant in the presence of human remains may seem an insensitive *modus operandi* but it is necessary to note that 0.8 to 1m of plough soil lay over the entire site. Excavation by hand of this depth of ploughsoil would not have been cost-effective. All human remains encountered during the mechanical stripping were recovered by hand and treated with due care and respect, and all ethical and professional procedures were rigidly adhered to on site.

*Excavation*

As preservation in situ is the preferred heritage option (SPP 2010, para 123), the primary aim of the excavation was that of rescue of disturbed remains and formal excavation and recovery of all in situ human remains deemed to be at risk from further agricultural work. Graves and other deposits deemed safe were left unexcavated, with only their positions being recorded. Other significant features were investigated via limited excavation to determine their nature and function. As we shall see, this approach has hindered our final interpretation of the site.

### 1.4.5 Walkover survey 2008

The site was accidentally ploughed again in January 2008 and further human bone and stone remains were brought to the surface. A second walkover survey was undertaken. Again, the extent of the damage was assessed by plotting the positions of disarticulated bones and displaced remains. The possibility that these had already been present in the plough soil was negated by the discovery within the new topsoil of three articulated infant remains and fragments of the terram matting used to cover the in situ remains after the excavation.

# CHAPTER 2

# THE EXCAVATED FEATURES

## 2.1 INTRODUCTION

At every stage of the fieldwork at Auldhame, the walkover survey, evaluation and excavation, significant archaeological remains were recovered (Figure 9).

The walkover survey recovered human bone lying on the surface over an area of approximately 900m$^2$ with the densest distribution on the southern side of the affected area and a more diffuse distribution toward the centre. None of the bone was articulated. A number of large stones were also found near the centre of the spread including several simple cross incised stones (Figure 71).

The test-pitting and subsequent excavation revealed the presence of at least 308 in situ graves, of which 242 were ultimately excavated (Appendix 2); it is highly likely that further as yet unidentified graves exist. The excavation and recovery of the human remains in these graves constituted the greater part of the fieldwork at Auldhame, accounting for roughly 90% of the time spent in the field. Within the centre of the graves were the remains of stone-built structures, interpreted as the chapel complex associated with the graveyard. A stretch of the large ditch previously observed as a cropmark on aerial photographs (Figure 3) was exposed within the excavation area, as well as a small range of other features, including six linear features of varying size, a possible hearth/oven, and a few pits and post-holes. These were all investigated to varying degrees.

An extensive radiocarbon-dating programme has demonstrated that the site was in use, in one way or another, for at least a millennium, from the late 7th century AD until the 17th century (Chapter 3). The excavated evidence is presented in this section, interpolated with the radiocarbon dates, but at this stage no attempt is made to present the evidence in chronological order, because the date of many of the excavated features remains unknown.

## 2.2 THE GRAVEYARD (Figure 9)

### 2.2.1 The extent of the graveyard

No clear, unambiguous boundaries to the graveyard were found during the AOC excavations, or during Hamilton's earlier investigations of the site. Nonetheless, its potential extent can be estimated. There were no graves visible in the northern and western baulks of the site, presumably because the cliff edge, which lies *c* 14m beyond the western baulk and 18m beyond the northern baulk (Figure 3), acted as the physical boundary to the graveyard to the north and west. The area between the cliff edge and the northern and western baulks was not investigated because it had not been ploughed and was in constant use by walkers and horse riders, so we do not know whether there had been a man-made boundary inside the cliff edge.

Ditch 1 appears to have formed the original southern boundary of the graveyard – the closely packed graves along its northern edge would suggest that this was so – but at some point the graves spilled over its edges and the graveyard expanded south. Test pitting did not reveal any further human remains along the southern edges of the plough soil spread (ie that containing skeletal remains) but Hamilton recorded skeletal remains apparently extending farther to the south-east (Figure 9). However, as was stressed above, there are difficulties in reconciling his sketch plan with the current plans. Furthermore, the sketch map was drawn prior to excavation and we do not know whether the spread represents ploughed-up *ex situ* remains rather than in situ graves. Nonetheless, the ditch, or perhaps some feature marking its original alignment, appears to have continued to form the southern boundary because there are no graves beyond its southern edge.

Test-pitting along the eastern edge of the ploughsoil spread also indicated that the AOC excavations had found the easternmost extent of the graveyard. Ditch 3

# LIVING AND DYING AT AULDHAME, EAST LOTHIAN

**Table 1**
**Radiocarbon dates listed in order of age**

| Context/skeleton | Material | SUERC Lab No. | Radiocarbon years | Calibrated age at 1σ | Calibrated age at 2σ | Contemporaneous? |
|---|---|---|---|---|---|---|
| 259 | Limpet | 13957 | 1680±35 | 665–745 | 640–800 | yes |
| SK321 | Human bone | 13822 | 1320±35 | 650–770 | 650–780 | yes |
| 503a | non-ID animal bone | 13827 | 1315±35 | 650–770 | 650–780 | yes |
| SK755 | Human bone | 13841 | 1305±35 | 660–770 | 650–780 | yes |
| SK1040 | Human bone | 18871 | 1295±30 | 670–770 | 660–780 | yes |
| 570 | non-ID animal bone | 13833 | 1290±35 | 670 770 | 650–810 | yes |
| SK394 | Human bone | 13825 | 1285±35 | 670–770 | 650–810 | yes |
| 567 | non-ID animal bone | 13832 | 1280±35 | 675–770 | 650–820 | yes |
| 205 | non-ID animal bone | 13817 | 1275±35 | 680–775 | 660–860 | yes |
| SK455 | Human bone | 13291 | 1275±35 | 680 -775 | 660–860 | yes |
| SK289 | Human bone | 10475 | 1240±35 | 680–860 | 680–880 | yes |
| SK293 | Human bone | 15601 | 1240±35 | 680–860 | 680–880 | yes |
| 35 | Bovine | 13815 | 1235±35 | 690 -860 | 680–890 | yes |
| 420 | Bovine | 13287 | 1235±35 | 690–820 | 680–890 | yes |
| 87 | Horse | 13322 | 1225±35 | 710–870 | 680–890 | yes |
| SK641 | Human bone | 10477 | 1215±35 | 770–880 | 680–900 | yes |
| 239 | Bovine | 13323 | 1205±35 | 775–880 | 690–940 | yes |
| SK843 | Human bone | 13303 | 1205±35 | 775–880 | 690–940 | yes |
| 536 | Ovine | 13324 | 1195±35 | 770–890 | 690–950 | yes |
| SK352 | Human bone | 13824 | 1185±45 | 770–900 | 690–750 | yes |
| SK752 | Human bone | 13292 | 1175±35 | 770–900 | 770–970 | yes |
| SK825 | Human bone | 15606 | 1145±35 | 820–980 | 770–980 | yes |
| SK1043 | Human bone | 18870 | 1115±30 | 890 -975 | 860–1020 | yes |
| SK104 | Human bone | 13313 | 1110±30 | 890–980 | 870–1020 | yes |
| SK216 | Human bone | 15600 | 1110±35 | 890–980 | 860–1020 | yes |
| SK122 | Human bone | 13314 | 1100±35 | 895–990 | 880–1020 | yes |
| SK626 | Human bone | 13317 | 1100±35 | 895–990 | 880–1020 | yes |
| SK219 | Human bone | 10470 | 1050±35 | 900–1030 | 890–1030 | yes |
| **SK467** | **Human bone** | **10476** | **975±35** | **1010–1150** | **990–1160** | **no** |
| SK798 | Human bone | 15605 | 970±35 | 1020–1160 | 990–1160 | yes |
| SK120 | Human bone | 13312 | 955±35 | 1020–1160 | 1010–1160 | yes |
| SK248 | Human bone | 13307 | 950±35 | 1020–1160 | 1010–1170 | yes |

# THE EXCAVATED FEATURES

Table 1
Radiocarbon dates listed in order of age (*cont.*)

| Context/ skeleton | Material | SUERC Lab No. | Radiocarbon years | Calibrated age at 1σ | Calibrated age at 2σ | Contemporaneous? |
|---|---|---|---|---|---|---|
| SK273 | Human bone | 10471 | 945±35 | 1030–1160 | 1020–1170 | yes |
| SK724 | Human bone | 13316 | 945±35 | 1030–1160 | 1020–1170 | yes |
| SK663 | Human bone | 13834 | 935±35 | 1030–1160 | 1020–1180 | yes |
| SK318 | Human bone | 13821 | 925±35 | 1040–1160 | 1020–1190 | yes |
| SK520 | Human bone | 13831 | 890±35 | 1040–1210 | 1030–1220 | yes |
| SK158 | Human bone | 13816 | 885±35 | 1250–1220 | 1030–1220 | yes |
| SK733 | Human bone | 13836 | 885±35 | 1050–1220 | 1030–1220 | yes |
| **SK669** | **Human bone** | **13835** | **735±35** | **1255–1290** | **1210–1380** | **no** |
| SK327 | Human bone | 13823 | 705±35 | 1260–1380 | 1250–1390 | yes |
| SK274 | Human bone | 13304 | 690±35 | 1270–1390 | 1260–1400 | yes |
| 503b | Ovine | 13956 | 685±35 | 1270–1390 | 1260–1400 | yes |
| SK868 | Human bone | 15607 | 660±35 | 1280–1390 | 1270–1400 | yes |
| SK883 | Human bone | 15608 | 655±35 | 1280–1390 | 1270–1400 | yes |
| SK426 | Human bone | 13826 | 645±35 | 1285–1390 | 1280–1400 | yes |
| SK915 | Human bone | 13311 | 640±35 | 1290–1390 | 1280–1400 | yes |
| SK708 | Human bone | 10478 | 635±35 | 1290–1400 | 1280–1400 | yes |
| SK742 | Human bone | 13837 | 620±35 | 1295–1395 | 1280–1410 | yes |
| **SK714** | **Human bone** | **13305** | **535±35** | **1320–1440** | **1310–1450** | **no** |
| **SK474** | **Human bone** | **13306** | **325±35** | **1510–1640** | **1470–1650** | **no** |
| SK585 | Human bone | 13321 | 305±35 | 1520–1650 | 1470–1660 | yes |
| SK900 | Human bone | 13293 | 300±35 | 1520–1650 | 1480–1660 | yes |
| SK852 | Human bone | 13315 | 260±35 | 1520–1800 | 1490–1960 | yes |

is the obvious boundary along this side; the ditch and its projected extension southwards encompass all the in situ graves – indeed, the alignment of the easternmost graves appears to mirror the alignment of the ditch (Figure 9). This picture is complicated by Hamilton's evidence, which suggests that skeletal remains were found east beyond the projected line of Ditch 3, but we must bear in mind the caveats expressed above.

Thus, if we accept that Ditch 1 and Ditch 3 formed the southern and eastern boundaries of the graveyard, while the cliff edge formed the northern and westernmost possible extents then the graveyard would have covered a roughly triangular area of approximately 900m².

### 2.2.2 Soils

A variety of soils were found throughout the graveyard (Figure 9). A compact dark brown clay silt [002], up to 1m deep, covered the northern part of the graveyard; while the eastern edge was covered by a deposit of mid-brown clay silt [350], up to 0.5m deep, which contained occasional small stones and marine shells. Their relationship is unclear, not least because they merge into each other. Both these soils were interpreted as buried agricultural soils (Chapter 6.4.1).

Both [002] and [350] overlay a compact dark grey silt layer [259] which contained marine shells dominated by dog-whelk (*Nucella lapillus*). The possible significance of these finds is discussed in Chapter 7.2.2. Significant numbers of white quartzite pebbles were also noted within this deposit. Deposit [259] lay around both the southern and northern sides of the chapel. Shell from [259] was radiocarbon dated to cal AD 640–800 (Table 1; SUERC-13957).

A deposit of compact orange/brown silt clay [291] lay between the south side of the chapel and the edge of Ditch 1; it lay under the southern edge of deposit [259] and to the west of the chapel it lay over a deposit of moderately compact brown clay silt [776]. This is interpreted as an in situ original ground surface (OGS) while [291] may be redeposited natural, possibly from the digging of Ditch 1 (see below – Chapter 2.5.1).

## 2.3 THE CHAPEL COMPLEX (Figures 10–14)

### 2.3.1 Introduction

Structural remains were located near the centre of the site on the top of a low mound. The stone-built remains were aligned east/west and covered an area of 15.5m east to west and 7.2m north to south (Figure 10). Three distinct styles of construction were apparent, identifiable by type and finish of stone and the bonding material used within the structure; consequently these distinctive building units have been called Buildings 2–4. An earlier structure, Building 1, was also tentatively identified.

As the imperative was to preserve in situ, minimal exploration of the complex of structures was undertaken and as a result no direct stratigraphic relationships between the different building units were uncovered. The chronology of the complex relies on the radiocarbon dating of those skeletal remains in direct relationship with the structural remains.

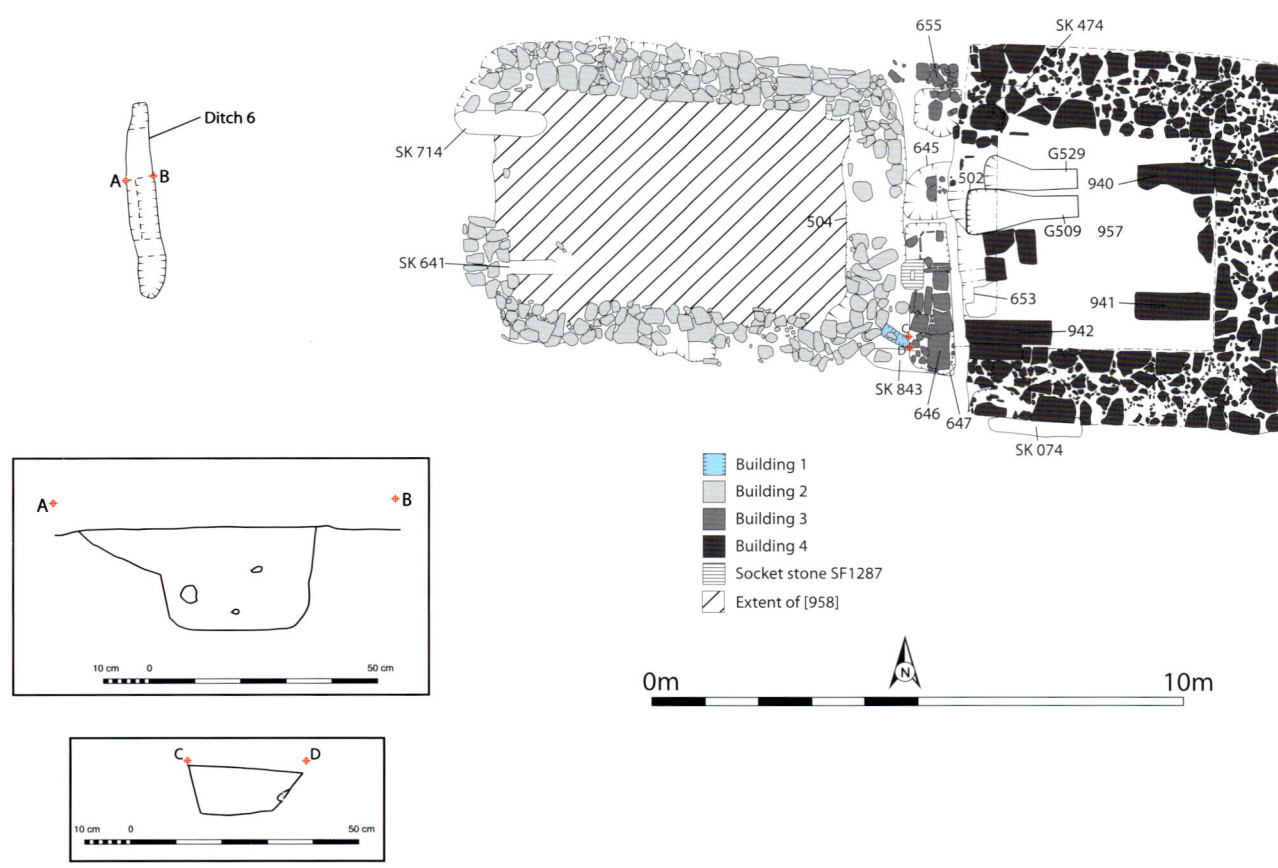

*Figure 10*
Plan of Buildings 1–4. Section A–B through Ditch 6. Section C–D through Building 1

# THE EXCAVATED FEATURES

*Figure 11*
View of the building complex looking east, Building 2 in the foreground. Burials SK714 and SK641 are also visible in the foreground

*Figure 12*
The relationship between SK641 and Building 2

### 2.3.2 Building 1

Removal of robber backfill (see below) in the centre of the building complex, between the eastern wall of Building 2 and the wall that represents Building 3, exposed a linear slot-like feature. Only 0.5m of its length was exposed but it appeared to lie on a NW–SE alignment. This feature contained a fill of firm mid-brown clay and measured 0.12m deep by 0.24m wide. The near-vertical sides and flat base of the feature (Figure 10; Section CD), together with the absence of artefacts from the fill suggests that this feature was a beam slot of an earlier, timber-built structure.

### 2.3.3 Building 2

Building 2 is rectangular in plan, with external dimensions of 8.4m east/west and 6.0m north/south. The walls of the building were between 0.85m and 1.1m thick and had been constructed of field stones (Figure 11). Many of the stones were rounded and possibly of glacial origin, given the numbers of erratics present (Paterson & McAdam 2005). The stones varied in size and were clay bonded. Although generally rectangular in plan, the structure had slightly rounded corners.

A section of the foundation of the eastern gable wall had been robbed out at some point and removal of the fill from the robber trench [504] showed that the foundations were up to 0.45m deep. Up to four layers of stone were observed but, given the nature of the stone used, these foundations probably did not have formal coursing and were rubble-built.

On the basis of comparisons with early church structures elsewhere (see Chapter 7.2.2) it is likely that the gap in the western gable wall was originally the entrance to the building but without excavation this could not be confirmed. However, the entrance is unlikely to have been as wide as the existing gap, which is in all probability the result of later stone-robbing. Within the confines of the building was a demolition deposit of compact yellow-grey clay silt [958], which contained flecks of mortar. This deposit sealed at least five burials but there may be more burials that were not detected. Two of the skeletons were radiocarbon dated. SK641, which had clearly been truncated by the construction of the western wall (Figure 12), returned a date of cal AD 680–900 (Table 1; SUERC-10477). SK714, which lay within the robbed-out entrance, returned a date of cal AD 1310–1450 (Table 1; SUERC-13305). Unfortunately, because the nature of the gap in the western gable wall is not fully understood, the stratigraphic relationship between SK714 and Building 2 remains ambiguous.

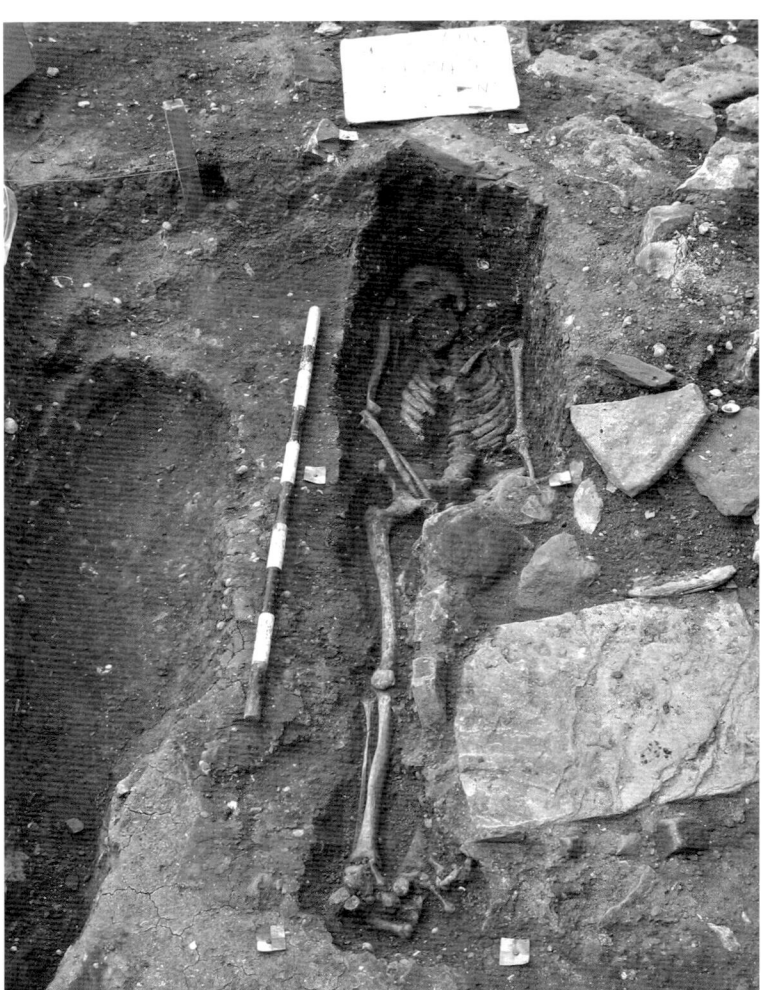

*Figure 13*
The relationship between SK843 and Building 3

### 2.3.4 Building 3

Between the remains of Buildings 2 and 4 were fragments of two mortared sandstone walls [655] and [646] (Figure 10). Both walls were constructed using a mixture of field stones and re-used building stone, and

# THE EXCAVATED FEATURES

*Figure 14*
View of building complex looking west, Building 4 in the foreground. The socket stone, SF 1287 is visible between Buildings 4 and 2

were bonded with a white lime mortar. The northern component [655] had been subjected to much stone-robbing and only a small length survived. Wall [646] was the better preserved. This section of wall had been built within a construction trench [647], which cut the shelly deposit [259] that surrounded the chapel. The construction trench had been lined with edge-set stones and these defined the northern extent of wall [646] giving it an overall length of 2.9m and a width of up to 0.9 m. The northern end of this wall lies on the same alignment as the break in the eastern wall of Building 1, and beyond this lay a small robber trench [645].

Set within the western face of wall [646] was a large sandstone boulder into which a rectangular socket had been carved (SF 1287 – Figures 10 and 14), probably a cross base. A similar cross base, SF 1280, was found on the edge of the promontory to the east of the site (Figure 72). Wall [646] overlay SK843 (Figures 10 and 13) so the radiocarbon date for this skeleton provides a *terminus post quem* of cal AD 690–940 (Table 1; SUERC-13303) for the construction of this building unit.

### 2.3.5 Building 4

Building 4 consisted of regular, well-built walls to the north, south and east, all 1.5m thick and made of dressed red sandstone blocks (Figures 10 and 14). The walls of Building 3 may have formed the western wall of Building 4 but no physical relationship could be determined. The building measured 7.2m east/west and 5.8m north/south.

Within the structure were three large sandstone slabs, [940], [941] and [942] (Figures 10 and 14), which are thought to be cover slabs for high status burials. These remained unexcavated as they were deemed to be safe from further damage. The latest deposit within Building 4 was a dark grey silt [957], which contained frequent coal fragments. At least two coffin burials, [503] and [509] (which were left in situ), had been cut through this deposit. [957] lay over a dense layer of unburnt coal fragments, which sealed G653. This grave was not excavated but clearly cut a sequence of mortared floor deposits.

The southern wall of Building 4 overlay SK074 (Figure 10), which was radiocarbon dated to cal AD

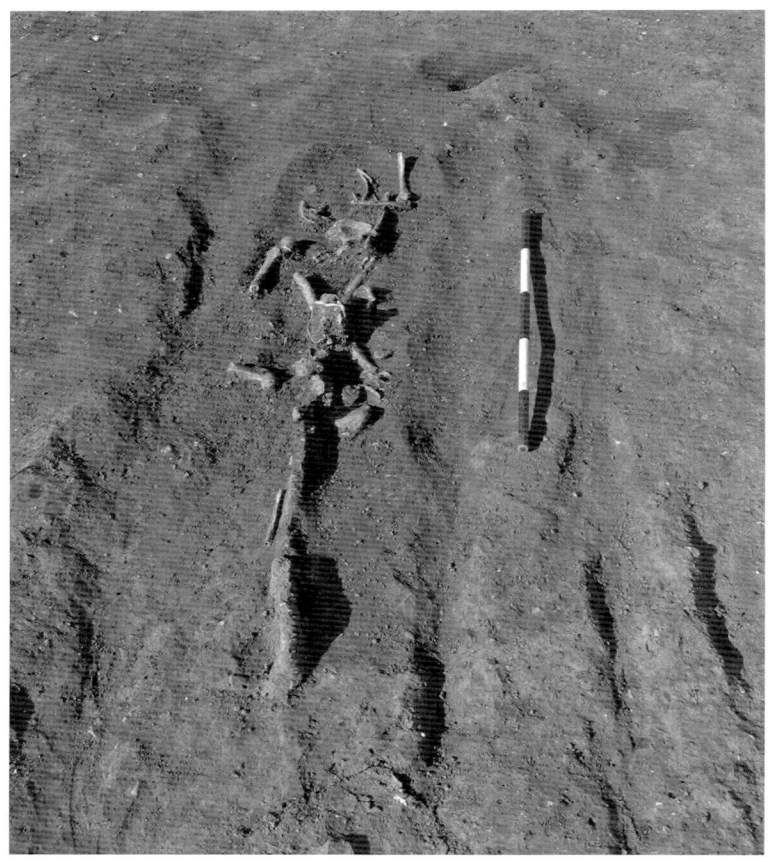

*Figure 15*
Plough damage to SK148. Note plough scars

were also clearly visible in the underlying deposits. This damage and truncation made the identification of grave cuts and their relationships extremely hard, and at times impossible, to define.

In total, 242 skeletons were recovered from the site and a further 66 known burials were left in situ because they were deemed safe at a depth of 0.3m below the lower limit of excavation set by Historic Scotland. Following ploughing of the site in 2008 another three disturbed skeletons were recovered. It is highly likely that further undiscovered human remains still survive on the site, and many more have probably been lost to erosion and other processes. A millennium of burial activity on the site has also had a significant impact on the coherence of the depositional sequence, and this is especially evident to the south of the chapel. Ploughing, erosion and burial have led to an average skeletal completeness of 58% within the recovered assemblage. Details of all the burials recovered from the site are presented in Appendix 2.

### 2.4.2 Grave alignment

Although the dominant alignment of graves was close to west–east with the head at the west (bearing of 270/90°), variations in the range of between 233/53° and 337/157° were recorded. Graves at or close to an east–west alignment occurred throughout all phases of the graveyard (Figure 42). The greatest variation occurred within the earliest burials on the site, those of Anglian date. Most of the variation in burials of this date was mainly toward a NW–SE alignment and, where these graves intersect with others and a physical relationship can be demonstrated, these burials tend to be earlier than their east–west counterparts. This group tends to occupy an area to the south-west of the building complex (Figure 9).

Graves with a SW–NE alignment all occur in one discrete area to the west of the chapel but the dated examples occur from the 10th century through to the 14th century (Figure 42), suggesting that this alignment has no chronological significance. The fact that these were mainly the burials of juveniles (Figure 29) may be more significant. The apparent isolation of this group hints at special treatment.

1260–1400 (Table 1; SUERC-13304), a date that is supported by the buckle, SF 301 (Figures 60 and 61) found within the grave. This grave provides a *terminus post quem* for Building 4. An Edward I silver penny (SF 955), minted between AD 1302–3 (Chapter 4.3.3), was recovered from the fill of burial [502] within the building and provides further evidence for a 14th-century or later *terminus post quem* date for its construction. A *terminus ante quem* for the abandonment of Building 4 is provided by SK474, which was inserted into the remains of the building (Figure 10) and was radiocarbon dated to cal AD 1470–1650 (Table 1; SUERC-13306).

## 2.4 BURIALS

### 2.4.1 Introduction

The vast majority of the graves displayed damage from ploughing, varying from slight to almost total removal of the skeleton (Figure 15). Modern plough scars

# THE EXCAVATED FEATURES

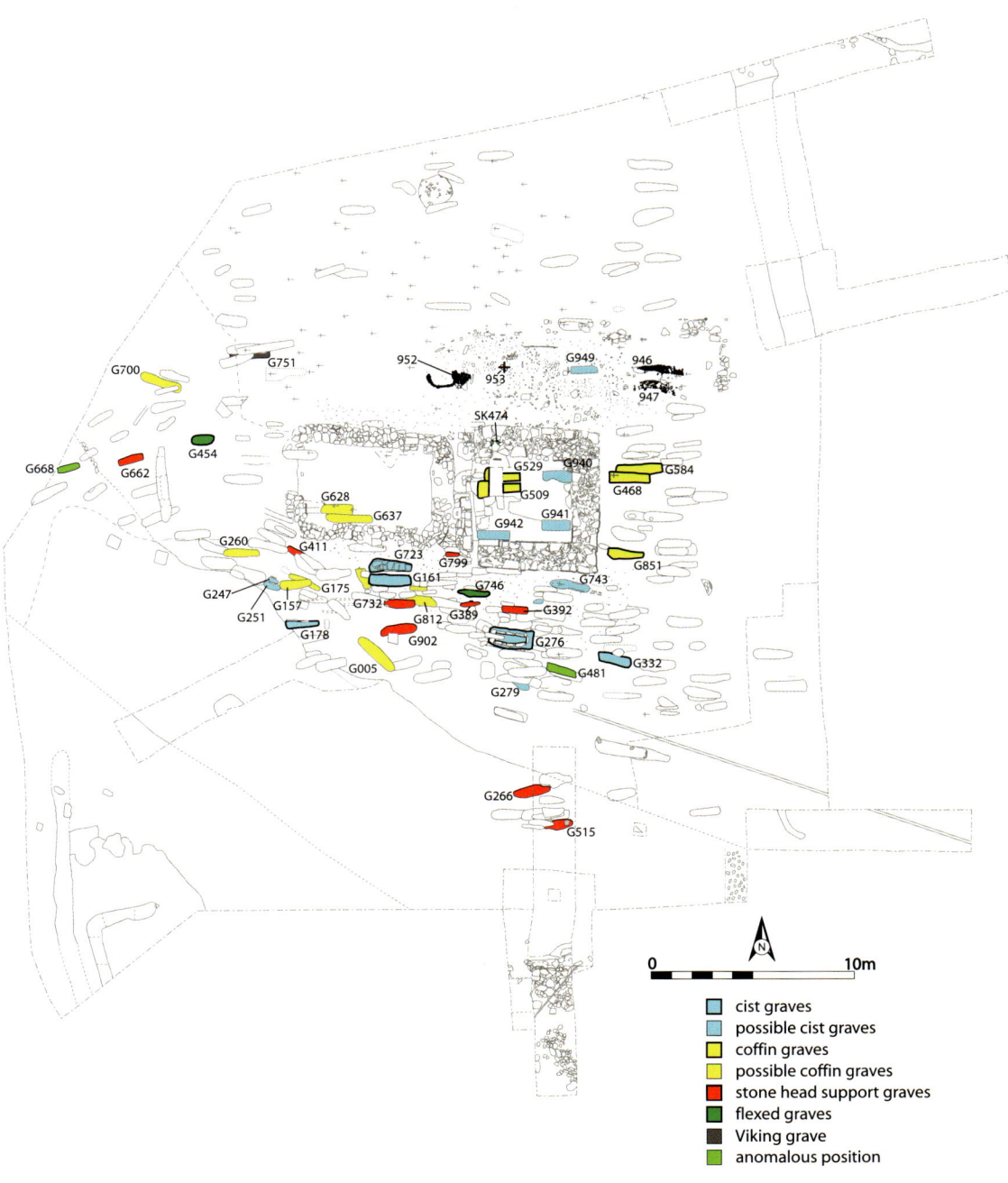

*Figure 16*
Plan showing location of different grave types. Only those graves mentioned in the text are numbered

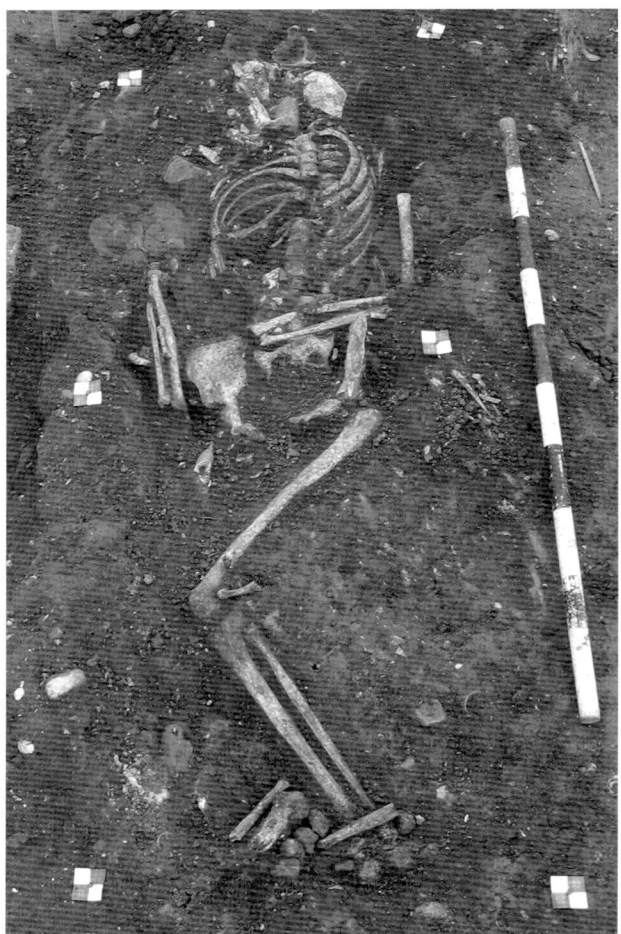

*Figure 17*
Flexed burial SK745

legs remained. These had been flexed to the south at approximately 45°. This burial has been dated to cal AD 660–860 (Table 1; SUERC-13291). The second flexed skeleton, SK745 (in G746), located just south of the Building 4 (Figure 16), was that of an almost complete middle-aged female (Figure 17). The third example was that of SK474, the infant burial found inserted into the remains of Building 4 (Figure 16) and dated to cal AD 1470–1650 (Table 1; SUERC-13306). In this burial the legs were flexed and the body turned but both arms remained by the sides.

Only two other skeletons displayed anomalous positions. SK480 (in G481) located at the southern limits of the graveyard (Figure 16) had been placed in the ground with the torso turned to the left and the left arm bent at 90° across the body but with the legs still placed side by side. A juvenile, SK669 (in G668), which lay on the very western edge of the excavated area (Figure 16), had been placed in a supine position but the elbows were bent so that the hands were by the chin.

### 2.4.4 Grave type

A range of different types of grave was found on the site; the majority were simple earth-cut graves but there were also cist burials, coffin burials and burials with pillow stones (Figure 16).

### 2.4.3 Body position

The dominant body position throughout all phases was that of an extended supine burial with the head at the west end and the feet side by side. The only real distinction was in the position of the arms, which were either crossed over the pelvis or lying by the side of the body. Where the position of the arms could be determined, those with crossed arms outnumbered those with arms by the side by 3:1. Two burials with crossed ankles were recorded, SK687 and SK699.

Of greater significance were three flexed burials. SK455 (in G454), located to the west of the building complex (Figure 16) had suffered much damage and only its

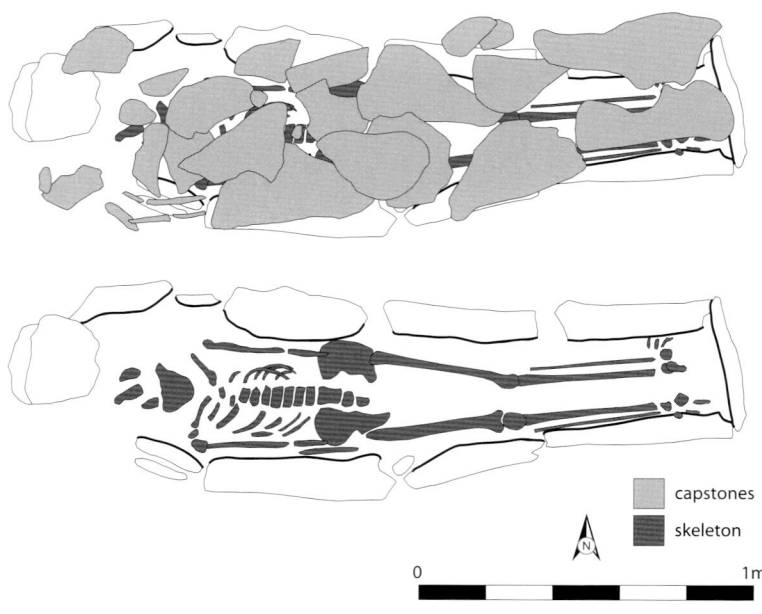

*Figure 18*
Plan of G161 with capstones in situ and after removal

# THE EXCAVATED FEATURES

partial remains represented by a few fragments of edge-set stones still in situ. The majority of cist burials were constructed from unworked slabs of field stone set around the edges of a sub-rectangular pit. Only one excavated cist, G161, had a cover still in place, but three large sandstone slabs, G940–2, within Building 4 (Figures 10 and 11) and a further slab, G949 to the north of the chapel (Figure 16) may also be single-slab cist covers. Only one excavated cist, G723, had a base.

The best preserved of the cist burials are described in detail below.

## G161

G161 was located to the south of Building 1 (Figure 16), immediately next to another cist, G723. The stone slab lid had shattered and collapsed into the cist so it was not possible to determine whether the covering consisted of a single slab or several slabs (Figure 18). The sides were constructed from unworked stones set on edge and angled slightly outwards (Figures 18 and 19). The fill of the cist was similar to the surrounding deposit [291] through which it had been cut and in consequence this fill contained many shells and quartz pebbles. Three nails and a possible gaming piece were also recovered from fill. The burial, SK190, was the remains of a middle-aged adult of indeterminate sex.

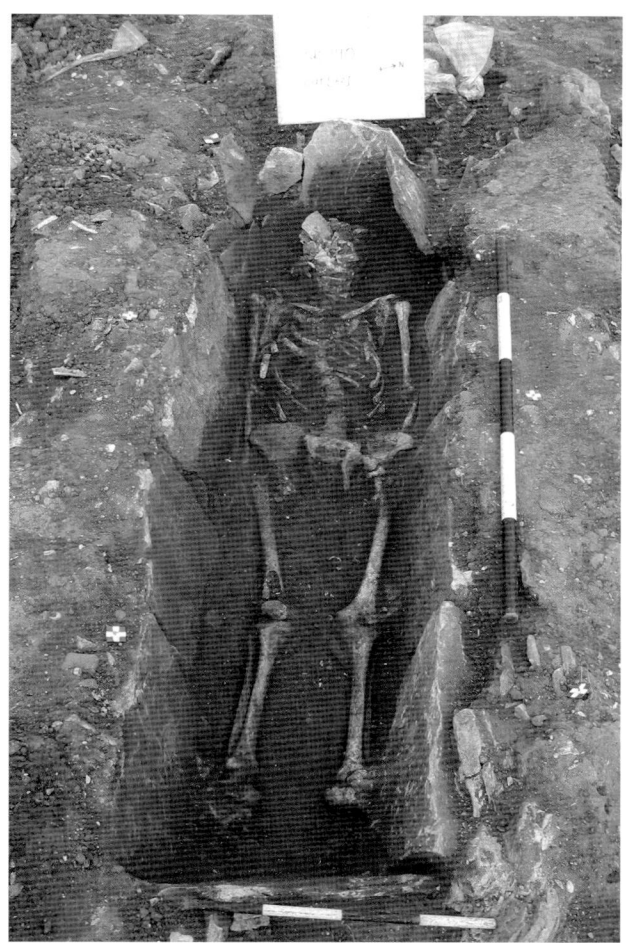

*Figure 19*
SK190 within G161

### Simple graves

Some 90% (216) of the excavated burials were simple earth-cut graves; ie the corpse was buried in a hole that had been dug just big enough to accommodate it, usually in an extended supine position although a small number of flexed burials were found (see 2.4.3). The bodies may have worn shrouds but no shroud pins were recovered. This type of grave was present in every phase of the graveyard and within each alignment group.

### Cist burials

There were at least five definite cist burials and a further nine possible cist burials. The reason for the uncertainty is that the condition of the cists ranged from well preserved to extremely

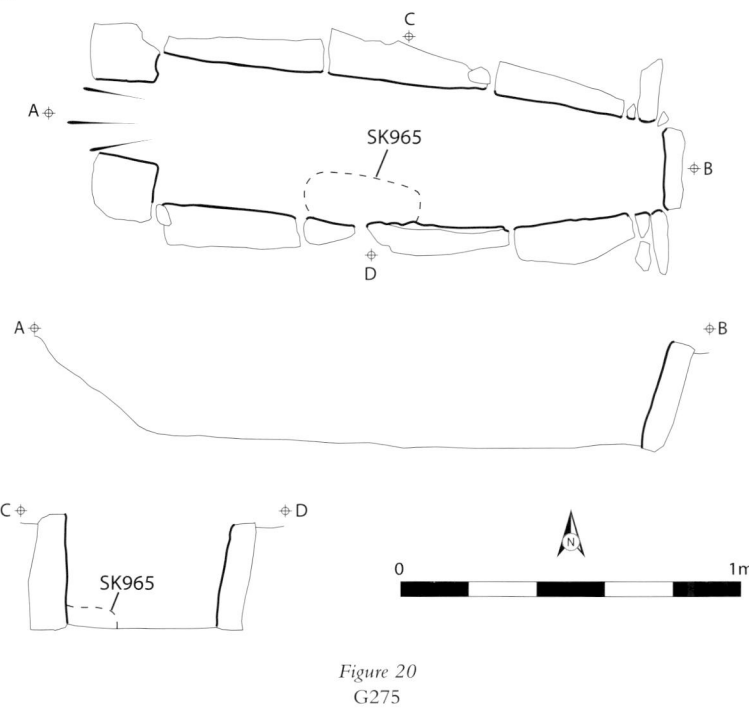

*Figure 20*
G275

*Figure 21*
G275

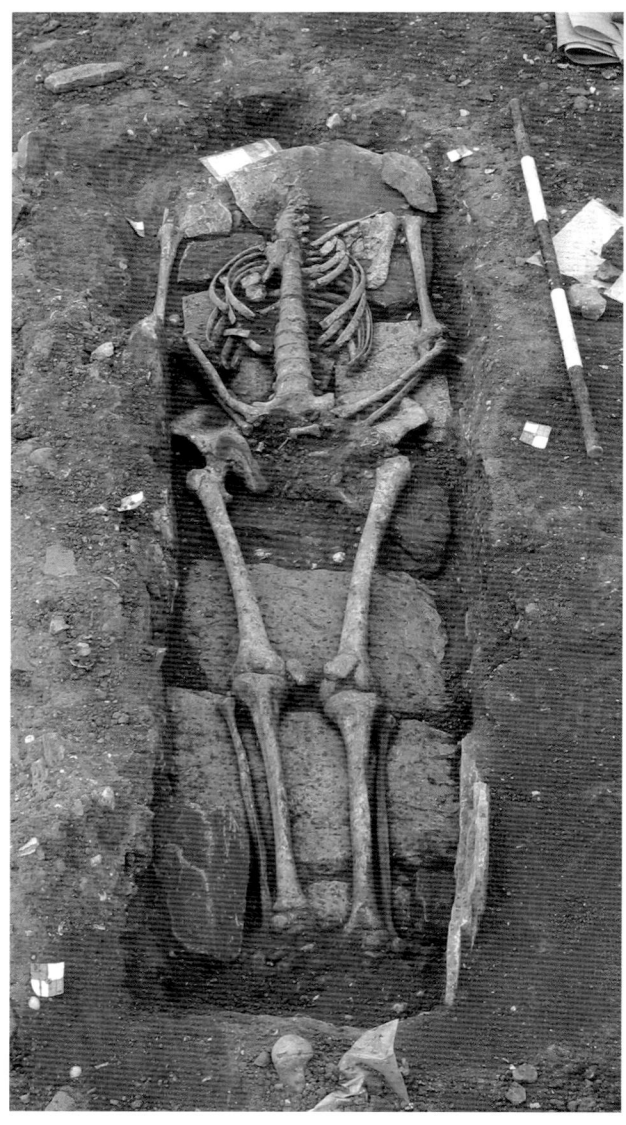

*Figure 22*
SK724 lying on the stone base of G723

When digging this cist the gravedigger must have cut through a recent infant burial, SK965 (Figure 20). The disturbed but still articulated remains were then re-interred within the cist. No evidence for a lid to this cist was found. It may be that it was removed when SK245 was interred or it may have succumbed to the plough. SK273 has been dated to cal AD 1020–1170 (Table 1; SUERC-10471).

G723

G723 was located close to G161 (Figure 16). Although badly damaged, this cist displayed quite different

G276

In comparison with the other excavated cists G276 was very well built (Figures 20 and 21). It was constructed from large, thick, edge-set square slabs bonded with light brown clay and set within a construction cut. The head of the cist was marked by two sub-square stones that acted as pillow stones set on either side of the head to keep it upright (see below).

The cist originally contained SK273, a female who may have died in childbirth, as the remains of a foetus, SK274, was found with its head within the pelvis. The skull of SK273 was subsequently removed and the body of a juvenile, SK245, was placed between the pillow stones so that its pelvis occupied the gap. An adult skull was found within the cist and is likely to be the one that was removed from SK273.

# THE EXCAVATED FEATURES

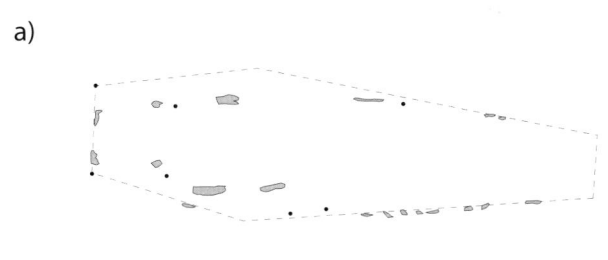

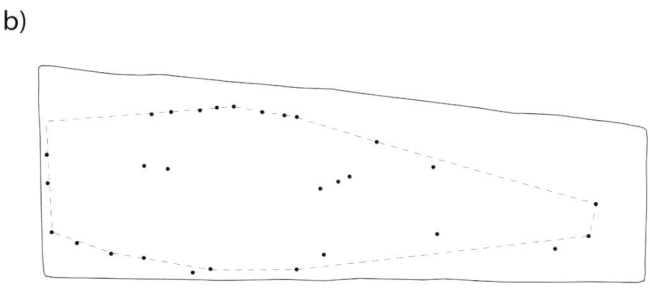

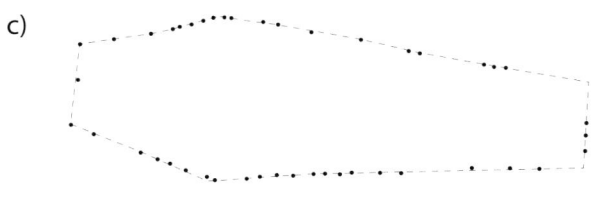

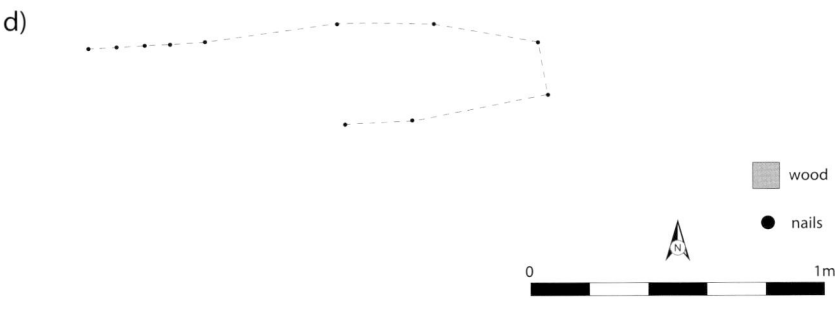

*Figure 23*
Wooden coffins: (a) G529; (b) G468; (c) G851; (d) G584

construction techniques to those of the other excavated cists. It had been truncated by the plough to such an extent that only the base and a few remnants of the sides survived. The base comprised flat rounded stone slabs on which the remains of two skeletons were found. The earliest of these and the most complete was SK724, a young adult male (Figure 22). SK720 lay directly over SK724 but had suffered so much plough

*Figure 24*
SK410 in G411 in which pillow stones have been used on either side of the head

damage that only the legs remained. The position of these skeletons might indicate a family burial plot. SK724 was radiocarbon dated to cal AD 1020–1170 (Table 1; SUERC-13316).

### HAMILTON'S CIST

Hamilton recorded a cist burial during his excavations (Figure 8). This appears to have been located in the south-east of the site along the line of the fence (Figures 8 and 9). It is described in the archive as constructed of edge-set upright stones between 1ft and 1ft 6in long, 1ft high and ½in to 1in thick, and that it had no cover or base. It was aligned east to west and contained no finds.

### SUMMARY

Despite the variation in construction style that these three cist burials display, the radiocarbon dates for this group are so similar as to suggest contemporaneity. The close alignment of two of the graves, G723 and G161, and their proximity to the chapel, together with the presence of a second burial within G723, is suggestive of a high status family plot.

The fashion for cist burial may have continued into the 14th century if another grave, G743 containing SK742, is interpreted as a cist grave. In this case, the cist-like construction consisted of a few broken edge-set stones on either side of the waist of SK742. These stones were very thin in contrast to those used in the other cist burials, so it is possible that this was not a cist at all but the remains of a collapsed cover. SK742 was dated to cal AD 1280–1410 (Table 1; SUERC-13837).

*Coffin burials*

Some 16 graves within the graveyard contain artefacts potentially associated with coffins and coffin fittings. However, in the majority of these graves the finds comprised a single nail, so the possibility that these finds were either residual from earlier periods or later intrusions could not always be eliminated, given the scale of the plough damage.

Only five graves provide unambiguous evidence of coffin burials. The coffins of these burials were seen in outline as decayed wood (Figure 23) but they were not excavated and remain in situ. Two of these, G509 and G529 (Figure 23a) were located within Building 4 (Figure 16).

Outside the eastern end of the building were another three coffin burials, G468 (with SK467), G584 (with SK585) and G851 (with SK852) (Figure 16), characterised by in situ coffin nails and traces of wood (Figure 23c–d). Skeletal remains from all three burials have been radiocarbon dated; SK467 to cal AD 990–1160 (Table 1; SUERC-10476), SK585 to cal AD 1470–1660 (Table 1; SUERC-13321) and SK852 to cal AD 1490–1680 (Table 1; SUERC-13315).

### G468

This grave was sub-rectangular in shape and contained the remains of a coffin defined by in situ coffin nails with wood attached (Figure 23b).

# THE EXCAVATED FEATURES

*Figure 25*
Graves marked by pebbles and shells? [946] (in the foreground) and [952]

G851

The cut for this grave could not be detected but it contained the outline for a six-sided tapered coffin in the form of in situ nails and wood fragments (Figure 23c).

G584

The cut for this grave was only partially observed due to plough and later burial activity (Figure 23d). It appeared to have been truncated by G468 but the radiocarbon dates indicate that the burial was interred 300 years later. Recovered from the fill of G584 was a pin (SF 1053; see Chapter 4.1.1) that has been dated to the early medieval period and therefore may be intrusive.

SUMMARY

Although coffin furniture was retrieved from 16 graves only five definitely contained coffins and, of these, only three were dated, one to the late 10th to mid-12th century and the other two to the late 15th to late 17th century. A variety of coffin furnishings was recovered from the graves (Chapter 4.3.4 and 4.3.5). Nails were used in the manufacture of the coffins, and wooden pegs may have also have been used as fixings. A number of L-shaped brackets were recovered; these may have been for decorative purposes and perhaps denote higher status burials, but it is also possible that the brackets were used to strengthen the coffin and could therefore indicate the transportation of bodies from some distance to the site. Hinges were also found; coffins are unlikely to have had hinged lids so this suggests the re-use of chests or other wooden containers as coffins.

*Burials with pillow stones*

Pillow stones, ie single stones placed on either side of the head (Figure 24), were identified in nine of the excavated graves and ranged from rough stones

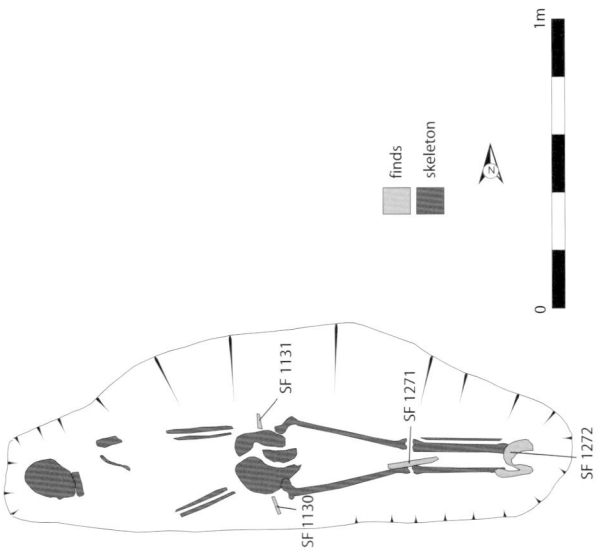

*Figure 26*
The Viking burial SK752

# THE EXCAVATED FEATURES

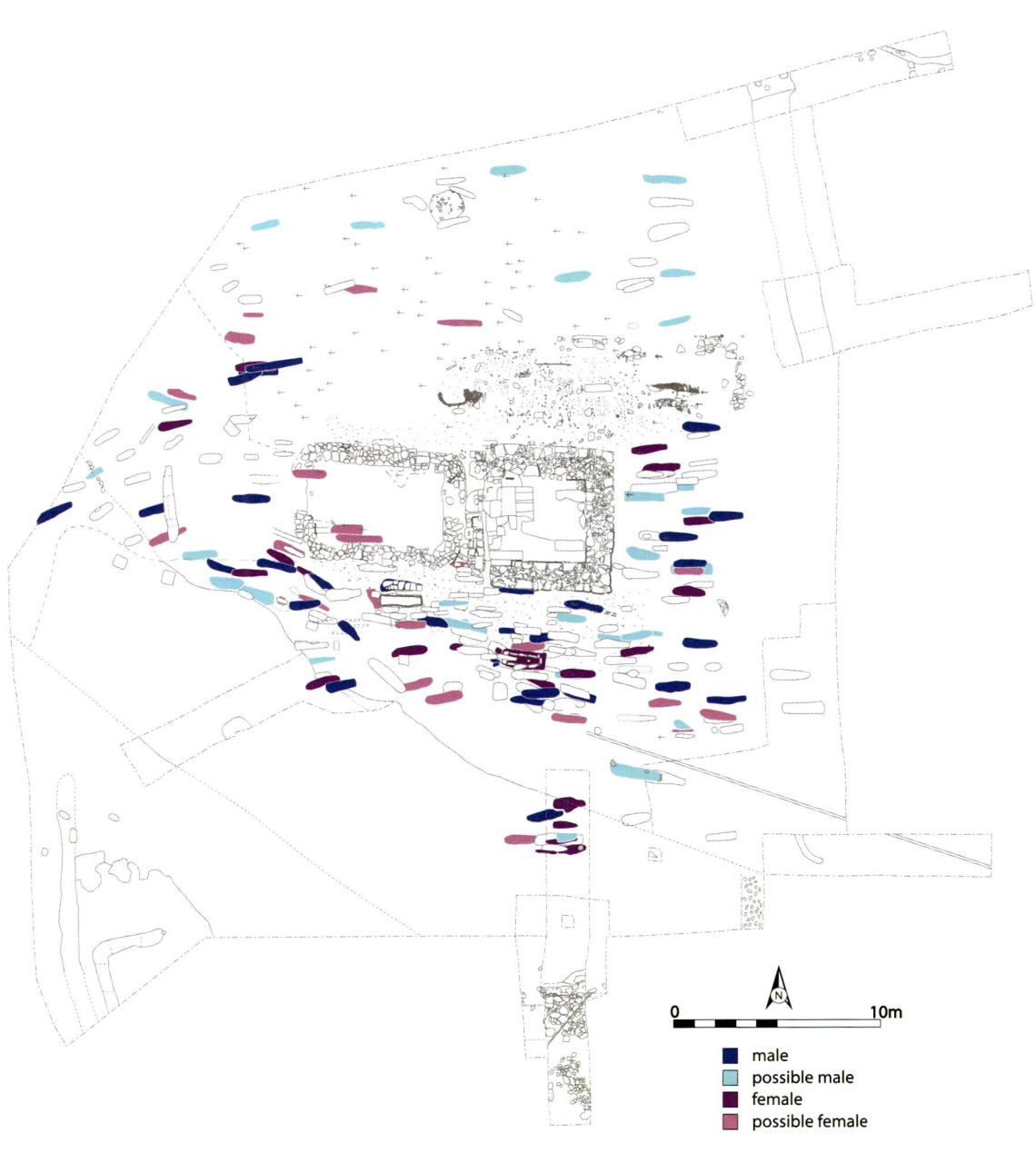

*Figure 27*
Distribution of males and females in the graveyard

# LIVING AND DYING AT AULDHAME, EAST LOTHIAN

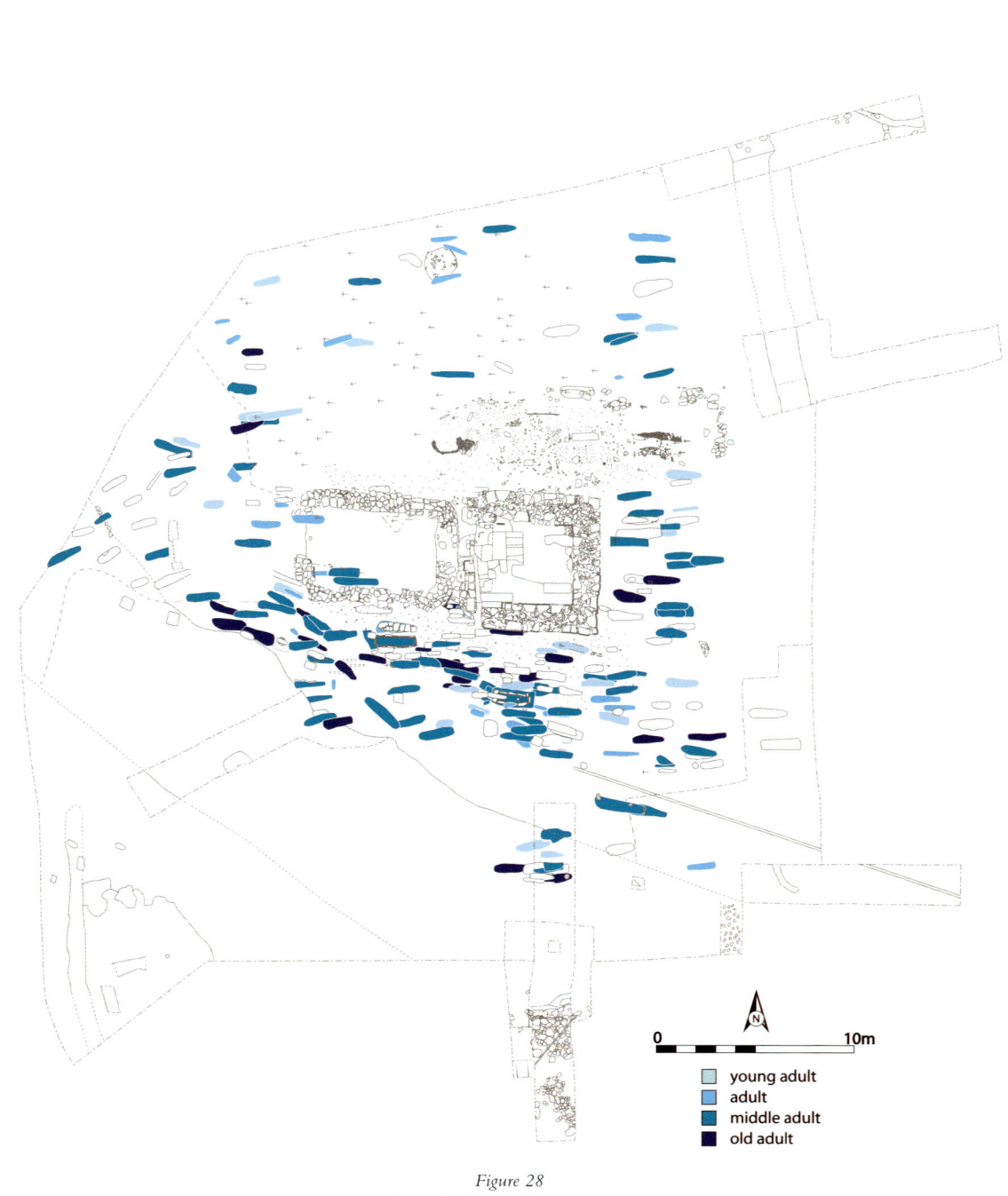

*Figure 28*
Age of adults in the graveyard

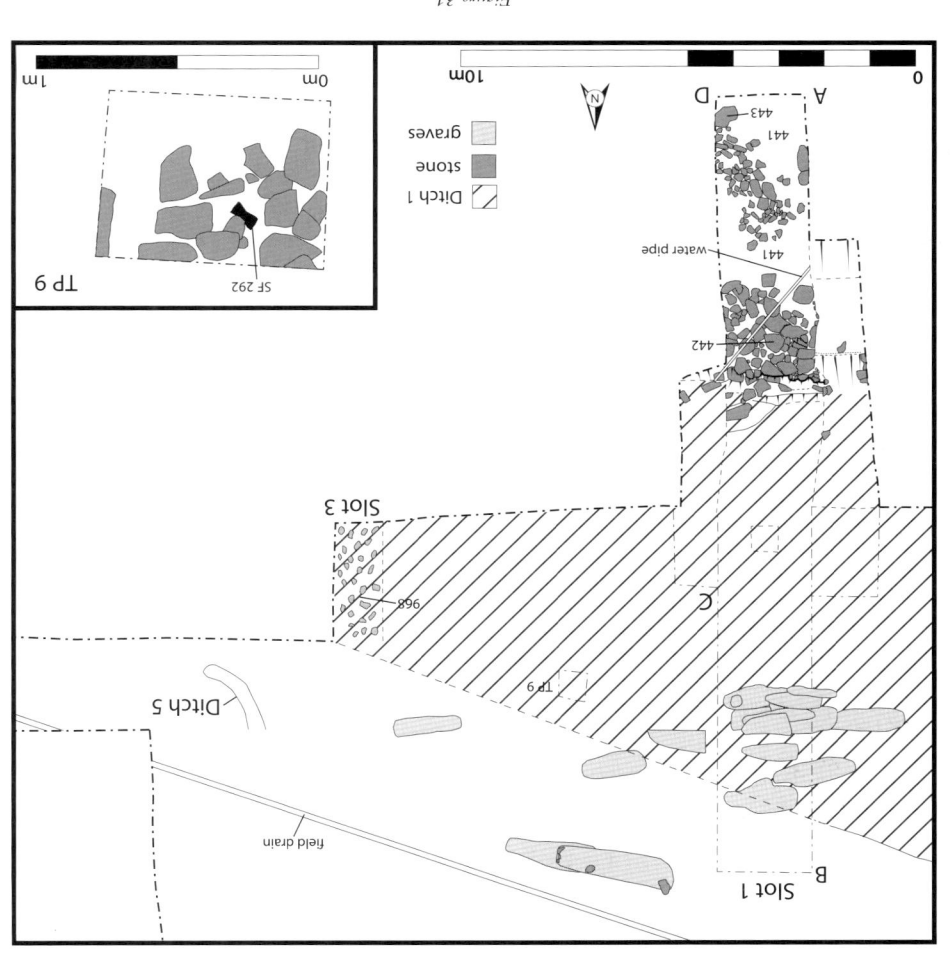

*Figure 31*
Zone 1

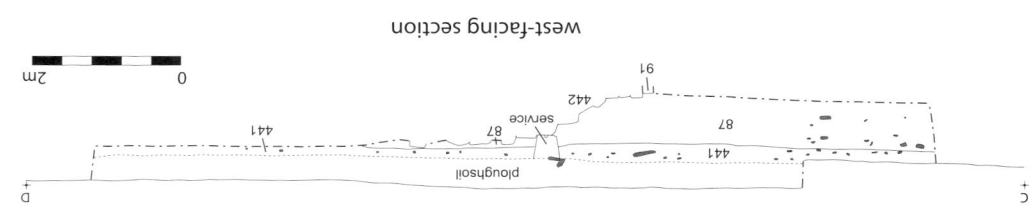

*Figure 32*
Sections across Ditch 1

THE EXCAVATED FEATURES

and see Chapter 4.2). A copper alloy ring buckle of 14th-century date (Figure 60), a pin (Figure 47) and a knife (Figure 67) were also found in three later graves. Three flat rounded water worn stones, one from G161 and two from a partially excavated grave, G034, could be gaming pieces (see Chapter 4.4.4).

### 2.4.7 Gender and age

The distribution of the skeletal remains in terms of gender and age is presented in Figures 27–29. There appears to be no segregation of burial in terms of gender or age (Figures 27 and 28). However, there is a distinct concentration of neonates and infants around the building complex, particularly along the southern walls (Figure 29). SK798 and SK825 were selected for dating from the base and top, respectively, of a sequence of five inter-cutting graves within the concentration of infant burials on the south side of the building remains. The two plough-disturbed burials, [1040] and [1043], were also found close to this location. The radiocarbon dates indicate that infant burial was practised at this location from the mid-7th to the mid-12th centuries AD. Similarly, the group of burials in the far west of the site, which are all aligned SW–NE (see 2.4.2) are predominantly juvenile yet, despite the apparent regularity in layout and orientation of this group of burials (Figure 29) they were interred over a time span of c 400 years (Chapter 3).

## 2.5 OTHER FEATURES

A range of other features were located on the fringes of the site away from the core of the graveyard. For ease of discussion the areas containing these features have been zoned as illustrated on Figure 30. The most important of these features, Ditch 1, spans several of these zones and is therefore described separately.

### 2.5.1 Ditch 1

Slots 1, 2 and 3, and Test Pit 9 were dug to investigate the ditch deposits.

The sections in Slot 1 (Figures 31 and 32) showed that Ditch 1 was sealed below a spread of dark grey clay silt [441] and that it cut through [291] along its northern edge. If [291] is indeed redeposited natural upcast during ditch digging, as suggested in Chapter 2.2.2, then this would suggest that Ditch 1 was a recut of an earlier ditch. The ditch was 9.5m wide in Slot 1. It was not bottomed but small sondages dug along the slot (Figure 33) indicate that the ditch is likely to

to edge-set rounded stones. There does not seem to be any correlation between the use of pillow stones and the age of the individual buried but it may be significant that where gender has been identified females outnumber males in these graves by 5:1. It is generally believed that these stones were used to keep the head upright so that on the Day of Judgement the deceased would rise up from the ground facing east and the newly risen Christ (Daniell 1997, 161). They occur in a range of grave types, in simple burials as well as cist burials (Figures 20 and 21). However, with only one radiocarbon date from a cist grave in which pillow stones were used, SK273 in G276 (cal AD 1020–1170 (Table 1; SUERC-10471), it is impossible to say whether their use reflects a particular fashion or whether their use was a matter of personal belief or aesthetic values.

### 2.4.5 Grave markers

No grave markers were found over any of the excavated graves. However, there were two distinct concentrations of shell and water worn pebbles, [946] and [947] which lie to the NE of Building 4 (Figures 16 and 25) and were visible within deposit [259], whose shape and size suggest that they mark graves. A third area of water-worn pebbles and shell, [952], which lies just N of Building 4, was more dispersed and amorphous in shape (Figure 16) but this may be due to plough damage. In all cases these deposits were associated with edge-set stones.

Two cross-inscribed sandstone slabs were found during the excavation. SF 270 had already been displaced (Figure 71b) but [953], which lies just N of Building 4, appeared to be in situ (Figures 16 and 71a) and was consequently left in place. Both these stones were unworked apart from simple crosses incised into one face (see Chapter 4.3.8).

### 2.4.6 Grave goods

The majority of the objects found in the graves relate either to the burial containers (ie coffin fittings) or have found their way into the graves through later redeposition and mixing of soils as grave cut through earlier graves.

Deliberately deposited grave goods are rare, presumably in keeping with Christian burial practices. There are a few examples, however, the most impressive of which are the copper alloy buckle and strap end, iron spearhead, spurs and associated attachments found in the late 8th–10th-century grave, G751 (Figure 26;

31

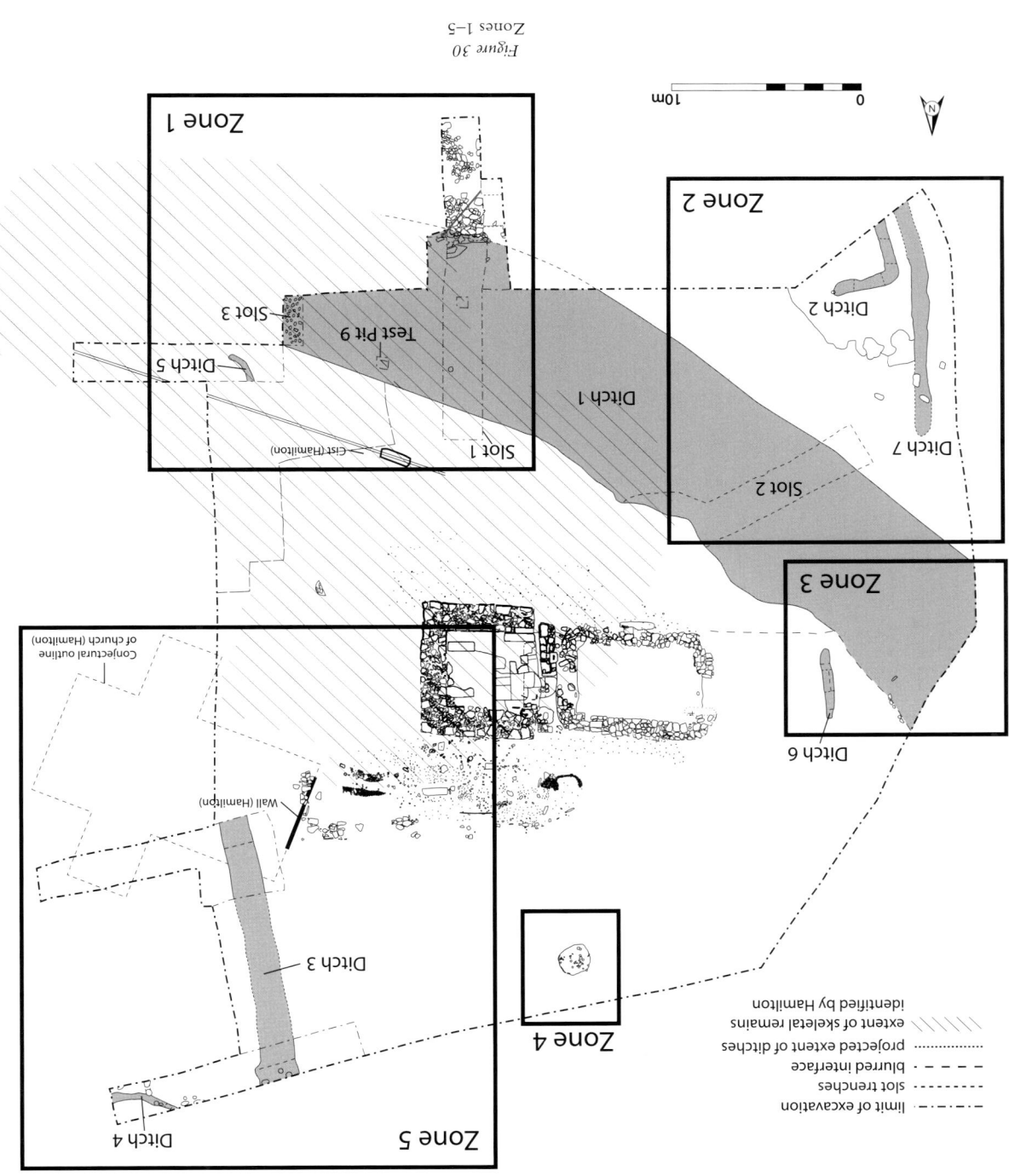

*Figure 30*
Zones 1–5

# THE EXCAVATED FEATURES

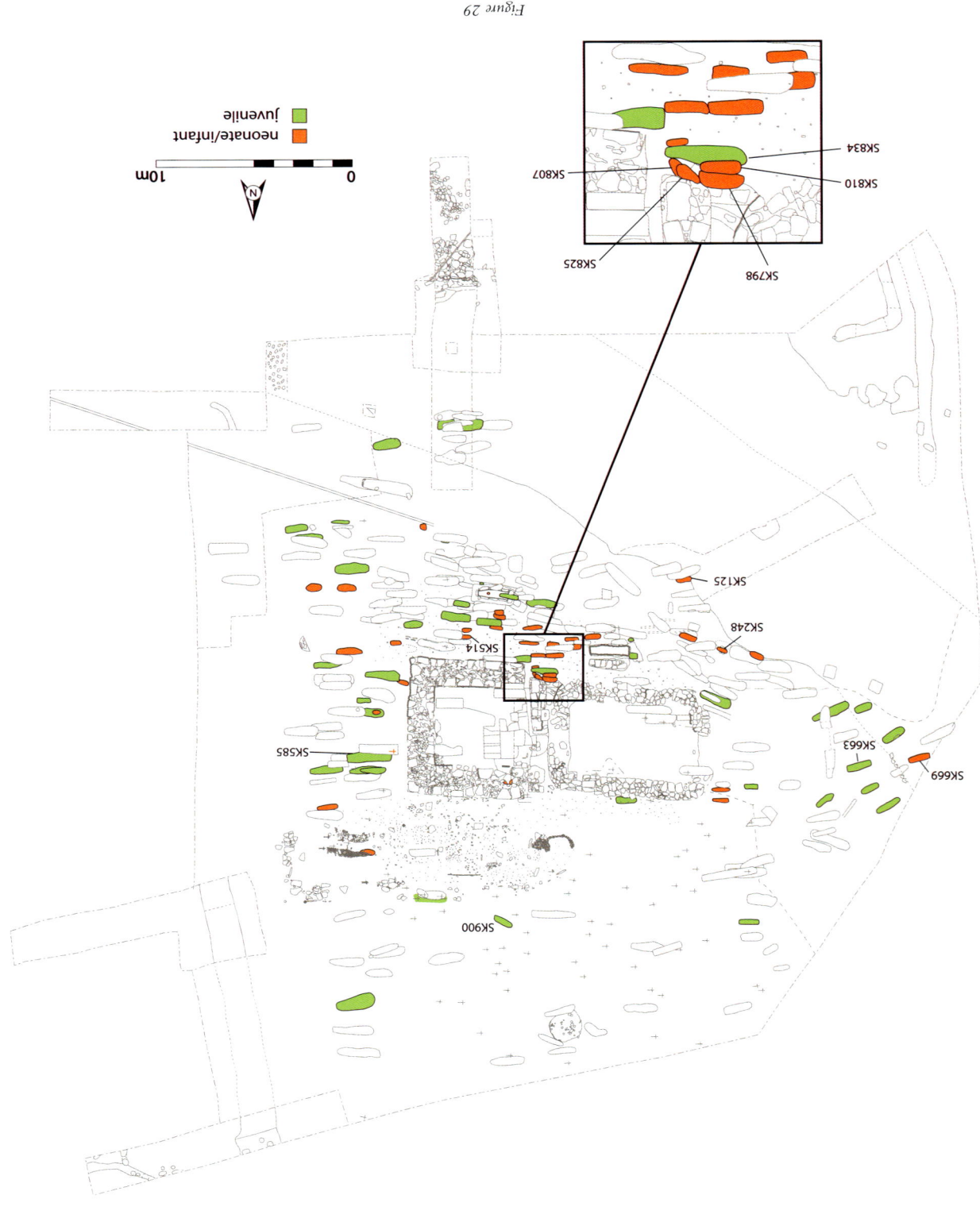

*Figure 29*
Distribution of juvenile and neonate remains

# THE EXCAVATED FEATURES

*Figure 33*
Ditch 1 during excavation, with revetment [442] in the foreground

be in excess of 1.9m in depth (it was recorded as 2m in depth when seen in section in the cliff face – see Chapter 1.3). The ditch contained three main fills. The lowest level encountered was [420]/[418], a yellow silty clay 0.3m deep which may represent deliberate back-filling. Animal bone recovered from this fill was dated to cal AD 680–890 (Table 1; SUERC-13287). In a small sondage in the centre of the ditch, a thin band of reddish-brown, sandy clay [419] 0.12m thick was observed lying over [420]. A thick deposit of dark brown clay silt, [087] sealed [420]/[418]. It was 1.4m deep and contained lenses of charcoal and yellow clayey sand, possibly hearth debris. There were also quantities of animal bone including cattle (*Bos taurus*) and sheep (*Ovis aries*). A bone fragment from this fill was radiocarbon dated to cal AD 680–890 (Table 1; SUERC-13322). The overlying deposit [441] extended as far as the northern edge of the ditch where it overlaid [291], which at this point appeared to be slightly banked. Graves had been cut into the upper fill of the ditch, but were undated.

A stone revetment or wall foundation [442] was found along the southern edge of Ditch 1 (Figures 31–33). This comprised a setting of mainly flat stones cutting fill [087]. These stones had been laid horizontally and several courses were apparent. A single sherd of Scottish White Gritty Ware was recovered from between the stones. These stones extended for a distance of 1.75m beyond the southern edge of Ditch 1 (Figures 31 and 32). Beyond this point lay a second deposit of stones [443]. Apart from surface cleaning these stones were not excavated; they may represent the remnants of a structure or possibly bank material. A small sondage was dug at the base of [442] through deposit [087] and a layer comprised almost entirely of periwinkle shells, [91] was encountered. This probably represents in situ dumping of domestic waste.

Stone rubble [070] was encountered on the northern edge of the ditch in Test Pit 9 (Figure 31). This lay in a similar position to that of [442] on the southern edge. SF 292, a medieval wood working axe, was recovered from amongst [070].

Slot 2 through Ditch 1 (Figure 34) was only excavated to a depth of 0.5m. As in Slot 1, the southern edge of the ditch was overlain by [441]; a few fragments of Scottish White Gritty Ware were retrieved from

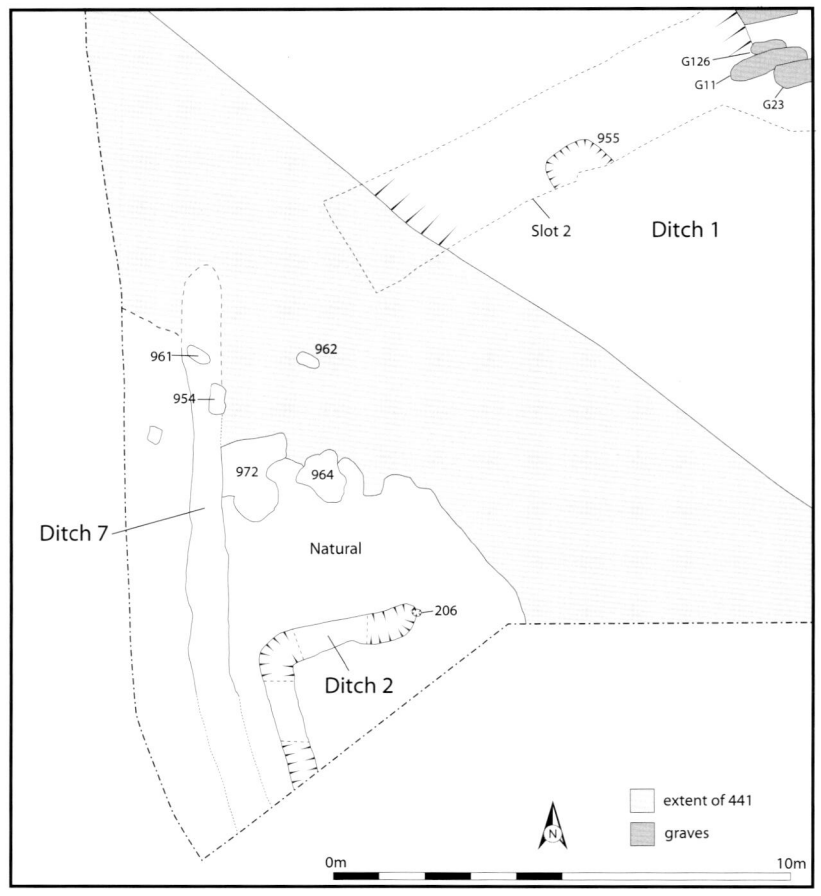

*Figure 34*
Zone 2

this layer. [441] was 0.31m deep at this point and overlay the dark brown clay silt, [087]. Excavation did not proceed beyond the surface of [087] in this slot.

[441] also sealed a stone filled pit [955], which is described in more detail in Chapter 2.5.3. At the eastern end of Slot 2, four graves overlay the inner edge of the ditch. Three of these were intercutting and the latest in the sequence, SK120 (G23), was dated to cal AD 1010–1160 (Table 1; SUERC-13312); as the other two graves in the sequence, G12 and G126, are clearly earlier then infilling must have been complete long before the 11th century AD.

In Slot 3, layer [441] was removed to reveal [968], a compact stony surface of medium sized stones (Figure 31). This layer was not excavated. The evidence from Test Pit 9 and Slot 3 suggests that the amount of stone over the ditch increases toward the southeast. This may explain why the cropmark that defines the ditch does not appear to traverse the whole of the promontory.

The western extent of Ditch 1 remained buried under unexcavated deposit [776]. A short line of stones, [619] appears to demarcate the northern edge of the ditch (Figure 35). Several graves had been dug over the ditch at this point and two of these have been dated; SK669 (in G668), dated to cal AD 1210–1380 (Table 1; SUERC-13835) and SK708 (in G707), dated to cal AD 1280–1400 (Table 1; SUERC-10478), provide a *taq* for the infilling of the ditch of at least the 13th–14th century AD.

### 2.5.2 Zone 1 (Figure 31)

*Ditch 5*

The remains of a curvilinear ditch was uncovered just beyond the northern edge of Ditch 1. A length of

2.2m was exposed, which appeared to end in a distinct terminus. It was filled with a mid-brown clay silt but was not excavated.

### 2.5.3 Zone 2 (Figure 34)

*Ditch 2*

This small rectilinear ditch, or bedding trench, lay to the south of Ditch 1 and was sealed below the modern plough soil. It was 'U-shaped' in profile and was 0.6m wide by 0.25m deep but became shallower toward its terminus. It extended north from the southern baulk of the excavation area for 3m before turning east and terminating after another 3.5m. The remains of a post-hole, [206] cut the terminus. Radiocarbon dates from animal bone from the fill of the ditch and the post-hole suggest infilling in cal AD 690–940 and 660–860, respectively (Table 1; SUERC-13323 and SUERC-13817). A single fragment of White Gritty Ware (12th–14th century) was recovered from one of the sections dug across the ditch but this is almost certainly intrusive, possibly from the overlying layer, [441].

Layer [441] partially sealed two deposits that were not excavated. [964] was a very dark and compact irregular spread which may represent in situ burning, while [972] was a dark grey clay silt possibly cut by Ditch 7.

*Ditch 7*

This ditch was unexcavated but it clearly cut deposit [441]. It was aligned north to south and extended from the southern baulk for a distance of 12m. It was 0.9m wide and was filled by a dark grey clay silt [967].

*Stone-filled pits*

A group of four stone-filled pits were found in this zone. Three of the pits [954], [961] and [962] were located in a cluster on the south side of Ditch 1, while the fourth [955] cut Ditch 1. [954] and [961] appear to cut Ditch 7. None of the pits were excavated, but fragments of medieval metalwork, SF 1022a, b and SF 1281 were recovered from the upper limits of the fill of [954].

Pit [955] was cut into the upper fill of Ditch 1 and was sealed by the layer [441]. This sub-circular pit was only partially excavated. It was approximately 1.4m in diameter with a sharp break of slope at its upper edge. The pit contained large angular stones which made up 75% of the fill, in a matrix of loose dark grey clay silt.

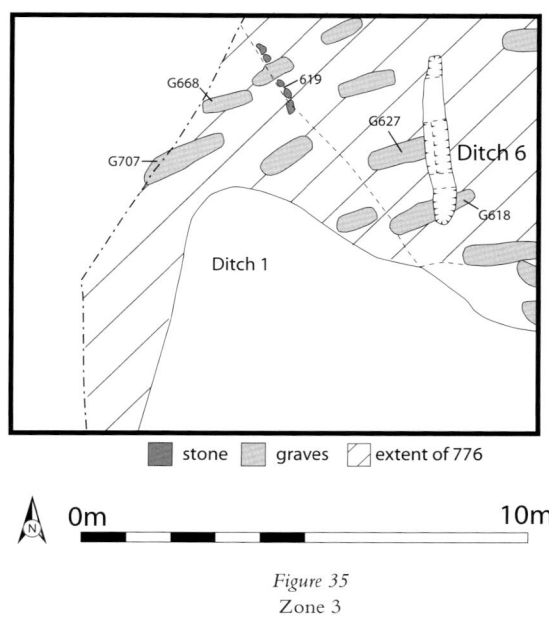

*Figure 35*
Zone 3

### 2.5.4 Zone 3 (Figure 35)

*Ditch 6*

Ditch 6 was a short linear feature aligned north to south. It was 3.85m long, 0.55m wide and 0.22m deep. It was virtually square in profile, with vertical sides and a flat base, except on the western side, which sloped in at an angle of 45° before becoming vertical. It had a single fill of mottled yellow-brown clay, which contained a number of disarticulated human bones. The bone is likely to have come from the two burials cut by this ditch, SK617 in G618 and SK626 in G627. SK626 was radiocarbon dated to cal AD 880–1020 (Table 1; SUERC-13317), providing a *tpq* for the cutting of the ditch.

### 2.5.5 Zone 4 (Figure 36)

*Hearth/oven*

The only feature within this zone was a sub-circular patch of burnt red clay [920] partially delineated by an arc of small upright stones. A charcoal-rich deposit, [921], lay immediately to the west. It is possible that [920] is the remains of a hearth or bread oven, [921] representing rakings from the fire. Both these features were unexcavated. [920] had been cut by two burials, SK915 and SK918, one of which, SK915, was radiocarbon dated to cal AD 1280–1400 (Table 1; SUERC-13311), providing a *taq* for the disuse of this feature.

*Figure 36*
Zone 4. Hearth/oven [920] looking south

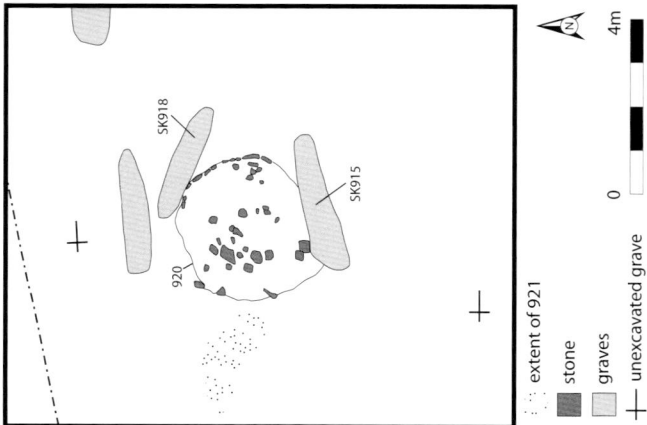

# THE EXCAVATED FEATURES

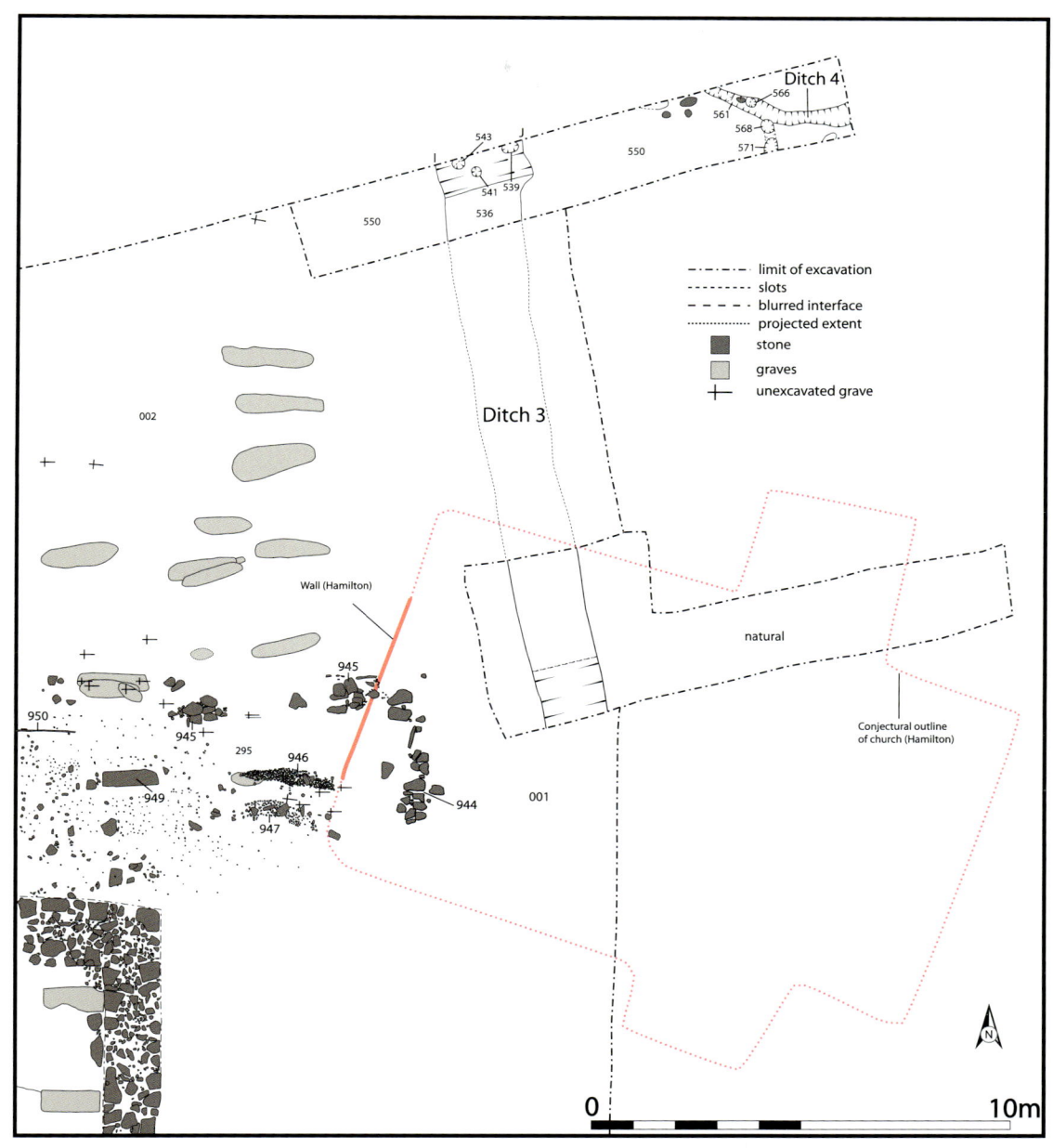

*Figure 37*
Zone 5

## 2.5.6 Zone 5 (Figure 37)

### Ditch 3

This shallow ditch ran north–south along the eastern edge of the site and continued beyond the limits of the excavation. It was cut into the natural boulder clay and was sealed below the graveyard soils, [002] and [350]. At the northern baulk it was 2.3m wide but only 0.18m deep, with gently sloping sides and an uneven base. At the southern end of the exposed length the ditch had narrowed to 1.7m but had increased in depth to 0.3m. It is likely that this ditch has been heavily plough-truncated. It was filled with a dark grey-brown, silty clay. Animal bone from the fill has been radiocarbon dated to cal AD 790–950 (Table 1; SUERC-13324).

Three stake-holes, [539], [541] and [543], were located in the base of the ditch. They varied in diameter from 0.05m to 0.1m and in depth from 0.05m to 0.1m, and were filled with a mid-grey/brown silty clay similar to the fill of the ditch. It was not possible to determine whether these were earlier features truncated by the ditch or whether they were stakes driven into the base of the ditch while it was open.

*Ditch 4*

Ditch 4 was a curvilinear gully/ditch lying to the east of Ditch 3. It was aligned east to west and was between 0.2m to 0.4m wide, and between 0.05m and 0.12m deep. The sides of the ditch were near vertical and the base gently rounded. It had a single fill of greyish-brown, clay silt from which a small amount of animal bone was recovered together with a fragment of undiagnostic pottery (SF 1014 – see Chapter 4.4.1). A post-hole, [566], 0.25m in diameter and 0.1m deep was found in the base of the ditch. As the fill of the post-hole was the same as the ditch fill, it was impossible to determine whether the post-hole cut the ditch or *vice versa*.

Post-holes [568] and [571] may be associated with [566]. [568] cut the southern edge of Ditch 4 and [571] lay 0.1m beyond it. Both post-holes were identical in size, with diameters of 0.35 to 0.4m and a depth of 0.08m. Animal bone recovered from these two post-holes produced virtually identical dates of cal AD 650–810 and cal AD 650–820 (Table 1; SUERC-13833 and SUERC-13832).

*Walls [944] and [945]*

Located to the north-east of the building complex were two linear areas of stonework, [944] and [945]. Both displayed a similar style of construction, which consisted of slabs placed upright along the edges of the foundation trench with an infill of rounded stones (Figure 38). This was the style of construction also used in Building 3 (see above). Neither of these features was excavated. It is perhaps significant that almost all in situ graves lie west of a line projected north–south from [944], while a line projected west from [945]

*Figure 38*
Walls [944] and [945]

would run along the boundary between the northern graveyard soil, [002], and the shell-rich layer, [259]. It is possible that the walls represent the corner of a former boundary wall to the graveyard during a period of contraction, although the method of construction seems overly elaborate for a boundary wall.

HAMILTON'S BUILDING

Hamilton found the remains of a building during his excavations. The foundation of a wall was found in one of the trenches and this was conjectured to be the gable wall of a possible church or chapel (Figure 8). Further excavation by Hamilton revealed the poorly preserved remnants of a drystone built structure which had been extensively robbed, leaving only a scattering of stones representing the side walls. It was 25ft (7.62m) wide and was flanked by a paved path. Ash and midden deposits on the paved surface, together with a decorated spindle whorl led Hamilton to conclude that the structure was not a church or chapel but must have had a domestic use. A spindle whorl labelled as 'from excavation of chapel site on cliff edge at Auldhame near North Berwick. April 1976.' has recently been found within the National Museum of Scotland and is probably the same artefact. This find is typologically of medieval or post-medieval date (Chapter 4.3.8 and Figure 73).

The location of Hamilton's building is something of a puzzle. It could potentially be the western gable wall of Building 2; the widths could be construed as similar, 7.62m compared to 6m. Building 2 is also of drystone construction but it is clay-bonded; Hamilton may simply have omitted to mention this detail but he would surely not have described the surviving walls as 'a scatter of stones'. It is unlikely that the wall was a component of either Building 3 or 4 as both these buildings were mortared and the walls are also still quite substantial. More significantly, no evidence of paving was found around the building complex, and there was no evidence of the trenches that Hamilton dug across the floor of the building. The alignment of features on his sketch plan and the recent survey would place his wall over wall [944] (Figures 9 and 37). However, if [944] is the wall of a building then it would form the eastern gable, with wall [945] as the northern wall. Again, no evidence of paving or of Hamilton's trenches was found in this area.

# CHAPTER 3

# CHRONOLOGY

## 3.1 AIMS AND OBJECTIVES

An extensive programme of radiocarbon dating was undertaken at Auldhame to disentangle the chronology of the chapel, graveyard and associated features. Some 54 samples were submitted for radiocarbon assay; 43 samples of human bone, 10 samples of animal bone and one of limpet shell (Table 1 and Figure 39).

The 54 samples were selected to answer specific questions about the site;

(i) Can phases of burial activity be identified in the graveyard?

(ii) Are the dug features seen around the periphery of the site contemporary with the graveyard?

(iii) Can the stone buildings be dated using the burials that lie under or over them?

(iv) Is there any relationship between chronology and the age and gender of the graves? Do specific genders dominate at particular times during the use of the graveyard?

(v) Is there any relationship between chronology and the variation in grave alignment? (See Chapter 2.4.2.)

(vi) Is there any relationship between chronology and the type of burial, ie coffins, cists and simple inhumations? (See Chapter 2.4.4.)

(vii) Does the concentration of infant burials at the south side of the building complex represent a single phase of interment? (See Chapter 2.4.7.)

(viii) Two of the burials displayed trauma that would have resulted in death (Chapter 5.2.7). Did this trauma occur at the same time or is there no connection between the two individuals? (See below and Chapter 5.4.3.)

Questions i–iv, above, are addressed in this chapter, and an overall chronology for the site is proposed.

### 3.1.1 Constraints on the evidence and analytical approach

John Barber

The 54 date-points relate to 43 interments and to animal bone and shell from a further 11 contexts. Two of the dated bone samples came from grave fills but it is improbable that the ecofactual dates have a defining taphonomic relationship with the interments and more probable that they are residual material accidentally included with grave fills. The shell date has been corrected for marine reservoir effect.

The remains of 43 individuals are thus dated, directly or indirectly from a graveyard population ($P_c$) comprising the 242 interments excavated and the 66 burials left in situ, and a large but unquantified number of human remains represented by the disarticulated and unstratified bone recovered from the ploughsoil. Thus, the 308 interments that have been identified must form the minimum estimate for the value of $P_c$. The limits of the graveyard were established and the partly excavated area comprises approximately 90% of the graveyard area. If we increase our estimate of $P_c$ proportionately to the whole area of the graveyard we arrive at a guesstimate of a graveyard population of 342, and if we further allow for an estimate of 100 interments amongst the disarticulated remains, a very rough guesstimate of the total graveyard population would be 450–500 burials. Thus, the dated sample represents roughly 9% to 10% of this population.

The dated sample is large enough to found upon provided that the geographical distribution of burial was not constrained over time. Thus, for example, if burials were inserted only in one restricted area of the graveyard in a particular century and we have not sampled that area, the sample may be biased. Only one indication of spatial segregation has been noted and that was the burial of infants (see Chapter 3.3). However, these fall into the general chronological

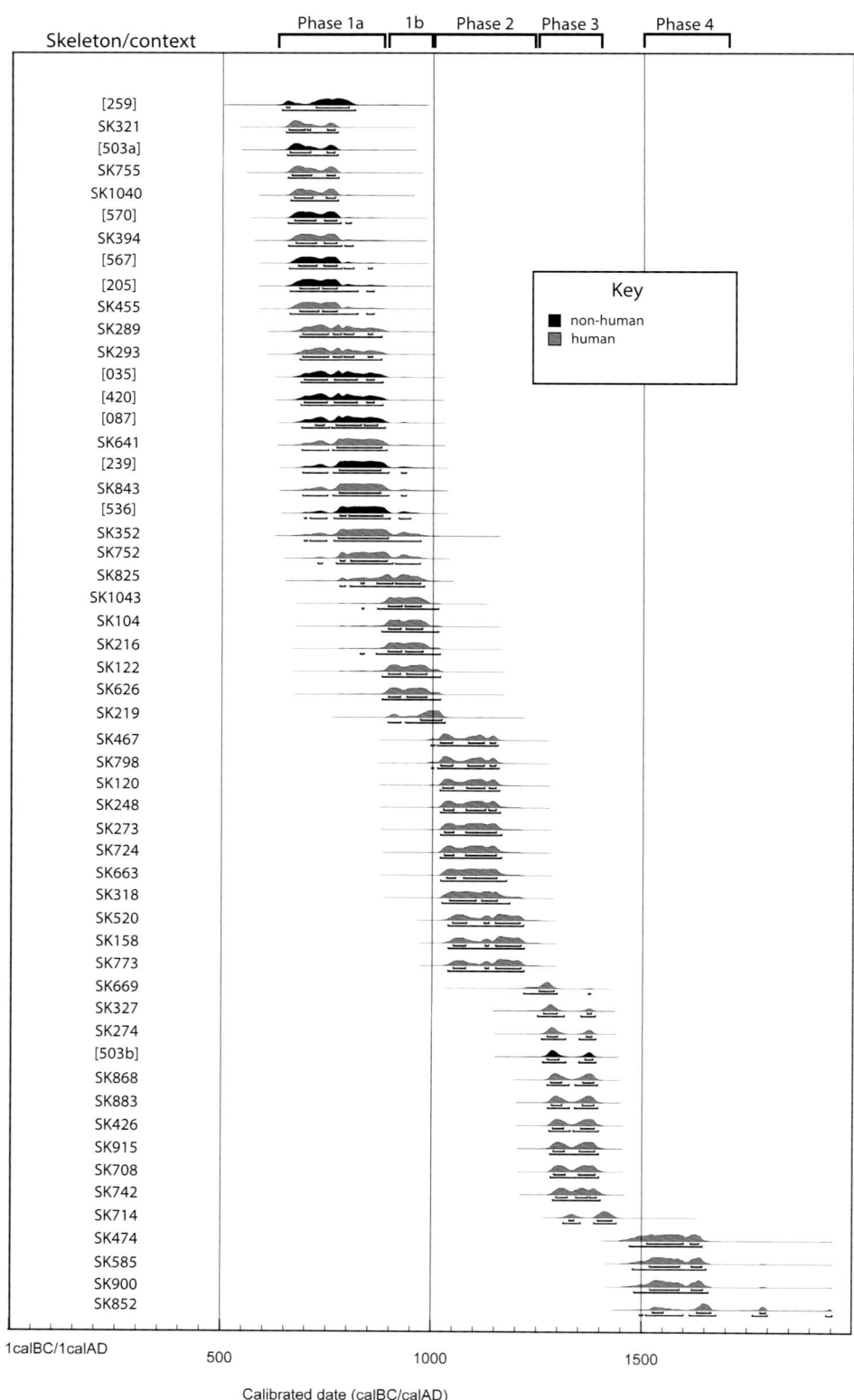

*Figure 39*
The radiocarbon dates (graph produced using OxCal v4 1.7 Bronk Ramsey 2010; r:5 Atmospheric data from Reimer et al 2009)

scheme and are not chronologically distinct. Our operating hypothesis is therefore that the dated sample is representative of the burial traditions of this graveyard over time and the discussion and conclusions that follow are predicated on that hypothesis.

With the reservations expressed above, it is argued here that the radiocarbon results have demonstrated that the graveyard was in intermittent use for approximately 1,000 years, from the late 7th century AD until the 17th century (Figure 39). Long and Rippeteau (1974) proposed statistical procedures for testing the hypothesis that groups of radiocarbon dates are contemporaneous, ie that they are separate attempts to assay the date of the same event. Their test measures the extent to which the differences between the dates in the group are significantly different from zero, given the imprecision of the radiocarbon method. Given an hypothesis that two particular radiocarbon dates represented the same event, the discovery that they could not legitimately be averaged, per Long and Rippeteau, would require the abandonment of the hypothesis (in the absence of any further evidence on the matter).

Where a sequence of dates represents a process that is continuous or that is subdivided by intervals too short to be resolved by the radiocarbon method, it is possible to use the Long and Rippeteau algorithm to explore issues of duration within the date series, even though it is clear that it would not be legitimate to average the whole of the series, or even where the difference between the earliest date and the latest is clearly significant with respect to the precision of the radiocarbon method. In Table 1, the radiocarbon dates are set out in chronological order. The legitimacy of averaging each adjacent pair was tested; where averaging was legitimate, the word 'Yes' has been inserted beside the older of the two dates and where it was not legitimate to average them the term 'No' has similarly been inserted. The 'No' determinations divide the date series into four groups, described as 'Phases' below (Figure 39). The reasonable objection that one burial cannot be averaged with another is correct but irrelevant, since this test explores the process of burial, not the quantum nature of individual acts of burial.

## 3.2 RESULTS

Figure 40 shows the location of all dated and phased skeletons. Figure 41 graphs the dates from animal bone and shell retrieved from non-burial features,

**Table 2**
**Graves phased by stratigraphic association with dated burials**

| Grave No. | Cut by | Phase |
|---|---|---|
| 808 | SK825 | 1 |
| 365 | SK321 | 1 |
| 251 | SK248 | 1–2 |
| 175 | SK159 | 1–2 |
| 12 | SK120 | 1–2 |
| 126 | G012 so by SK120 | 1–2 |
| 735 | SK733 | 1–2 |
| 812 | SK733 | 1–2 |
| 815 | G812 so by SK733 | 1–2 |
| 787 | G817 so by SK733 | 1–2 |
| 316 | SK273 | 1–2 |
| 769 | SK273 | 1–2 |
| 835 | SK798 | 1–2 |
| 811 | SK798 | 1–2 |
| 835 | G811 so by SK798 | 1 - 2 |
| 515 | SK520 | 1–2 |
| 873 | SK883 | 3 or 4 |
| 870 | SK883 | 3 or 4 |

while Figures 42, 43 and 44 graph the dates according to grave alignment, age and gender, and burial type respectively (note that the dates for the two plough disturbed burials, SK1040 and SK1043, have only been plotted on the age and gender graph as it was not possible to tell from the remains what their original alignment was or what type of burial had taken place).

As might be expected in a crowded graveyard there was much intercutting and consequently some of the dated skeletons can provide *taqs* for undated skeletons by virtue of their stratigraphic relationships. However, the *taqs* must necessarily be broad, encompassing both the phase to which the dated skeleton was assigned and the earlier phases. Thus, a grave cut by a Phase 3 grave could belong to either Phases 1, 2 or 3, unless there is evidence to suggest otherwise. Graves provisionally dated in this way are listed in Table 2 and shown on Figure 40.

# LIVING AND DYING AT AULDHAME, EAST LOTHIAN

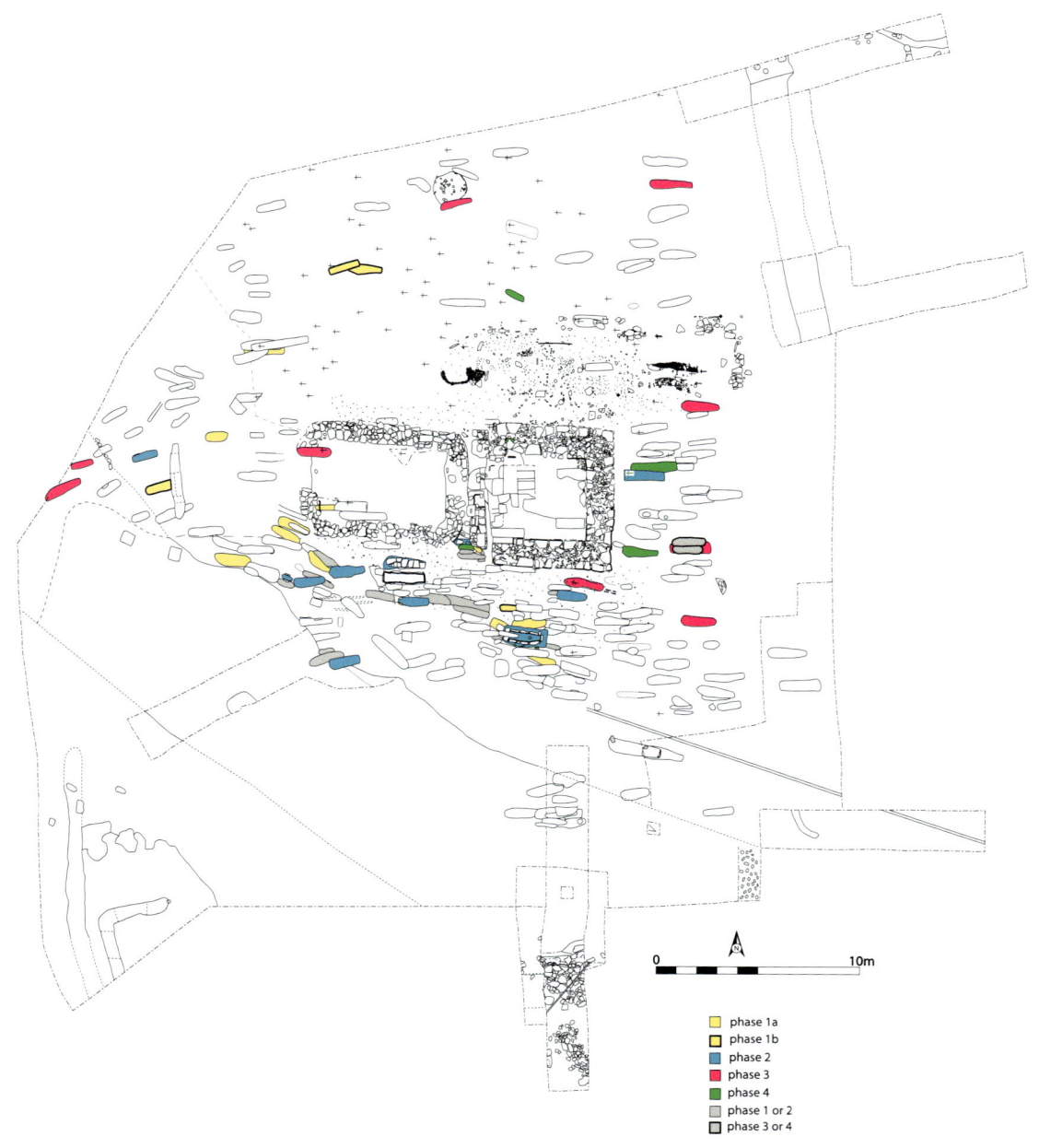

*Figure 40*
Radiocarbon-dated burials and burials provisionally dated by stratigraphic relationships

### 3.2.1 Phase 1; AD 650–1000

All but one of the dated samples of animal bone belongs to this phase (Figure 41). The animal bone invariably came from the dug features on the site, from the fills of Ditches 1, 2 and 3 and from the post-holes associated with Ditch 4. The single shell date places the shell-rich deposit, [259] in this phase. The animal bone, together with other food remains (see Chapter 6) represents the accumulation of domestic refuse and implies the presence of a settlement on the site. This is likely to have been an ecclesiastical settlement, the evidence for which will be drawn together in Chapter 7.2.2. The radiocarbon dates suggest that midden accumulation, and by implication the settlement, had ceased c AD 850–900.

44

# CHRONOLOGY

Of the dated burials, 18 belong in this phase. All the burials, with the exception of the two plough-disturbed infant burials, SK1040 and SK1043, were simple inhumations (Figure 44). Twenty-two per cent of the skeletons were either neonate/infants or juveniles. Adult males and females were present in roughly equal numbers, although gender could not be confidently determined for many of the skeletons in this phase (Figure 43). The dated graves are of mainly E–W orientation but most of the dated graves with a NW–SE orientation occur in Phase 1 too (Figure 42). Some variation in burial rite is seen during this phase; the Viking burial, SK752 with its burial goods, and the flexed burial, SK455, date to this phase.

The chronological distribution of the dated burials suggests continuous, uninterrupted use of the graveyard for most of this phase. However, towards the very end of this phase there is a group of five burials (SK1043, SK104, SK216, SK122 and SK626) whose radiocarbon dates are virtually identical and could therefore legitimately be averaged together, suggesting that they represent a single event, ie they were all buried at the same time. This group displays no apparent bias in terms of gender, age or

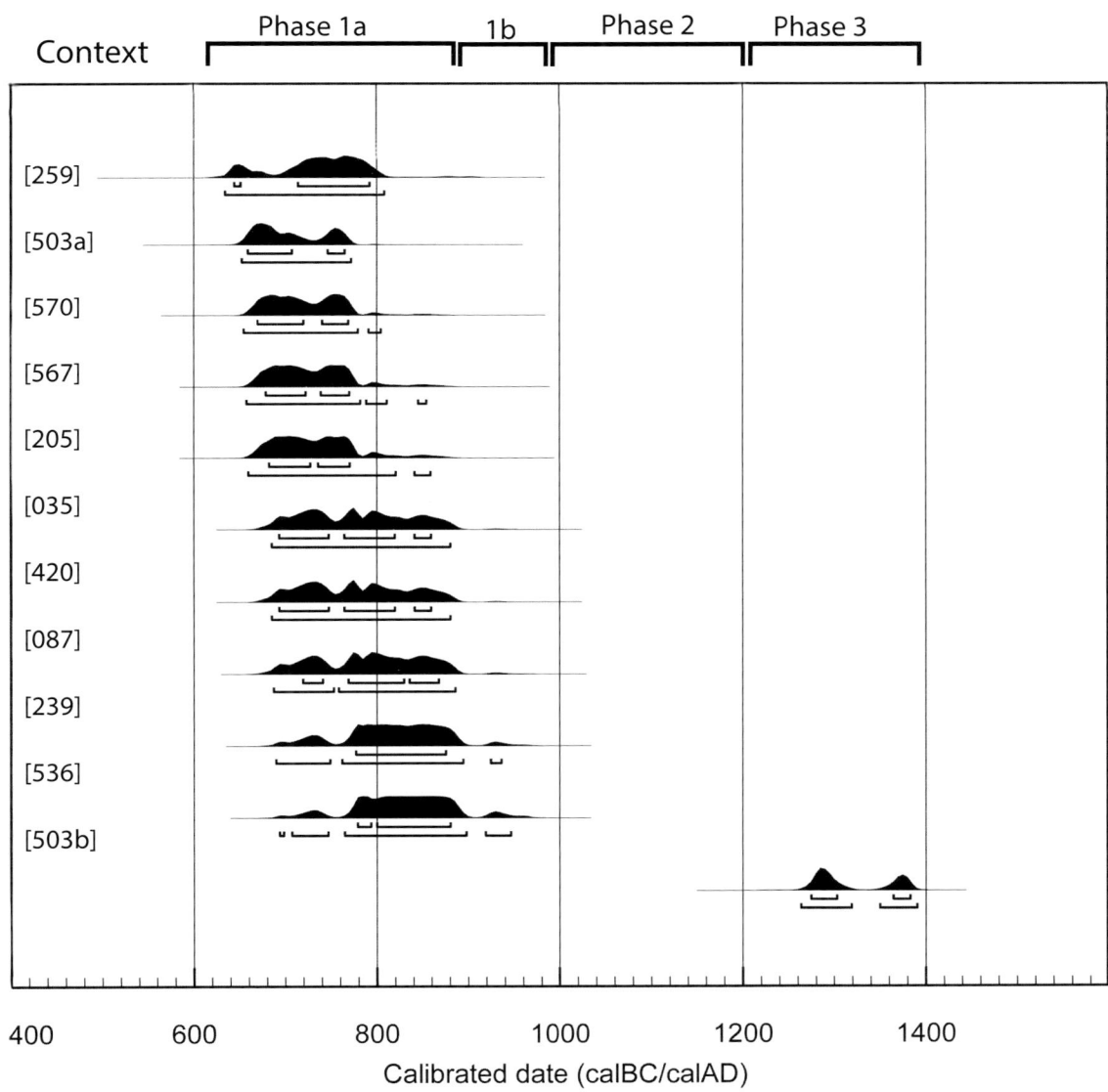

*Figure 41*
Radiocarbon dates from animal bone and shell

# LIVING AND DYING AT AULDHAME, EAST LOTHIAN

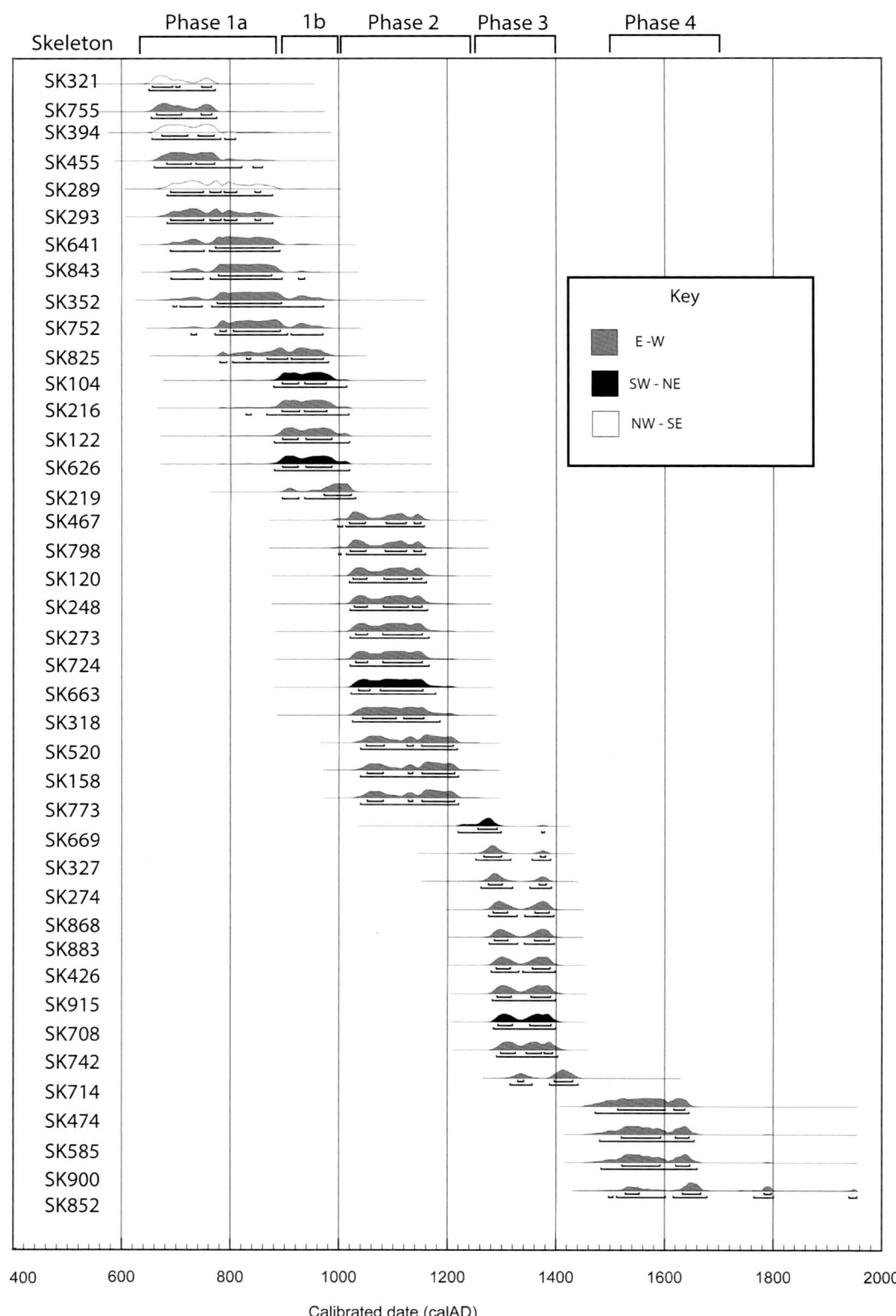

*Figure 42*
Grave alignment by phase

# CHRONOLOGY

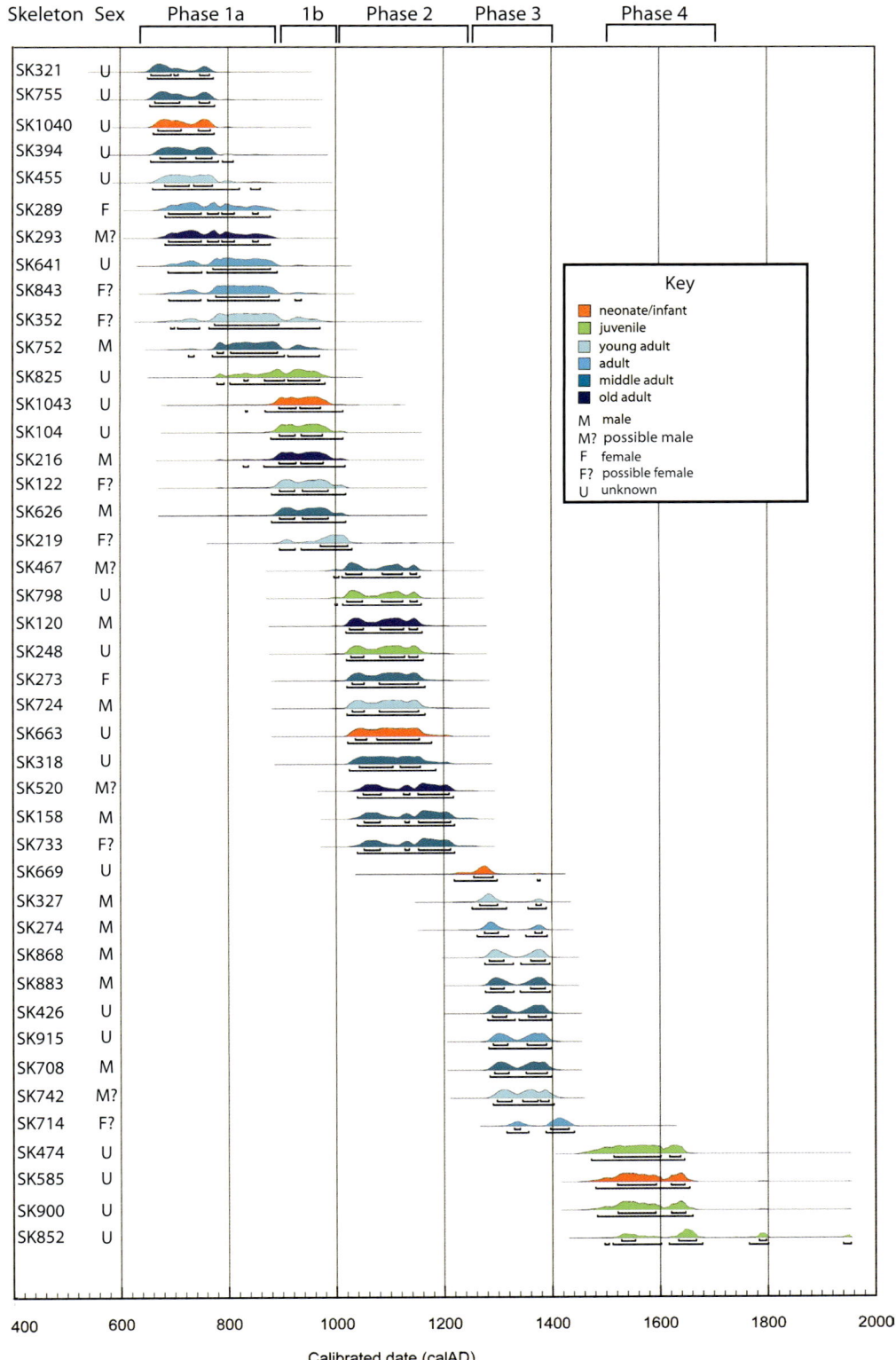

*Figure 43*
Age and gender by phase

# LIVING AND DYING AT AULDHAME, EAST LOTHIAN

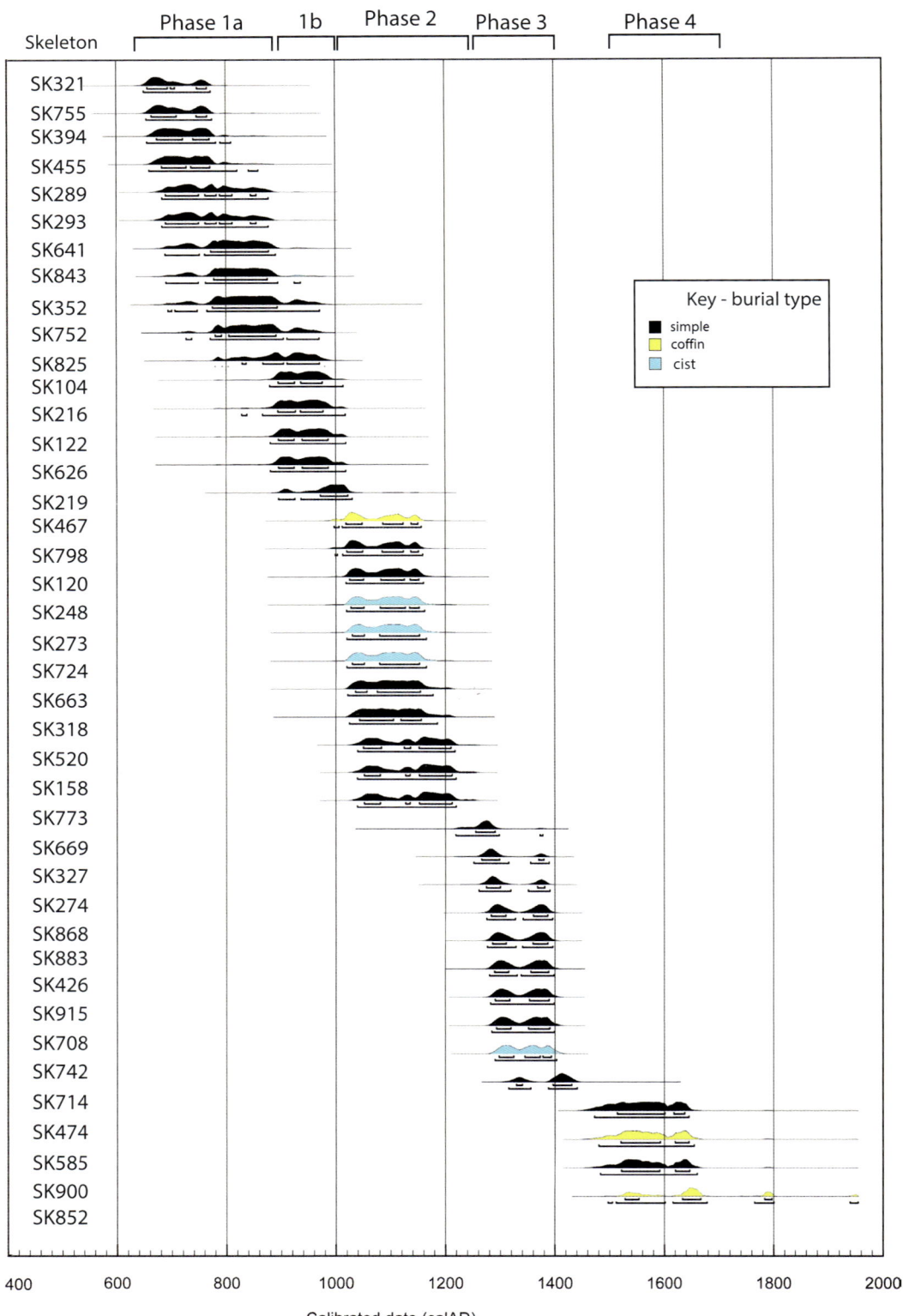

*Figure 44*
Burial type by phase

pathology (Figure 43; and see Chapter 5.2.7) but it may be significant that one of these skeletons, SK216, was one of those that had suffered fatal injury from a sharp weapon (Chapter 5.2.7), while two, SK104 and SK626, had been buried in graves with slightly aberrant orientations, ie NW–SE. If the ecclesiastical settlement ceased *c* AD 850–900, as the animal bone dates suggest, it is possible that these burials, together with the slightly later burial SK219, represent *ad hoc* interments in an otherwise abandoned churchyard, their orientation simply reflecting the absence of management in the graveyard. This phase has therefore been subdivided into Phases 1a and 1b to reflect this apparent change in the rate and nature of burial activity on the site.

### 3.2.2 Phase 2; AD 1000–1200

There are 11 dated burials in this phase. Again they are mainly E–W in orientation but there are also examples of NW–SE and SW–NE orientation present (Figure 42). In this phase there are at least twice as many adult males as females (Figure 43).

The greatest variation in grave type is seen in this phase, which includes a coffin burial, SK467, and three cist burials, SK248, SK273 and SK724 (Figure 44). It has been proposed above (Chapter 2.4.4) that the contemporaneity of the radiocarbon dates for these three burials, together with their close alignment and proximity to the chapel, and the re-use of one of the graves is indicative of a family plot.

One of the graves dated to this phase, SK120 (in G23), had been dug over the inner edge of Ditch 1, thus providing a *taq* for its backfilling (Figure 34).

### 3.2.3 Phase 3; AD 1200–1400

Phase 3 is represented by ten dated burials. Apart from a cist burial, SK742 (Figure 44), all the burials were in simple dug graves, oriented mainly E–W apart from two that were SW–NE (Figure 42). As in Phase 2, adult males dominate (Figure 43). One skeleton, SK868 had suffered a fatal injury from a sharp weapon, similar to the injury encountered on one of the Phase 1 skeletons, SK216.

Statistical analysis indicates that SK714 is distinct from the other Phase 3 burials and must represent a separate event, although still within Phase 3. While there are probably other undated burials associated with this event, the fact that there is only a single dated representative suggests that burial activity reduced quite dramatically towards the end of Phase 3.

### 3.2.4 Phase 4; AD 1500–1700

There are only four burials dated to this phase, two in coffins SK585 and SK852 and two in simple dug graves (Figure 44). The age profile of the dated burials is distinctive, with an infant and three juveniles present (Figure 43). Orientation is E–W except for one oriented NW–SE (Figure 42).

### 3.2.5 The date of the buildings

Some of the dated burials have provided *terminus ante quem* and *terminus post quem* dates for construction and disuse of the buildings but their chronology still remains fluid and does not dovetail neatly into the phases of graveyard activity outlined above. However, although we cannot unambiguously tie the buildings into the various phases of burial activity it seems unlikely that changes to the chapel, the focal point of the graveyard, are not connected to pulses of burial activity. The following chronology is proposed for the development of the chapel complex, drawing on other strands of evidence where necessary.

*Building 1*

We have no secure dating evidence for Building 1 except that it predates all the other buildings. If it does represent a small wooden chapel or oratory, and that is the likeliest explanation, it can only be associated with the earliest burials on the site, in Phase 1. It appears to lie on a NW–SE alignment, which may explain why so many of the Phase 1 burials lie on this alignment.

*Building 2*

There are two pieces of dating evidence for Building 2. SK714 (cal AD 1310–1450) lies across the line of the western gable wall and could therefore represent a *terminus post quem* date for its construction, at the end of Phase 3. However, the stratigraphical relationship between the burial and the gable wall is very ambiguous as the wall no longer exists at this point (Figure 10), and such a late date for Building 2 would conflate the available chronology for the later buildings. Furthermore, by the 14th century, mortar was routinely used in building construction and it seems unlikely that a drystone building would have been erected at so late a date (see below). Rather, we propose that Building 2 was built some time in Phase 1. It lies over a Phase 1 burial, SK641, but as Phase 1 spans 350 radiocarbon years, it is quite feasible that Building 2 could also have been constructed during this phase. An earthfast timber building, such as that indicated for Building 1, is unlikely to have lasted unaltered for nigh on four centuries and so we surmise that it was replaced by a building with more durable foundations.

Building 2 had clay-bonded drystone foundations but it may have had a timber superstructure. The rather tenuous evidence for this lies in our interpretation of Ditch 6 (Figure 10). This short trench lies parallel with the western gable wall of Building 2, at a distance of some 6m, and it does not extend beyond the projected north and south walls of that building. The space within is relatively free of burials (Figure 9) and it is suggested here that it represents a timber extension to Building 2. It does have the distinctive square profile of earthfast timber constructions (Figure 10 – Section AB; and see Chapter 7.3.2) As Ditch 6 cuts through SK626, one of the late group of Phase 1 burials, it must have been constructed in Phase 2, implying that Building 2 continued in use throughout this phase. A transition from earthfast timber construction to stone-footed timber buildings has been noted on other contemporary sites. At Whitby (Rahtz 1976, 461), Hartlepool (Daniels 1988, 175–81) and Hoddom (Lowe 2006, 183), this transition occurs in the mid-to later 8th century AD, while at Dunbar it occurs some time between the mid-8th and mid-9th century (Perry 2000, 319) (see Chapter 7.2.2 for further discussion). Building 2 may have been built around the same time and its timber extension added in Phase 2 when the graveyard came back into use.

*Building 3*

The only dating evidence for Building 3 is that it lies over a Phase 1 burial, SK843. However, it is likely to be later than Building 2, simply because it is of mortared construction. The proposition that Building 2 had a timber superstructure helps to make sense of Building 3. It is represented by two lengths of walling, [655] and [646], which appear to replace the eastern gable wall of Building 2, but it extends the footprint of the latter by no more than a wall's width (Figure 10). If the timber superstructure of Building 2 had decayed away during the hiatus in graveyard activity between Phases 2 and 3 then walls [655] and [646] may be all that remains of a mortared sandstone building that was built over the drystone foundations of Building 2, the eastern gable wall being fully replaced because it was in such a state of decay. The terminal of wall [646] implies an entrance into an eastern extension which now lies under Building 4. Building 3 thus marks the renewed use of the headland in Phase 3, probably as a parish church and graveyard (see Chapter 7.3.3). This phase of activity had ended by the time SK714 (cal AD 1310–1450) was inserted across the foundations of the western gable wall, when Building 3 was presumably in ruins.

*Building 4*

The southern wall of Building 4 lies over a Phase 3 burial, SK074 (Figure 10). This building was probably built to coincide with the final pulse of burial activity in Phase 4 which begins *c* 1500. The disuse of this building is marked by the insertion of the infant burial, SK474 (cal AD 1470–1650) into the north wall. The graves cut through the coal-rich deposits within the building (see above) may also date to the same period as SK474, suggesting that the locus continued to have a significance even after the buildings were abandoned.

## 3.3 SUMMARY

A broad chronology of activity on the headland can now be proposed.

Phase 1 (AD 650–1000) sees the establishment of an ecclesiastical settlement on the headland. A small timber oratory is built (Building 1) and burials take place in a graveyard located mainly to the south and west of the oratory. One exception to this general pattern is the Viking grave, SK752, which lies to the north. The timber oratory is eventually replaced by a stone-footed chapel (Building 2), probably some time in the mid-8th to mid-9th century AD, if analogy with other sites is correct. The ecclesiastical settlement has been abandoned by AD 900 but there is a late episode of burial in the graveyard when at least five bodies are interred probably simultaneously. The chapel and graveyard may have been abandoned for a short period after this event.

In Phase 2 (AD 1000–1200) burial activity in the graveyard recommences. The dilapidated structures of the ecclesiastical settlement are probably levelled and the ditches deliberately backfilled at the beginning of this phase. Building 2 continues in use as the chapel, but with the addition of a timber nave at its western end. Again, there is a period of abandonment at the end of this phase, during which Building 2 decays.

# CHRONOLOGY

When burial activity is renewed in Phase 3 (AD 1200–1400), the chapel is rebuilt in mortared masonry (Building 3). The timber nave at the western end is abandoned but a new chancel may have been added at the eastern end. The graveyard spreads north and east of the chapel. The chapel and graveyard are once more abandoned around AD 1400 and a century elapses before the site is used again. During this time Building 3 tumbles down and a burial is inserted in the decayed west gable wall.

As is argued in Chapter 7.3.1, Phase 4 is probably associated with the acquisition of the Auldhame estate by Adam Otterburn in the early 16th century. He probably had Building 4 erected over the footprint of the Building 3 chancel as a burial aisle, and over the next century there is a small amount of burial activity, mainly on the eastern side of the graveyard. The building itself may have fallen derelict after Otterburn's death in 1548 but the locus continued in use as a place of burial, as witnessed by the infant burial in wall and the later burials cut into the coal-rich deposits within the building.

### 3.3.1 Age and gender over time

MELISSA MELIKIAN

Analysis of the dated burials indicates that more adults were buried at Auldhame throughout Phases 1 to 3 than in Phase 4. The number of dated adult interments decreased by half between Phase 1 and Phase 2 but remained stable at the lower rate into Phase 3. It is unclear whether specific factors influenced the health of the adults between Phases 1 and 2 (such as epidemics of disease or poor harvests linked to dietary deficiency or famine). Periods of violence can result in higher number of adult deaths, particularly of males. The two clear episodes of violent death in the assemblage were not, however, dated to the same period, as SK216 was dated to Phase 1 and SK868 to Phase 3. This dating also clarifies that there is no apparent connection between the two burials with weapon-related injury at the site.

Interpretations of a peak in adult mortality followed by a phase of relative stability between Phases 2 and 3 are indicated only by the dated burial sample. While the adopted hypothesis of this research is that the dated sample is representative of the burial traditions of the graveyard, the dated sample broadly represents only 9–10% of the burial population. It remains unknown as to how the mortality rates may actually have varied by phase if the whole excavated assemblage had been dated.

The assemblage of the dated skeletons contained more adult males (19) (amalgamated with probable males) compared to females (12) (and probable females). This generates an imbalance in the sex of the dated burials by a ratio of 1.6:1. Although the dated assemblage represents only a sample of all of the burials excavated, it is revealing to see that the difference in sample numbers between the sexes is reflected throughout the whole assemblage with a ratio of 1.3:1 in favour of the males.

Similar numbers of males and females were buried in Phase 1. The male bias among the dated burials is evident in Phases 2 and 3. The number of dated male burials that occurred between Phase 1 and Phase 3 remained largely consistent. The more significant change in the dated sample was the higher number of female burials that occurred in Phase 1 compared to later phases. Following this difference, there is quite marked uniformity in the number of adult males and females buried between Phase 2 and Phase 3 (5M, 1F; 5M, 2F respectively for burials in each phase rather than mixed phasing).

It is unclear why there were similar numbers of males and females buried at Auldhame during the earliest phase of cemetery use. It is possible that individuals were using the monastery as a focus for treatment and support during ill-health. If so, the isotope data from the burial assemblage indicate that people were not travelling far to get to the monastery as the population was predominantly local. The dating suggests that there were two periods of burial activity within Phase 1, one corresponding to the establishment and use of an ecclesiastical settlement on the headland between AD 650 and AD 900, and the second post-AD 900 after the abandonment of the settlement. The reasons for continued burial at the site following the abandonment of the settlement are not clear, but may have influenced the burial numbers compared to those highlighted in the later phases of cemetery activity.

Juvenile (<18 years) burials were present as 13 of the 43 dated burials (30.2%) The ratio of juvenile to adult burials in the dated sample is similar to the demographic profile of the whole burial assemblage, in which 33.4% of the sample was represented by juveniles. Thirteen of the dated child burials were of neonates or infants. The remaining six dated burials were juveniles aged 6–17 years. The high number of burials that occurred at a young age is likely to be due to the suite of factors influencing infant mortality including the risk of disease occurrence, particularly of infectious diseases, and the quality of available nutrition (see Chapter 5.4.2). It is interesting, however, that there are no clear fluctuations in the number of juvenile burials across the dated assemblage. In particular, there is no evidence for a marked increase in juvenile mortality in Phase 4 relative to the preceding phases.

Although there were no adults represented in the dated sample from Phase 4 it is untenable to interpret from this that no adult burials were made at Auldhame during this phase. If the cemetery activity in Phase 4 had been specifically for juvenile burials in contrast to the preceding periods, an increase in the number of child interments would perhaps have been expected relative to the previous phases to define such a phase of activity better. As outlined above, the juvenile mortality rate in the dated sample remained relatively consistent.

# CHAPTER 4

# THE ARTEFACT ASSEMBLAGE

Excavations at Auldhame produced a wide range of material types including ceramic, glass, non-ferrous and ferrous objects, bone and stone. This chapter brings together the catalogues and discussions of artefacts, as well as pertinent analytical work. The material is presented in three broad chronological assemblage: Anglo-Saxon; Viking; and medieval and later. A category of miscellaneous finds is included so that discussions and comparisons within and between periods can be made.

In the course of the individual specialists' discussions, attention is drawn to particular aspects of the assemblage, particularly chronology, function, use and manufacture. Where appropriate, wider parallels are drawn. In Chapter 7 all of these salient points are pulled together to create a picture of living and dying in Auldhame over two millennia.

## 4.1 ANGLO-SAXON

### 4.1.1 Copper alloy

ALICE BLACKWELL

The Anglo-Saxon assemblage consists of a decorative cloisonné mount, two copper alloy pins and a further copper alloy pin shaft section.

Cylindrical cloisonné stud (Figures 45 and 46)
(Scientific analysis by Tate et al 2010)

SF 300

Small gilt copper alloy cylindrical setting with four translucent red glass cloisonné inlays, surrounded by a second gold-silver alloy cylinder with 'dog-toothed' edge and a double filigree collar. No means of attachment survives. Bubbles are visible in the inlays, indicating glass rather garnet, and this was confirmed by analysis that indicated a soda-lime-silica glass. The bubbles do not appear to resolve into lines. The surface of the insets is shiny and, although there are slight scratches, no polishing marks are visible. On one inset a slight raised line is visible on the surface of the glass. Hatched gold foils, which are commonly found behind Anglo-Saxon garnet cloisonné work, are absent on the Auldhame mount, and neither do there appear to be plain gold cell bases. A small portion of a thin dark

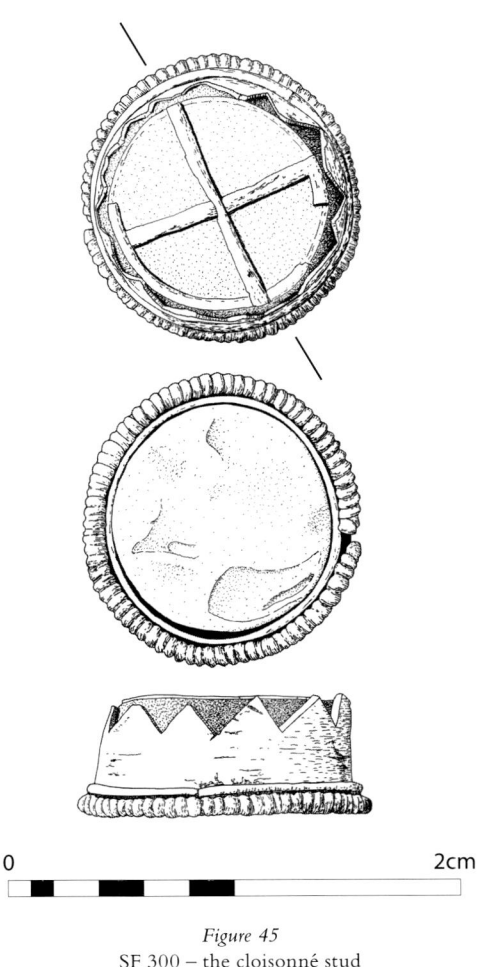

*Figure 45*
SF 300 – the cloisonné stud

*Figure 46*
(a) the front of the stud © Trustees of National Museums Scotland; (b) the back of the stud © Trustees of National Museums Scotland

grey sheet is visible where the copper alloy cylinder is particularly corroded; this may be a metal foil behind the glass that reaches up the side of the inset (found in gold on some garnet cloisonné) or, alternatively, it may be a product of differential corrosion causing lamination of the cylinder body.

The four inlays are divided by gilt copper alloy cell walls forming a cross shape. One wall is a single piece, the other formed by two pieces with joins clearly visible on X-ray but partially covered by surface gilding. These walls expand slightly over the edge of the insets, holding them in place. X-rays suggest that the main, single-piece cell wall appears to extend down to the base plate, whereas the two-piece subsidiary wall does not. This is usual among copper alloy cloisonné where secondary walls are bedded into filler rather than soldered to the base plate. Two of the glass insets now appear to be a darker shade of red, which may be because they remain more firmly fixed in their settings than the lighter two, which have shifted and sunk slightly. X-rays also suggest the two-piece wall may be bent at right-angles within the mount, producing flaps that might aid the structural integrity of the cloisonné.

The copper alloy cylinder reaches to the base of the setting, where it is attached to an unperforated copper alloy base plate. The plate has corroded through in places to reveal a crystalline substance behind, likely to be a cement or filler used to support the inlays in their settings. A very small patch of gilding survives near the edge of the base plate: in light of the lack of any other areas of gilding on the plate, and its location very near the edge, this seems more likely to relate to gilding on the outside surface of the copper alloy cylinder (just visible to the eye near the base), rather than indicate the base plate was gilded.

Surrounding the gilt copper alloy cylinder is a second cylinder of gold-silver alloy. The upper edge of this cylinder is cut to form triangular teeth with apices roughly level with the top of the mount. Cut marks are clearly visible at the bases of many of the cut-away sections. Some of the teeth have not been cut sharply, leaving a u- rather than v-shaped trough. Further possible cut marks are visible near the apices of three 'teeth', running roughly parallel with the upper surface of the mount.

The teeth of the gold-silver cylinder are bent inwards slightly to clasp the copper alloy cylinder.

The base plate does not extend to the outer cylinder, leaving a small gap between the two cylinders around most of their circumference. This suggests the clasping teeth are the only means of fixing the outer cylinder to the inner mount.

At the base of the gold-silver cylinder are two encircling filigree collars. The upper is a single line of plain wire; immediately below is a line of beaded wire, flush with the base of the mount. The beaded wire appears silvery on the underside whereas the rest of its visible surface is bright gold; there is a clear 'tidemark' between the two colours, which is consistent around the circumference of the collar. While the spacing between beads is fairly regular, the degree to which the beads have closed varies. On the underside, the beading is relatively crisp and where the beads have not closed there are sharp medial grooves. In contrast, the gold-coloured areas of the beading seem smoother, and the beads more rounded and less affected by medial grooves. This suggests that the beaded wire has been gilded, and that the gilding has covered and smoothed some of the imperfections. SEM results support this conclusion. Several small areas of additional, gold-coloured alloy are visible on the (silver-coloured) underneath of the beading; these might be stray patches of gilding material.

One end of the beaded wire is loose, leaving the collar in a fragile state. It appears that the beading was soldered to the plain wire collar as well as the gold-silver cylinder, perhaps for strength given the challenges of the small surface area presented by beaded wire. The plain wire collar is the same gold colour as the upper areas of the beaded wire; no underside is visible. Joins in both filigree lines are visible. D at base including filigree 12.6mm, D at top 10.9mm, H 5.3mm. Unstratified.

There are several indications that this object may be comprised of two different elements, a reused central gilt copper alloy glass cloisonné cylinder and the outer gold-silver cylinder with filigree collars. Firstly, the combination of the two different materials in a single small mount is very unusual and there is no apparent structural reason for it. Secondly, the two elements differ in quality; the gilt copper alloy cloisonné is of a good quality, and differs markedly to the crudeness of the teeth cut-marks visible on the outer surface of the gold-silver cylinder. Thirdly, the only join between the two cylinders appears to be the clasping teeth; if the object was conceived as a whole the base plate might be expected to extend to the outer cylinder to strengthen the whole. Finally, although now hidden, the outer walls of the copper alloy cylinder are gilded near the base, suggesting originally the whole of the inner cylinder was intended to be seen.

No means of attachment survive, relating to either the original copper alloy cloisonné mount or the altered mount in its present state. This hinders identification of the function of the mount(s), although they will have formed part of larger objects. The central cloisonné setting lacks the pierced back plate required for attachment by rivet, which is relatively common on mounts from composite Anglo-Saxon objects. Cylinder-shaped mounts are far less common than domed mounts, the latter featuring fairly regularly, for instance, on composite disc brooches and buckles. The simple cross-shaped division of four insets is also relatively unusual, but can be paralleled on a gold and garnet cloisonné domed mount from Barham (Suffolk), found by a metal detector and not closely dated (West 1998, 7, fig. 5.47).

Translucent red glass insets are rare among Anglo-Saxon jewellery, where garnet is far more common. There has been only limited recent research into the incidence and significance of the use of transparent red glass inlays, imitating garnets, in Anglo-Saxon cloisonné. Bimson regarded the use of red insets as rare, but noted it does occur occasionally on Continental material (Bimson & Freestone 2000, 131). Aside from the Sutton Hoo *millefiori* insets, translucent red glass appears as insets on a small group of material from England, including: a mount from Bidford-on-Avon, Warwickshire (Wise & Seaby 1995, Pl. 1, fig. 1); a Continental heart-shaped buckle-plate from Abingdon, Oxfordshire (Evison 1982, 9); a cabochon mount from Hamwic (Hinton 1996, 54, fig. 22); one or possibly two insets on St Cuthbert's pectoral cross (Bruce-Mitford 1956, 542–4); the Kingston brooch (Evison 1982, 8–9); a pinhead from Flixborough, Humberside (Webster & Backhouse 1991, 96, No. 69d); a similar pinhead from Whissonset, Norfolk (*Treasure Annual Report 2004*, fig. 124); and a pin from Sancton, Lincolnshire (*Treasure Annual Report 2004*, fig. 119). (It is possible, however, that the insets on several of these pieces, for instance St Cuthbert's pectoral cross and Kingston brooch, are not ancient, given their extended biographies.) Given the identification of glass rather than garnet on two of these objects in 2004 during routine analysis, it seems likely that other occurrences of glass have gone as yet unrecognised.

The origin of the translucent red glass insets has been debated – there appears to be very little translucent red Roman glass, and red glass is not produced in Britain until the general development of bright and deep colours in the late 7th–8th century; this is semi-opaque and streaked, not clear and garnet-coloured. Translucent red glass had been dated to the 8th century or later, but Evison noted that the appearance of red on Sutton Hoo *millefiori* indicated its use in the first half of the 7th century (Evison 1982, 9), albeit used in a different way. Evison suggested that the difficulty in finding rare Roman glass in the correct shade to match garnets raised the possibility of Insular manufacture. More recently, work has emphasised the reuse of Roman glass in coloured glass inlays and enamel from this period (I Freestone pers comm; Bimson & Freestone 2000; Freestone et al 2008). Analysis of the Sutton Hoo *millefiori* confirmed the colour was produced by manganese. The quantities of manganese detected in the Auldhame mount are significantly lower but this may be explained by leaching (I Freestone pers comm).

Copper alloy cloisonné occurs on some Anglo-Saxon composite disc brooches, and Pinder emphasises that it is not safe to assume that copper alloy examples necessarily are a degenerate form of the gold (Pinder 1995). Cloisonné patterns (rather than the setting of a single, isolated inset) are, however, more commonly found in gold than copper alloy. Analysis of the uncleaned, corroded base plate suggested a copper-silver alloy, which seems relatively unusual among other analysed Anglo-Saxon copper alloys (although most of the analysed material dates to the early Anglo-Saxon period). The outer cylinder also contains a significant amount of silver. The crispness of the silver-coloured underside of the beaded wire, and the clearly defined change in colour to gold-coloured metal and smoother beads with apparently filled medial grooves on the upper portion suggest a gilded silver-rich metal. This appears to be unique among early medieval filigree. The use of a plain, unbeaded or untwisted wire collar is also unusual and rarely occurs among Insular filigree work (Whitfield 2007, 21).

The corrosion of the base plate reveals a crystalline substance that seems highly likely to be a filler, commonly used in cloisonné objects to support the insets by filling hollow spaces below them. It has not yet been possible to analyse the composition of this substance, but this is very desirable as previous analysis has focused on substances found within gold rather than copper alloy cloisonné (Pinder 1995, 8; Arrhenius 1985). Practical considerations suggest that those found within copper alloy objects may have had different properties, particularly adhesiveness, to counter the lack of burred edges on some disc brooches to hold the insets in place. On the Auldhame mount the cross cell walls appear to help hold the glass insets in place, perhaps reducing the need for an adhesive, although it appears that the secondary cell wall pieces still required bedding in the filler.

The 'dog-toothed' edges of the decorative cylinder can be paralleled on a number of other garnet cloisonné pieces: on the scabbard mount from East Linton (East Lothian; NMS FE 106), thin gold sheet triangles disguise the fact that some of the garnet inlays have cut-away portions on their lower edges. More structural triangles surround the base of a pair of similar scabbard mounts from Sutton Hoo (Bruce-Mitford 1978, fig. 222). Gold triangles clasp the large garnet slab insets of a buckle from Tostock (Suffolk), and the central setting of the Sarre brooch (Bruce-Mitford 1956, Pl. XVI) and some cabochon pendants. St Cuthbert's pectoral cross uses three-dimensional tooth decoration running along the edge of the cloisonné arms (Bruce-Mitford 1956, Pl. XVI). There does seem to be a Northumbrian fashion for this decorative feature, although it was evidently also popular farther south. With the exception of St Cuthbert's cross, teeth on the other objects cited serve a similar purpose, clasping the

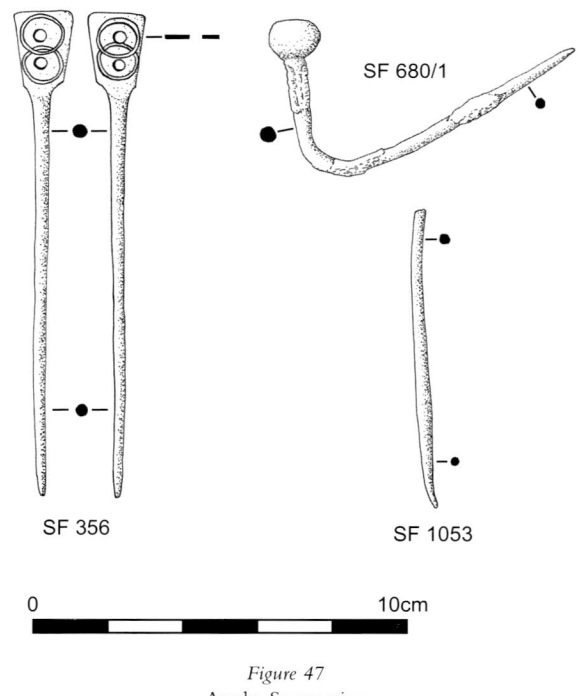

*Figure 47*
Anglo-Saxon pins

# THE ARTEFACT ASSEMBLAGE

garnet insets, or alternatively creating that effect in the case of the Sutton Hoo and East Linton mounts.

Dating the Auldhame stud is difficult because of the number of unusual features it exhibits, which remain hard to parallel, because of the probable reuse of the central cloisonné cylinder and because it is not clear what object(s) it was once part of. The use of red translucent glass inlays has previously been ascribed to a decline in the garnet trade, but this is not founded on closely dated material and so remains open to question. Further consideration of the alloys might aid dating. At present a 7th–8th-century date range might be suggested to encompass the original mount and the alterations that produced the object as it is today.

*Pins (Figures 47 and 48)*

(Scientific analysis by Christopher Brooks and Jim Tate)

### SF 356

Complete cast copper alloy pin with hipped shaft and thin wedge-shaped head. The head has two perforations, one above the other, each of which is surrounded on both faces by two indented concentric circles. The upper set of circles overlies the bottom on both faces. The head is not quite symmetrical, and there is no collar between the head and shaft. The shaft is circular-sectioned along most of its length but is flattened and tapers near the head. It is gently swollen just below the mid-point. Very slight facets run along the length of the shaft, upon which, at right angles, are what appear to be fine file marks. Less fine file marks run diagonally across the head. L 66.6mm, shaft D at mid-point 1.6–1.8mm, shaft D at hip 2.4mm, head T 0.7mm, head max W 7.9mm, head L 10.0mm. Alloy: bronze. Unstratified.

### SF 680/1

Cast copper alloy pin, originally in two pieces, with bent shaft, and undecorated ball-shaped head with flattened top. The shaft swells slightly at around two-thirds of its length, although this area is corroded on one side. Corrosion also affects the upper portion of the shaft around the bend and near the head, but despite this there does not appear to be a collar between head and shaft. The head is smooth, and the flattened top does not produce a facet. L 60mm, shaft D at mid-point (uncorroded) 2.0mm, shaft D at hip 2.7mm, head D 6.6–6.8mm, head H 5.1–5.2mm. Alloy: leaded bronze. Unstratified.

### SF 1053

Short section of copper alloy round-sectioned pin shaft, with very slight possible hip. L 41mm, shaft D near break 1.8mm, max shaft D 2.2mm. Alloy: leaded bronze. Grave fill [584], [586].

The two copper alloy pins both have hipped shafts, indicating an early medieval date. Neither have collars between the shaft and head, a feature commonly (but not always) found on Anglo-Saxon pins. SF 356 does not fit easily within Ross' typology of Anglo-Saxon pins (Ross 1991). Ross' 'wedge-headed' type, which comprises a single pin from Castledyke (Humberside) cemetery only, is similar to Auldhame although the head expands smoothly from the shaft. The head is somewhat reminiscent of styli erasers, but the Auldhame head is too thin to have functioned in this way. A better parallel for the shape of the head of SF 356 is an incomplete pin from South Newbald (Yorkshire),

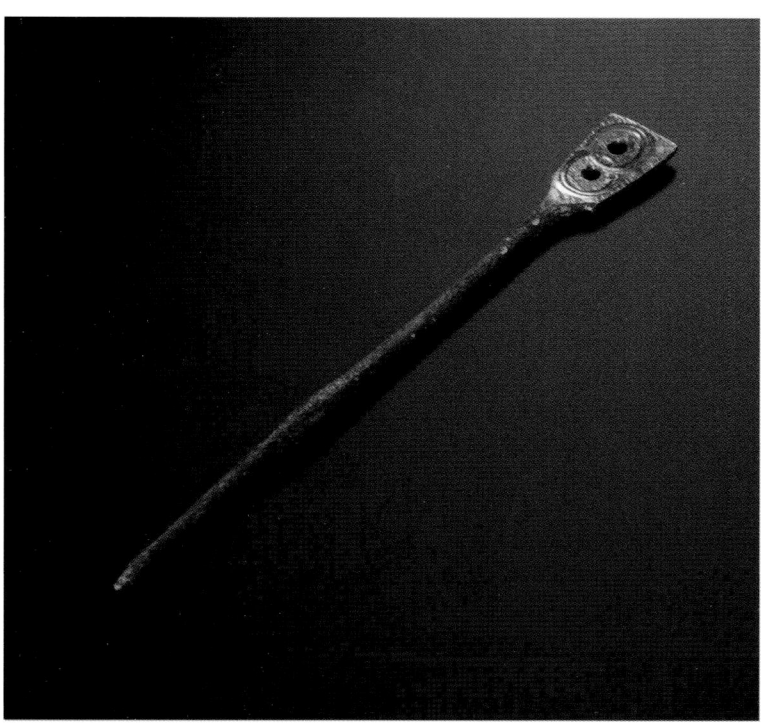

*Figure 48*
Pin SF 356 © Trustees of National Museums Scotland

which also lacks a collar (Leahy 2000, fig. 6.8 No. 17) but features two similarly arranged perforations surrounded by rings. A similar pin was found in the fill of a 9th-century *Grübenhaus* at Thwing (Yorkshire) and a further is known from Hotham (North Humberside) (Leahy 2000, 71), suggesting perhaps it is a northern type. A further pin with a similarly shaped but thicker and unperforated head, decorated with two ring-and-dots one above the other, is known from York, where it was regarded as an Anglo-Scandinavian type dating to the 10th to mid-11th centuries (Mainman 2000, 2578, fig. 1274).

Simple ball-headed pins, some with flattened tops, are a common type discussed by Ross. The simple head shape and lack of decoration means that close dating is not possible, but Ross regards the type generally as firmly established by the 8th century, if not slightly before, continuing into the 9th and possibly the 10th centuries (Ross 1991, 228–95). While collars are a very commonly occurring feature, an example from South Newbald also lacks one. The possible hipping on the section of pin shaft (SF 1053) suggests it too is likely to be from an early medieval pin. The diameter is comparable with that of SF 356.

*Discussion*

This small Anglo-Saxon copper alloy assemblage, together with the glass inkwell (see Campbell, Chapter 4.1.2 below), is particularly important given the dearth of other material known from this period in northern Northumbria. The only other Scottish material of similar date, aside from the 9th-century Trewhiddle-style strap-ends, comes from Aberlady (East Lothian), and includes a very high-quality gilt-copper alloy openwork Mercian-style disc-shaped pinhead and several other middle-Saxon copper alloy pins more comparable to those from Auldhame.

### 4.1.2 Glass

Ewan Campbell

*Inkwell*

SF 748

Two joining sherds forming the top part of cylindrical decorated glass inkwell (Figure 49). Slightly dished upper surface with central hole, diameter 7mm. Although broken at the shoulder, there is no sign that the body was other than cylindrical. Metal light blue-green, good quality, shiny surfaces with scattered bubbles. Around the central hole is decoration of a single fully marvered opaque yellow spiral trail. The trail contains a thin black line caused by impurities. Size 47 × 48mm, T 1.5–3.0mm. Estimated diam *c* 7cm. Unstratified.

Glass inkwells of the Anglo-Saxon period have only recently been identified as a type (Evison 2000, 82) and are extremely rare. The Auldhame find is therefore unusual, both for the artefact itself and as the only example of the type from Scotland. Anglo-Saxon glass inkwells developed from Roman prototypes but seem to lack the handles of their predecessors, and may have been produced in England rather than being imported from the Mediterranean region. Only a handful of examples are known: one from Lurk Lane,

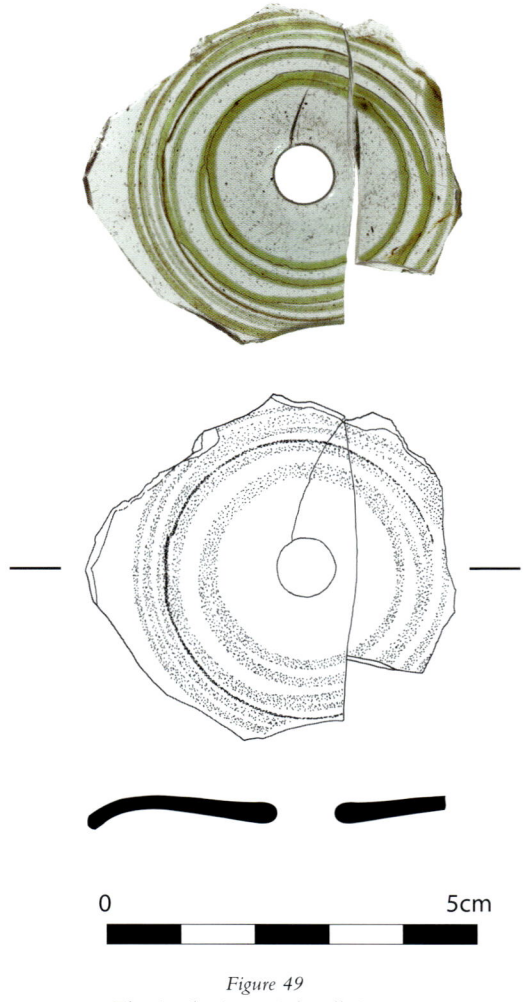

*Figure 49*
The Anglo-Saxon inkwell, SF 748

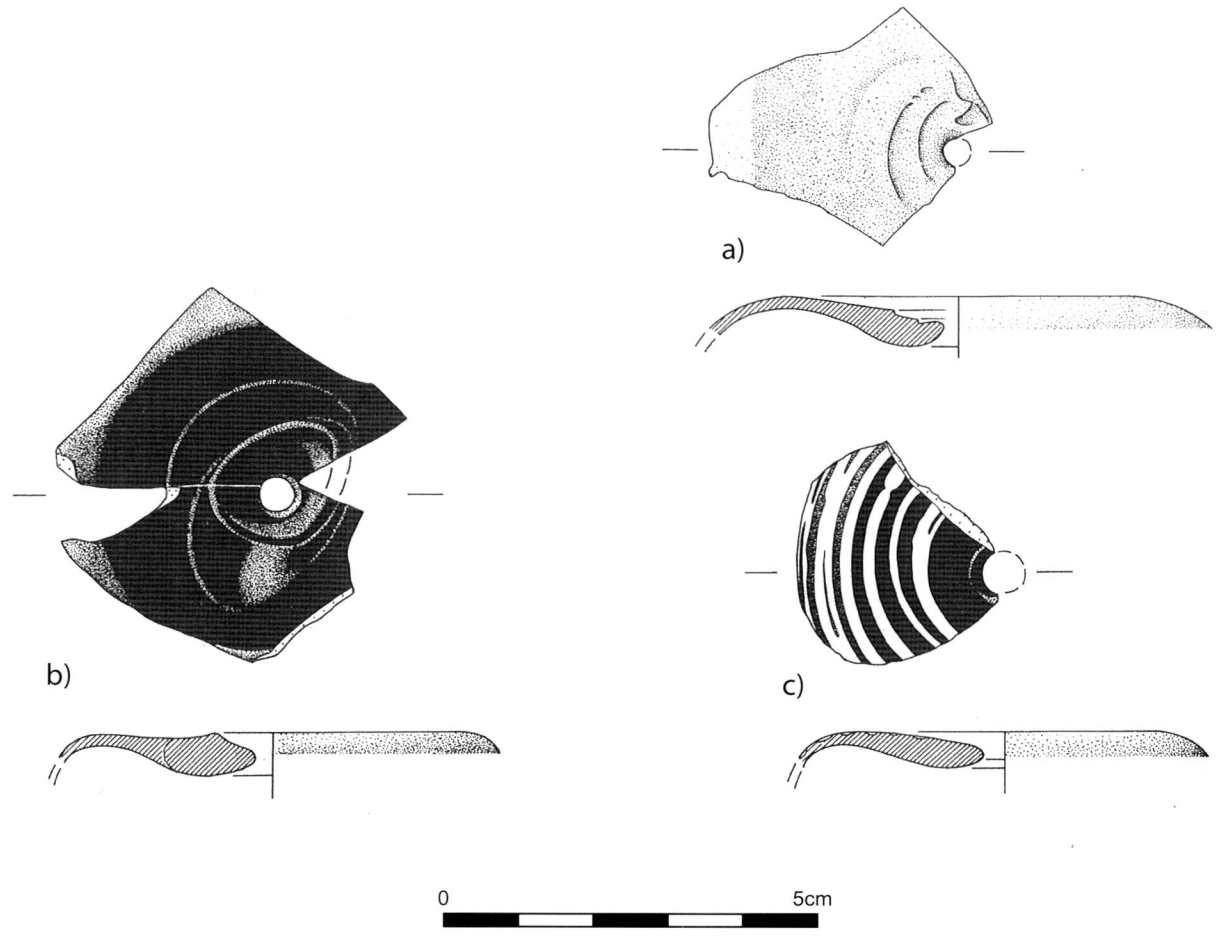

*Figure 50*
Anglo-Saxon inkwells from Lurk Lane, Beverley (a) and Brandon, Suffolk (b and c)

Beverley (Henderson 1991, 126, No. 217); three from Brandon, Suffolk (Evison 2000, 82, fig. 14c, d) (Figure 50); and two from *Hamwic*, Saxon Southampton (Hunter & Heyworth 1998, 16; Pl. 5; fig. 13, 24/510; Pl. 8, fig. 13, 169/770).

The colour scheme of the inkwell, of light blue-green glass with opaque yellow trails, is characteristic of mid-Saxon period glass, and a similar colour scheme is found on one of the Southampton inkwells. Other examples are in black or blue glass, with or without yellow trails. All these English examples are from 8th- or 9th-century contexts, and this is the likely date of the Auldhame vessel. It is possible that the form may have continued into the Late Saxon period, but this period has little surviving glass because of a change in composition to potash glasses, and the Auldhame vessel is clearly of the earlier soda-lime glass. A survey of later medieval glass vessels recorded no inkwells of this form (the single putative inkwell of this period is of quite different form) (Tyson 2000, 173, fig. 36, g1134), suggesting the glass inkwell form is characteristic of the mid-Saxon period.

Both the Brandon and Beverley examples came from monastic contexts, which is not surprising given the need for writing materials in these establishments. The Southampton examples came from the Six Dials area of the mid-Saxon trading settlement, where there is some debatable evidence for glass vessel production (Hunter & Heyworth 1998, 26, 61), so these examples may have been either produced or traded here. The presence of an inkwell at the Auldhame site suggests that it was monastic at this period, as such a piece of writing technology would be inappropriate for a site functioning purely as a chapel and burial site. The

# LIVING AND DYING AT AULDHAME, EAST LOTHIAN

commonest indicator of literary activity at this period is the stylus, examples of which are found widely on monastic sites in England, but which are very scarce in Scotland and Ireland (Campbell 2010).

## 4.2 VIKING

The Viking Age grave (G751) is a very welcome addition to the 130 or so Viking graves from the country, the Auldhame inhumation being the most southerly example in Scotland. The grave also expands the extremely sparse archaeological evidence for Viking activity in south-east Scotland. The significance of this find will be more fully discussed in Chapter 7. Here, individual objects found in the grave are catalogued and discussed, with wider parallels drawn.

### 4.2.1 The copper alloy belt set and associated organic materials

PENELOPE WALTON ROGERS (scientific analysis by Christopher Brooks and Jim Tate)

The belt set from G751 includes a buckle, matching strap end, remains of the belt, and a fragment of the

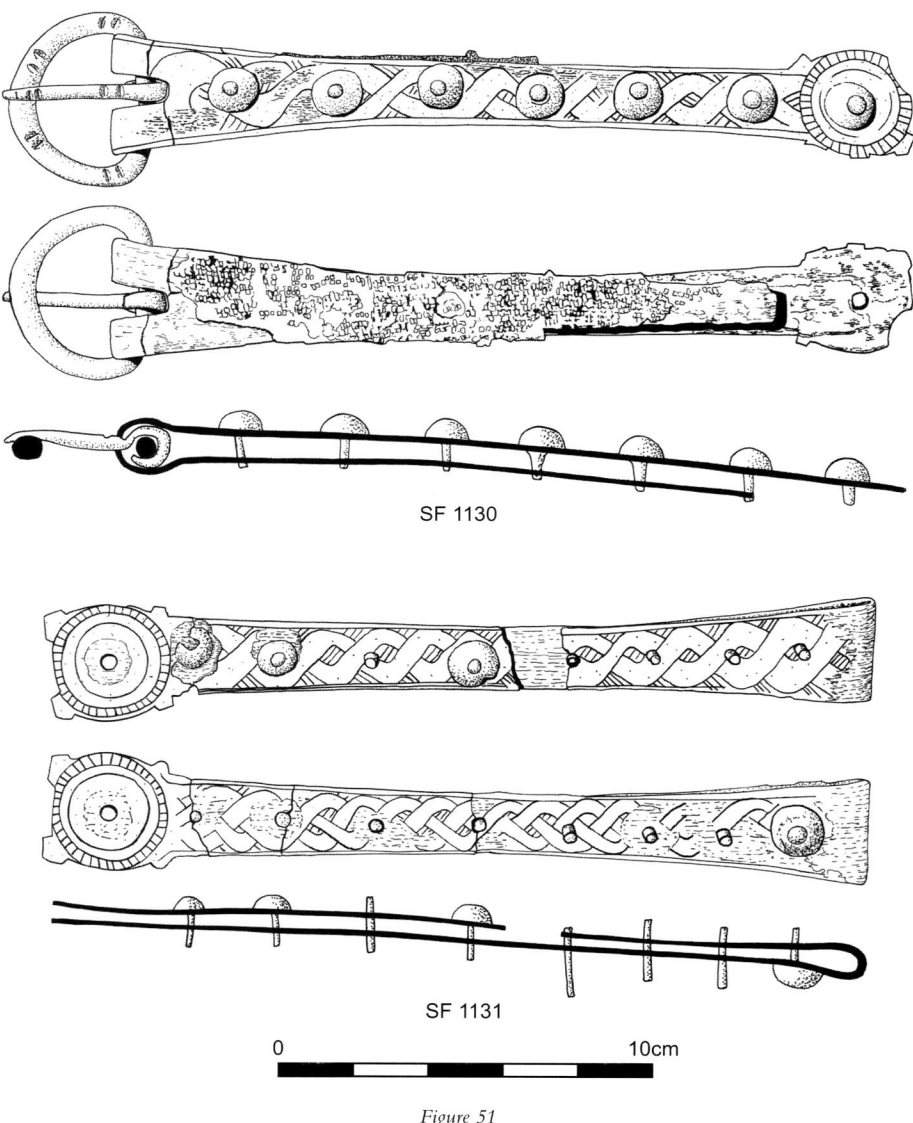

*Figure 51*
The Viking belt set; the buckle SF 1130 and the strap end SF 1131

garment that the belt fastened. The complex was found at the waist of the body, the buckle, SF 1130, on the body's right and the strap end, SF 1131, on the left. The two belt fittings represent metalwork made in the British Isles, possibly in one of the Norse settlements in Ireland, and the garment fragment can be compared with textiles from other Viking Age graves in Britain and Scandinavia. The tooled leather belt, on the other hand, forms a new addition to our knowledge of the costume of the period.

The buckle, SF 1130, has a D-shaped loop and a long narrow belt plate that has been folded around the loop axis and fixed with a row of seven dome-headed rivets (Figures 51 and 52). At the front the plate narrows in the middle, and at the back it tapers towards the rear edge. Decoration is reserved for the front half of the plate, where there is an incised two-strand cord, with hatching in the interstices and a lobed roundel towards the rear edge. There are also transverse incised lines in pairs on the buckle loop and tongue.

The strap end, SF 1131, is similar to the belt plate, but it is reversible. It is made from folded sheet metal, and the front and back halves of the plate are the same shape, with a roundel at the end of both faces; there is a medial row of nine rivets, with dome heads on front and back; and the decoration is a two-strand cord on one face and a three-strand plait on the other. Both the buckle-plate and the strap end have been determined as leaded bronze with a tinned surface, but the core metals have different compositions and the buckle loop and pin are different again. This supports the view that these are reworked elements, assembled from other objects.

This set belongs to a distinctive group of metalwork found in Viking Age sites around the Irish Sea and in the Scottish Islands (Grieg 1940, 48–58, 67–9; Bersu & Wilson 1966, 19–26, Pls V-VI; Graham-Campbell 1973; Laing 1993, 38–9, 84–8; Thomas 2001, 45–6; 2004, 4–5; Paterson 2001, 127–9). It is characterised by roundels separated by panels of ribbon interlace, and a profile that swells around the roundels and narrows in between. The roundels are usually pierced for rivets and, where present, the rivets have dome heads. The objects are often ornamented on both faces and there is sometimes a zoomorphic terminal, although this is absent from the Auldhame set. In common with most Insular metalwork, the raw material is bronze or gunmetal, brass being largely limited to metalwork made in Scandinavia or late phases of the Danelaw (Bayley 1992, 809–10; Paterson 2001, 125–6, 131).

*Figure 52*
The buckle SF 1130 © Trustees of National Museums Scotland

Buckles, strap ends, and bridle and harness fittings have all been found with these features. Their style and construction was clearly influenced by 9th-century Irish metalwork, but most examples must have been made by or for the Norse (Thomas 2001, 45; Paterson 2001, 128). They have been found in graves dated to the late 9th and 10th century, and in occupation levels of 9th- and 10th-century Dublin (Thomas ibid; Paterson ibid) and early 10th-century Whithorn, Galloway (Nicholson & Hill 1997, 371–2), while variants have appeared in Danelaw England (Thomas 2001, 45–6; 2004, 4). The Auldhame example lies on the eastern edge of the group's distribution.

The purpose-made strap ends have been cast in a mould and the Auldhame example, made from folded sheet metal, has almost certainly been reworked from horse tack. The fold has been rolled over a former, to make space for the attachment of a ring or distributor, a feature that appears in the harness fittings from Kiloran Bay, Colonsay (Grieg 1940, objects v–z and aa, 53, 57–8; Bersu & Wilson 1966, Pl. VII), dated to the late 9th century (Paterson 2001, 128). The Kiloran

Bay objects and the bridle fittings from Balladoole, Isle of Man (Bersu & Wilson 1966, Pls V–VI) are, like most examples of this group, riveted only through the roundels, but a further comparison can be made with a belt set from a 10th-century burial at Kneep (Cnip), Uig, Isle of Lewis (Welander et al 1987, 158–9, 162, 170). This lacks the panels of interlace, but has the extra rivets seen in the Auldhame example. It has nine rivet-heads on one face of the belt plate and nine on both faces of the strap end; it has the same rolled bulge at the fold; and it has paired cross-markings on the buckle loop and tongue. Another example has been recorded from an area of disturbed burials at St Michael's, Workington, Cumbria (housed at St Michael's Church; information from L Hodgson at St Michael's; to be published in P Flynn in prep). This has a buckle-plate with a single framing line interrupted by punched dots and no interlace but six rivets, and a buckle loop with incised cross-markings.

The Kneep fittings were found in a well-furnished woman's burial, which is a common occurrence for reused Insular harness mounts in graves in Scandinavia (Wamers 1998, 38, 42), but most comparable finds in the British Isles come from burials with male-gender accessories (Welander et al 1987, 153, 170). In one study of burials in Norway, spurs (SF 1272) showed a slight bias towards males, and spearheads (SF 1271) were regarded as diagnostic of the male gender (Løken 1987, 56–7; see also Heald, Chapter 4.22 below and Chapter 7.2.3). This accords with the identification of the body as a young adult male (Chapter 5.2.3).

To summarise, the buckle and strap end from G751 are likely to have been made for horse bridles or harnesses somewhere in the Irish Sea region, possibly even in Dublin, in the late 9th or 10th century. They may have reached East Lothian with a traveller, as merchandise, or by down-the-line exchange, but somewhere along the way they were removed from the horse tack, reworked and refitted on a belt.

Remains of the leather strap were visible inside the buckle-plate and the strap end, but only the piece behind the roundel of the buckle-plate could be removed (Figure 53). It has a tooled lattice pattern on the grain side, and the thickness of over 3mm suggests that it was derived from cattle. Few leather belts have been preserved from this period (Cameron 2000, 4–5; Ewing 2006, 46–9, 102), although a buckled strap from Anglo-Scandinavian York is plain, 9mm wide and made from calf (Mould et al 2003, 3400). Leather sheaths, on the other hand, have been recovered more often and a variety of tooled lattice patterns have been recorded on sheaths from Late Anglo-Saxon and Anglo-Scandinavian England (Cameron 2000, 64–8, 201–18) and from Hiberno-Norse Dublin (Cameron 2007, 101, 103). The position of the strap end in relation to the buckle suggests that the pendent end of the strap was c 40mm long.

Lying flat against the back of the buckle-plate is a single layer of textile (Figure 51). It covers most of the back of the plate and laps on to the edges, and there were less well preserved remains in the earth around the object. The textile is a tabby repp, $25/Z \times 20/Z$ threads per cm, and the rib of the repp weave runs lengthways along the buckle-plate. The fibre is a fully processed plant fibre, almost certainly flax from *Linum usitatissimum* L. (ie linen). A coarser example of plain tabby, probably linen, was recovered from the outer face of the spurs. In clothed (as opposed to shrouded) burials there was a shift towards linen tabby across north-west Europe in the 7th century (Walton Rogers 2007, 107). By the Viking Age, tabby made from Z-spun yarn, of which the major part is assumed to be linen, represented 75% of all Danish textiles from burials, and formed a significant proportion of textiles from burials in Norway and Sweden (Bender Jørgensen 1992, 136–7). In Scotland, tabby and tabby repp have been recorded in several Viking burials, most recently at Kneep (Bender Jørgensen 1987, 166) and Scar, Sanday, Orkney (Gabra-Sanders 1999a and 1999b).

*Figure 53*
Fragment of the leather strap behind the roundel of the buckle plate. The tooled lattice pattern on the grain is visible

# THE ARTEFACT ASSEMBLAGE

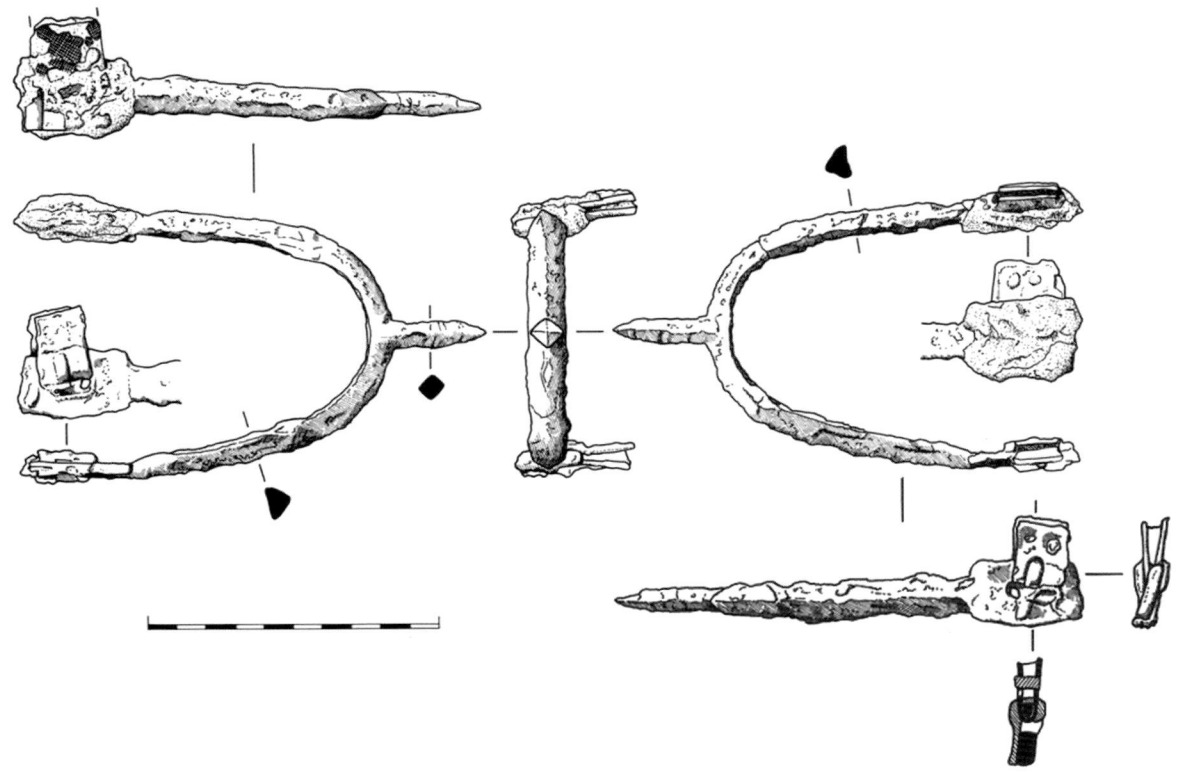

*Figure 54*
The Viking spurs, SF 1272a

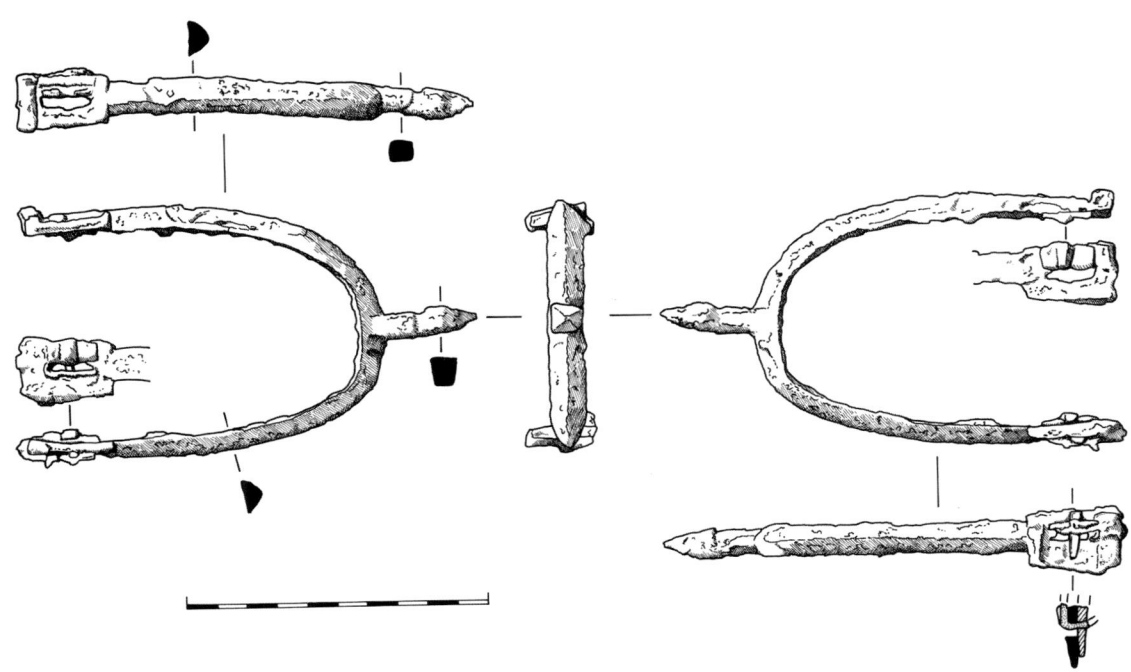

*Figure 55*
The Viking spurs, SF 1272b

Tabby repp gives a more robust fabric than ordinary tabby. The garment the textile represents is uncertain, as a range of belted clothing was worn by both men and women (Ewing 2006, 46–7, 78–92, 102).

### 4.2.2 The iron artefacts

ANDREW HEALD and CAROLINE PATERSON

*Iron spurs with buckles*

A pair of iron spurs (SF 1272) was recovered by the feet of the body (Figures 54 and 55). The earliest use of spurs in Britain is shown by finds from Roman sites (Shortt 1959, 61–76). In the 8th century Carolingian influence revived the fashion for wearing spurs on the continent where they were worn by mounted retainers of the Carolingian nobility or *milites* (Thomas 2012, 489). The fashion for wearing spurs, together with its attendant status then spread to Britain under Viking influence as reflected in the Carolingian copper alloy spur fittings from Balladoole, Isle of Man (Bersu & Wilson 1966, 36–9, Pl. vii, b–d). There is also a particular concentration of spur finds in the Viking graves of Cumbria (Paterson et al 2014, 140). These finds are made of tinned iron and were most probably manufactured within the Danelaw (ibid). By the Middle Ages, gilded spurs were used in the ceremonies of knighthood and had become symbolic of that rank (see Ellis 2002; and examples in Graham-Campbell 1980, 259).

These are the first examples of Viking Age prick spurs from modern day Scotland, although they form part of a wider group in use from the Viking era with their association with Bernicia and Northumbria of particular note (see below). The spurs are characterised by the point or goad and terminals. The general characteristics of the Auldhame spurs, particularly the straight arms when viewed from the side, the goad alignment in the same plane, the form of terminals and goad (Figure 57) suggest that they should be viewed within the general types in circulation across Europe between the 8th and 12th centuries AD (see Ellis 2002; LMCC 1940, 95, fig. 28). As Paterson et al (2014, 140) remind us, spurs are relatively rare grave finds in Scandinavia, where they are largely restricted to 10th-century burials and usually have rather longer, slender necks and goads (Ottaway 1992, 701) In Denmark, there are 15 recorded burials containing spurs placed at the feet of the deceased, suggesting that here they were worn at the time of burial, presumably like the Auldhame example.

Comparable examples from northern Britain are rare although the numbers have increased over the last two decades. The most recent examples are from two Viking Age graves in Cumwhitton, Cumbria, where the occupants of Graves 3 and 5 were both buried with fine sets of spurs with attendant strap fittings (Paterson et al 2014, 52, 87, 104–6, 140). Although it was not possible to apply scientific dating methods to the material, the recovered artefacts suggest that the Cumwhitton cemetery as a whole dates to *c* AD 850–1000. The short spur goads, and early form, may suggest a late 9th-century date for these two graves (Paterson et al 2014, 153). Indeed, the number of spurs found in Cumbrian graves is notable and is discussed further below (see Chapter 7.2.3). Spurs have also been found in other nearby areas, the Balladoole spurs on the Isle of Man being good examples (Bersu & Wilson 1966, 35–6, fig. 25). The excavators dated the Balladoole grave to around the 9th and 10th centuries AD (Bersu & Wilson 1966, 39; see also the recent discussions by Wilson 2008, 38–46 and Griffiths 2010, 83–6). Various spurs were also recovered from Anglo-Scandinavian contexts from Coppergate, York (Ottaway 1992, 698–704). Although recovered from Viking graves and settlements, spurs were neither a Scandinavian introduction nor exclusive to Scandinavian warriors but their presence in such contexts would appear to reflect their Carolingian ideals (see Paterson et al 2014, 140).

*Iron strap guide*

A strap guide was found around the feet of the body, beside the prick spurs (Figure 56a). Strap guides were usually set in a buckle-plate behind a buckle. When the strap had passed through the buckle it would then pass through the strap guide, which held it securely in place. Often, strap guides form part of the spur attachments and given their association at Auldhame this seems the best interpretation of this find. A 10th–11th-century strap guide of the same bi-lobate form, which too is part of a spur attachment, was recovered from Northampton (Goodall 1979, 273, fig. 121, 121) with other examples from Flaxengate, Lincoln and Coppergate, York (see Ottaway 1992, 689, fig. 297: 3777, 3781 & 3783).

*Buckle-sets*

Two iron buckle-sets were recovered from the grave (Figure 56b and c). Buckles can be associated with a range of fittings, from everyday dress accessories

# THE ARTEFACT ASSEMBLAGE

through to horse equipment. Iron buckles are common finds from sites of the mid-9th to 11th century and are frequently found in Scandinavian Viking Age graves as part of bridles and spurs or stirrup fittings (see Ottaway 1992, 683–4 for a list of Scandinavian and English examples). The recovery of this pair from beside the deceased's feet suggests that the buckles were, at the very least, associated with footwear. Moreover, their close proximity to the spurs and strap guide suggests that they were probably used for fastening the spur leathers. There are not many examples of such fittings surviving in association with spurs in England, though tinned bronze examples were associated with the Balladoole spurs (Bersu & Wilson 1966, 37, Pl. VII d), and tinned iron buckle sets with associated strap guides were recovered from Graves 3 and 5 at Cumwhitton, Cumbria (Paterson et al 2014, 87–8 Figs 63–4, 105–6, Pl. 57). Carolingian spur fittings on the continent frequently include copper alloy strap-slides and strap-ends (Bersu & Wilson 1966, 37–8; Giesler 1974). The form of the Auldhame iron strap-ends is hard to discern, but they would appear to have been decorated with transverse lines or ribbing with a sub-triangular terminal, and X-rays indicate that they were originally tinned, with tinning surviving in the recessed ornament. Although of a different form, the Cumwhitton buckle plates were also tinned and decorated with linear ornament. As with the spurs, the tinned iron composition of these fittings would indicate that they were manufactured somewhere within the Danelaw, possibly York, where there is evidence for the manufacture of tinned dress fittings (Ottaway 1992, 704).

*Iron spearhead*

A spearhead (Figure 58) was found lying just inside the right knee of the body; it was lying in parallel with the body, the tip of the spear pointing down towards the feet.

Spearheads of a range of shapes and sizes are known from a number of Scottish Iron Age–Norse sites, but they have not been systematically studied. The tendency is to look for parallels in the better-studied Anglo-Saxon series (Swanton 1973; Campbell 1998) or rely heavily on the almost hundred-year-old study by Petersen (1919, 22–36). The corrosion makes classification difficult but it appears that the Auldhame example is a socketed iron spearhead with a narrow neck and slender blade of lozenge-shaped cross-section.

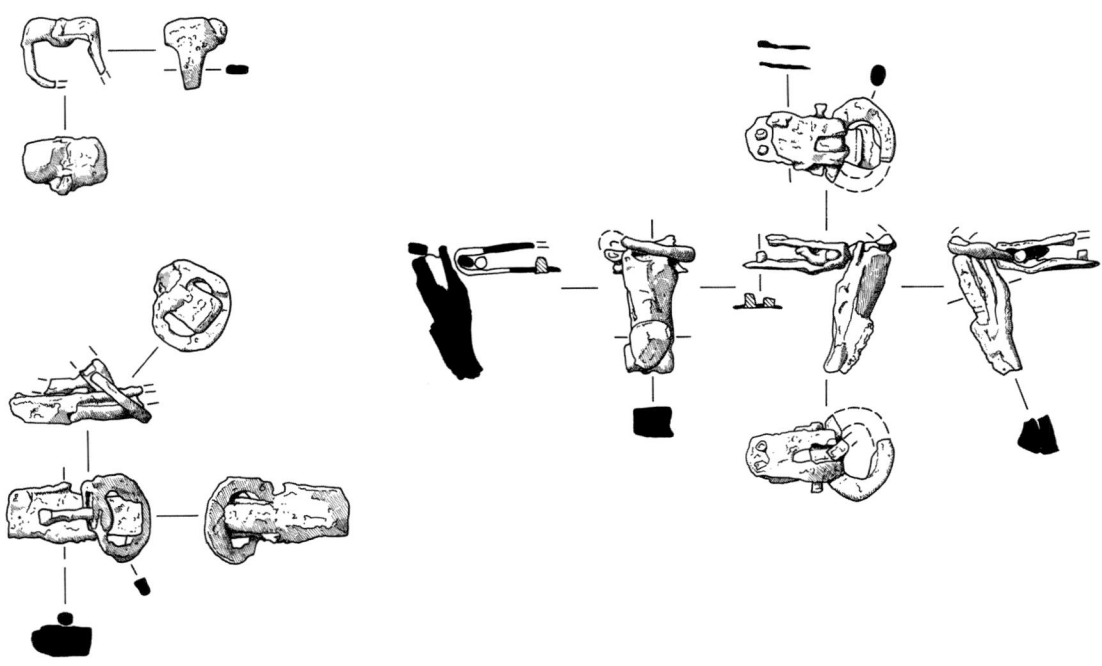

*Figure 56*
(a) strap guide, SF 1272c; (b and c) buckles and strap-end mount, SF 1272d and e

65

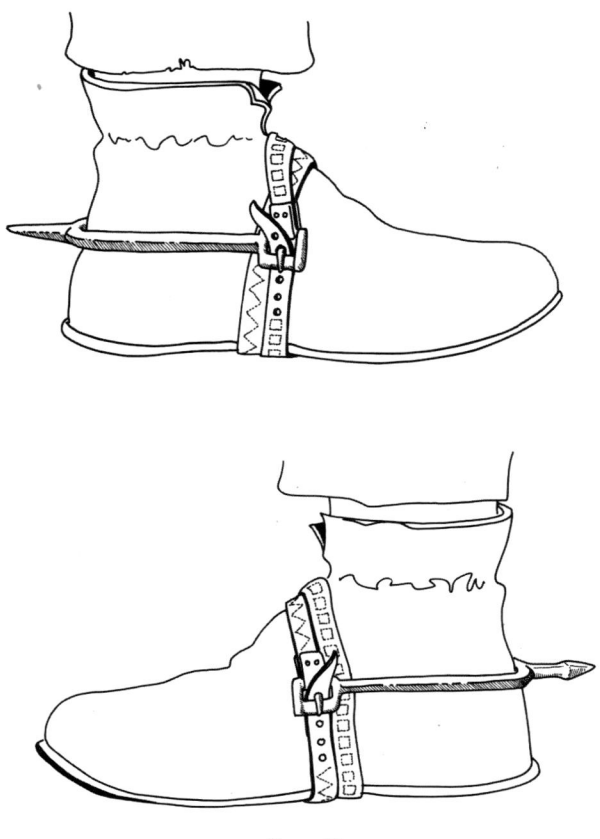

*Figure 57*
Reconstruction of the spurs

The angle of the shoulder appears slightly asymmetrical, but this could be as a result of damage or corrosion. These features most closely align the Auldhame spearhead with Petersen's type K, a light throwing-spear (1919, 31–3) of late 9th- or early 10th-century date. The Auldhame example is relatively small and slender, but paralleled by other spears of this type of similar dimensions such as that from Grave 5, Cumwhitton, Cumbria (Paterson et al 2014, 109).

The absence of a prominent midrib and defined shoulders, also observed on some spearheads from the Isle of Man and Ireland has led to the proposal that this particular form may be of Insular as opposed to Norwegian manufacture (Bøe 1940, 26; Bersu & Wilson 1966, 57–8). Harrison (pers comm) proposes that this group may have been manufactured in Dublin, based on a concentration of the type within the Dublin graves, including D 369 and D 375 from Kilmainham 1845. Although it is uncertain whether the Auldhame spearhead was also manufactured in Dublin, it would certainly appear to be linked to this group, together with several examples from the Scottish graves, including the examples from Balnakeil (Batey & Paterson 2013, 643) and Westness (Graham-Campbell & Paterson forthcoming).

*Miscellaneous*

Three miscellaneous iron objects were also recovered from the grave. None has any recognisable shape or form.

### Catalogue of artefacts from the grave

*Buckle (Figures 51 and 52)*

SF 1130

Copper-alloy buckle, complete, with damage at rear edge of plate. The D-shaped loop and tongue are cast;

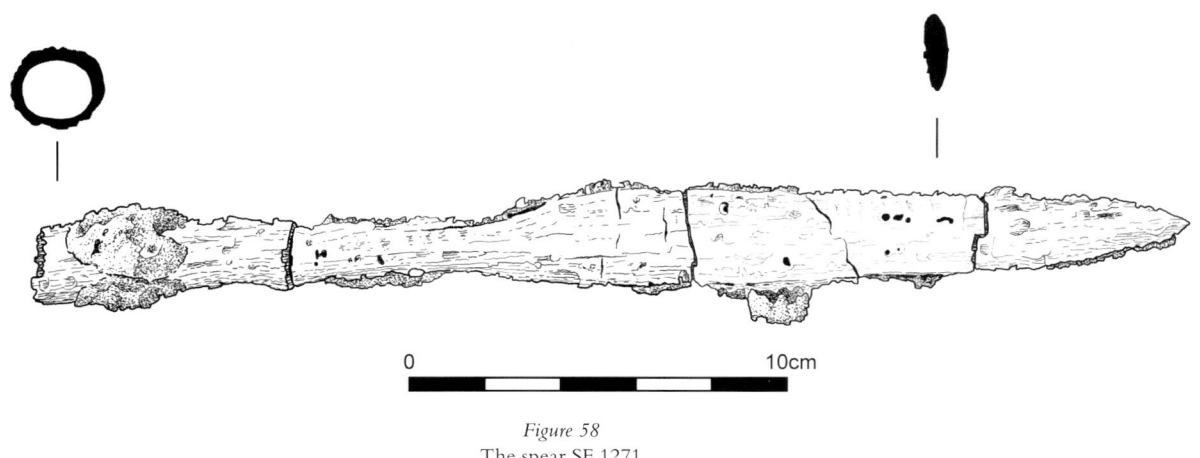

*Figure 58*
The spear SF 1271

the loop has four pairs of transverse incised lines and there is another pair on the tongue. The plate is a long strip of sheet metal folded around the axis of the buckle loop. The plate is widest at the fold and on the front it flares again at the rear edge; on the back it tapers towards the rear edge. Front and back parts of the plate are held together by a row of seven copper alloy rivets, each *c* 2mm thick. Each rivet has a separately made dome-shaped cap, *c* 2.5mm tall and 6.5mm diameter, with a central perforation; on the back the end of the rivet has been hammered flat. The incised ornament at the plate rear edge is a roundel made up of three concentric rings, the space between the outer two rings being filled with radiating lines. Between the roundel and the buckle loop runs an irregular attempt at a two-ply twisted cord, with oblique hatching lines in the interstices. The motif is framed by a single incised line parallel to the plate edge, with no ornament in the border. Length of plate 100mm; width at folded end 14mm; width of loop 25mm; thickness of sheet metal 1mm; space between plates 3.0–3.5mm.

XRF and SEM-EDX analysis: Belt plate: leaded bronze, tinned surface; rivets and rivet caps: copper alloy, probably tinned. Buckle loop: leaded bronze, but not same composition as belt plate. Buckle tongue: copper alloy including small amount of silver, tinned.

Recovered from between the plates is a fragment of leather, 10 × 10mm, with a tooled lattice pattern on the grain surface. The flesh side has partially decayed, but it was probably originally more than 3mm thick.

Lying flat against the back of the plate is a single layer of textile, woven in tabby repp, 25/Z × 20/Z threads per cm. The rib of the repp weave runs lengthways along the plate. Examination of the fibre by optical microscopy at ×400 magnification shows it to be a fully processed plant fibre, almost certainly flax, from *Linum usitatissimum* L.

*Strap end (Figure 51)*

SF 1131

Copper-alloy strap end, complete, pair to buckle, SF 1130. Made from a strip of sheet metal, folded in two, and fixed with rivets as on SF 1130, except that there are remains of nine rivets on both sides. The two faces of the plate are shaped in the same way and both have incised ornament. On one face the ornament is a two-strand spiral, as on SF 1130, but on the opposite face it is a three-strand interlace, with hatching in the interstices. In both instances the motif is framed by a single line parallel to the long edges. A roundel is present on both faces and both roundels have four, squared, equidistant lobes around the edge (broken on SF 1130). Length 110mm; width at fold 14mm and across roundel 16mm; thickness of sheet metal 1mm; space between plates 2.0mm.

XRF and SEM-EDX analysis: Strap end: leaded bronze with significant levels of zinc, tinned. Rivet cap: bronze with low zinc, tinned. Rivet: bronze with low zinc. Leather was still present between the plates, but it was trapped by the rivets and could not be removed for examination.

*Iron spurs (Figures 54 and 55)*

SF 1272a

Badly corroded spur. Consists of a simple splayed U-shaped hoop the arms of which are of triangular/D-shaped cross-section. X-rays indicate that the spur arms may originally have been decorated with clusters of incised diagonal lines located on the upper arms to either side of the goad and also just above the slotted rectangular terminals. Tinning may also survive in these areas as indicated on X-ray. X-ray reveals the goad to have a ribbed collar below to a biconical lobe ending in the prick itself. The arm terminals are rectangular in shape with one longitudinal piercing, similar to London Museum Medieval Catalogue Type C (LMCC 1940, fig. 28; 95). X-ray reveals the lower edges of the terminals to have a rolled profile. At least in one terminal gap are the remains of part of the attachment fitting, specifically the buckle-plate and tongue/pin. H: 152mm; W: 84mm; T: 12mm. Terminals: H: 31mm; W: 18mm; T: 3mm.

SF 1272b

Badly corroded spur. Consists of a simple splayed U-shaped hoop the arms of which are of triangular/D-shaped cross-section. X-rays indicate that the spur arms may originally have been decorated with clusters of incised diagonal lines located on the upper arms to either side of the goad and just above the slotted rectangular terminals. Tinning may also survive in these areas as indicated on X-ray which reveals the goad to have a ribbed collar below a biconical lobe ending in the prick itself. The terminals are rectangular in shape with one longitudinal piercing, similar to London Museum Medieval Catalogue Type C (LMCC 1940, fig. 28, 95). Within both terminal slots are the remains of the spur leather attachment fittings; one has adhering textile impressions. The attachments consist of a folded and riveted metal sheet with a tongue allowing them to function as a buckle, which would have joined the spurs to their leathers in the manner of a reconstructed example from York (Ottaway 1992, 702–3, fig. 305). H: 161mm; W: 92mm; T: 14mm. Terminals: H: 38mm; W: 22mm; T: 3mm.

On the outer face of the buckle-plate, running diagonally across the plate, in patches over an area 20 × 15mm, mineralised textile in tabby weave, 12/Z × 10–12/?Z per cm. Fibres fine, 10–11 microns diameter, possibly flax. Inside buckle-plate and pierced by tongue, remains of strap more than 16mm wide and 4–5mm thick. Its thickness suggests that it is made from adult cattle skin.

*Iron strap guide (Figure 56a)*

SF 1272c

Bi-lobate strap guide, badly corroded. Both terminals broken at tips. L: 18mm; W: 10mm; H: 15mm.

*Buckles (Figure 56b and c)*

SF 1272d

Iron buckle, buckle-plate, and strap-end mount. The buckle set consists of a buckle-plate made from sheet metal, bent over the hoop of an oval or D-shaped loop, to which a strap-end mount is corroded. There is evidence of the attachment slot, a small part of the pin, and two rivets, which would have secured the buckle-plate to its strap. Corroded to the buckle at an angle of $c$ 40 degrees is a strap-end mount, suggestive of it having just passed through the loop. The mount is badly corroded and spalling, but X-rays indicate that it tapers to a sub-triangular terminal and that its body was decorated with ridges or transverse lines. Its profile would suggest it has a split end. L: 46mm; W: 18mm; T: 4mm. Loop: L: 31mm; W: 25mm; T: 3mm.

SF 1272e

Iron buckle, buckle-plate, and strap-end mount of same construction as above. The buckle set consists of a sheet metal buckle-plate with an oval or D-shaped loop. The pin is bent back away from the loop and corroded to the buckle-plate. The buckle-plate is overlain by a strap-end mount which would appear to have just passed through the loop. This is probably of the same type as SF 1272d, with a sub-triangular terminal and ridged or decorated with transverse lines along its back. L: 46mm; W: 18mm; T: 4mm. Loop: L: 31mm; W: 28mm; T: 3mm.

*Spearhead (Figure 58)*

SF 1271

Spearhead. Badly corroded. The blade is narrow and has a lozenge-shaped cross-section. The midrib is not particularly pronounced but does exist. The blade is $c$ 30mm at its widest point, but is corroded in an asymmetrical fashion; the angle of the shoulder appearing more acute on one side than the other. The cylindrical socket is complete with a narrow neck from which it extends 114mm. Organics/wood impressions survive on the inside of the socket. Mineralised wood corroded to the exterior of the spearhead may be indicative of a wooden bier or coffin on which the body was laid, or possibly the spear shaft if it was broken so as to be accommodated within the burial. Surviving L: 302mm; socket dia: 20mm.

## 4.3 MEDIEVAL AND POST-MEDIEVAL

### 4.3.1 Pottery (Figure 59)

Derek Hall

The excavations produced 85 sherds of pottery; 84 are of medieval date while the other is from a post-medieval stoneware vessel. All the material has been identified by eye and assigned to a recognised fabric type. Ten sherds of whiteware were submitted for ICPS (chemical sourcing).

*Scottish White Gritty Ware*

Sixty-five of the sherds are from vessels in this fabric, and jugs are more common than jars (cooking vessels). Recent chemical sourcing and typological analysis has suggested that the manufacture of this pottery type was more widespread across Scotland than previously thought (Jones et al 2006). The closest identified production centre is at Colstoun near Haddington, which lies some 15km to the south-west of Auldhame (Hall 2007, 35–76).

*Yorkshire Type Ware*

Vessels in this fabric type are amongst the most popular medieval imported wares on the Scottish east coast in the 13th and 14th centuries (Jennings 1992). There are only two sherds in this assemblage from a jug ([282]) and an unidentified vessel form from FN 937.

# THE ARTEFACT ASSEMBLAGE

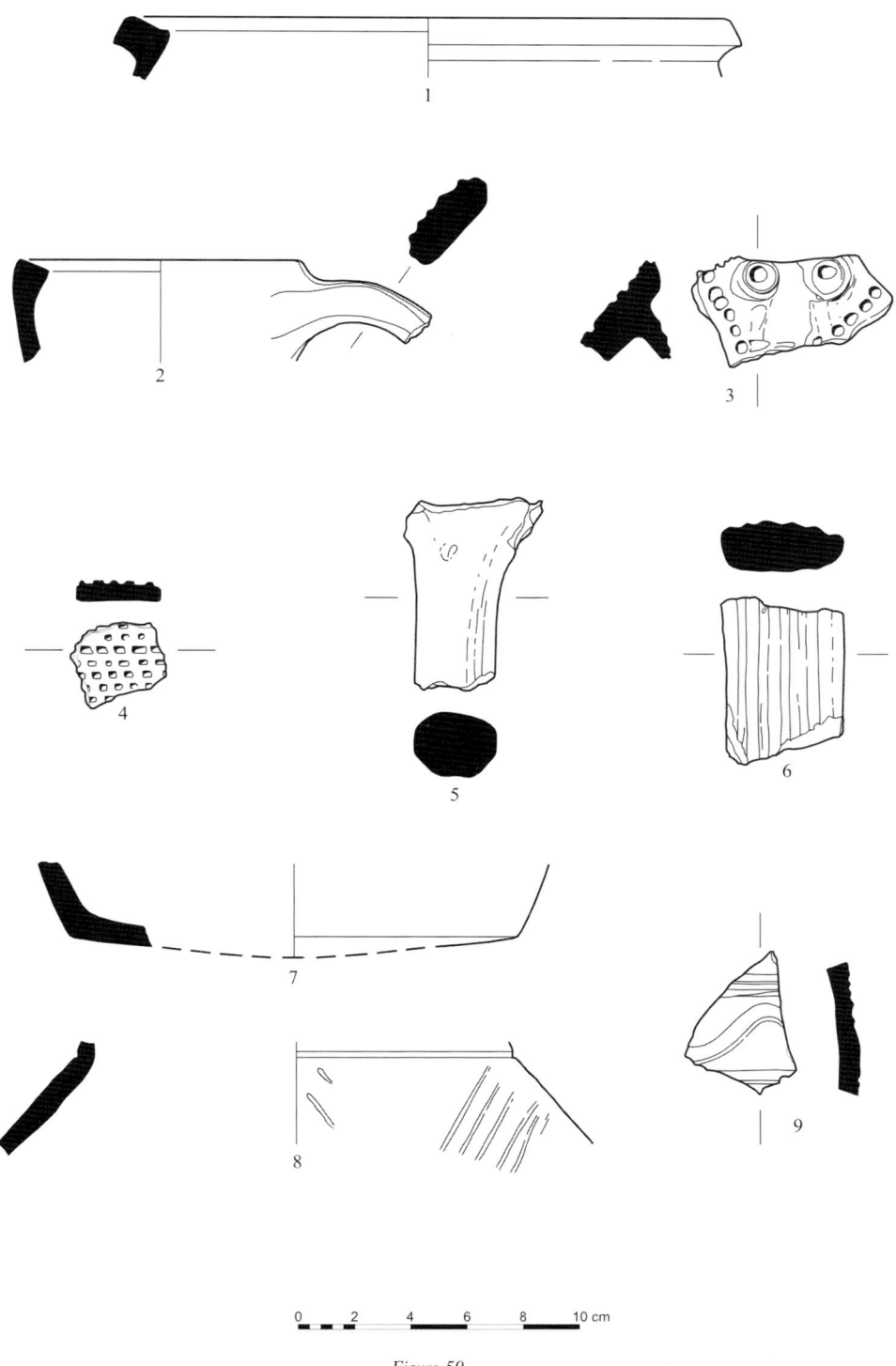

*Figure 59*
Medieval and post-medieval pottery

*Developed Stamford Ware*

This fabric has been recovered from sites in Perth (Hall 1996, 952–9) and from excavations in Aberdeen (Murray 1982, 123). The vessels represented are very well-made glazed jugs, and the fabric dates to the late 11th to early 12th century (Kilmurray 1980). There is a single bodysherd from a jug ([008]) in this fabric.

*Unidentified*

There are 15 body sherds that are not large enough to accurately source.

All of the pottery from Auldhame would appear to be of 13th- or 14th-century date with a small residual earlier component as indicated by the presence of a single sherd of Developed Stamford Ware. The dominant fabric is a Scottish White Gritty Ware, possibly of local manufacture. Aside from a single sherd of Post-Medieval Stoneware (SF 264) there is nothing to suggest a later date.

*Illustrated Pottery Catalogue (Figure 59)*

SCOTTISH WHITE GRITTY WARE

1. Rimsherd from jar, [001] (SF 275)
2. Rim and ribbed strap handle junction from splash glazed jug, [086] (SF 622)
3. Green glazed facemask from jug, [001] (SF 758)
4. Bodysherd from splash glazed jug decorated with rouletted notches, [001] SF 758
5. Rod handle from splash glazed jug, [001] (SF 758)
6. Ribbed strap handle from splash glazed jug, [001] (SF 554)
7. Basal angle from jar, [001] (SF 476)

UNIDENTIFIED

1. Bodysherd from unglazed globular vessel with incised line decoration, [001] (SF 1075)
2. Bodysherd from jug glazed speckled green and decorated with incised lines, [086] (SF 622), Yorkshire Type ware?

### 4.3.2 Copper alloy

DAWN MCLAREN and FRASER HUNTER (scientific analysis by Christopher Brooks and Jim Tate)

Eleven medieval copper alloy objects were recovered during the excavations at Auldhame. Most are ornaments, especially brooches and pins, but there is also a small quantity of decorative mounts and vessel fragments.

*Brooches (Figures 60 and 61)*

SF 305

Small cast annular brooch, oval in section, decorated on the external face with a series of regular transverse lines that were cast rather than incised later. Each line has been formed by a series of strokes, not always perfectly aligned. The decoration is smoothed and worn at one edge from contact with the pin tip. The ring has two opposed indents that form a narrow strip over which the cast pin has been fitted. This has a flat rounded head expanding into a distinct raised shoulder, which then tapers to a fine circular-sectioned pin with a small oval facet at the tip where it rests on the broach. The shank curves slightly downwards in the middle, probably from use. A very similar brooch of silver came from a hoard in Dumfries, believed to have been deposited about 1310 (Callander 1924, 160–3, fig. 1:2). The size and form is typical of a 13th–14th-century date (Biddle & Hinton 1990, 639). Brooch D 26.5 W

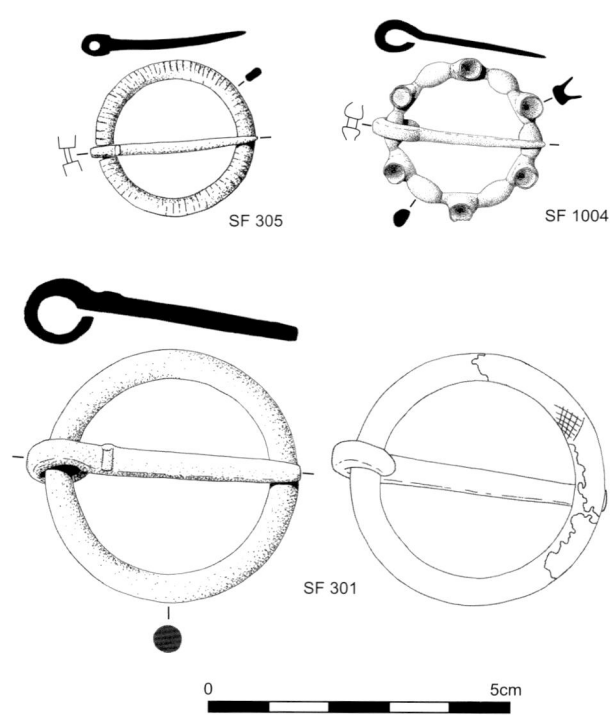

*Figure 60*
Medieval buckles and brooches © Trustees of National Museums Scotland

# THE ARTEFACT ASSEMBLAGE

3 T 2mm; pin L 28 D 2mm. Alloy: leaded gunmetal. Ditch fill, [076].

SF 1004

Intact cast annular brooch, its hoop comprising alternating raised cups and ovoid mouldings. There are six regularly spaced cups (D 2.5–3.5 H 4–5mm), originally set with coloured glass or semi-precious stones. Opaque yellow paste remains in one setting only. The pin is circular in section, and has been hammered out of a rod; it may be a replacement. A fragment of a silver brooch with a similar but more ornate hoop, came from a hoard in Dumfries deposited about 1310 (Callander 1924, 160–3, fig. 1:5). Brooch alloy: leaded gunmetal. Pin alloy: leaded gunmetal with trace amounts of silver. Brooch D 26.5 W 2–3.5 T 2.5–3mm; pin L 28.5 D 1.5mm. Unstratified.

*Buckle (Figure 60) Penelope Walton Rogers*

SF 301

Cast copper alloy ring buckle, complete with intact, cast, pin. The ring is plain with a circular section. The pin has a sub-circular section, a blunt, squared tip and an inner rebate at the point where it has been looped around the buckle frame. Alloy: leaded gunmetal. Diameter 43mm; ring width 5mm; pin length 46mm; pin thickness 4.5mm tapering to 3.0mm.

On the back of the ring there is an imprint in the corrosion, 15 × 6mm, of textile woven in tabby, 12/Z × 12/Z threads per cm. Some fibres, separate from the main imprint, are plant-stem in origin and probably flax (identified by polarised light microscopy).

Buckle located under hand, on the lower right hip of SK074 within fill of G079, [075].

Plain ring-buckles were in use in north-west Europe between the later 13th century and the mid-15th century, although the larger examples, of the type seen here, mainly come from the period *c* 1350–1450 (Thordeman 1939, 117–28; Egan & Pritchard 1991, 22–3, 57–65; Mould 2011, 626, 631). They were sometimes used singly on belts, which could be low-slung, but they also commonly occur in men's graves in pairs between the lower hip and mid-thigh (Thordeman 1939, figs 117–18; Mould 2011, fig. 700; Gilchrist & Sloane 2005, 85–6). In the case of SK074, the left side of the skeleton was destroyed during the construction of Building 4 (Figure 10) and it is highly likely that a second buckle has been lost from the left hip.

Pairs of buckles in this position were used to fasten the leather straps that attached the man's long hose to his *brygyrdyl* (Russell-Smith 1956). The *brygyrdyl*, or breche girdle, was the belt used to support the breche or braies, which at this date were baggy linen underpants (Strutt 1796, 225; Cunnington et al 1960, 24). Buckle fastening on hose was a 14th-century fashion that was displaced by tie-fasteners during the final third of the century (Russell-Smith 1956, 221). The size of the buckle and its

*Figure 61*
Brooches SF 305 and SF 1004

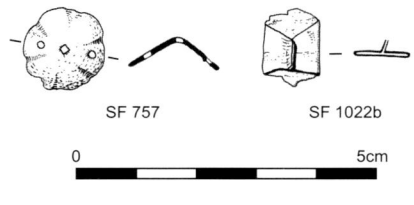

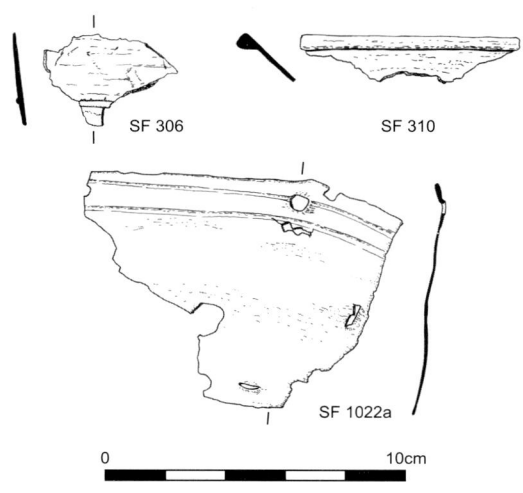

*Figure 62*
Decorative mounts and fittings – SF 757 and SF 1022b. Lead vessel fragments SF 306, SF 310 and SF 1022a

position on the body therefore fit the second half of the date range indicated by the radiocarbon dating of the human bone (Table 1; SUERC-13304). The presence of the buckle suggests that the body was at least partially clothed when it was buried and the linen textile most probably represents the fabric of the man's braies.

*Pin*

SF 286

Badly corroded pin shank fragment, circular in section; head and tip lost. L 28 D 3mm. Alloy: bronze, low-lead. Fill of G041, [039].

*Decorative mounts and fittings (Figure 62)*

SF 757

Six-petal domed flower stud with two small diametrically-opposed perforations (D 1mm), one slightly distorted, possibly from wear. Slight damage to one edge and top of dome. This is a decorative mount once attached to leather or textile, such as a belt fitting (Gilchrist & Sloane 2005, 84–5, fig. 44). Similar decorative studs come from Linlithgow Carmelite Friary (Stones 1989, 157, illus 96:109a), St Giles' Cathedral, Edinburgh (Franklin & Collard 2006, 55, illus 40:4) and Whithorn, Dumfries and Galloway (Nicholson 1997a, 375–6). They were in common use throughout the 14th and 15th centuries in London (Egan & Pritchard 1991, 186–92, fig. 119). D 13 H 4.5 T 0.2–0.3mm. Alloy: leaded gunmetal, trace silver. Ploughsoil, [001].

SF 304

Slightly domed oval or circular mount, centrally perforated (D 2mm) with a larger circular perforation (D 3.5mm) 2mm from one edge. The opposite edge has been damaged. L 26.5 H 2.5 T 0.5mm. Alloy: leaded gunmetal. Ploughsoil, [001].

SF 1022b

Paperclip rivet, arms broken, head a flattened hexagon. L 3mm; head W 12.5 × 10 T 0.5mm; shank L 2.5mm. Pit fill, [954].

*Vessels (Figure 62)*

SF 306

Cast vessel fragment from the body of a slightly rounded vessel with traces of a horizontal decorative rib (W 3mm). L 44.5 W 31.5 T 2mm. Alloy: leaded bronze with significant antimony. Ditch fill, [076].

SF 310

Rim fragment of a large shallow cast dish or bowl with a triangular slightly out-turned rim. Post-casting hammering is visible on the external surface. The original diameter of the vessel is approximately 250mm. L 73 W 26.5 T 2–6mm. A similar rim fragment comes from Brough of Deerness, Orkney (Morris & Emery 1986, 341, illus 25) and is suggested as late medieval in date. Alloy: leaded bronze with significant antimony. Ploughsoil, [001].

SF 1022a

Fragmentary flat sub-rectangular patch, cut from a sheet vessel. One edge comprises the slightly irregular but fairly straight flattened rim of the vessel; the other three sides are cut. Two corners have been lost, displaying recent breaks. The original vessel form is uncertain because it was flattened, but the rim was

# THE ARTEFACT ASSEMBLAGE

Table 3
Types of medieval copper alloy objects present

| Feature | Ornament | Decorative mounts & fitting | Vessel |
| --- | --- | --- | --- |
| Grave fill [041] | Pin fragment (SF 286) | | |
| Grave fill [079] | Buckle (SF 301) | | |
| Ditch fill (c 076) | Cast annular brooch, decorated (SF 305) | | Cast vessel fragment with decorative rib (SF 306) |
| Pit fill (c 954) | | Paperclip rivet (SF 1022b) | Fragment of sheet vessel, reused as patch (SF 1022a) |
| Ploughsoil (c 001) | | Six-petal domed flower stud (SF 757); Oval or circular mount (SF 304) | Rim fragment from cast vessel (SF 310) |
| Unstratified | Cast annular brooch, decorative settings (SF 1004) | | |

probably everted or flat (W 11–16.5 T 1mm) with regularly spaced decorative rivets similar to medieval examples from Balgone, North Berwick and Denny, Stirlingshire (*PSAS* 3 (1857–9), 245–6; *PSAS* 6 (1864–66), 107–8). No decorative rivets remain in situ but two perforations, 70mm apart, one complete (D 4mm), the other on the cut edge of the patch (D 3.5mm) are present on the rim. A third ripped perforation is visible on the edge of the rim. Hammer marks are visible from the manufacture of the vessel, particularly around the rim where there is a small linear tear (9.5 × 2–3mm), which is likely to have occurred during production of the rim. The internal surface of the vessel has been smoothed and slightly polished for display. Later, the vessel was hammered flat and this sub-rectangular sheet cut off to be reused as a patch. Parallel to two cut edges are rectangular perforations (6 × 1.5mm); these have been punched through from the external surface of the sheet. The patch would have been attached by fixing paperclip rivets (eg SF 1022b) through these holes. A further two perforations are visible on the broken edges. Four sheet fragments with recent breaks were recovered from the same context and are likely to be further fragments of this patch but no longer join. L 106 W 78 T 0.2–1mm. Alloy: brass with tinned surface (detected in analysis; no longer visible). Pit fill, [954].

*Discussion*

The medieval finds comprise two brooches, a buckle, a pin fragment, two decorative mounds, a paperclip rivet and three vessel fragments, two from cast vessels and one a sheet vessel that has been reused as a repair patch (Table 3).

Very few objects (only two) were recovered from graves, as is typical of medieval Christian burials where grave goods are rare. These comprised an intact buckle from G079 and a pin fragment (probably residual) from G041. The buckle is a common medieval type of 13th–15th-century date (Whitehead 1996, 16); examples with such large diameters are likely to be from the later half of this period (Egan & Pritchard 1991, 57–65). Such simple buckles could have been used as belt buckles, reused as brooches or, when found in pairs, as fastenings for breeches or hose (Gilchrist & Sloane 2005, 85–6). Walton Rogers (above) has argued that this buckle was one of a pair, the other having been removed during the construction of Building 4 (Figure 10), and that the position in which it was found, by the thigh, makes it more likely that this was a hose fastening. The traces of textile preserved on the rear suggest that the deceased was interred fully clothed rather than being buried in a simple shroud.

Two brooches, one decorated with transverse ribs, the other with raised settings (originally holding glass paste or semi-precious stones) and ovoid mouldings, are typical medieval ornaments. These were both recovered from undated contexts, one from the fill of Ditch 1 ([076]) and the other from spoil.

Fragments of both cast and sheet vessels were recovered. Most notable was a fragment from a sheet vessel, which was reused as a repair patch. It was recovered from an undated pit alongside a paperclip rivet and an iron collar fitting (SF 1281). It is likely

Figure 63
Coins

bottom basin with an everted thickened rim similar to that from Dowalton Loch, Dumfries and Galloway (NMS: HU 4; Hunter 1994, 60–1, fig. 7) but perforated by decorative rivets. Such bowls are a long lived type but the rivets in the rim are a medieval style. Similar bowls come from Balgone, North Berwick and Denny, Stirlingshire (*PSAS* 3 (1857–9), 245–6; *PSAS* 6 (1864–66), 107–8). Repair patches for sheet metal vessels are more commonly found than intact vessels (cf examples from late medieval deposits at Meal Vennel, Perth; Cox 1996, 769–70, illus 19); a heavily patched sheet bowl with in situ paperclip rivets was recovered from late deposits at Linlithgow Carmelite friary (Stones 1989, 160, illus 101). The bowls from Balgone were recovered during draining operations in an area of boggy ground. They were found in association with animal bones and a suite of other bronze vessels, including two flagons that have been dated to the 14th or 15th centuries. All three vessel fragments from Auldhame derive from domestic vessels and are unlikely to be ecclesiastical objects.

The suite of ornaments, vessel fragments and mounts are all broadly datable to the 13th to 15th centuries.

### 4.3.3 Silver

Nicholas M McQ Holmes

*Coins (Figure 63)*

SF 1266

William the Conqueror silver penny, BMC type vii (profile/cross and trefoils), Eadwine, London (1080–1083?)
19.5mm; 0.91 g; die axis 5°

Obv.: +PILLELMREX; crowned bust to right with sceptre
Rev.: +EDPIONLIINDNI; short cross pattée with annulet in middle; voided trefoils in angles
Very slightly buckled; unworn
Ploughsoil, [001]

that the rivet relates to the use of the patch. Such rivets are common in the medieval period (as in late 14th- and 15th-century contexts from Perth: Ford 1987, 129, No. 39–41, fig. 63). Although it is not possible to determine the original dimensions of the vessel, it is likely that it was a flat- or dished-

# THE ARTEFACT ASSEMBLAGE

SF 1129

Another similar, Ælfwine, probably London, but possibly Lewes

19.0mm; 0.93 g; die axis 45°

Obv.: +PILLELMREX

Rev.: +[ ]ELFPINEONLI[ ]

Poorly struck; reverse double-struck; probably only slight wear

Mixed graveyard soil, [750]

SF 995

Edward I silver penny, class 10ab3 (uncertain subclass), London (c 1302–23)

19.0 × 18.5mm; 1.46 g; die axis 150°

Slightly uneven striking; all-over dark accretion; moderate wear

Grave fill [502], [500]

SF 355

Another, class 10cf2b, London (c 1306–07)

18.5mm; 1.26 g; die axis 210°

Slightly chipped; slightly buckled; fairly worn

Ploughsoil, [001]

DISCUSSION

This site is so far unique in a Scottish context in producing two English silver pennies of William the Conqueror. Only one other example of a coin of this king has so far been recorded – from excavations on the Isle of May (Bateson & Holmes 2003, 260). Both the coins from Auldhame belong to the relatively rare type BMC vii, minted during the period 1080–1083(?) and, while one of them is too poorly struck for the amount of wear in circulation to be accurately assessed, the other shows no evidence of wear at all and is therefore likely to have been lost from circulation in the early 1080s. These coins predate the commencement of the Scottish regal coinage by more than half a century, and it is evident from the extreme scarcity of finds that there was effectively no circulating currency in Scotland at this period.

The other two coins are Edwardian pennies from the first decade of the 14th century, such as are common finds all over Scotland. Coins of this type clearly continued to circulate until well into the second half of the century, as demonstrated by hoard evidence. At least two other Edwardian pennies have recently been found by metal detectorists in close proximity to the excavation site.

### 4.3.4 Iron

Dawn McLaren and
Fraser Hunter

Aside from the iron objects found in the Viking grave G751 discussed above, another 201 iron fragments were recovered from the excavations at Auldhame. This assemblage is dominated by nails (173 fragments, representing a minimum of 105 nails) and coffin fittings. There are also a few knives, bar fragments and possible tools. A large quantity of material was recovered from graves, most of which appear to be coffin fittings; only one further grave good has been identified. Very little of this assemblage is chronologically distinctive, but those objects which can be broadly dated (the knives and the axe) would fit a later medieval date.

The objects have been grouped into functional categories where identifiable: fittings, nails, tools and miscellaneous. Measurements (in millimetres) are largely taken from X-rays, using the abbreviations: L length, W width, T thickness, H height, D diameter.

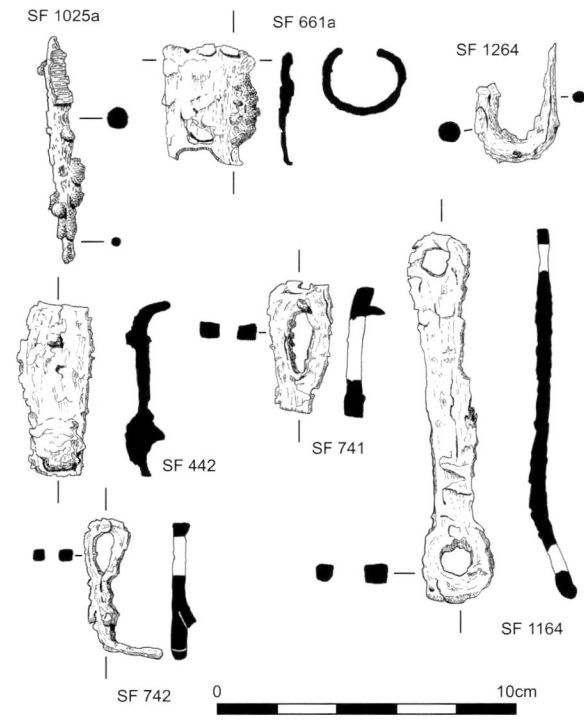

*Figure 64*
Miscellaneous iron objects

# LIVING AND DYING AT AULDHAME, EAST LOTHIAN

*Tapering rods*

SF 1025a

Fitting? Square-sectioned rod, tapering at both ends to a blunt narrow point. Wood traces present on shank. L 78 W 6.5 T 6.5mm. Grave fill [468], [466]. (Figure 64)

SF 1031a

Fitting? Square-sectioned rod, tapering at both ends to blunt narrow points. Wood traces present on shank. L 70 W 5 T 4mm. Grave fill [468], [569].

SF 1031b

Fitting? Square-sectioned rod, tapering at both ends to blunt narrow points. L 67 W 5 T 5mm. Wood traces present on shank. Grave fill [468], [569].

DISCUSSION

These three examples were all recovered from the same grave fill, [466], in association with a large suite of nails. It is likely that these are all coffin fittings but exactly how these tapering rods functioned is unclear. Each example has wood traces over the whole length of the shank, the grain of the wood running transversely across the width of the rod, suggesting that each end was fixed into separate wooden components to join them together. There is no sign of clenching of the ends, indicating that the full length of each point was driven into the wood.

*Collars*

SF 1281

Plain, slightly uneven iron ring, a thicker area indicating the weld position. Similar examples are interpreted as bindings for pivots or the ends of heavy wooden shafts and

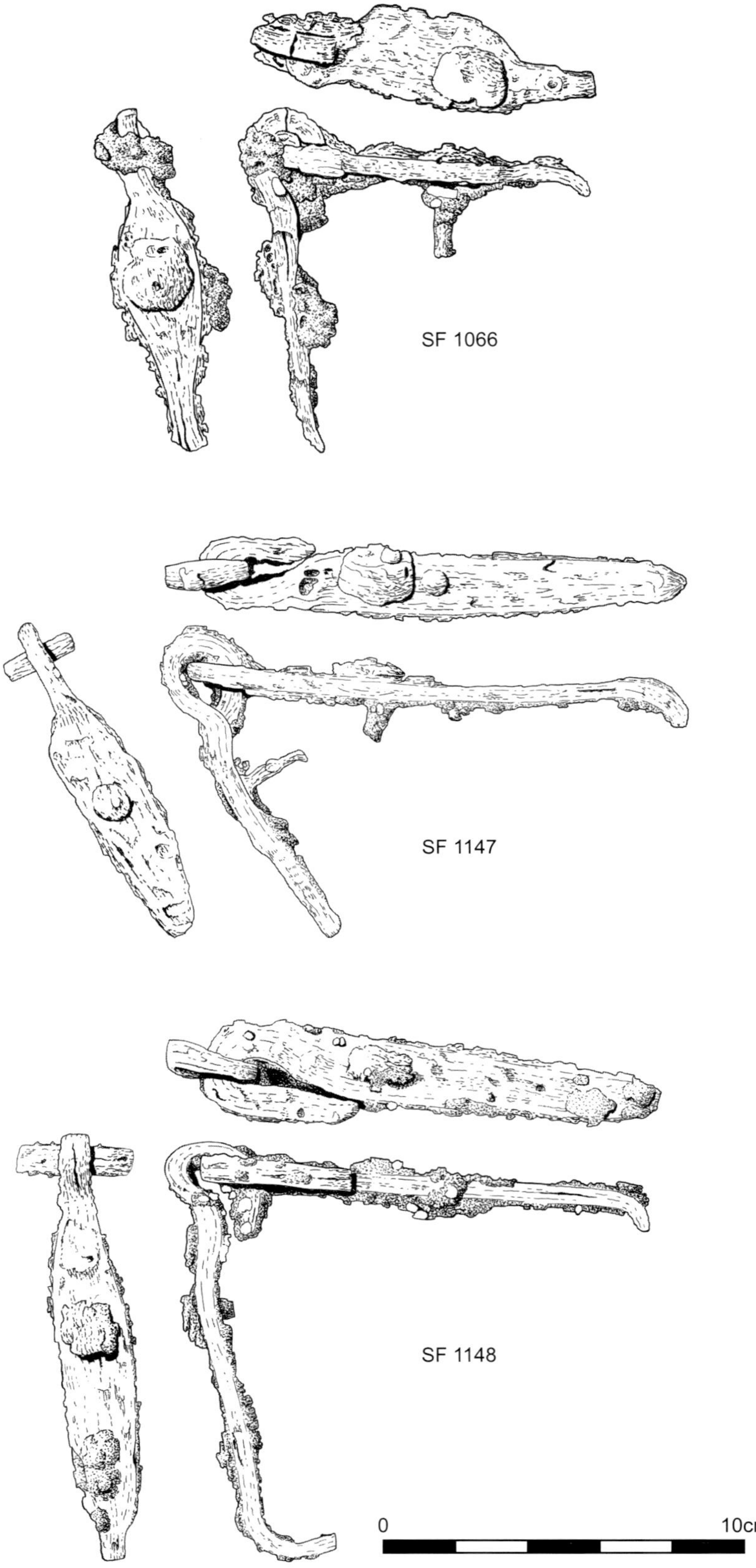

SF 1066

SF 1147

SF 1148

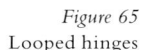

*Figure 65*
Looped hinges

76

handles (Manning 1985b, 140). D 34 H 12.5mm. Pit fill, [954].

SF 661a

Open C-shaped collar, damaged in antiquity. One edge has been folded inwards to create a thickened, strengthened edge (T 3.5mm); the opposite edge is slightly flared (T 2.5mm). A small square perforation (D 4mm) in the centre of the collar, opposite the gap, would have secured it to the base of a wooden pole or shaft to protect it from wear. A similar ferrule comes from Fishergate, York (Rogers 1993, 1419, fig. 695). L 38.5; thickened end: external D 28mm, flared end: external D 23.5mm. Coal-rich layer, [096]. (Figure 64)

*Hooks*

SF 1264

Hook or staple. Fragment of a thick square-sectioned rod that has been bent back on itself to form an open hook. One end is lost; the remaining end tapers to a straight, blunt, slightly flattened tip. Although there are no wood traces remaining on the shank, this is likely to be a fitting from a coffin or structural timber, used to join pieces of wood together. Similar examples come from St Ronan's, Iona (O'Sullivan 1994, 339, illus 6) and Whithorn, Dumfries and Galloway (Nicholson 1997b, 413), and were used to secure loop-headed iron fittings to wooden chests or coffins. L 74.5 W 3.5–7.5 T 5–7.5mm. Ploughsoil, [001]. (Figure 64)

*Brackets*

Four fragmentary brackets or straps were recovered during the excavation, all from disturbed contexts. Three (SF 442, 539, 533a) are fragments of L-shaped brackets, and it is likely that the fourth (SF 768) was of similar form. Each arm or strap is perforated with a single nail hole, the nail remaining in situ. Two have traces of wood on the interior surfaces, confirming that the fittings were deposited attached to their wooden components. Despite their recovery from disturbed contexts it is likely that these were coffin fittings similar to those from the medieval cemeteries at St Ronan's, Iona (O'Sullivan 1994, 340, illus 7) and Whithorn, Dumfries and Galloway (Nicholson 1997b, 412–13, illus 10.93), and from the chapter house at Jedburgh Abbey, Borders (Caldwell 1995b, 91, illus 81:111).

SF 442

Fragment of L-shaped bracket; one arm has been lost but the remaining fragments indicate it was bent upwards at 90°. The remaining flat rectangular arm tapers slightly to a squared end with rounded corners, which curves slightly upwards. 11.5mm from remaining end is a small rivet hole with nail in situ. Wood traces visible on interior surface. L 58 W 19–21 T 3.5mm. Ploughsoil, [001]. (Figure 64)

SF 539

Fragment of L-shaped bracket? Flat rectangular strip, heavily damaged by corrosion. Both ends are broken, one bending upwards at 45°. 15mm from the opposite end is a hole with in situ nail. L 48.5 W 17 T 13.5mm. Ploughsoil, [001].

SF 533a

Five fragments, no longer joining, of an L-shaped binding strip or bracket. The arms appear to be symmetrical, flat rectangular-sectioned strips, expanding towards perforated rounded ends with in situ nails. Wood traces are present in the interior surfaces and around the nails. Both broken ends are bent at 90°. Arm 1: L 52 W 12.5–17.5 T 4mm; Arm 2: remaining L 29 W 15.5 T 4mm. Ploughsoil, [001].

SF 768

Flat rectangular strip, bent and distorted, with in situ nail at rounded end, which bends upwards at 90°. Both ends are broken. L 35 W 19.5 T 4mm. [232].

*Loop-headed fittings*

SF 741

Loop-ended fitting. Fragment of a flat elongated oval loop (L 38 W 21.5mm), formed by bending a thin flat strip (W 19 T 5mm) back on itself; tapers into a flat narrow strip (W 9mm), broken at both ends. L 44 T 5mm. Prior to conservation, mineral-preserved wood and a white material were visible on the surface. Grave fill [175], [177]. (Figure 64)

SF 742

Loop-headed fitting or bar. Square-sectioned shank (4.5 × 4.5mm), bent at 90° mid-shank; one end is bent back on itself to form an oval loop (L 24.5mm) with an elongated tear-shaped eye (L 14.5 W 3.5mm), the other tapers to a blunt rounded tip. Fitted to wood a maximum of 20mm thick. L 60mm. Grave fill [175], [177]. (Figure 64)

## SF 1164

Double loop-headed strap. Flat, rectangular strip with expanded round perforated terminals, slightly bent at one end, perhaps from removal. Very similar examples were associated with a chest/coffin at Whithorn (Nicholson 1997b, 413, fig. 10.93). L 126 W 13 T 4.5mm; terminal W 21mm, 19.5mm; perforation D 10.5×9mm, 9×7mm. Unexcavated layer, [776]. (Figure 64)

*Looped hinges (Figure 65)*

## SF 740

L-shaped hinge composed of two interlocking loop-headed straps, both broken; one is flat (T 4mm) and rectangular in section (L 43 W 8mm), the other is a thicker (T 7mm), square-sectioned rod (L 35 W 7mm) with wood traces, broken across a right-angled bend. Grave fill [175], [177].

## SF 1066

Two interconnecting loop-headed straps forming a right-angled hinge, with nails in situ. Wood is present on the interior surfaces and around the nails. Arm 1: L 101 W 10–24mm T 4mm; Arm 2: L 86.5 W 20–29 T 4.5mm. Grave fill [637], [639]. (Figure 65)

## SF 1104

Two interconnecting loop-headed straps with one in situ nail. Both straps are flat but differ slightly in shape. Wood is present on the interior surfaces and around the nail. Arm 1: L 93.5 W 12–28.5 T 6mm; Arm 2: L 108 W 26 T 5mm. Grave fill [700], [698].

## SF 1147

Two interconnecting loop-headed straps, bent at a 45° angle to each other. Arm 1 is a rectangular strap, tapering at one end, which is bent at 90° and broken. Wood traces remain on both sides of the tip, suggesting it had been hammered into the timber. Off-centre, 32mm from the loop is a perforation housing a small nail. Arm 2 is a flat, asymmetrical oval strap; one end is broken, the other tapers into a narrow rod bent into a loop, which interconnects with that on arm 1. 26mm from the start of the loop is an in situ nail. Wood is present on the interior surfaces and around the nails. Arm 1: L 113.5 W 5–19 T 5mm; Arm 2: L 97 W 20 T 5.5mm. Compact dark grey layer, [259]. (Figure 65)

## SF 1148

Two interconnecting loop-headed straps, bent at 90° forming an L-shaped hinge, of very similar construction to SF 1147. These may be a pair. Both arms have a single perforation housing in situ nails. Wood traces remain on the interior surfaces of each arm. Arm 1: L 133.5 W 4.5–19.5 T 4.5–8mm; Arm 2: L 123 W 8.5–20 T 5.5mm. Compact dark grey layer, [259]. (Figure 65)

## DISCUSSION

Although a variety of strap shapes, sizes and loop forms are present, all are variations on a basic design comprising pairs of oval or sub-rectangular flat straps with interconnecting looped heads. Each strap or arm has a single perforation to allow the strap to be attached to timber by a small iron nail (see below). All five examples have nails in situ; wood traces on the interior surfaces indicate they were deposited attached to wood that rotted in situ, suggesting their function as hinges for chests or

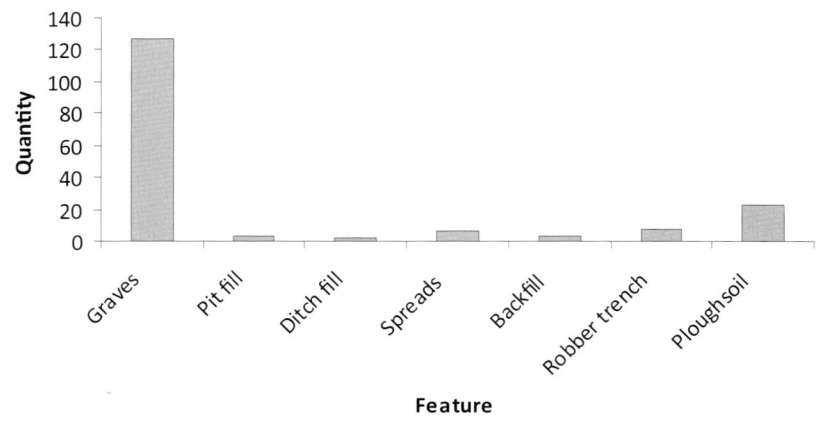

*Figure 66*
Range of features from which nails were recovered

# THE ARTEFACT ASSEMBLAGE

coffin lids. Similar looped or linked hinges come from Fishergate, York (Rogers 1993, 1415–16, fig. 692).

*Nails*

The most common iron find from the site were nails, with 173 fragments representing a minimum of 105 examples. They have been categorised by head morphology and dimensions; all have square-sectioned tapering shanks and square or sub-square heads except where noted. Square-sectioned bar fragments with no further identifiable features have been interpreted as nail fragments. A full catalogue can be found in the archive; only a summary is outlined here.

The 57 stratified intact nails form the basis for this discussion; those from topsoil have been disregarded as they are likely to be modern. Length ranges from 13.5 to 76.5mm (average 39mm). The heads measure from 3 to 22mm in width and from 1.5 to 6mm in thickness (average 12mm by 3mm). Shank sizes range from 1.5 to 6mm in diameter (average around 4mm). Seventy-seven per cent (40) of the intact nails have mineralised wood traces preserved on the shanks. Just over 20% (12) of the intact nails were bent, most at 90°, indicating that they were deposited in situ within their wooden fittings. Only four were curved and twisted, indicating that they had been removed.

The small proportion of large nails (four examples) over 70mm in length in this assemblage is to be expected as these were more likely to be removed and reused (Manning 1985a, 134–5) and are often under-represented in the archaeological record.

A small quantity of more unusual nail types are present within the assemblage:

SF 244

Twisted and bent rectangular-headed tack. L 8mm; head W 6; shank D 4mm. [003].

SF 282

Heavy duty tack with sub-oval head and a short, robust tapering shank. Head damaged but otherwise intact. L 21mm; head: W 24 T 3mm; shank D 7mm. [032].

SF 309

Small sub-square headed nail with square-sectioned shank. L 53.5mm; head W 6mm; shank D 5.5mm. [76].

SF 724

Heavy duty nail or tack with large flat head and short tapering shank. Similar to SF 282 and 1142 but with a longer shank. L 31mm; head: W 21 T 3mm; shank D 4.5mm. [160].

SF 929

Small square-sectioned tack. L 24mm; shank D 3.5mm. [403].

SF 1142

Heavy-duty decorative tack with sub-square head and a short, robust tapering shank. L 26mm; head: W 23 T 4mm; shank 11mm. [750].

DISCUSSION

Seventy-three per cent (127) of the nail fragments were recovered from grave fills (Figure 66), representing a minimum of 74 nails. Eighty-nine per cent (114) of those from graves had substantial wood traces remaining around the shank, indicating that the nails were deposited within their wooden fittings and rotted in situ. It is likely that most, if not all, of these are coffin fittings. Some were in situ within iron brackets and fittings.

A further 46 nail fragments were recovered from a range of other excavated features; half came from ploughsoil. Other examples came from secondary contexts, mainly ditch fills, pit fills, robber trenches and spreads. It is likely that these nails were either from disturbed graves or dismantled structural elements of the chapel itself.

*Bar fragments*

SF 1165

Square-sectioned tapering bar fragment; broken at one end, the other squared with rounded corners. Possible off-cut. L 37.5 W 19 T 6.5mm. Unexcavated layer, [776].

SF 1060

Rectangular tapering slightly curved bar fragment, broken at one end, the other rounded. L 28 W 6–7 T 2mm. Found amongst skeletal remains within G627, [676].

*Tools*

SF 291

Fine circular-sectioned rod, one end rounded, the other tapering to a blunt end, bent mid-shank. Possibly

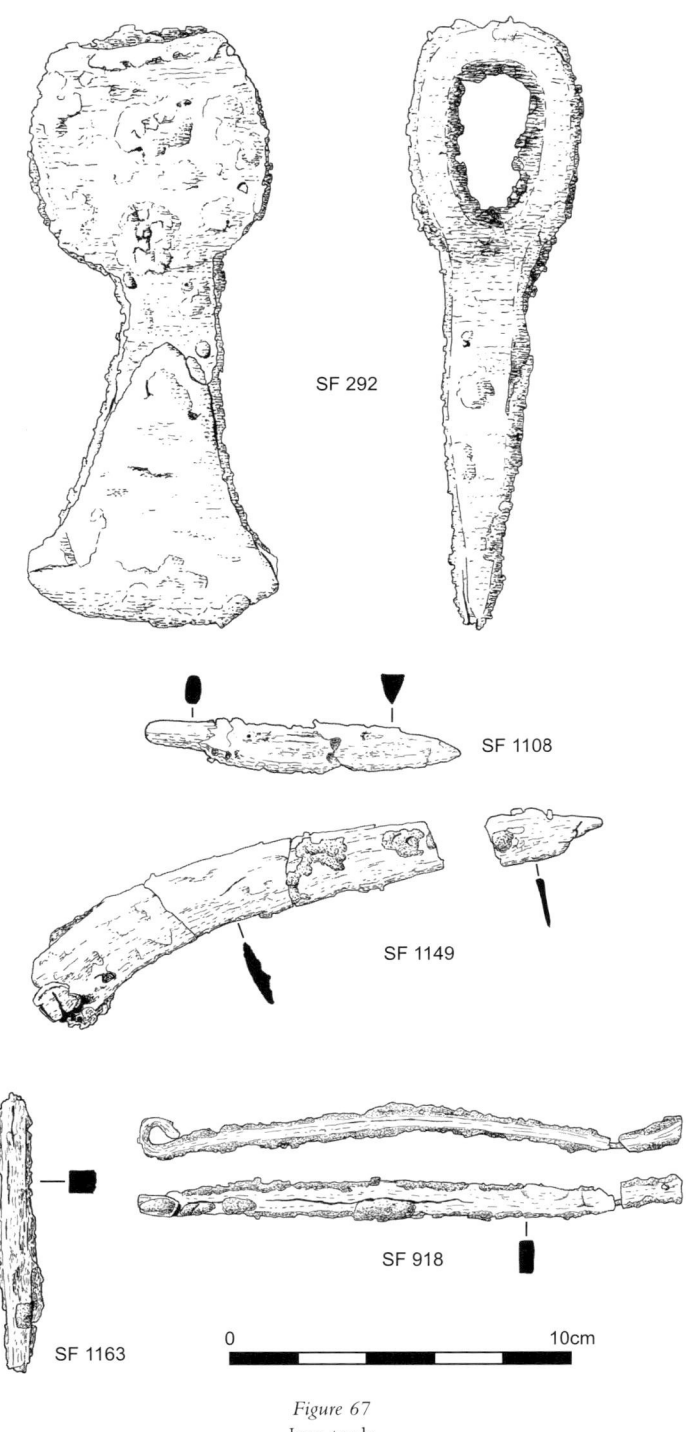

Figure 67
Iron tools

a fine punch for use in leather- or bronze-working. L 107 D 5mm. Ditch or pit fill, [069].

SF 292

Axe-head. Large sub-square socket with rounded ends and rectangular-sectioned perforation (44 × 24.5mm), with blade aligned centrally on the socket. The blade is slightly asymmetrical and quite narrow where it meets the socket, expanding gradually to the edge. It was made by folding a sheet of iron, with the weld line butt and blade clearly visible. The edge has been strengthened by welding a thin (T 7mm) wedge-shaped iron plate (L 90mm) to one side of the blade. L 185mm; socket L 61 W 67 T 6–12.5mm; blade L 124 W 26.5–73 T 3.5–31mm. The form is consistent with medieval wood-working axes from London (Wheeler 1954, 55–6, fig. 12:4) and Exeter (Goodall 1984, 337, fig. 189). Deposit of stone above ditch or pit fill, [70]. (Figure 67)

SF 1108

Knife. Slightly curved blade with straight back tapering to the tip. The tang is intact, rectangular in section, tapering to a blunt rounded point with wood from the handle remaining on both sides. The tang joins the back of the blade with a distinct shoulder. The blade is short and convex, indicating it had been extensively resharpened. Consistent with Ottaway's type C3 (1992, 570). L 93mm; blade: L 44mm, W at shoulder 16mm, T 6mm; tang: L 44mm W 11, T 7mm. Grave fill [716], [718]. (Figure 67)

SF 1149

Reaping hook? Two fragments, no longer joining but plausibly from the same bladed tool. Upright, lentoid-sectioned blade, expanding and curving slightly to the broad rounded tip, with cutting edge on the inner surface. The end has a very short tapered tang. The form is unusual, but the curved shape and concave cutting edge are consistent with identification as a reaping hook (cf Manning 1985b, 51). The tang is surprisingly short, but the handle could have extended onto the blade. L 148 W 17–22 T 2–3mm; tang: L 14 W 5–11 T 3.5mm. Possible trample layer, [766]. (Figure 67)

# THE ARTEFACT ASSEMBLAGE

**Table 4**
**Range of iron objects present**

| Function | Quantity | Types |
|---|---|---|
| Fittings | 17 | Double-ended pins, collars, hooks, brackets, loop-headed fittings, hinges |
| Nails | 173 fragments | Minimum of 105 nails represented |
| Bars | 2 | |
| Tools | 6 | Axe, two possible fine punches, knife, blade and tang fragments |
| Miscellaneous | 3 | Handle fragment, strip fragment, unidentified fragment. |

SF 1163

Square-sectioned rod, tapering to a blunt rounded point at one end, broken at the other. Possibly a punch. L 79.5 W 8 T 8mm. Unexcavated layer, [776]. (Figure 67)

*Handles*

SF 918

Handle. Long, thin, rectangular-sectioned rod, gently curved along its length. One end tapers slightly in width towards a looped terminal (D 11mm), forming an open loop 6mm in diameter, which curves slightly upwards. The other end has been lost but also tapers and curves upwards, suggesting a similar looped terminal was originally present. L 159.5 W 9 T 5mm. Ditch fill, [419]. (Figure 67)

*Miscellaneous*

SF 661B

Strip/sheet fragment. Two conjoining fragments of iron strip or sheet, one original straight edge remaining. L 38 W 26 T 3mm. Coal-rich layer, context 096.

SF 760

Unidentified rod fragment. Elongated thin tapering iron rod curving towards rounded tip, broken at other end. L 43 W 4 T 2.5mm. Ploughsoil, [001].

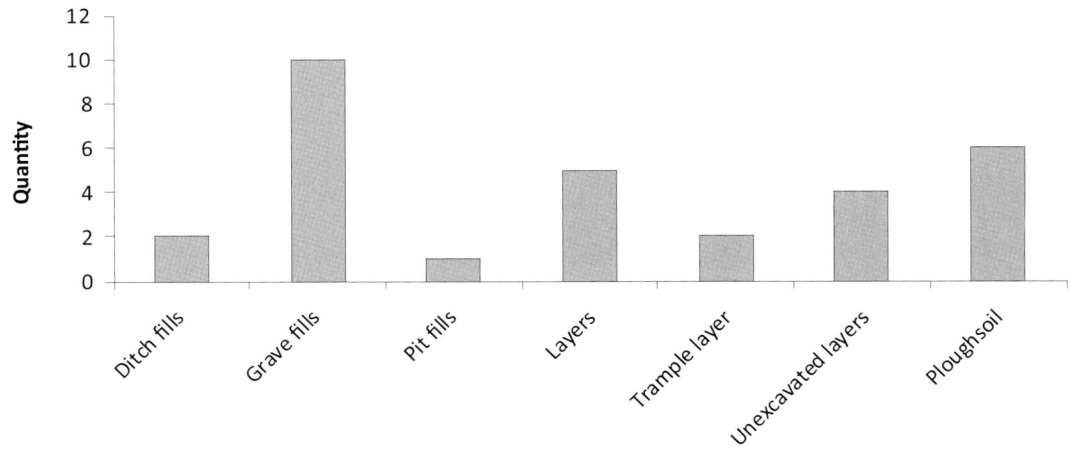

*Figure 68*
Contexts of iron objects recovered (excluding nails)

# LIVING AND DYING AT AULDHAME, EAST LOTHIAN

DISCUSSION

This discussion looks at the iron objects (Table 4) recovered from graves and other locations, apart from the objects from the Viking grave, G751.

The majority of the finds came from graves (Figure 68) in the form of coffin fittings such as nails and brackets. Aside from the richly furnished burial within G751, only one further grave good was identified amongst the iron finds, an intact knife with a wooden handle in mineralised condition associated with G716. Knives of this type are only broadly datable but it is consistent with a medieval date (Cowgill et al 1987, 80–2, fig. 55). Knives and tools in general are very rarely found as grave goods within medieval burials (Gilchrist & Sloane 2005, 177–8), although there are examples from Whithorn and Barhobble, Dumfries and Galloway (Hill 1997, 74; Cormack 1995, 81–3).

*Coffin furniture*

Despite the large number of burials excavated, iron fittings (nails and various brackets, hinges and looped fittings) were recovered from only 16 graves (Table 5). Gilchrist and Sloane (2005, 111) note that although wooden coffins were the most common container for burials during the 11th to 16th centuries, most medieval burials were not furnished with a container.

Large quantities of nails were recovered from G468 (dated to AD 990–1160 at 2σ), G584 (AD 1470–1660 at 2σ) and G851 (75% probability of 1490–1680), in which wooden coffins were detected by staining and fragments of mineralised wood. The shape of the grave pit for the former two indicates that these coffins were the usual shape, being wide at the shoulders and gently tapering towards the feet. The few graves with significant quantities of associated nails makes it difficult to draw any further conclusions but it is

Table 5
Iron objects and fittings recovered from graves

| Feature | Quantity | Types |
|---|---|---|
| Grave fill [005] | 1 | 1 intact nail |
| Grave fill [157] | 1 | 1 intact nail |
| Grave fill [175] | 3 | Loop-headed hinge (SF 740), loop-headed strap fragment (SF 741), loop-headed rod (SF 742) |
| Grave fill [260] | 1 | 1 intact nail |
| Grave fill [389] | 1 | 1 fragment |
| Grave fill [405], severely truncated | 3 | 3 fragments (min. of 1 nail) |
| Grave fill [468] | 42 | 39 fragments (min. of 19 nails), 3 tapering rod fittings (SF 1031 a&b, SF 1025a) |
| Grave fill [502] | 8 | 8 fragments (min. of 4 nails) |
| Grave fill [584] | 18 | 18 fragments (min. of 12 nails) |
| Grave fill [627] | 1 | Bar fragment (SF 1060) |
| Grave fill [637] | 4 | 3 fragments (min. of 3 nails), Loop-headed hinge (SF 1006) |
| Grave fill [700] | 1 | Loop-headed hinge (SF 1104) |
| Grave fill [716] | 1 | Intact knife with traces of wooden handle (SF 1108) |
| Grave fill [747] | 1 | 1 fragment |
| Grave fill [799] | 1 | 1 intact nail |
| Grave fill [812] | 1 | 1 fragment |
| Grave fill [851] | 49 | 49 fragments (min. of 31 nails) |

clear that no standardised quantity of nails was used. Rodwell (1981, 152) notes that a minimum of 12 nails are required to construct a nailed coffin, but the limited number within many burials at Auldhame suggests that coffins were produced using a combination of traditional carpentry techniques, with wooden pegs to secure joints as well as iron nails.

The small quantity of nails recovered from other graves (eg G005, G157, G260, G389, G405, G747, G799 and G812) makes the presence of a coffin hard to substantiate. In eight examples, only one nail was recovered. This could be the result of accidental inclusion due to mixing of material when the grave pit was excavated, slumping post-deposition, later disturbance or the reuse of timber for coffins, with nails left in situ. The reuse of wood for grave linings has been noted previously at Perth Carmelite friary (Boyd 1989, 117).

A range of brackets, hinges and looped fittings was also recovered from grave fills. Four fragmentary L-shaped brackets came from disturbed contexts, but it is likely that these were reinforced coffin or chest fittings similar to those from St Ronan's, Iona (O'Sullivan 1994, 340, illus 7) and Whithorn, Dumfries and Galloway (Nicholson 1997b, 412–15, fig. 10.93). Gilchrist and Sloane (2005, 113) discuss some southern examples dating from the 11th to 16th centuries and their possible purpose either as functional reinforcements for coffins that needed to travel long distances or as decorative embellishment. As the Auldhame examples were not in situ, it is not possible to reconstruct the coffin furnishings.

G468, dated to AD 990–1160, had three tapering rod fittings and a large suite of nails. Each of these fittings had wood traces covering the shank, the grain running transverse to the rod. The ends of the points have not been clenched, indicating that the full length of each point was driven into the wood. It is likely that these fittings were used to join two adjacent planks, perhaps the lid, but why only three are present, and why only in this burial, is unclear.

The most significant fittings from the Auldhame graves are the hinges. These hinges, taking the form of two interconnected looped straps, would have been fitted on to the wooden box with a single nail in each arm and the bent, narrow terminals driven into the timber. One arm was fitted vertically on the back of the box with the loop or eye at the top. The second arm was fixed horizontally across the top of the container, its loop threaded through that of the first arm, forming a hinge which would allow the lid to be lifted. The presence of such fittings is significant as a hinged lid would not have been necessary for a coffin (Rogers 1993, 1433) and suggests that some burials at Auldhame were deposited within reused chests or other wooden containers.

*Other iron objects*

A limited quantity and range of other iron objects were also recovered from the excavation at Auldhame. These include a small number of tools, fittings unconnected to coffin furnishings, a bucket handle and unidentified bar and strip fragments. The most impressive find is the intact axe head; the remaining objects were fragmentary and most were recovered from secondary contexts such as ditch fills, pit fills and trample layers. They provide few clues to the activities taking place on the site although the tools indicate a range of craft activities: a wood-working axe and punches, a fine one probably for leather-working and a heavier duty one more suited to metalworking.

Table 6
**Dated graves containing iron objects. Displayed in order of date, earliest to latest**

| Feature | Types | Date |
| --- | --- | --- |
| Grave fill [627] | Bar fragment (SF 1060) | AD 880–1020 at 2σ |
| Grave fill [468] | 39 fragments (min. of 19 nails), 3 tapering rod fittings (SF 1031 a&b, SF 1025a) | AD 990–1160 at 2σ |
| Grave fill [157] | 1 intact nail | AD 1030–1220 at 2σ |
| Grave fill [584] | 18 fragments (min. of 12 nails) | AD 1470–1660 at 2σ |
| Grave fill [851] | 49 fragments (min. of 31 nails) | AD 1490–1680 (75% probability) |

## Table 7
### Range of lead objects recovered by context

| Context | Casting waste | Off-cuts | Patches | Strips/sheets | Window came fragments |
|---|---|---|---|---|---|
| Ploughsoil (001) | 4 | 4 | 1 | 9 | 1 |
| Ditch fill (076) | | | | 1 | |
| Layer (259) | | | | 1 | |

*Chronology*

Very few of the iron objects are closely datable. A small number of burials associated with iron finds were dated (Table 6); the wide range (from the 9th to the 17th centuries AD) suggests that the graveyard was in use, perhaps sporadically, for over 800 years. The axe head and intact knife are consistent with a medieval date but cannot be closely dated.

Taphonomic issues with the iron finds from graves have already been discussed above, including possible disturbance of burials, accidental inclusion of objects during backfilling and the reuse of old wood containing iron fittings. The dates derived from the skeletal material cannot in all examples be directly related to the finds but can provide us with a useful *terminus ante quem* for their deposition.

### 4.3.5 Lead

DAWN McLAREN and FRASER HUNTER

The majority of this small assemblage of lead fragments was recovered from ploughsoil or unstratified contexts (Table 7); many may relate to the structural fittings of the chapel structure or its demolition. A full catalogue can be found in the archive.

Folded strips and sheet fragments dominate the assemblage. Only two were stratified: one from a compact spread or layer, [259], which covers a large area around the chapel; and one from [076], an upper silt infill of Ditch 1. It is likely that these relate to the structure of the chapel itself and may indicate the deliberate stripping of lead from the roof during its abandonment or deconstruction. One repair patch is also present; a tear in the rivet hole suggests it too was removed deliberately from the structure. Only one fragment of window came is present, recovered from ploughsoil.

A small quantity of nodular casting waste and off-cuts suggests that a limited amount of lead-working was taking place on the site, although its date is unclear as the finds are unstratified; it could be connected to reuse of the material or the chapel's abandonment.

*Catalogue of illustrated items (Figure 69)*

SF 302

Off-cut from rounded end of rectangular-sectioned bar. L 16 W 14.5 T 10.5mm. Ploughsoil, [001]

SF 313

Sub-rectangular lead patch with iron rivets within two perforations (9 × 7mm, 8 × 7mm); one is ripped, perhaps leading to its discard. A thin incised marking-out line runs parallel to, and 2.5mm from, the original edge. L 45 W 28 T 2.5mm. Ploughsoil, [001]

SF 359

Corner of sheet, broken across perforation (D 5mm). L 23 W 17.5 T 2mm. Ploughsoil, [001]

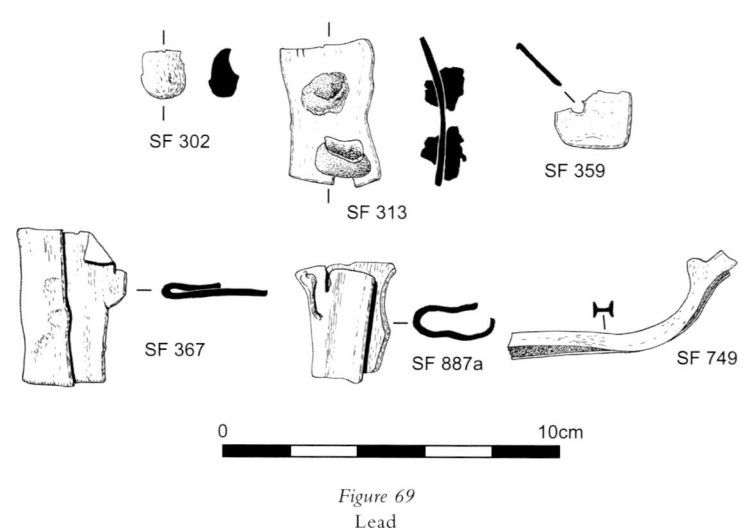

*Figure 69*
Lead

# THE ARTEFACT ASSEMBLAGE

SF 367

Rectangular sheet, folded in half and flattened, with tool marks on the folded edge. A strip has been cut off the opposite edge. L 47 W (unfolded) 43.5 W (folded) 31.5 T 2.5mm. Ploughsoil, [001]

SF 887a

Rectangular strip folded in half and slightly flattened, with distinct linear tool marks (11 × 1.5mm) from flattening. L (unfolded) 55 L (folded) 29 W 33.5 T 2mm. Ploughsoil, [001]

SF 749

H-sectioned lead came, bent, bifurcated at one broken end. L 73 W 6.5 T 5.5mm. Unstratified.

### 4.3.6 Vitrified material

DAWN MCLAREN

A small quantity (1119g) of vitrified material (Table 8) was recovered during the excavations at Auldhame, the majority from secondary contexts and ploughsoil. Although a little iron-working debris is present, many of the fragments cannot be related to iron-working activities and are likely to be residues from hearths or another high-temperature process.

This material was broadly categorised on criteria of morphology, density, colour and vesicularity and has been described using common terminology (eg McDonnell 1994; Starley 2000). A full catalogue is given in the archive report.

**Table 8**
**Vitrified material classification**

| Type | Weight (g) |
|---|---|
| Plano-convex hearth bottoms | 477.5 |
| Unclassified slag | 532 |
| Amorphous burnt plant material | 108 |
| Unworked coal | 1.5 |

*Plano-convex hearth bottoms – smithing?*

Smithing hearth bottoms are an accumulation of slag formed in a pit as the result of high temperature reactions between the iron, iron-scale and silica from either the clay furnace lining or sand used as a flux by the smith. They are recognisable by their characteristic plano-convex form, having a rough convex base and a smoother, vitrified, upper surface. Smithing hearth bottoms are typically smaller in size and lighter than furnace bottoms from smelting (McDonnell 1994, 230). The size and weight of those from Auldhame are consistent with smithing hearth bottoms. Only one fragmentary hearth bottom and a second possible example were recovered. One (SF 653) is an amalgamation of at least two superimposed slag cakes, indicating multiple phases of use of a single hearth.

*Unclassified slags*

The remaining bulk slags (532g) are fractured and small. Such slags are a common component within

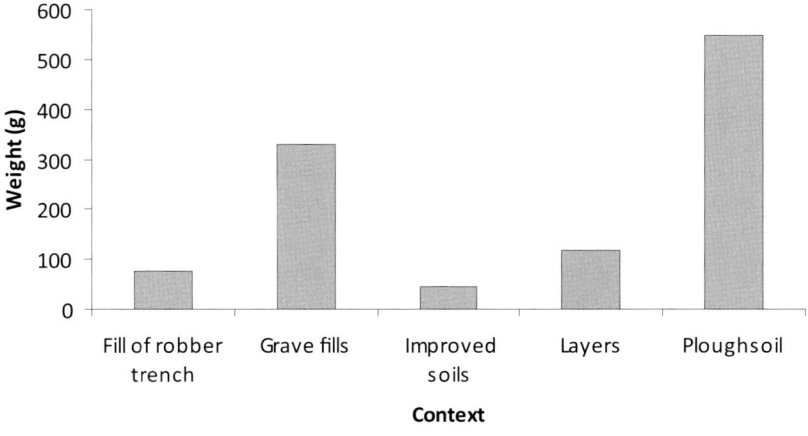

*Figure 70*
Quantity of material by context

85

a slag assemblage and can be produced during both iron smithing and smelting. Differentiating between the two through visual examination alone is difficult and for this reason such slags are often referred to as undiagnostic slags.

*Other materials*

Many items classed as 'slag' during excavation cannot be directly related to iron-working. This accounts for 109.5g of material from Auldhame, of which a significant amount (108g) is amorphous burnt plant material. Also amongst the assemblage is a fragment of unworked coal or shale, perhaps used as fuel.

*Discussion*

Only a small amount of material diagnostic of iron-working was recovered from Auldhame in the form of one, possibly two, hearth bottom fragments. It is likely that these are the product of smithing. The unclassified slags, many of which have significant quantities of coal and gravel inclusions, may also be the result of a similar process. The bulk samples from all stratified contexts were re-examined for hammerscale and magnetic residues, but no further vitrified material was recovered.

All of the vitrified material from the site appears to have derived from secondary contexts, primarily ploughsoil and grave fills (Figure 70). This, with the lack of micro-debris such as slag spheres and hammerscale, or any fragments of hearth structures from the site, confirms that the material is residual and not indicative of in situ iron-working. It is likely that iron-working was taking place in the vicinity of the chapel during its use but the location of this activity remains unknown.

The presence of significant quantities of vitrified material within grave fills, including one hearth bottom, indicates that most if not all are medieval in date. The coal inclusions within many of the unclassified slag fragments are consistent with this date.

### 4.3.7 Bone

DAWN MCLAREN

*Bone bead or button core*

SF 839

Thin disc of bone with central circular perforation (D 4mm), surfaces lightly polished. The articular surface of the bone is visible on one face. Similar bone discs are known from medieval contexts at Edinburgh Castle (Clark 1997a, 148, illus 127:3), Jedburgh Abbey (Caldwell 1995a, 83, illus 77:12) and Perth (Bowler & Cachart 1994, 484, illus 9:45). D 16.5 T 2.5mm. [328].

### 4.3.8 Stone

DAWN MCLAREN and ANDREW HEALD

*Cross-incised stones (Figure 71)*

SF 270

Cross-incised stone. Sub-square slab. The stone is smooth, but irregular, and measures 0.38m long by 0.39m wide by 90mm deep. The cross is not symmetrical; one arm is 0.22m in length, the other 0.30m long. The grooved channel is smooth and round-bottomed.

[953]

Cross-incised stone. Roughly diamond-shaped slab. The stone measures 0.33m long by 0.56m wide. The stone was left in situ, hence the depth cannot be ascertained. The cross is not symmetrical; one arm is 64mm in length, the other 126mm long.

DISCUSSION

Incising a simple cross into stone has been common practise for many centuries. For example, a great variety of linear incised crosses is known across Scotland, Ireland and Wales, carved during the 7th and 9th centuries AD (Fisher 2001, 12–13). Similar cross-incised stones to those recovered from Auldhame have been found at, for example, Hoddom, Dumfriesshire (Craig 2006, 131, Pl. 5.11) and Mote of Mark, Kirkcudbrightshire (Laing 1973, 124). As Craig (2006, 132) states, as expressions of personal devotion by amateur carvers, such simple incised stones are difficult to date, but a date in the early medieval period is not impossible.

*Socket stones (Figures 10, 14 and 72)*

SF 1280

Socket stone. This sub-square boulder has a flat, upper surface and chamfered edges. It is 0.69m wide, 0.69m in breadth and 0.30m in height. The rectangular socket is 0.23m by 0.11m and 0.10m in depth.

# THE ARTEFACT ASSEMBLAGE

a)

b)
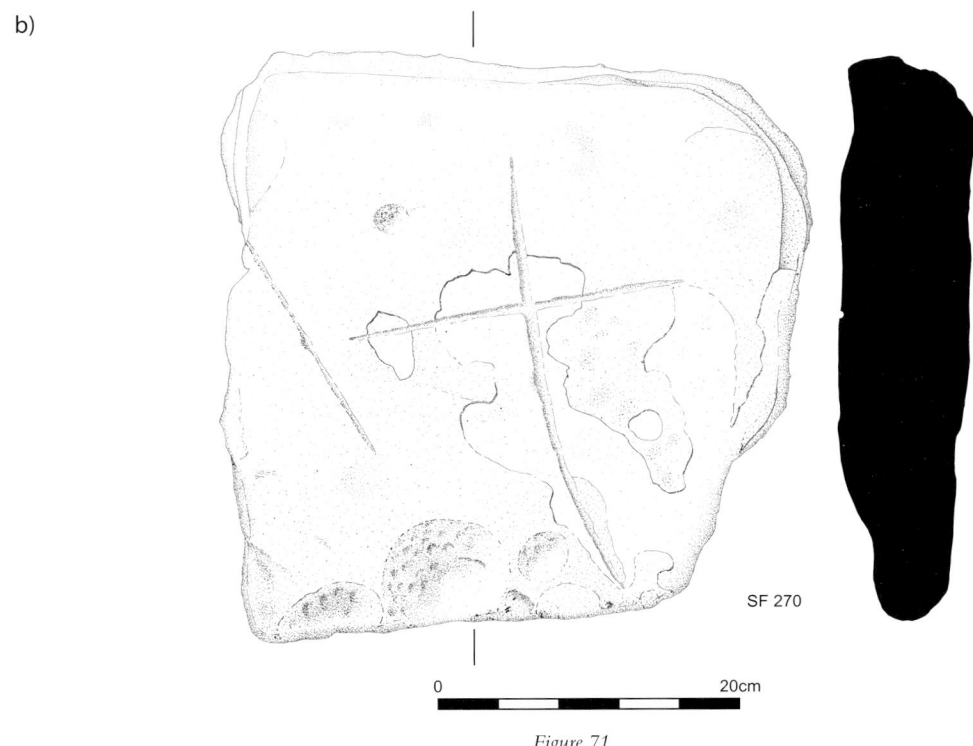

*Figure 71*
(a) The cross-incised stone [953] in situ; (b) The cross-incised stone, SF 270

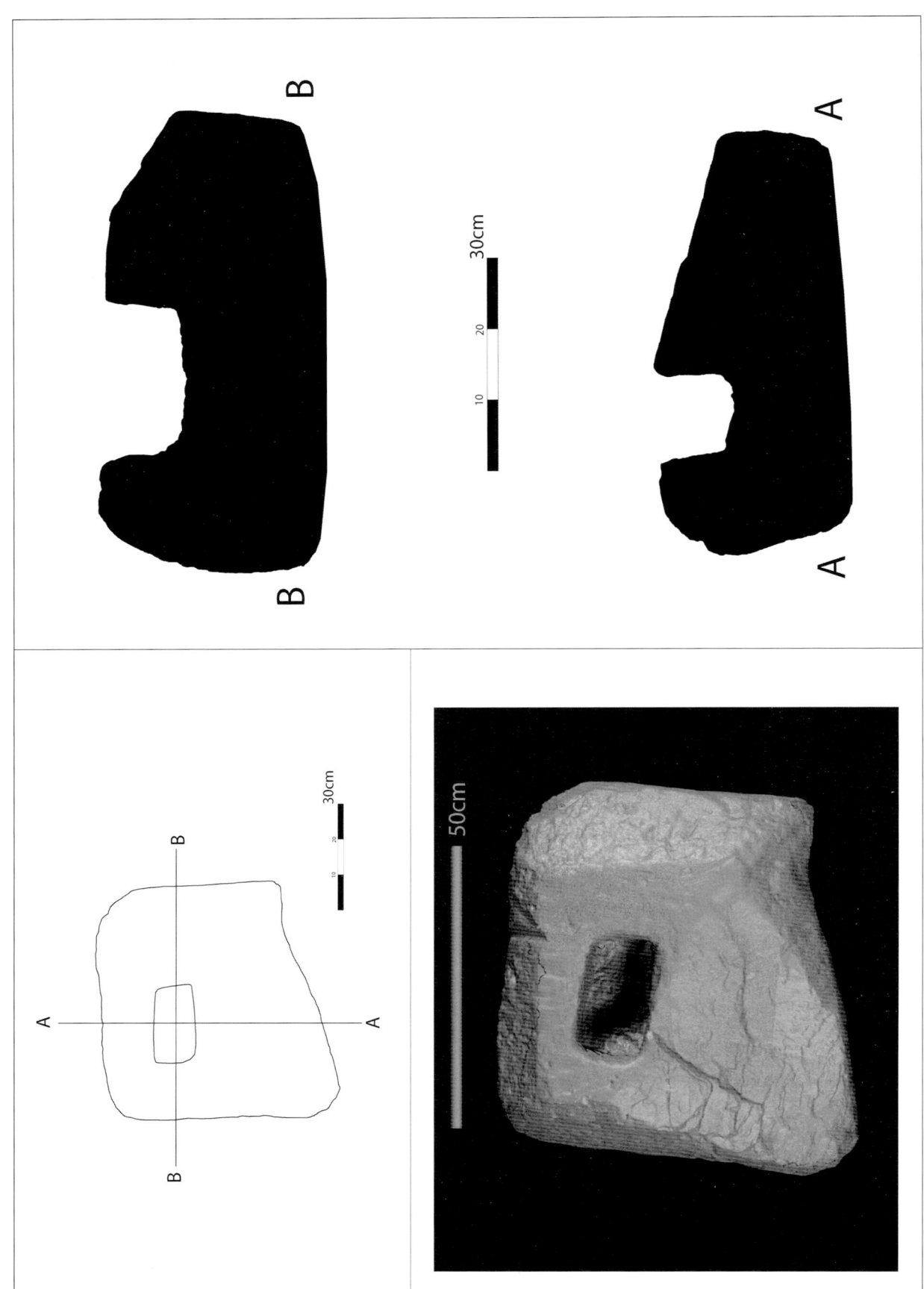

*Figure 72*
The socket stone SF 1280

# THE ARTEFACT ASSEMBLAGE

SF 1287

Socket stone. This rectangular boulder was built into the wall of Building 3 but left in situ. It is 0.42m wide with a breadth of 0.585cm. As it was not excavated, the object's height could not be ascertained. Its upper surface was originally flat but is now damaged. The roughly rectangular socket is 0.20m by 72mm.

DISCUSSION

Socket stones have previously received scant attention in the archaeological record. However, recent surveys from western and eastern Scotland (Fisher 2001, 54–5; Borland et al 2007) have begun to shed light on these enigmatic artefacts. A socket stone is a large boulder or slab containing a hollow (the socket) in its upper surface in which the foot of a stone or wooden pillar or slab could be housed, securing it against excessive lateral movement (Borland et al 2007, 100). The difficulty in interpreting socket stones is that the structure(s) that provided their *raison d'être* are missing. Identification of date, function and role is, therefore, difficult and dependent on the physical form of the socket stone itself, its location and comparison with similar monuments.

Both examples from Auldhame are similar to examples from, for example, Camperdown, Inverkeilor and Monifieth, Angus (see Borland et al 2007, 100–5, illus 2 and 3). All three have been interpreted as bases for holding free-standing crosses, probably of early medieval date. These parallels suggest that the Auldhame examples probably also housed free-standing crosses, as opposed to cross-slabs. The shapes of the sockets vary, suggesting a more slab-like shaft in SF 1287 and a square shaft in SF 1280. It is not clear whether SF 1287 was simply reused as building material in the wall of Building 3 or whether it carried a cross in that position within the church.

*Spindle whorl (Figure 73)*

BE 618

Bun-shaped decorated siltstone whorl, with central drilled conical perforation (D 7–9.5mm). The shape of the whorl and elements of its decoration appear to have been lathe-produced. The decoration consists of two incised concentric lines encircling the central perforation on the upper surface. Below these are an evenly-spaced series of triangular bands, infilled with crudely incised zig-zag lines. A slight miscalculation

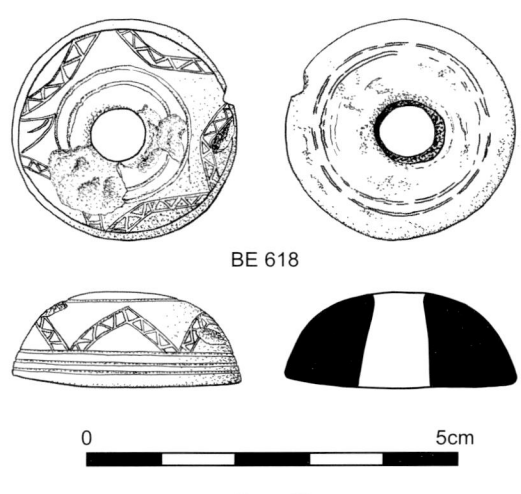

*Figure 73*
The decorated spindle whorl, BE618

in spacing resulted in the sixth triangular band being reduced to a plain incised triangle due to lack of space. Below these are a series of three concentric incised lines running parallel to the edge of the whorl. Overlapping incised concentric lines encircle the perforation on the base. D 31 T 13.5mm. A similar whorl comes from Castle Park, Dunbar (Cox 2000, 141, illus 100:331), likely to be medieval or post-medieval in date. NMS: BE 618. Recorded as 'from excavation of chapel site on cliff edge at Auldhame near North Berwick. April 1976'.

### 4.3.9 Building materials

DAWN MCLAREN (with lithological identifications by Fiona McGibbon)

*Floor tile*

SF 990

Fragment of a tabular granodiorite, only one original edge remaining; this is straight but rounded towards the lower surface with small peckmarks remaining from manufacture. One face is flat and smooth with patches of high polish from contact wear, the other is unmodified. The stone is not local and is likely to have been quarried from an outcrop, perhaps in the Southern Uplands. L 111.5 W 141 T 33mm. 837g. [76].

*Mortar*

Only a small amount of mortar was recovered (460g) from the excavations (Table 9). Most pieces are small

# LIVING AND DYING AT AULDHAME, EAST LOTHIAN

Table 9
Summary catalogue of mortar fragments

| Context | Weight (g) | Type | Description |
|---|---|---|---|
| 96 | 4 | A | 5 small amorphous lumps |
| 927 | 409.4 | B | Large amorphous fragment, no original surfaces remaining |
| 32 | 41.5 | C | Multiple small rounded fragments, abraded. |
| 87 | 0.3 | C | Small fragment, edges abraded |
| 124 | 4.7 | C | Multiple small rounded fragments, abraded. |
| u/s | 0.3 | C | Multiple crumbs |

and fragmentary, making identification difficult. Despite this, three distinct types were identified: type A is abraded agglomerate consisting of *c* 90% small rounded gravel within a soft white matrix; no tile or shell is present. Type B consists of *c* 90% abraded and rounded shell fragments, 2% rounded gravel in a soft white matrix. A couple of terracotta-coloured flecks may be crushed tile. Type C is a fairly soft agglomerate of white-grey coloured cement with few gravel inclusions (<10%).

## 4.4 MISCELLANEOUS DATE

The following assemblage is difficult to date and relates to a few sherds of ceramic and stone objects.

### 4.4.1 Pottery

Ann MacSween

Two body sherds and a fragment were recovered, neither of which is diagnostic as to age.

SF 982

Abraded body sherd from a coil-constructed vessel with diagonal junctions. The fabric is sandy clay with occasional rock fragments, which has fired hard and is grey with red margins. Th 15mm; Wt 28g. [482]

SF 1014

Abraded body sherd and fragment, from a coil-constructed vessel with diagonal junctions. The fabric is sandy clay, which has fired hard and is grey with a red exterior margin. The interior surface is sooted. Th 12mm; Wt 22g. [534].

### 4.4.2 Fired clay

Rob Engl

SF 651

Fired clay. [110] 32 × 44.7 × 32.4mm Roughly oval lump of fired clay.

### 4.4.3 Chipped stone and quartz pebbles

Rob Engl

*Chipped stone*

The chipped stone assemblage consisted of three pieces of flint, all recovered from the ploughsoil. With one possible exception, all the pieces appear to be of local origin and represent material commonly found on sites along the east coast of Scotland. The exception is a large primary chunk of fresh dark grey chalk flint. Material of this type is occasionally found on local beaches along the Forth. This flint probably represents either material from the Low Countries brought to Scotland as ships' ballast in the 18th/19th centuries or is derived from offshore chalk deposits within the North Sea.

Given the paucity of finds and the fact that they were all recovered from the ploughsoil, little can be said regarding the date and nature of the assemblage. The chipped stone artefacts would appear to be confined within the general area to the north of the chapel. It is probable that the material originated within the original ground surface [002], a deposit rich in shell. The presence of the narrow retouched blade and bipolar core may indicate Mesolithic activity within this general area of the promontory.

# THE ARTEFACT ASSEMBLAGE

*Quartz pebbles*

Quartz pebbles were observed in the majority of the grave fills in varying quantities and also in the ploughsoil. This was at odds with the apparent lack of quartz in the surrounding fields or in the subsoil, and suggests that the quartz was deliberately being brought into the graveyard from the nearby beach. Quartz pebbles within graves are often given a ritualistic meaning. At Whithorn, locally derived, rounded quartz pebbles were recovered from many of the Period V graves (Chadburn & Hill 1997, 472). Though common within the site, the pebbles were too few to suggest their use as grave covers and it has been suggested that they were treated as burial 'talismans' or tickets of admission to the afterlife. Chadburn and Hill (ibid) quote references from the Bible and from Bede that allude to the use of white stone, so it clearly had sacred connotations. Certainly, their occurrence in Christian graveyards is not uncommon (Crowe 1982) and they have been recorded in graveyards throughout the UK (Nowakowski & Thomas 1992).

### 4.4.4 Coarse stone

ROB ENGL

*?Gaming pieces*

SF 693

Small stone disc/gaming piece. [160] Sandstone. 20.7 × 5.8mm. Small, circular stone with roughly ground rounded edges and flat faces.

SF 287.1

Possible stone gaming piece [032] 24.4 × 12mm Igneous rock. Small circular pebble of smoothed water-worn stone.

SF 287.2

Possible stone gaming piece [032] 24.2 × 22.3 × 10.8mm. Igneous rock. Small, roughly circular pebble of smoothed water-worn stone.

*Manuport*

SF 663

Elongated cobble. [006] Micaceous sandstone. 141.3 × 48 × 35.5mm. Elongated water-worn cobble with no signs of wear.

*Hammerstone*

SF 496

Fragment. [001]. Micaceous sandstone. 90.8 × 51 × 30.3mm Elongated, water-worn cobble with horizontal break. The artefact is partially symmetrical, and has a dense concentration of percussion scars applied to the unbroken end. These run horizontally along the artefact edge.

*Discussion*

The coarse stone has a wide distribution over the site with the three possible gaming pieces associated with grave fills alongside the fired clay (see above). The two cobble tools were recovered from the ploughsoil and ditch fill respectively.

## 4.5 SUMMARY OF THE ARTEFACTUAL EVIDENCE

ANDREW HEALD

Each of the artefact categories has already received a full discussion in the relevant sections, and more pertinent points are drawn out in Chapter 7, particularly in relation to the burials. For now, it is worth summarising a few other points, as way of a convenient summary.

### 4.5.1 Chronology

A good proportion of the material, particularly the metal objects, are chronologically undiagnostic, but some are more useful.

The presence of the narrow retouched blade and bipolar core may indicate Mesolithic activity within the general area of the promontory. A few sherds of pottery and possibly some other stone tools may indicate Iron Age occupation.

The influence of the Angles is reflected in the recovery of various items. The cylindrical cloisonné stud is likely to date to around the 7th to 8th centuries AD, and the glass inkwell may date to between the 8th and 9th centuries AD. The copper alloy pins appear to have been in use around the 8th to mid-11th centuries AD.

The Viking objects also fall within this broad period; the strap end is likely to date to between the 9th and 10th centuries AD, and it is best to view the prick spurs and the spearhead within this general time frame.

Typology and associations indicate that many of the remaining objects are likely to be medieval in date. The suite of medieval copper alloy ornaments, vessel fragments and mounts are all broadly datable to the 13th to 15th centuries. Although a good proportion of the iron objects are chronologically undiagnostic, many appear to be medieval. The coinage falls into two recognisable groups; the two English silver pennies of William the Conqueror were minted during the period 1080–1083(?) whereas the two Edwardian pennies date to the first decade of the 14th century. The pottery from the site appears to be of 13th- or 14th-century date with a small residual earlier component represented by a single sherd of Developed Stamford Ware. Aside from a single sherd of post-Medieval stoneware there is nothing to suggest activity after the 15th century.

### 4.5.2 People and place

The concentration on burials obviously leads any discussion on the site to issues of death, belief and ritual (see below). However, some of the finds do hint at other areas of life. Storage, cooking and consumption of food and drink are suggested by the pottery fragments and copper alloy vessels. Agriculture is suggested by the reaping hook; and the two collars, which may be associated with wooden handles, may also be related to tools. The spindle whorl is indicative of textile working while the axe must be associated with wood-working. Leather- or bronze-working is suggested by the fine punch and the more robust punch is probably associated with metalworking. The two hearth bottoms are indicative of iron-working in the vicinity and the broken iron bar may be associated with this activity. The small quantity of nodular casting waste suggests that a limited amount of lead-working was taking place on site.

Ornamentation is fairly sparse although the Anglo-Saxon copper alloys, the two medieval brooches and to a lesser extent the bone bead are good examples.

A few finds also give insight into possible structures on the site. The majority of the small assemblage of lead fragments may relate to the structural fittings of the chapel structure or its demolition. Folded strips and sheet fragments may indicate the deliberate stripping of lead from the roof during its abandonment or destruction. The window came is also likely to be associated with the chapel. The floor tile, mortar and nails from non-grave contexts also add to our understanding of building materials in use at Auldhame.

# CHAPTER 5

# OSTEOARCHAEOLOGICAL STUDIES

Melissa Melikian

## 5.1 INTRODUCTION

The human remains recovered at Auldhame were subjected to detailed osteological analysis. Although four phases of burial activity over the course of a millennium have been identified (Chapter 3) the burials have been considered as one assemblage for the purposes of the osteological analysis, as only a small proportion of the total assemblage was sampled. The findings are compared with analyses in published reports from regional cemeteries that are contemporary with the medieval date ranges of these burials to identify any osteological or funerary trends within the data.

The Early Historic period in southern Scotland is characterised by the influxes of new peoples, in particular the Anglo-Saxons. Thus, stable isotope analysis of bone and tooth strontium and analysis of oxygen isotopes were undertaken to identify the composition and origins of the Auldhame population, and its variation over the time span of the graveyard use. Stable isotope analysis of carbon and nitrogen isotopes was also undertaken to investigate the dietary composition of the buried population and

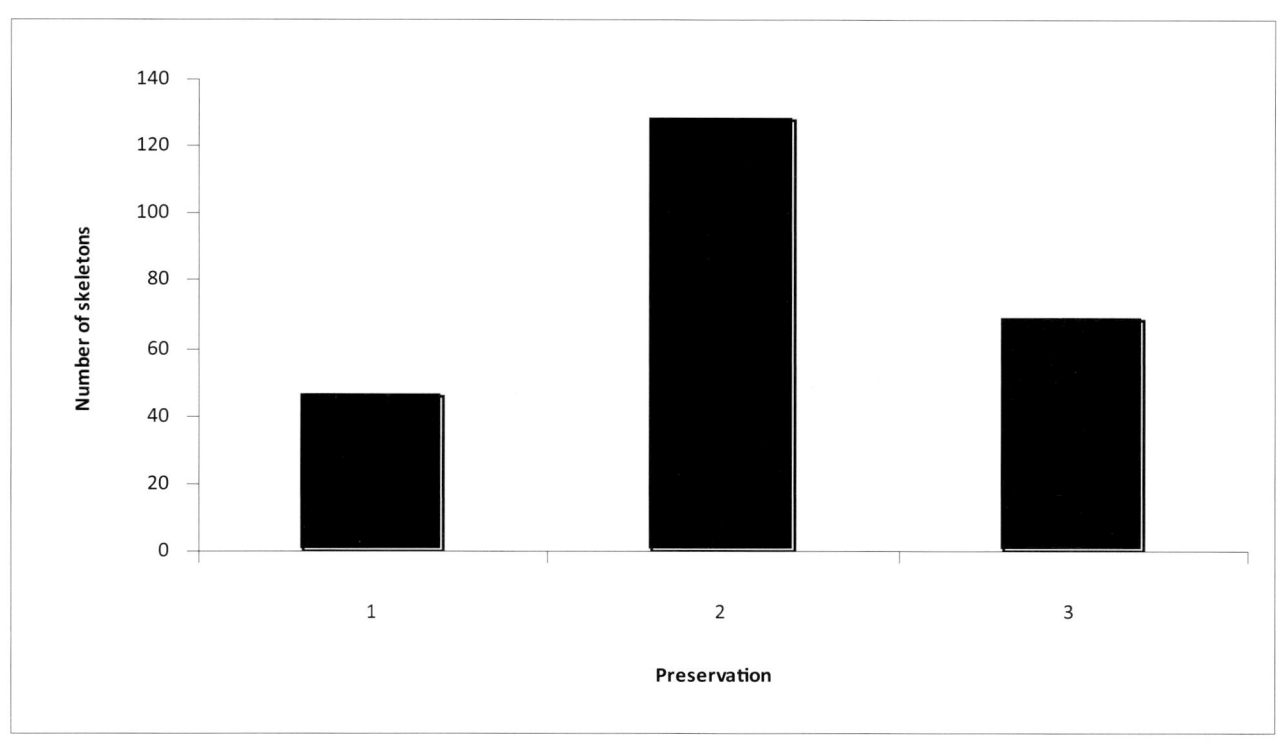

*Figure 74*
Preservation of the Auldhame skeletons

whether this changed over time or varied spatially across the graveyard, as this may reflect on status-based differences in the inhabitants of the population buried at Auldhame. The methodology used in the osteological analyses is presented in Appendix 3 while all tables referred to in this section can be found in Appendix 4.

## 5.2 RESULTS

The total assemblage consisted of 242 individuals (Appendix 2). The results of the osteological and isotope analyses are presented below.

### 5.2.1 Preservation and completeness

The preservation levels of the Auldhame skeletons are shown in Figure 74. The majority (*n*. 128) of skeletons were in a moderate state of preservation (52.8%). A total of 68 skeletons (28.0%) were in a poor state of preservation and 46 skeletons displayed good preservation (19.0%). A number of skeletons displayed weathering and bleaching. The changes were probably due to the disturbance of the graveyard by ploughing and exposure of the bones to the elements. The bones of several skeletons demonstrated erosion of the bone surfaces due to root activity in a similar manner to changes documented by McKinley (2004, 15).

Many of the burials at Auldhame were inter-cutting and 151 skeletons (62.4%) were recorded as incomplete due to truncation. These factors are reflected in the range of completeness scores shown in Figure 75, and the results demonstrate that 42.1% of individuals were recorded as 50% complete or less.

### 5.2.2 Demographic results

The age at death distribution for the assemblage is presented in Figure 76. The sample consisted of 161 adults (66.5%) and 81 sub-adults (33.4%). A total of 73 of the 81 sub-adults could be categorised into an age group. The mortality profile indicates that age at death for the juveniles was relatively consistent across the age groups with only a slight peak evident for those aged 6–11 years at death (Age Category 5). The prevalence of the neonate or foetal deaths is 4.5% when expressed as a percentage of the total sample, or 15.1% of the total aged juvenile sample. The adult data indicate that the majority of adults were dying in age groups 26–35 years (Age Category 8), representing 26% of the total adult sample, and 36–45 years (Age Category 9), representing 27.9% of the total adult sample.

### 5.2.3 Sex determination

The results of the sex determination of adults aged over 18 years from the Auldhame assemblage are shown in Figure 77. The assemblage consists of 58 adult males or probable males and 47 adult females or probable females. A total of 10 adults were classed

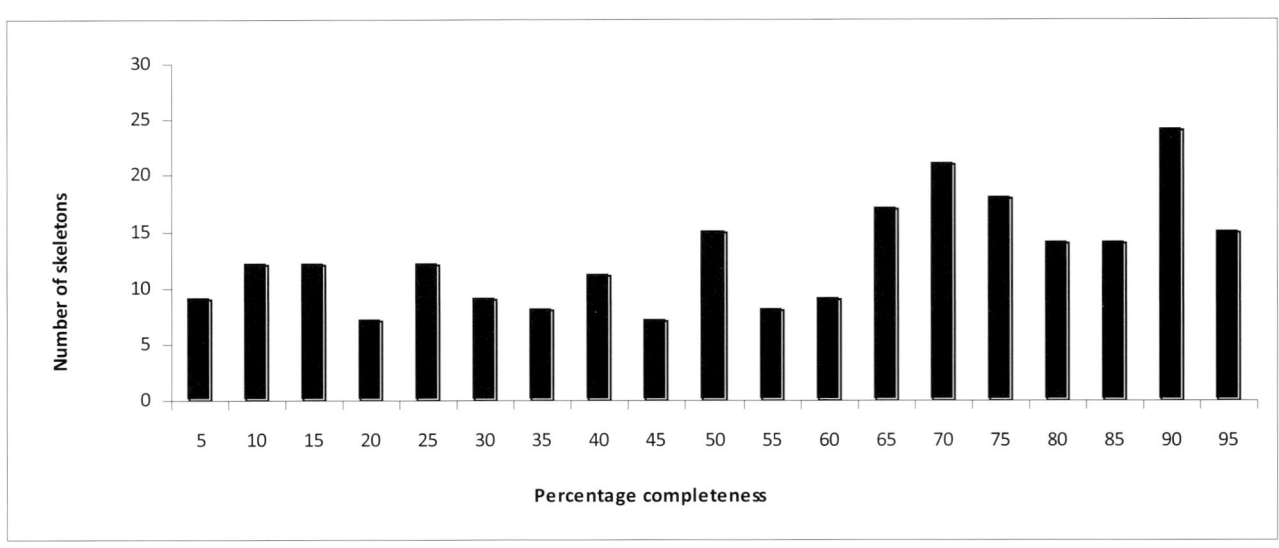

*Figure 75*
Completeness of the Auldhame skeletons

# OSTEOARCHAEOLOGICAL STUDIES

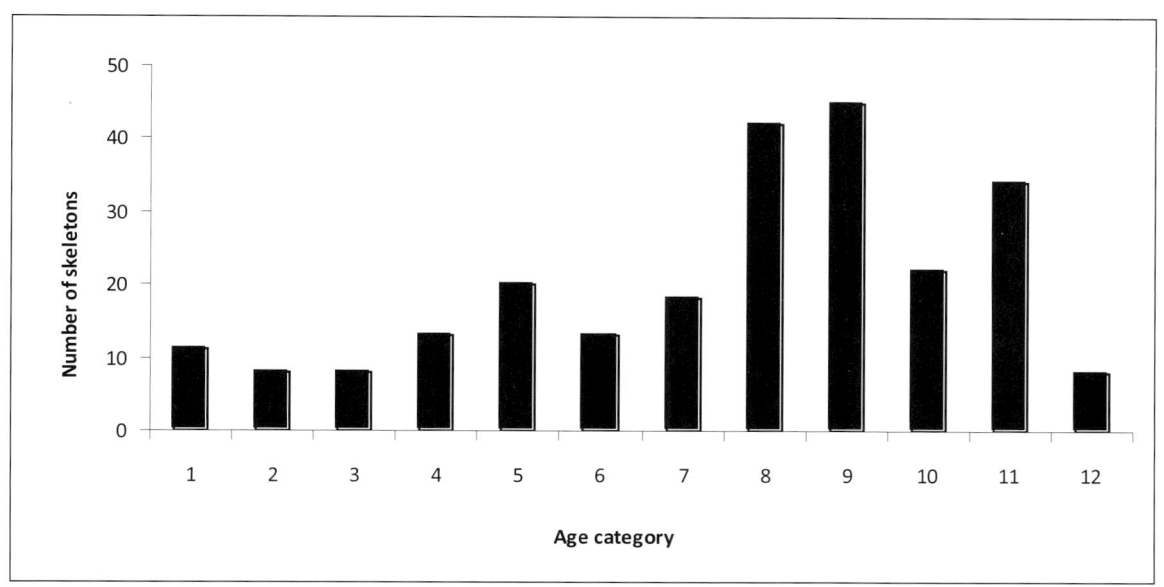

*Figure 76*
Mortality profile of the Auldhame skeletons

as indeterminate sex, while 42 adults were classed as probable males or females. The Auldhame assemblage shows a slight bias, with a sex ratio of 1.3:1 in favour of males. A 1:1 ratio is to be expected in any 'normal' population where sex is simply governed by genetic factors. The difference in numbers of male and female burials is not statistically significant ($\chi^2$ (1) = 1.71, p = 0.191).

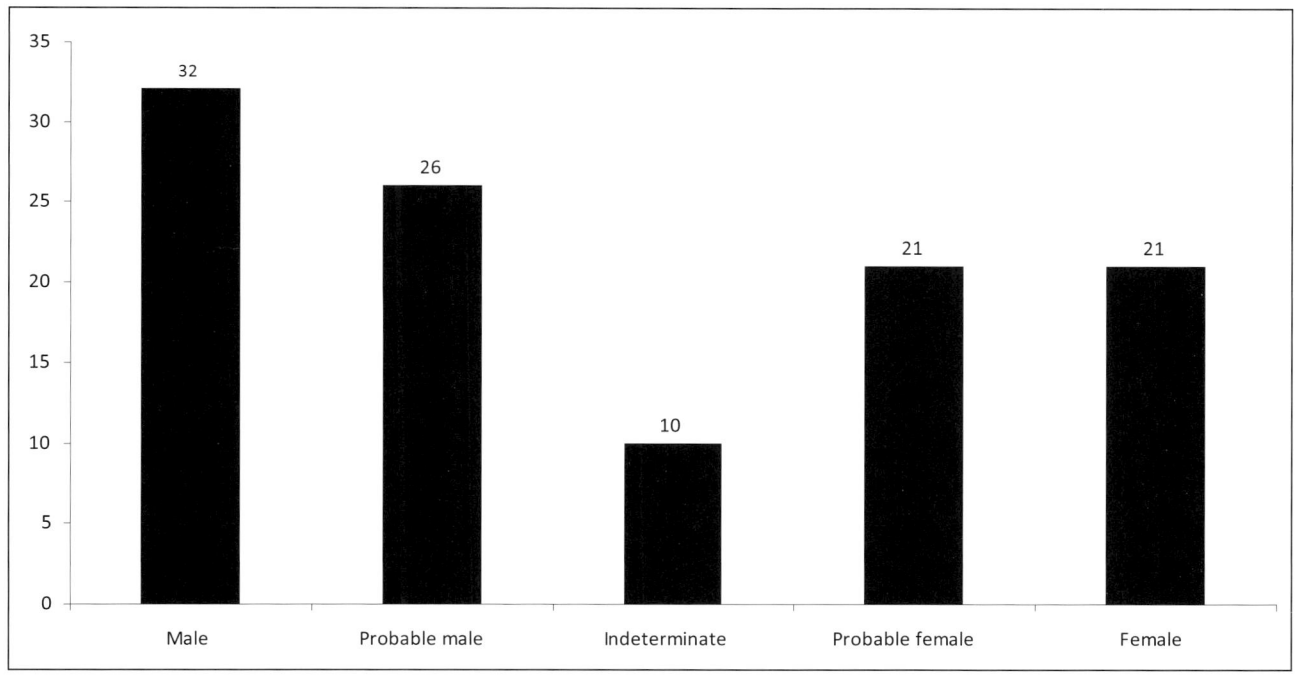

*Figure 77*
Number of adults (18+ years) in each sex category from Auldhame

The results of demographic profiling of the assemblage are shown in Table A4.1. Six individuals aged 12–17 years (Age Category 6) were assigned a sex and these are included in Table A4.1. The sex of a large number (*n*. 126) of individuals remains undetermined. This includes 75 juveniles (59.5% of the undetermined samples). The remaining 51 adults (40.4%) of undetermined sex were affected by low levels of preservation on site and the high degree of truncation. The demographic data indicate that, in general, men were dying younger than women. There were more males dying at ages 18–25 years and 25–35 years than females. There were, however, fewer old adult females (46+ years) than males.

### 5.2.4 Metric data

*Stature*

Stature estimates for the adult assemblage from Auldhame are presented in Table A4.2. The mean stature for males and probable males was 169.9cm (5ft 6in) and for females or probable females 158.6cm (5ft 2in).

*Other metric traits*

The majority of skulls were fragmented, limiting the range of cranial metrical analyses that could be undertaken on this assemblage. One skull of an adult female (SK859) was sufficiently intact to retrieve metric data. The cephalic index, which gives an estimate of the shape of the skull relative to cranial length and breadth, was 75.1, and falls within the mesocephalic index range (Brothwell 1981, 87). A summary of indices calculated from the Auldhame assemblage is shown in Table A4.3. Individuals with gross pathology that affected the lower limbs were excluded from this part of the analysis. Platymeria, or antero-posterior flattening of the femur, is classified by an index below 84.9. Platycnemia as transverse flattening of the tibia is classified by an index up to 62.9 following Brothwell (1981, 88–9). The results in Table A4.3 indicate that the mean male and female femoral indices are platymeric, indicating some degree of antero-posterior flattening of the shaft of the femur. In contrast, the mean male and female tibiae scores are not platycnemic.

### 5.2.5 Non-metric traits

Tables A4.4 and A4.5 present the frequency of cranial and post-cranial non-metric traits identified in adults from the Auldhame assemblage. Four adults (4/57: 7%) presented a retained metopic suture (metopism) along the midline of the frontal bone. This trait is formed by a failure of the two halves of the frontal bone to fuse. This fusion normally occurs during early childhood and can range between 1 and 4 years (Scheuer & Black 2000, 107). Occasionally, the suture line does not fuse and remains open into and during adulthood. The frequency of this trait can be variable. For example, rates from other medieval Scottish sites range from 5.5% (The Hirsel – Anderson 1994) to 25% (Isle of May – Battley et al 2008). The trait is symptomless and the reasons for retaining a suture line at this location, including biomechanics or genetic factors, are at present poorly understood (Brothwell 1981, 93; Scheuer & Black 2000, 105).

Of the post-cranial non-metric traits observed in the adults from Auldhame, several present a higher prevalence in left bones than in right bones (for example *os acromiale* and septal aperture). As the development of non-metric traits can be influenced by both environmental and genetic factors it is often difficult to suggest a specific cause of these features. One condition, *os acromiale*, however, is represented by non-fusion of the tip of the acromion of the scapula and has been documented in individuals who have been known to perform repeated actions of the shoulder and arm, such as archery, during childhood and adolescence (Stirland 2000; Roberts & Cox 2003, 152). Additional evidence of *os acromiale* was identified in a medieval assemblage from Towton (Coughlan & Holst 2000, 73; Knüsel 2000, 115), which they attributed to severe stress on the rotator cuff muscles of the shoulder during adolescence.

### 5.2.6 Dental health

*Calculus*

Dental calculus is formed on tooth and root surfaces following the mineralisation of plaque deposits. Plaque comprises both micro-organisms and proteins from saliva, and the accumulation of mineralised deposits of plaque can be increased by diets high in protein and/or carbohydrates (Roberts & Manchester 2005, 71). Poor oral hygiene practices may allow the build-up of large mineralised plaque deposits on teeth and root surfaces (Hillson 1996, 259). The data for calculus presence or absence, severity and age distribution of individuals with one or more teeth affected by calculus are shown in Table A4.6.

The results indicate that, of the individuals with teeth observable for calculus deposits (scores 1–4, Table

A4.6), over half of the deposits observed were scored as mild (50/95: 52.6%). Of these, 26- to 35-year-olds had the highest number of observed teeth with calculus (38% of the total mild scores). In comparison, severe deposits comprised only 13.6% of the recorded deposits. There appears to be a slight trend for old adults (Age Category 10) to have more severe calculus deposits (Grade 4) than at other ages but the differences are not significant.

The results of calculus deposits present on one or more teeth observable and divided by the sex of the osteological sample are presented in Table A4.7. The data indicate that males had more recorded deposits of calculus than females except for the most severe accumulations (Grade 4), in which the same prevalence of teeth affected per individual recorded were identified (38.5% for males and females). The differences in calculus prevalence between the sexes at Auldhame was not statistically significant ($\chi^2$ (1) = 0.38, p = 0.5376).

*Alveolar disease*

Alveolar disease, also referred to as periodontal disease or gingivitis, is characterised by resorption or loss of alveolar bone from the mandible or maxilla. It is caused by the inflammation of the soft tissues in the jaw, which progresses into the bone. If severe, it can loosen the periodontal ligaments and soft tissues attached to the teeth, leading to ante-mortem tooth loss (Roberts & Manchester 2005, 73–4). Alveolar disease is often related to the adjacent accumulation of bacterial infection or micro-organisms derived from caries or calculus deposits. The condition tends to be age-related and thus increase with old age, but can also be affected by poor oral hygiene practices (Hillson 1986, 305–9). The results of the assessment of alveolar disease from the Auldhame assemblage are shown in Tables A4.8 and A4.9.

The results demonstrate there were more individuals (47/85: 55.2% of individuals with teeth observable) without evidence of alveolar disease than individuals with graded expressions of alveolar resorption (38/85: 44.7%). The difference in numbers of alveolar disease presence or absence is not statistically significant ($\chi^2$ (1) = 0.64, p = 0.4237). Of the data that demonstrate alveolar disease presence, the majority of individuals were recorded as showing only mild changes (28/38: 73.6%). There was no clear age-related increase in the severity of alveolar disease in the sample, as shown in Table A4.8. Adults aged 26–35 years showed the highest prevalence of alveolar resorption (30% of all individuals with evidence of alveolar resorption).

The results demonstrate that slightly more females showed no evidence of alveolar disease than males (Grade 1), although this slight difference is not statistically significant ($\chi^2$ (1) = 0.08, p = 0.7773). At all grades of alveolar disease presence, males are more affected at Auldhame than females (total 19/30 compared to 11/30). This difference between the sexes in alveolar disease expression is not statistically significant ($\chi^2$ (1) = 1.43, p = 0.2318).

*Ante-mortem tooth loss*

Ante-mortem tooth loss is generally the result of periodontal disease or dental caries. In the current study, ante-mortem tooth loss was scored for each tooth position where applicable. Table A4.10 illustrates the frequency of ante-mortem tooth loss per tooth in the adult sample.

Ante-mortem tooth loss was observed at 107 tooth positions, giving a prevalence of 107/1973 (5.4%) for the Auldhame adult assemblage. The results indicate that the prevalence of ante-mortem tooth loss was higher in the mandible than in the maxilla for both right and left sides. The difference in ante-mortem tooth loss, however, is not statistically significant between the maxilla and mandible ($\chi^2$ (1) = 1.96, p = 0.1615). Ante-mortem tooth loss was predominant in the left mandibular first molar (22.2%), followed by the right mandibular first molar (14.7%). Table A4.11 shows the distribution of ante-mortem tooth loss for each tooth position in the maxilla by adult age category.

The results of ante-mortem tooth loss by age in the maxillary dentition show a trend for increased tooth loss with age, with high levels of tooth loss in adults aged 46+ years (Age Category 10). The results of ante-mortem tooth loss by age category in the mandible are shown in Table A4.12.

The mandibular data also demonstrate high levels of ante-mortem tooth loss in old adults (46+ years; Age Category 10). The overall prevalence for each age can be found in Table A4.13.

The overall results confirm that the prevalence of ante-mortem tooth loss is higher in the older age groups. Table A4.14 shows the distribution of maxillary ante-mortem tooth loss per tooth position by sex, and Table A4.15 presents the distribution of mandibular ante-mortem tooth loss by sex. The prevalence of ante-mortem tooth loss differs slightly between the sexes. The males have a prevalence of 5% and the females 6.3%.

*Dental abscess*

A dental abscess, a body of pus surrounded by denser tissue, can form in response to a number of stimuli. For example, dental caries can lead to a dental abscess through exposure of the pulp cavity. Periodontal disease, severe attrition or trauma can also predispose the development of a dental abscess. Table A4.16 presents the frequency of dental abscesses in the adult sample.

The presence or absence of dental abscesses could be scored for 1973 tooth positions. Evidence for abscesses was detected in 25 tooth positions; a total prevalence of 1.3%. The prevalence for the maxillary and mandibular sites was relatively similar; 1.5% and 1.1% respectively. The most common tooth position for abscesses was the right first maxillary molar (9.4%). Table A4.17 shows the prevalence of abscesses for each tooth position in the maxilla for each age category and Table A4.18 shows the data for abscesses in the mandible by age category. Table A4.19 shows the total prevalence for each age category. The results show that the prevalence of dental abscesses is high in the older age groups.

Table A4.20 shows the distribution of dental abscesses in the maxilla per tooth position by sex and Table A4.21 presents the equivalent data for the mandible. The prevalence of dental abscesses was relatively similar in each sex; 1% in the males and 1.4% in the females. In both sexes, dental abscesses were more common in the maxillary than the mandibular teeth.

*Dental caries*

Dental caries is a common dental disease that results from the fermentation of food sugars by bacteria contained on teeth in dental plaque (Roberts & Manchester 2005, 65). Acids produced from such fermentation can demineralise tooth enamel, resulting in either opaque spots or large cavities (Hillson 1986, 287; Larsen 1999, 65). Areas of teeth that are difficult to clean, such as the fissures of the molars and inter-proximal contact areas between adjacent teeth, often lead to the accumulation of plaque, which can predispose to carious destruction.

In the current study, the presence or absence of dental caries and the location of any lesions were recorded for each tooth. Table A4.22 presents the prevalence of caries per tooth observed for the adults from Auldhame. Dental caries was identified in 64 teeth out of 1,629 observed (3.9%). Caries was most frequently identified in the right maxillary third molar (13.9%), followed by the left mandibular third molar (13.3%). Table A4.23 shows the caries initiation site. The highest number of carious lesions was represented by gross destruction of the tooth crown (*n*. 23), which prevents the identification of the initial site of enamel destruction. The results in Table A4.23 also indicate that the inter-proximal contact points at the mesial (*n*. 11) and distal (*n*. 13) aspects of the tooth crowns exhibited high numbers of caries. It is likely that poor oral hygiene practices limited the manner of cleaning food debris from the very back of the mouth and between the teeth, which contributed to the caries rates observed at Auldhame.

The difference in caries frequency between the maxilla (32/746) and the mandible (32/883) is not statistically significant ($\chi^2$ (1) = 0.44, p = 0.5071).

The results in Table A4.24 show that the prevalence of dental caries is generally higher towards the older age groups, with a peak of 7.3% in Age Category 9. The full prevalence data for caries in the maxilla per tooth position are shown in Table A4.25 and for the mandible in Table A4.26.

Table A4.27 shows the distribution of dental caries per tooth position in the maxilla by sex; Table A4.28 shows the same distribution for the mandible. There was a difference in the prevalence of dental caries between the sexes; 2.7% in the males (20/728) and 5.1% in the females (36/703). This difference is statistically significant ($\chi^2$ (1) = 4.95, p = 0.0261).

*Enamel hypoplasia*

Enamel hypoplasia is a condition where the enamel of the tooth has not developed properly. This is usually due to some 'stress' occurring at the time the tooth was developing. This can be due to a deficiency disease or a serious illness such as scarlet fever. Enamel hypoplasia was identified in six individuals from Auldhame; a crude prevalence rate of 4.4% (*n*. 135).

### 5.2.7 Pathology

*Joint disease*

OSTEOARTHRITIS

Osteoarthritis (OA) is a progressive joint disease characterised by the loss of joint cartilage and subsequent degenerative and reactionary changes in the joint surfaces and surrounding bone. The distribution of the arthritic changes to the extra-spinal skeleton of the adults can be found in Table A4.29. Table A4.30 summarises the prevalence of OA by age category. Further details of osteoarthritis prevalence in the hands and feet and data per joint and by age are presented in the Auldhame archive report.

The most common site for OA in the adults was the right acromioclavicular joint of the scapula (31.2%), followed by the right acromioclavicular joint of the clavicle (25.9%), the left acromioclavicular joint of the clavicle (23.9%), the left acromioclavicular joint of the scapula (14.6%), the left PIP joint of the fourth phalanx of the foot (14.3%), the left PIP joint of the fifth phalanx of the foot (12.5%), the left sacroiliac joint (11.5%) and the right sacroiliac joint (10.9%). There was no OA in Age Categories 1–5 (sub-adults) or 12 (un-aged sub-adults). OA was most frequent in Age Category 9 (adults aged 36–45 years); 8.8%. Table A4.31 shows the prevalence of OA for each joint by sex. The prevalence of OA was higher in the females (4.8%) then the males (2.2%). The most common joint affected in males was the left acromioclavicular joint of the scapula (25%), followed by the right acromioclavicular joint of the clavicle (21.7%) and the left acromioclavicular joint of the scapula (19%). The most common joint affected in females was the right acromioclavicular joint of the clavicle (21.7%), followed by the right glenohumeral joint of the humerus (17.2%) and the right femoral head (16.2%). This difference in OA sites may indicate a difference in activity between the sexes.

VERTEBRAL PATHOLOGY

The presence of osteoarthritis (OA), osteophyte, fusion, intervertebral disc disease (IVD), Schmorl's nodes and ligamentum flavum were recorded for each individual for each vertebra. The analysis of the data for OA, Schmorl's nodes and IVD is discussed here. The definition of OA has already been described in the previous section. The frequency of OA in the vertebrae can be found in Table A4.32. The results are shown for each vertebral body (C1–S1). Table A4.33 shows vertebral OA by sex. The most common site for vertebral OA for the adults was T8 (23.8%), followed by C3 (20%) and T7 (19.7%). The frequency of OA tended to increase with age, with vertebral OA first appearing in Age Category 6.

The prevalence of vertebral OA was higher in the females (15.1%) than the males (9.2%) and the pattern of OA varied between the sexes. In the males the most commonly affected site was C3 (21.9%), followed by T5 (17.6%) and T8 (16.2%). In the females the most commonly affected site was T8 (30.3%), followed by T11 (27.3%) and T7 (27.2%).

Table A4.34 shows the prevalence of IVD and Schmorl's nodes in the adults for each vertebra. The analysis of IVD indicates that most commonly affected site was $C_5$ (24%), followed by $C_6$ (19.2%) and $C_3$ (18.6%). Table A4.35 shows IVD for each vertebra by age and Table A4.36 by sex. As is to be expected, the frequency of IVD tended to increase with age, with IVD first appearing in Age Category 6. The frequency of IVD varied slightly between the sexes, with a prevalence of 7.6% in the males and 6% in the females. In the males the most commonly affected site was $C_5$ (29.4%), followed by $C_3$ (24.2%) and $C_4$ (21.6%). In the females the most commonly affected site was $C_7$ (20.6%), followed by $C_6$ (18.2%) and $C_5$ (15.6%). The prevalence of Schmorl's nodes indicates the most commonly affected site was T8 (58.5%), followed by T11 (52.3%) and T9 (51.8%). Table A4.37 shows the frequency of Schmorl's nodes for each vertebra by age and Table A4.38 by sex. The frequency of Schmorl's nodes tended to increase with age, with Schmorl's nodes first appearing in Age Category 6. The frequency of Schmorl's nodes was 25.7% in the males and 17.9% in the females. For the males the most commonly affected site was T8 (66.7%) followed by T11 (64.3%) and T7 (60.5%). For the females the most commonly affected site was T7 (54.5%) followed by T8 (48.4%) and T9 (43.8%).

OTHER JOINT DISEASE

A number of other joint diseases were observed in the assemblage. SK264, a male aged 46+ years at death, had evidence of Scheuermann's Disease in the fourth and fifth lumbar vertebrae. This condition is characterised by osteochondritic erosion of the anterior-superior aspect of the vertebral body (Aufderheide & Rodríguez-Martin 1998) and is relatively common. Most people with Scheuermann's Disease will have an increased rounded back caused by forward curvature (kyphosis) of the spine but it is not associated with pain.

SK361 had evidence of bilateral sacroiliitis; a condition where the sacroiliac joint is inflamed and painful. A wide range of factors may cause sacroiliitis, including trauma, infection or specific joint conditions such as spondyloarthropathies. The affected individual

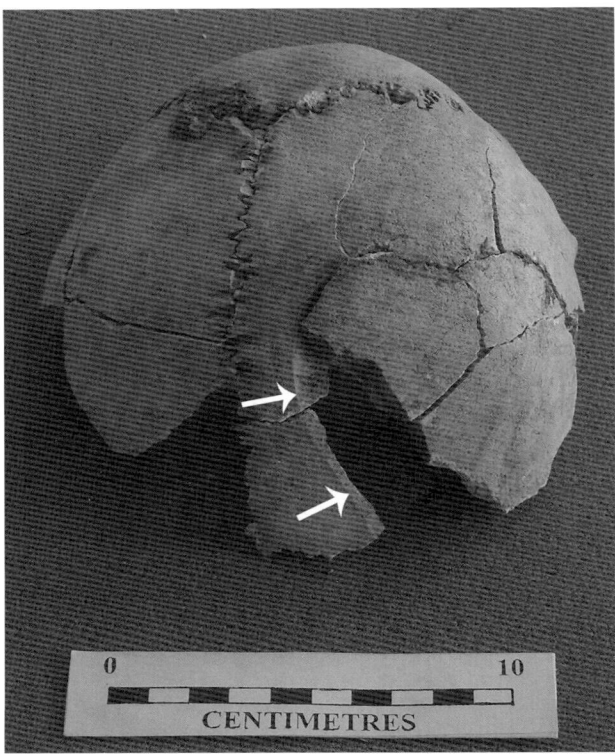

*Figure 78*
Evidence of sharp blade cuts that passed straight through the left parietal of the skull (arrowed) with residual radiating fractures. There is no evidence of new bone formation on the bone margins indicating the injury was fatal. (SK216, a 46+ years male)

*Evidence of trauma*

## INTERPERSONAL VIOLENCE

Traumatic conditions can be defined as any bodily wound or injury, including fractures, abnormal placement or dislocation of a bone and the disruption in a nerve and/or blood supply (Roberts & Manchester 2005). Two skeletons in the Auldhame assemblage displayed evidence of sharp force weapon trauma. SK216, a male aged 46+ years at death, had a linear, clean cut to the left parietal measuring at least 800mm (Figure 78). The weapon had passed through the bone and the lack of new bone growth indicates this injury would have been fatal. SK868, a male aged 18–25 years at death, had three linear cuts to the skull that had passed clean through the bone. These were located at the left zygomatic arch, on the parietals and frontal bone near bregma (measuring 65mm anterior-posterior) and at the occipital (Figure 79). Again there was no healing

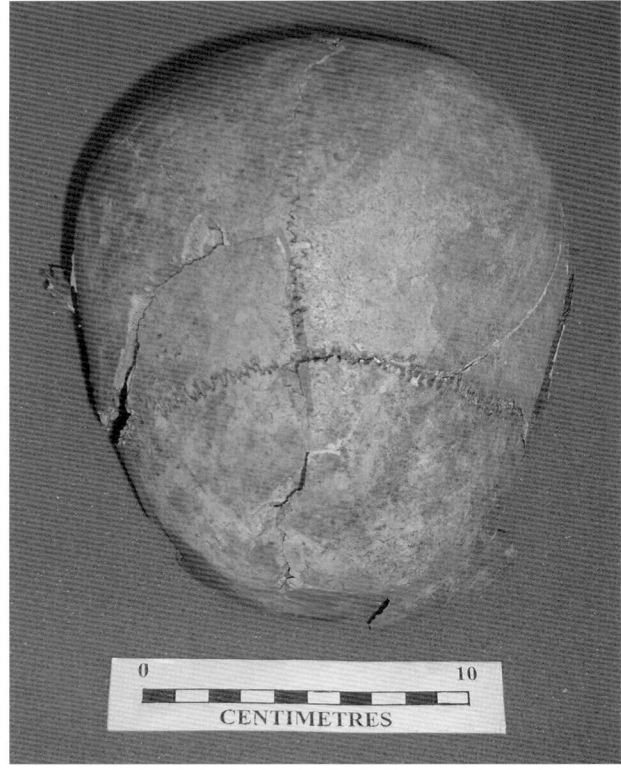

*Figure 79*
Evidence of sharp force trauma to the frontal, parietals and occipital bones, and which also involved the left zygomatic arch. The injuries are from a sharp blade, which cut through the bone. There is no evidence of bone healing, indicating the injuries were fatal. (SK868, a 18–25 years male)

from Auldhame was aged 18–25 years at death and of indeterminate sex with no other evidence of joint disease or gross pathology. SK816 had protrusio acetabuli of the left hip with osteoarthritis. Protrusio acetabuli is an uncommon developmental condition where the socket of the hip joint is too deep and bulges into the cavity of the pelvis. Secondary OA can often develop as a result of the condition as in this example from Auldhame. It is usually asymptomatic, except for a slight limitation of movement of the joint. SK733, a probable female aged 36–45 years at death, had bilateral pseudoarthroses between the calcaneus, talus and cuboid. This is a developmental condition where an additional joint has formed. OA was present on many of the metatarsals and phalanges and this may have been secondary to the pseudoarthrosis. Each of these conditions was seen in only one adult individual; a crude prevalence rate for each condition of 0.4% when calculated as a percentage of the assemblage as a whole (*n.* 242) or 0.6% as a percentage of the adult sample (*n.* 161).

of the bone, indicating that these wounds were fatal. The location of the injuries suggests the person who inflicted the injuries was right-handed. These two instances were both found in adults; a crude prevalence rate of 0.8% for the total assemblage (*n.*242) and 1.2% for the adults (*n.*161).

ACCIDENTAL TRAUMA

There were a number of fractures observed within the assemblage, seen in both males and females. SK629, a probable female aged 26–35 years at death, displayed evidence of a fracture to the right mandibular head. There was slight mal-union of the bone and both temperomandibular joints displayed OA, which was probably secondary to the trauma. There were two instances of fractured clavicles: SK234, a male aged 36–45 years at death; and SK545, an individual of undetermined sex aged 36–45 years at death. Both instances were mid-shaft fractures and the area surrounding the fractures sites was bulbous with shortening of the bone. This is the most common fracture site of the clavicle and is generally caused by a fall on the shoulder or the outstretched hand (Crawford 1987). Four individuals had evidence of fractured ribs (SK155, SK336, SK401 and SK871). Fractures of the ribs are relatively common and are caused by direct injury or a fall against a hard object (Crawford 1987).

SK520, a probable male aged 46+ years at death, had a mid-shaft fracture of the humerus and two fractured ribs. The humerus was well aligned, with a small amount of additional bone surrounding the fracture site (Figure 80). SK293, a probable male aged 46+ years at death, had a fractured left radius. The fracture was mid-shaft and the fracture site was enlarged; the bone displayed some shortening. The cause of this type of injury may be either an indirect force such as a fall on the hand or a direct blow to the forearm (Crawford 1987). This individual also had a fractured rib and osteoporotic collapse in the vertebra (see below). Osteoporosis is a condition where the bones become thinned and weaken and are consequently more susceptible to fractures. Broken wrists, hips and spinal bones are the most common fractures in people with osteoporosis.

SK886, a female aged 36–45 years at death, had a fracture to the shaft of the left ulna. The bone was slightly angulated with a small raised spur of smooth bone present on the fracture site. This individual also had bony ankylosis of an unidentified proximal and

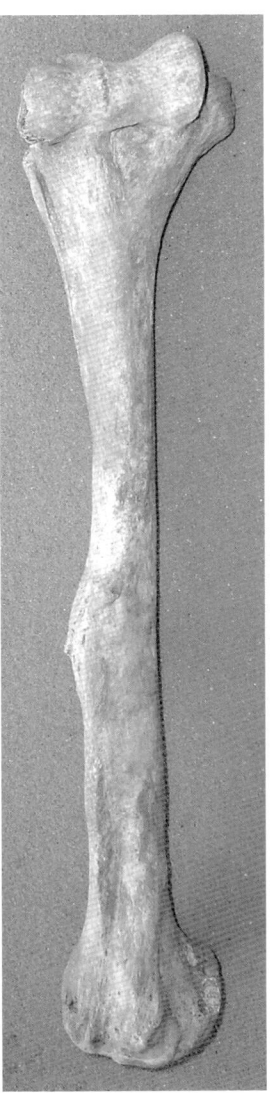

*Figure 80*
A left adult humerus with a well-healed fracture at the mid-shaft visible with ossified fracture callus on the lateral aspect towards the top of the image

intermediate phalanx. The bones were fused in a flexed position and are likely to be due to an infection of the joint or trauma-related. Another fracture of the ulna was seen in SK843, a probable female aged 36–45 years at death. The fracture was at the distal portion of the shaft of the right ulna. The bone was well aligned and the fracture site was slightly enlarged. As with fractures to the radius shaft, the cause of this type of injury may be either an indirect force, such as a fall on the hand, or a direct blow to the forearm (Crawford 1987).

SK299, an individual of 36–45 years at death, had an oblique fracture of the shaft of the left fourth proximal phalanx. This individual also had heterotrophic ossification (HO) on the dorsal aspect of the shaft of the left third proximal phalanx. HO is trauma related and may be due to the same injury that caused the fracture on the same hand.

A transverse fracture of the right patella was present in SK467, a probable male aged 36–45 years at death. The fracture was largely healed and only visible on the anterior surface. Fractures of the patella are generally caused by two types of injury, a sudden violent contraction of the quadriceps muscle or a fall or blow directly to the kneecap (Crawford 1987). A fracture of the right patella was also seen on SK708, a male aged 26–35 years at death. The fracture was transverse, approximately midway across the bone, with osteophyte and new bone present at the fracture site. The fracture was a clean break with non-union of the two fragments. This individual also had a fractured fourth right metatarsal. The fracture was at the distal portion of the shaft with slight malunion and angulation. Most metatarsal fractures are caused by direct violence from a heavy object; other causes are a twisting injury or repeated stress (Crawford 1987).

SK333, an individual of undetermined sex aged 18–25 years at death, had a fractured right fibula at the distal portion of the shaft. The type of fracture could not be identified, as the bone was well healed with an area of *c* 43mm of new bone. A fracture of the right fibula was also present in SK426, an individual of undetermined sex aged 36–45 years at death. The fracture site was at the distal portion of the shaft and, again, due to remodelling and new bone, the fracture type was not identifiable.

A total of 16 adult individuals displayed evidence of fractures, a crude prevalence rate of 6.6% of the total assemblage (*n*. 242) and 9.9% of the adults (*n*. 161).

SK452, a female aged 36–45 years at death, had an ankylosed third left digit (all three phalanges) due to subluxation. Subluxation of a joint occurs when its articular surfaces are partially displaced but retain some contact with each other (Crawford 1987). It is likely this injury was caused by hyperextension.

A traumatic lesion of the right first metacarpal was present in SK438, an adult probable male. A small, smooth, raised area of bone was present on the posterior surface of the shaft, measuring *c* 10mm proximal-distal. The cause of this lesion is unknown but may be the result of an overlying infection.

Myositis ossificans traumatica was present in three individuals; a crude prevalence rate of 1.2% (*n*. 242). This lesion is usually produced by avulsions of tendinous and/or muscle attachments to bone generating a hematoma; this hematoma may become calcified or ossified (Aufderheide & Rodríguez-Martin 1998). SK621, a sub-adult, had this lesion on the distal portion of the shaft of the left humerus, measuring 9mm. SK883, a male aged 26–35 at death, had bilateral myositis ossificans of the tibia on the medial surface of

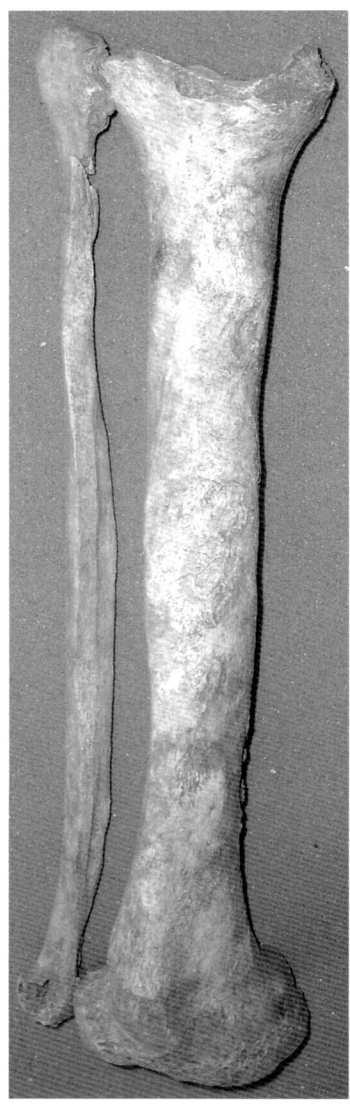

*Figure 81*
An adult left tibia and fibula with evidence of swelling and bone formation over the entire shaft of the tibia. The changes are indicative of a non-specific infection

# OSTEOARCHAEOLOGICAL STUDIES

the shaft at the same level as the tibial tubercle. SK210, a male aged 46+ years at death, had two small spurs of bone on the medial surface of the distal portion of the right tibia. This individual also had periosteal bone on the right fibula. Other traumatic lesions include heterotopic ossification in a rib fragment of a male aged 26–35 at death (SK198).

*Infectious disease*

Bone infections can be caused by a specific or known condition such as leprosy or tuberculosis, or a treponemal condition such as venereal syphilis. Alternatively, infectious evidence in the skeleton can derive from a range of non-specific causes and are instead characterised by the type of lesion they represent. These include periostitis, where new bone formation is laid down on the external bone surface, which in life is adjacent to the periosteal membrane; and osteitis, in which more extensive internal and external involvement of a bone occurs. There were no examples of the specific infections of tuberculosis, leprosy or any treponemal disease in the skeletons from Auldhame.

There were two cases of the non-specific infection, osteomyelitis, in the assemblage. Osteomyelitis is an inflammation of the bone and bone marrow caused by pus-producing bacteria. The affected bones show simultaneous destruction and reparative formation and often demonstrate a draining sinus (cloaca), which extends from the internal bone structure to the external bone surface (Roberts & Manchester 2005, 168). SK164, a probable male aged 46+ years at death, had evidence of osteomyelitis in the left tibia with an 8mm diameter cloaca. SK589, a probable male aged 17–25 years at death, had evidence of osteomyelitis in the left femur and the right and left tibiae and fibulae (Figure 81). These two examples give a crude prevalence rate of 0.8% of the whole assemblage (*n*. 242) and 1.2% of the adults (*n*. 161).

There were four instances of periostitis – a crude prevalence rate of 1.7% of the total assemblage (*n*. 242) and 2.5% of the adults (*n*. 161). Periostitis is non-specific inflammation of the bone and is relatively common in skeletal assemblages. The inflammatory process invokes a reaction in the periosteal membrane that covers most of the external bone surfaces, which causes the formation of new bone on the bone surface. The bone formation can either be remodelled into long, narrow, vertical striations, or comprise plaque-like raised layers of smooth or porous new bone (Roberts & Manchester 2005, 172). This condition can be caused either by a localised trauma and inflammatory reaction or by a non-specific infectious process, although often it is not possible to be specific about the particular etiology. Periostitis was seen in the distal portion of the left fibula of SK629, a probable female aged 26–35 years. SK611, a female aged 26–35, and SK724, a male aged 26–35 years, had periosteal reactions on all the leg bones. SK210 has already been discussed above.

*Neoplastic disease*

A neoplasm is an abnormal growth of localised tissue. There were two examples of neoplastic disease in the assemblage from Auldhame. SK155, a probable female aged 26–35 years, had a large cystic swelling in the right ilium measuring *c* 49mm in diameter (Figure 82). The lesion was smooth-sided with no destruction present. The most likely diagnosis is that

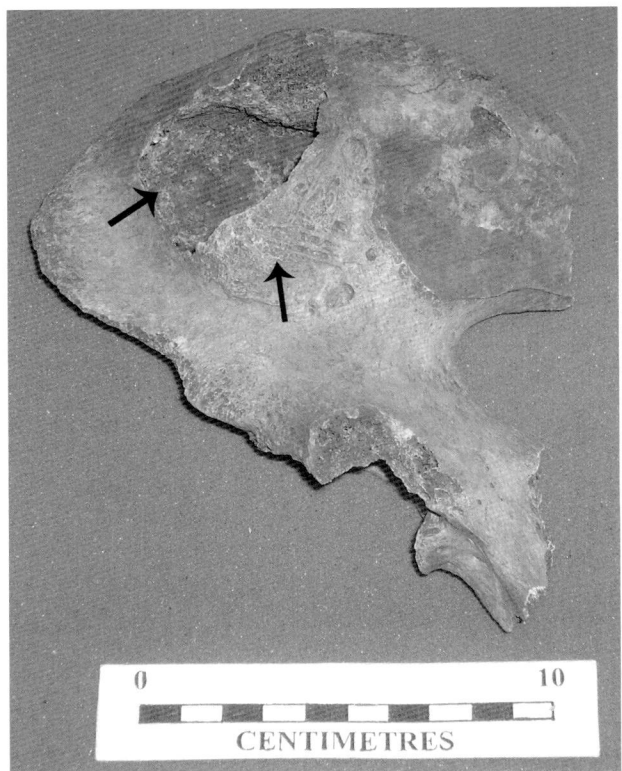

*Figure 82*
A right adult pelvis with post-mortem damage having separated the anterior pubis. Remnants of a large, rounded bone covered swelling or cyst are evident on the medial or internal aspect of the ilium as indicated by black arrows. There is some post-mortem damage to the bone covering the cyst. The internal surface is smooth with no bone formation and is likely to have been fluid-filled

this represents a slow-growing bone cyst. A bone cyst is a benign fluid-filled cavity in the bone. SK672, a probable female aged 36–45 years at death, had two lesions on the first thoracic vertebra measuring 4mm and 9mm in diameter. A similar lesion was also seen on the vertebral end of the right first rib. It is thought these lesions are attributed to a soft tissue lesion of some kind – a swelling or tumour. Each of these conditions was seen in only one adult individual; a crude prevalence rate for each condition of 0.4% when calculated as a percentage of the assemblage as a whole ($n.$ 242) or 0.6% as a percentage of the adult sample ($n.$ 161).

*Circulatory disorders*

The only circulatory disorder identified in this assemblage was osteochondritis dissecans and this was seen in five individuals; a crude prevalence rate of 2.0% ($n.$ 242). Osteochondritis dissecans is a condition characterised by small epiphyseal areas of bone necrosis (Aufderheide & Rodríguez-Martín 1998). SK011, a female aged 36–45 years at death, had bilateral osteochondritis dissecans of the lateral condyle of the femora. SK144, a probable female aged 15–16 years at death, had osteochondritis dissecans on the distal articular surface of the left humerus. SK370, a male aged 18–25 years at death, had bilateral osteochondritis dissecans on the proximal articular facet of the radii. SK492, a probable female aged 46+ years at death had osteochondritis dissecans on the patellar surface of the right femur. SK520, a probable male aged 46+ years at death, had bilateral osteochondritis dissecans of the lateral condyle of the tibiae. The aetiology of the disease is unknown but may be related to a traumatic episode that affects the blood supply to the bone or joint surface (Aufderheide & Rodríguez-Martin 1998). The most frequent sites for the condition are the femoral condyle and the elbow.

*Congenital anomalies*

Congenital skeletal anomalies are determined during the intrauterine phase of development; they may be observed at birth or develop years later. These anomalies can be minor or more serious, with both medical and cosmetic implications. Two individuals (CPR 0.8%, $n.$ 242) had Klippel-Feil syndrome, a rare condition where two or more cervical vertebral segments are fused. The condition is congenital and shortening of the neck is uniformly present, often with restricted mobility. The two individuals from Auldhame that had the condition were SK318, an individual of indeterminate sex aged 26–35 years at death, and SK608, a juvenile aged 6–11 years at death.

Two other congenital anomalies were identified, which are likely to have gone unnoticed by the individual. SK140, a male aged 26–35 at death, had partial fusion of the laminae of the sacrum. SK312, a male aged 26–35 years at death, had a malformed left facet joint of the fifth lumbar (L5) and first sacral vertebra (S1). The articular facet of S1 is absent and L5 articulates with S2.

Spina bifida occulta was seen in 24 individuals, a crude prevalence rate of 10% ($n.$ 242). This is a relatively common condition involving the incomplete fusion of the posterior neural arch, and can involve one or more sacral segments. The defect is often asymptomatic. Spondylolysis was present in three individuals, a crude prevalence rate of 1.2% ($n.$ 242). Spondylolysis is the ossification failure of the *pars interarticularis* of the vertebra, resulting in the separation of the posterior part of the vertebra. The aetiology is believed to be a combination of congenital and traumatic factors. The condition is relatively common, occurring in 4–8% of the general population (Aufderheide & Rodríguez-Martín 1998). In most instances the defect does not cause symptoms.

*Metabolic diseases*

The metabolic bone diseases encompass a variety of pathological conditions, ranging from nutritional deficiencies to diseases mediated by environmental conditions or demographic composition of the affected population sample (Brickley & Ives 2008). In the Auldhame sample, three adults presented evidence of age-related osteoporosis, providing a crude prevalence rate of 1.9% of the total assemblage ($n.$ 242) and 1.2% of the adults ($n.$ 161).

Osteoporosis was considered manifest in these individuals through the presence of vertebral compression and wedge fractures. In SK293, a probable male aged 46+ years at death (who is described above as having a fractured left radius), the eighth and ninth thoracic vertebrae were wedge-shaped and fused. The centrum of the fifth lumbar vertebra was also collapsed. These are thought to be osteoporotic compression fractures. This individual had also sustained a fracture to the left radius. This fracture occurred at the mid-shaft level of the radius and was well healed, and may have occurred prior to the skeletal osteoporosis. Osteoporotic fractures were also seen in the eleventh thoracic and first lumbar vertebrae of SK492, a probable female aged 46+ years at death. An early osteoporotic fracture was seen in the first lumbar vertebra of SK558, a probable male aged 46+ years at death.

These osteoporotic fractures would have produced a bending of the spine (kyphosis). Osteoporosis is a condition where the bone mineral density is reduced. The aetiology of osteoporosis is multifactorial; it may be affected by diet, lifestyle, age, ethnicity, genetic factors and other diseases. The condition is more common in women than men and more frequent in older individuals.

SK611, a female aged 26–35 years at death, displayed evidence of having suffered from vitamin D deficiency (rickets) as a child. Vitamin D can be obtained by exposure of the skin to sunlight or by eating eggs or oily fish such as salmon. A deficiency of vitamin D causes poor bone mineralisation, leading to skeletal weakening and softening. This disease can be manifest as bending bones in affected children due to weight-bearing on weakened bone tissue. The case of vitamin D deficiency from Auldhame indicates the female did not get enough sunlight exposure or dietary vitamin D during her childhood.

In some instances, disturbances of calcium intake may also increase the risk of a vitamin D deficiency. When children with rickets put weight on the bones, particularly long bones, through crawling or walking, the bones can bend and deform under the pressure and lead to a range of characteristic features throughout the skeleton (Ortner & Mays 1998; Mays et al 2006; Brickley & Ives 2008). Where deformities are severe, the skeleton may not be able to remodel the evidence of rickets, which may remain visible in the adult skeleton. In the case from Auldhame, the femora demonstrated anterior bending of the shaft. This case presented the only evidence for vitamin D deficiency from Auldhame as no sub-adults present evidence for healed or active cases. This result produces an individual prevalence of 0.4% (1/242 individuals).

Two skeletons, SK309 and SK1003, showed cribra orbitalia, both occurring in the left orbits of the affected individuals. The individuals affected were an infant aged 7–11 months, SK1003, and a juvenile aged 15–16 years, SK309 (CPR 0.8% n. 242). Cribra orbitalia is characterised by small holes or pitting in one or both orbits.

*Miscellaneous conditions*

Several miscellaneous conditions were observed in the Auldhame assemblage. Four individuals had evidence of rotator cuff disease; a crude prevalence rate of 1.7% of the total assemblage (n. 242) and 2.5% of the adults (n. 161). The rotator cuff is the group of four tendons that stabilise the shoulder joint. Rotator cuff disease occurs when the rotator cuff is damaged, for example from an injury or repetitive overhead motions. This condition is one of the most common causes of shoulder pain. People with rotator cuff disease usually find it difficult to lift the arm away from the body fully. SK170, a probable female aged 36–45, SK492, a probable female aged 46+ years, SK498, a male aged 26–35 years and SK859, a female aged 26–35 years, all had bilateral rotator cuff disease.

Paget's disease was seen in SK563, a male aged 36–45 years (CPR 0.4%, n. 242). The disease was monostatic, affecting only the skull. The right temporal, parietal and occipital was thickened, to 14mm at its maximum depth. Paget's disease is a condition of 'unknown aetiology characterised by a profound increase in both bone resorption and new bone formation' (Aufderheide & Rodríguez-Martín 1998, 413). Clinically, it is more common in older individuals and is found in 2–3% of adults over the age of 40 years (ibid).

Hyperostosis frontalis interna was found in SK548, a 26- to 35-year-old of undetermined sex (CPR 0.4%, n. 242). This individual had raised thickened areas of bone on the internal surface of the right frontal bone. The aetiology of the condition is unknown. It is found almost exclusively in women, with a prevalence of c 5% (ibid).

SK822, a male aged 26–35 years at death, displayed an unusual wear pattern on the canines, which is thought to be activity-related.

## 5.3 ISOTOPE ANALYSIS

Jane Evans

### 5.3.1 Introduction

*Background to principles of oxygen and strontium stable isotope analysis*

In this study, oxygen and strontium isotope analyses were conducted on samples of tooth enamel. Oxygen and strontium isotopes are fixed in enamel biogenic phosphate at the time of tooth formation. Biogenic phosphate is extremely robust. The isotopic signature of enamel does not change during life and is not altered in the burial environment. Oxygen isotopes are derived primarily from ingested fluids, and they reflect the isotopic value of available meteoric/ground/drinking water. Strontium isotopes are derived from both solid and liquid food and relate to the soil-derived bio-available strontium, which, in the absence of any surficial deposits such as peat, loess or tills, is related to the geology of the area where the food was produced. As strontium and oxygen isotopes behave independently of one another, they provide two parameters for investigating an individual's place of origin and migration patterns.

*The local bedrock geology*

Auldhame is underlain by rocks of the Carboniferous Limestone series and close by is an area of Carboniferous andesite and basalt volcanic rock. The underlying rocks release strontium into the biosphere with values in the range 0.7082–0.7085 as recorded by the leachate of soil sample provided from the burial site, and from the dentine, which will equilibrate with pore fluids after burial.

*Principles of carbon and nitrogen isotope dietary studies*

The reconstruction of past human diets from stable isotope analysis is based on the principle that the relative abundance of the two main carbon isotopes, carbon-12 and carbon-13, is indicative of plant types ($C_4$ vs $C_3$ plant types) and different ecosystems such as terrestrial and marine. Nitrogen isotope ratios increase by approximately 3‰ for each step up the food chain (as a key component of amino acids and hence protein). It is therefore possible to use bi-variate discrimination diagrams of carbon and nitrogen isotopes to constrain and identify dietary inputs and regimes. Samples of bone collagen were extracted from a sample of skeletons from Auldhame for dietary reconstruction.

Fifty bone and 20 tooth enamel samples were submitted for chemical analysis. The methodology

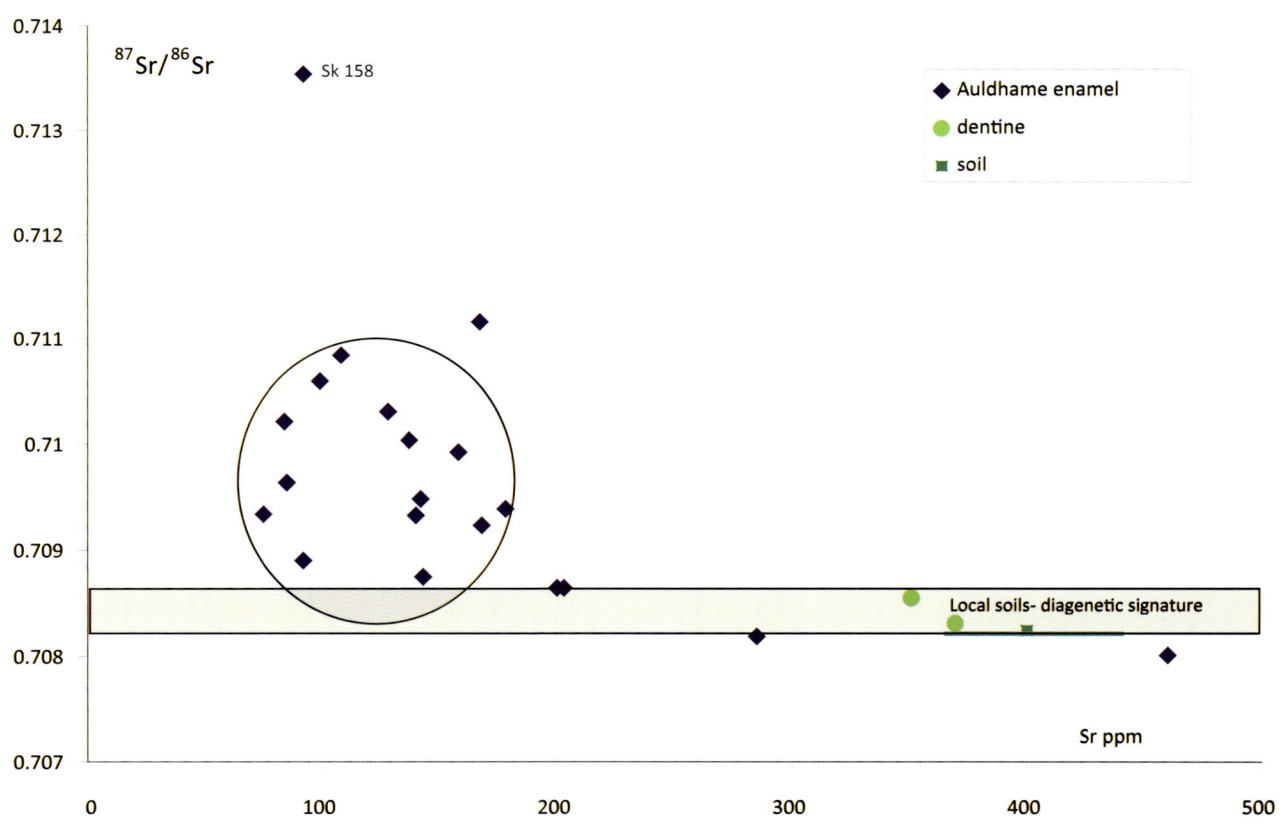

*Figure 83*

$^{87}Sr/^{86}Sr$ plotted against strontium concentration for samples from Auldhame. The predicted isotope composition for digenetic fluids is highlighted, and is based on the values derived from a soil leach and dentine values (see Appendix 5)

# OSTEOARCHAEOLOGICAL STUDIES

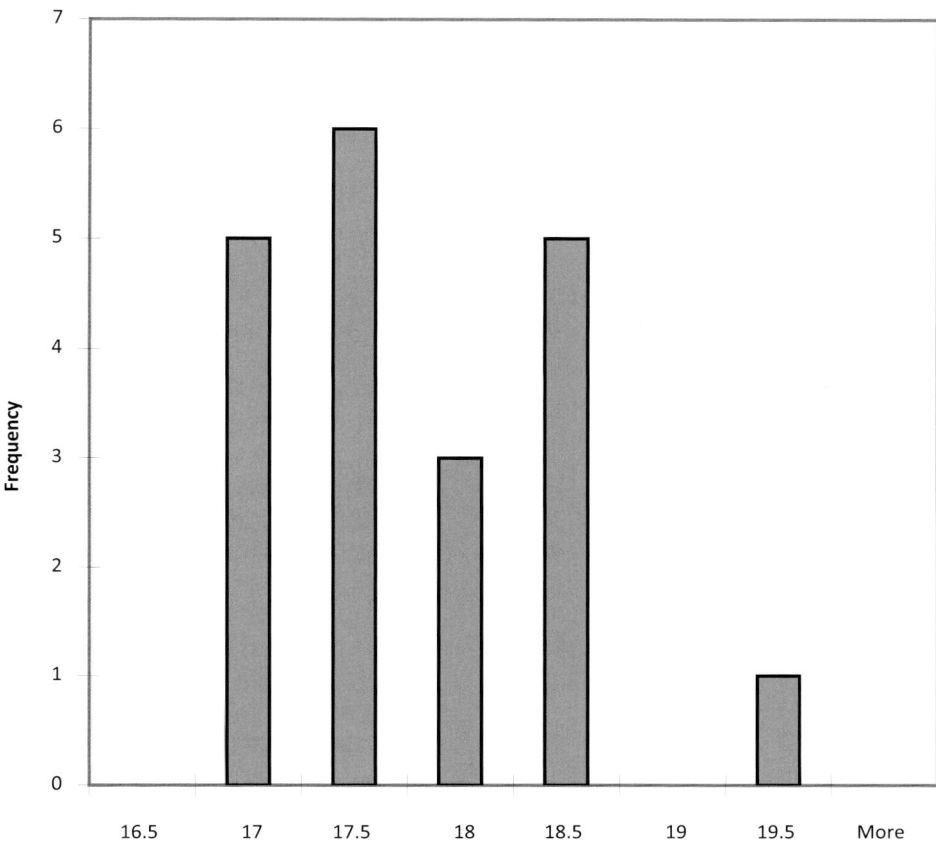

*Figure 84*
Histogram of $\delta^{18}O_{SMOW}$ values for enamel samples from Auldhame

used in the isotope analyses and results are presented in Appendix 5.

### 5.3.2 Results

*Strontium isotope results*

The data from the strontium analysis are presented in Figure 83 and Table A5.1. The majority of the tooth enamel samples plot between Sr concentrations of 75–160 ppm with an isotope range of 0.70875–0.71084 (Figure 83). There are two outliers from these data: a high point, sample SK158, which has an $^{87}Sr/^{86}Sr$ ratio of 0.71354; and SK868, which has a slightly elevated $^{87}Sr/^{86}Sr$ ratio of 0.71116.

The main field of data suggests a predominantly static population, with outlier SK158 appearing more clearly 'exotic', having spent their childhood in a more radiogenic setting (Lamb et al 2012). The value of 0.71354 is typically derived from Palaeozoic or older rocks, or granites (Evans et al 2010). The closest source of such rocks would be possibly the Palaeozoic sequences of the Southern Uplands, or the areas of Perthshire and Aberdeenshire to the north.

*Oxygen isotope results*

The oxygen isotope data from the Auldhame individuals describe a roughly normal data distribution (Figure 84) with $\delta^{18}O = 17.4 \pm 1.4$‰ ($2\sigma$, n = 16) for all the data, and 17.3 ± 1.2‰ ($2\sigma$, n = 15) if outlying sample SK327 is excluded. The value of 17.3‰ converts to a drinking water range for this population

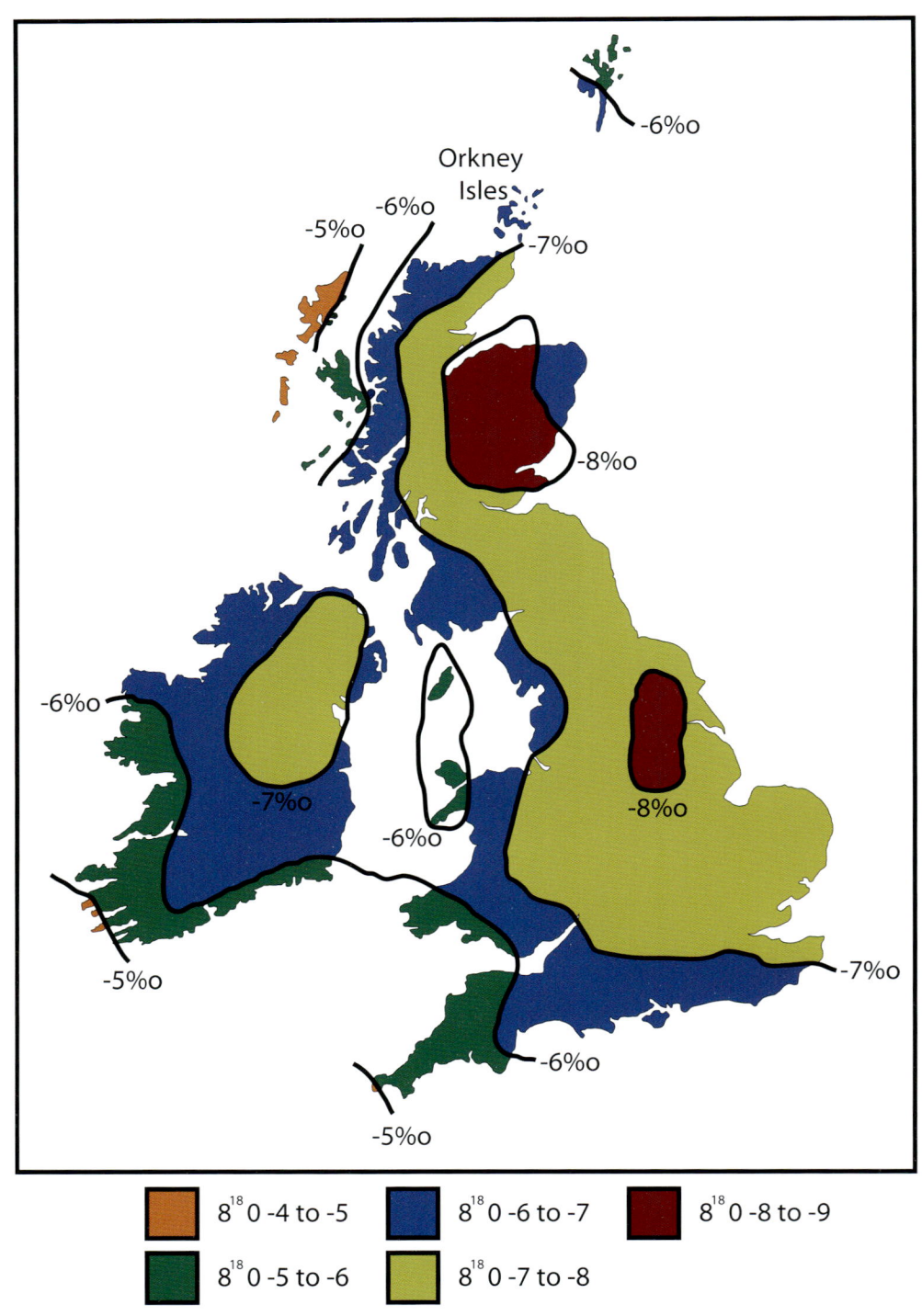

*Figure 85*
Average drinking water values for the UK (compiled by Carolyn Chenery)

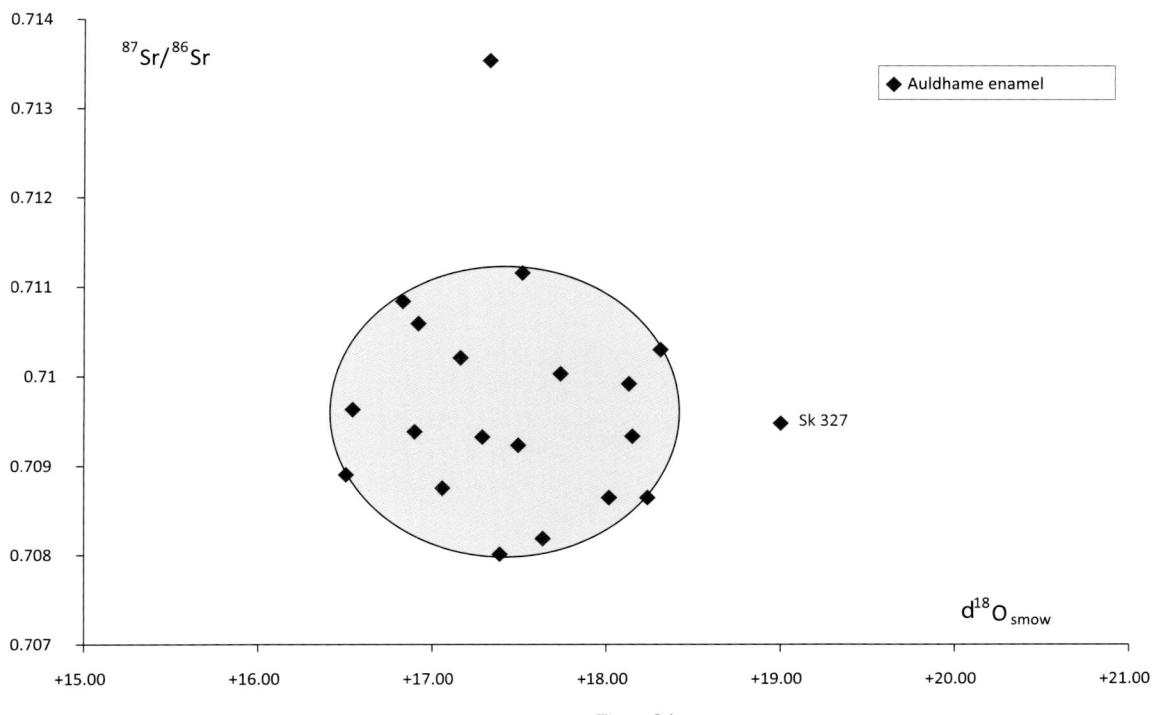

*Figure 86*
The field of Auldhame data in $^{87}Sr/^{86}Sr$ vs $d^{18}O_{SMOW}$ highlighting the two main outlying samples SK158 and SK327

of −7.1 ± 1.85‰ (2SD), which is consistent with drinking water values for the Lothian area of Scotland (Figure 85). When plotted against strontium isotope ratios, the majority of the data forms a coherent group with two outliers caused by the high strontium isotope ratio of SK158 and the high $\delta^{18}O_{SMOW}$ of SK327 (Figure 86). Individual SK868, with an elevated strontium level, was confirmed by the oxygen isotope analysis to be local to Lothian. Two individuals (SK318 and SK352) appeared to have drinking water equivalents potentially indicative of central European or Scandinavian values although the strontium results for both individuals were within local ranges.

The unusually high $\delta^{18}O$ value of +19.0‰ in SK327, which would convert to a drinking water value of −4.5‰, is outside the range of average British drinking water values and is more typical of warmer, Mediterranean environments. Drinking water values are based on the assumption that the main source of water into the body is from an unaltered rainwater source, either directly or from aquifers. If, for some reason, such a source is not the main water intake (for instance, in the case of breastfeeding babies) then the value can be modified. We therefore have the following possibilities in interpreting the results for SK327:

(i) SK327 comes from a warmer climate where the Sr isotope systematics are indistinguishable from those in Lothian

(ii) SK327 is a random statistical outlier in the population

(iii) the water intake of SK327 was modified in some way such that it did not conform to the model of unmodified UK water source.

The strontium and oxygen data of the remainder of the sample support the theory that all these individuals, with the exception of SK158 and possibly SK327, are from the Lothian area of Scotland. There were no changes in the mean stable isotope results throughout the period of cemetery use, as established by radiocarbon dating. The lack of change in strontium and oxygen isotopes at the site over time, in particular, further confirms there were no apparent large-scale changes to the structure of the local population during the time of graveyard use.

## LIVING AND DYING AT AULDHAME, EAST LOTHIAN

*Carbon and nitrogen isotope results*

The carbon and nitrogen results are presented in Figure 87 and Table A5.1 and A5.2 (see Appendix 5), and are compared below with data from medieval populations from three Northern England sites (Müldner & Richards 2005); medieval burials from Wharram Percy (Richards et al 2002) and Fishergate Priory, York (Müldner & Richards 2007a, 2007b); and a multi-age site from Newark Bay, Orkney (Richards et al 2006). An Iron Age assemblage from East Yorkshire is also shown (Jay & Richards 2007). Data fields for cattle and freshwater and marine fish collagen (Müldner & Richards 2005) are also included. The collagen atomic C/N ratios fall into the expected range for well-preserved bone (DeNiro 1985), apart from two individuals (SK104 and SK426), which fall just outside of this range. Individual SK327, who had an undepleted oxygen isotope of +19.0‰, also had a high carbon isotope composition of −17.9. This supports the interpretation that this individual had a more unusual and more $C_4$-enriched diet than the majority of the population. As a result, individual SK327 may have been non-British.

The paleodietary results from the Auldhame sample fall into the range identified previously from medieval Orkney, in which fish was identified as having contributed to the diet in additional to cereals and animal protein (Richards et al 2006). The Auldhame data also define overlapping fields with the other medieval sites from Northern England. While these results suggest some consumption of fish protein following the model proposed by Müldner and Richards (2005), the largely terrestrial carbon isotope results indicate that other factors made a contribution to diet rather than significant consumption of marine fish.

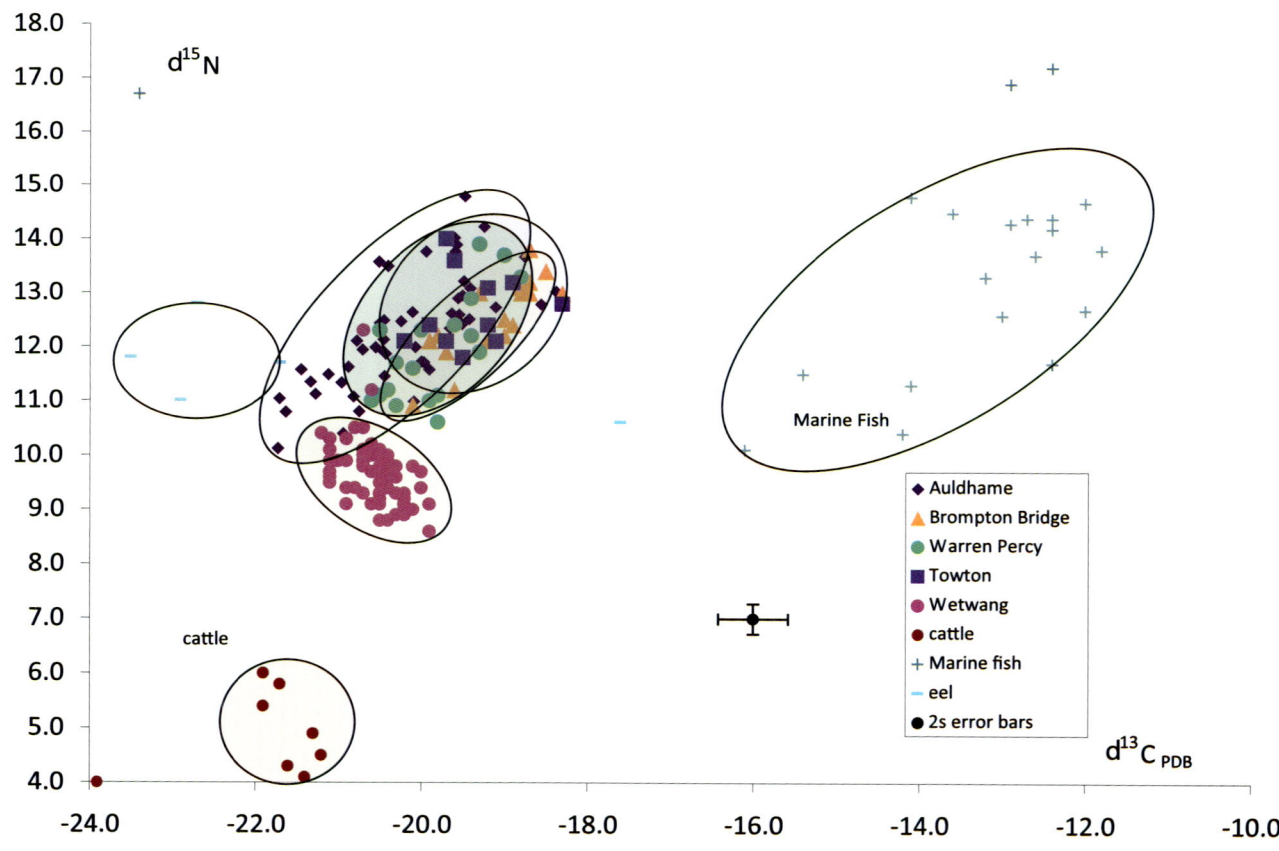

*Figure 87*

$\delta^{13}C_{PDB}$ vs $\delta^{15}N_{AIR}$ of the Auldhame samples compared with data from northern English Medieval population, a multi-age Orkney assemblage, Iron Age human populations and various faunal data (data from Müldner and Richards 2005, 2007; Richards et al 2002; Richards et al 2006; Jay and Richards 2007).

## 5.4 DISCUSSION OF THE HUMAN REMAINS FROM AULDHAME

MELISSA MELIKIAN

### 5.4.1 The assemblage

The size of the skeletal assemblage from Auldhame facilitates a range of interpretations of funerary evidence bearing upon the life and funerary practices of a medieval population, which spanned one thousand years of graveyard use between the 7th and 17th centuries AD. The sample size permits interpretations of the demographic profile of the population as well as a survey of the health challenges faced by the population. The results are integrated and discussed below, together with the results of the chemical analyses undertaken to investigate the origins of the population sample from the graveyard and to provide insights into the dietary composition from the period.

The paleopathological inferences derived from this study are well supported by a programme of radiocarbon dating, which clarifies the periods of use and burial phasing from this graveyard (Chapter 3). A recent survey of health derived from skeletal analyses from medieval sites highlighted the predominance of English parallels; out of 72 early medieval sites referred to by Roberts & Cox (2003), only four (5.5% of their sample) were Scottish sites. The publication of osteological investigations from sites such as Castle Park, Dunbar (Perry 2000), Isle of May (James & Yeoman 2008), Thornybank graveyard (Rees 2002), Orkney (Stevens et al 2005), Inchmarnock (Lowe 2008) and Parliament House (Roy et al forthcoming) also serve to expand the interpretations of life and health in Scotland during the medieval period. The findings from the investigation of the human remains from Auldhame therefore significantly add to these perceptions.

### 5.4.2 Population origins and demographic composition

The isotopic analysis of the samples from Auldhame demonstrated that the group were largely a local population, with the strontium and oxygen isotope results indicating a group local to the Lothian region. The strontium results did identify two individuals from Auldhame as possible outliers to this model, indicating an origin elsewhere than Lothian. Of these, one individual, SK158, derived from a region with Palaeozoic or older rocks or granites, which is likely to indicate areas of the Southern Uplands or areas of Perthshire and Aberdeenshire, a finding also confirmed by the stable oxygen isotope analysis. The second individual, SK868, however, was confirmed by oxygen isotope analysis to have been local to Lothian in contrast to the strontium results. SK327 was identified by oxygen analysis as possibly non-British, having come from a warmer, Mediterranean environment. It is not yet clear how extraneous factors may potentially influence the oxygen isotope composition of bone or tooth samples, such as the environmental regulation over water supplies, cultural behaviours in the manner of storing or using water (eg heating) or physiological states such as pregnancy (White et al 2004). Such factors are at present only beginning to be investigated further (Evans pers comm).

The oxygen isotope results also indicated that two individuals (SK318 and SK352) had drinking water equivalents potentially indicative of central European or Scandinavian values. In contrast, the strontium results for both individuals were within local ranges. It is not clear whether broad similarities in strontium isotope signals between Scandinavia and Eastern Scotland may actually hinder the differentiation of non-local individuals that may be highlighted in the oxygen data. This is of interest regarding SK752, who was buried with grave goods suggestive of a Viking origin (Chapter 4.2) but was identified as of local origin to East Lothian by Sr and O analysis.

The Auldhame skeletal assemblage revealed more adults (66.5% of total sample) than sub-adults (33.4% of total sample). The mortality profiles demonstrated low numbers of neonate and infant deaths. Individuals of these very young ages are often expected to show a high susceptibility to illness due to the developing immune system, as well as the dependence on others for adequate nutrition. Waldron (2001, 41) has suggested that prior to the advances in hygiene, nutrition and medical services often seen in many modern developed countries, it would be expected that high levels of neonate and infant mortality would exist. It is possible that specific areas of the graveyard were retained for the burial of infants and young children. For instance, a comparative medieval assemblage from a rural graveyard that spanned AD 950–1850 at Wharram Percy, north Yorkshire, demonstrated a trend for infants below the age of 18 months to be buried on the north side of the church (Mays 2007, 189). Juvenile burials at Auldhame are present across all four phases of graveyard use but predominate in the last phase (Figure 43). Whether this highlights a change in burial practice at this time to only or mainly juvenile burials in the graveyard is not clear.

As is the case in many graveyard excavations, the burial assemblage from Auldhame does not represent a complete sample of the original buried population. At the time of excavation a further 66 burials were identified and preserved in situ and the burial ground may have extended farther to the north and west beyond the limits of the excavated area. This can add tremendous complexity in terms of the interpretations of health and past lives made from osteological analyses as argued by Wood et al (1992) and as reviewed more recently by Wright and Yoder (2003). However, interpretations made from the analysis of the human burials where contextualised with the population group under study and utilising multiple strands of osteological evidence, such as dietary reconstruction and health indicators, can enable meaningful insights to be attained (Goodman 1993; Cohen 1994; Larsen 1999; Waldron 2001; Roberts & Cox 2003).

The assemblage from Auldhame consisted of 161 adults (66.5%) and 81 sub-adults (33.4%). The percentage of sub-adults in the sample from Auldhame is quite high. The rate is, however, lower than the 45.3% of juveniles documented by Anderson (1994) from a medieval graveyard from The Hirsel, Coldstream, Berwickshire (Cramp & Douglas-Home 1980). Radiocarbon dating indicates the graveyard was in use from around the 11th century to the 14th century, with one identified from the 17th century (Rosemary Cramp pers comm). The group from Wharram Percy (Mays 2007, 89) also presents a high percentage of juveniles (under 16 years) in the skeletal assemblage (n. 312, 45% of the total burials).

A much smaller assemblage of juveniles was identified at the priory on the Isle of May, where a total of 56 skeletons were excavated. Burials were recovered from multiple phases including from a long-cist graveyard (AD c 430–680) and a cairn burial phase (7th–12th century), as well as later coffined graves (12th–17th century). Comparative data from this assemblage derived from two groups: A) dated to 5th–12th century (n. 42); and B) 12th–17th century (n. 14) (James & Yeoman 2008). Juveniles from Group A comprised 9.5% of the burial sample and from Group B 9.5%. A recent study of burials from a comparable rural community at Inchmarnock (Henderson 2008) also demonstrated high numbers of sub-adults in the skeletal assemblage as 56% of the sample. Such low numbers of sub-adult burials, especially when compared to the Auldhame data, may either indicate that a selective burial area for sub-adult graves existed in this burial ground or reflect on the demographic composition of the individuals associated with the priory during the periods investigated. The Isle of May is sufficiently small that it is improbable that tenants or farmers other than the monks occupied it. Thus, the numbers of juveniles available for burial may have been artificially small. The number of sub-adult burials recovered from the Cistercian Newbattle Abbey at Dalkeith, Midlothian (Gooder 2004) was 23% of the total number of burials (n. 127), which is also lower than the proportion identified at Auldhame. Newbattle Abbey was founded by David I in 1140 and was secularised in the 16th century. At Kirkhill, St Andrews, Fife, the proportion of sub-adult burials (20%) was also lower than at Auldhame. The burials at Kirkhill represented a 5th–12th-century graveyard group associated in the early phases with a Pictish religious centre (Rains & Hall 1997). A further sample from the medieval Gilbertine priory of St Andrew's at Fishergate, York, presented a lower proportion of sub-adults to adults (22.4%) (Stroud 1993) than was present at Auldhame. The proportion of sub-adults from Auldhame can also be compared to medieval cemeteries associated with urban contexts. At St Helen-on-the-Walls in York, for example, the proportion of sub-adults was very similar to that from Auldhame, as 30.5% of the total sample (Dawes 1980).

At Auldhame, the mortality profile shows that age at death for juveniles is relatively consistent throughout the age groups until a slight peak forms (n. 20) in Age Category 5 (6–11 years at death). This trend could indicate that perhaps poor nutrition or recurrent disease epidemics had affected this population group. At The Hirsel, over two-thirds of juvenile deaths occurred before the age of 6 years, with the greatest mortality occurring in the 0–2 year age group, 50% of which died before reaching c 6 months of age (Anderson 1994). The mortality profiles for the York assemblages are more closely comparable with the highest mortality for the juveniles at St Helen-on-the-Walls in the 6- to 10-year-olds (Dawes 1980). At Fishergate the mortality profile for juveniles was more evenly spread (Stroud 1993). The Newbattle Abbey mortality profile for the juveniles is fairly evenly distributed, with a peak (34%) in the 14- to 21-year-olds. There were no individuals aged below 7 years identified at the Isle of May (Battley et al 2008). Of the 56 juveniles at Kirkhill, St Andrews, 23.2% were neonate, 7.1% were aged 2 months to 2 years, 50% 2–10 years, 12.5% 10–18 years and 7.1% 18–22 years (Rains

& Hall 1997). At Wharram Percy, Mays (2007, 189) found that almost 15% of the whole skeletal assemblage (*n.* 687) were infants. At Inchmarnock, a large number of sub-adults were infants aged 0 to 1 years (50.9% of juvenile sample) (Henderson 2008, 214), indicating a high infant mortality. This comparative data suggest that young infants were probably buried in an area of the graveyard not fully excavated at Auldhame.

The adult sample at Auldhame consisted of 58 males, 42 females, 10 of intermediate sex and 51 of unidentified sex. Auldhame shows a slight bias with a sex ratio of 1.3:1 in favour of males. At The Hirsel the ratio was 1:1, which is to be expected in any normal population. There was a slight difference at Fishergate with a male to female ratio of 0.9:1. At Newbattle Abbey there was a marked bias towards the males with a ratio of 2.2:1. This is, perhaps, to be expected on a monastic site. At the Isle of May the ratio of males to females for Group A was 8:1, and for Group B it was 3:1 (Battley et al 2008), which again reflects the monastic setting but is perhaps amplified by the island's isolation from the secular population. The male to female ratio at Kirkhill, St Andrews, was somewhat unusual, with a male to female ratio of 0.4:1 (Rains & Hall 1997). The reason for the ratio is unknown and it may have resulted from under-identifying males. The sex ratio at Inchmarnock (Henderson 2008) was 1.7:1 in favour of males, although this was derived from quite a small sample of burials (*n.* 43 adults).

The mortality profile of the adults indicates that more males than females died in young adulthood. However, fewer females than males lived into old adulthood. It is difficult to identify accurately the possible factors that contributed to these trends. In other medieval graveyard groups, large numbers of males dying quite young in adult life has indicated a group affected by warfare or interpersonal violence (eg Fiorato et al 2000). While two adult males had evidence for violent injury at Auldhame (see below), one had survived into old adulthood and there is little evidence in the assemblage as a whole for weapons-related injury or violence. The mortality pattern of men dying younger than women is comparable to the pattern found at St Helen-on-the-Wall and Wharram Percy. In contrast, the assemblage from The Hirsel suggested that women in general died younger than men. At Newbattle Abbey the mortality profiles for the men and women were similar, with a slight peak around the 36–49 years age category. At Kirkhill, St Andrews, there was a fairly even distribution of females in each of the adult age groups. More men (58.3%, *n.* 28) died in the middle-age category. At the Isle of May the sample sizes were too small to assess age at death by sex.

The smaller numbers of females in the assemblage at Auldhame in both young adulthood and old adulthood could be illustrative of the trend of female migration towards more densely populated urban areas, owing to the demands of domestic service and craft industries. This interpretation was recently suggested by Mays (2007, 91–2) as a possible factor explaining the smaller numbers of females (*n.* 140) than males (*n.* 211) in the assemblage from Wharram Percy. Comparisons with data from the Scottish sites outlined above, however, do not appear to demonstrate this trend, and analysis of large urban sites local to Auldhame would be needed in order to investigate whether this is a viable possibility for this sample.

High mortality in young adult females would have been expected because of the risks associated with pregnancy and childbirth. Skeletal investigations have contributed to the recognition of such outcomes. For example, a recent survey from graveyard reports from the early medieval period (defined as *c* AD 410–1050 by Roberts & Cox 2003, 164, 166) identified six females found with associated foetal bones, and 10 possible cases of obstetric-related deaths from the later medieval period (*c* AD 1050–1550 ) (Roberts & Cox 2003, 221, 253). Three cases from Wharram Percy discussed recently by Mays (2007, 86) also illustrate females found with foetal remains. One young adult female from Inchmarnock was also found with foetal remains in situ (Henderson 2008, 219). None of the female burials identified from Auldhame was found associated with foetal remains, although SK273 was found with the remains of a small infant, SK274, overlying the pelvis. The age at death of this young child was between 1–6 months and it is suggested that the remains may represent a mother and child who potentially died at similar times and so were buried together.

### 5.4.3 Skeletal pathology

*Dietary and environmental inferences*

Recent comparative analyses of the composition of diets in the medieval period, as identified by stable isotope analysis, emphasised the role of aquatic resources as routine foodstuffs (Müldner & Richards 2005; 2007a, 2007b). This study was significant in identifying this trend as relatively consistent across medieval groups with seemingly little regard for any status-related differences in the diet (Müldner & Richards 2005, 45). These authors, together with Mays (2007), have speculated on the extent to which there was an increased consumption of fish during liturgical fasting periods during which meat consumption would have been forbidden.

The dietary results from Auldhame show a relatively high nitrogen isotope contribution together with a largely terrestrial carbon isotope signature. This does not suggest a significant amount of marine fish was present in the Auldhame medieval diet. Müldner and Richards (2005) have suggested that omnivore consumption (eg of pigs), or consumption of freshwater fish together with a terrestrial plant component may represent this type of isotopic signature. Interestingly, the paleodietary results from Auldhame are within the range identified for burials from medieval Orkney, in which fish contributed to the diet together with cereals and animal protein (Richards et al 2006). This combination of dietary isotopes has previously been suggested to be unusual for the medieval period, but the data here suggest it may have been more common than originally perceived.

There are, however, a number of extraneous factors evident at Auldhame that may have influenced the isotopic signatures established for the site. It is possible that intensive manuring to improve the local soil quality (see Chapter 6.4.1) may have altered the nitrogen signatures in the soil, which could subsequently alter the nitrogen component in cereals and animals grazing on the land (Bogaard et al 2007; Van Klinken et al 2000). This could enhance the nitrogen composition of the isotope samples from human bone, although these processes are at present incompletely understood. In addition, sea-spray may also affect nitrogen in the soil in a similar manner to manuring (Richards et al 2006). As such, these interpretations must remain tentative until further comparative research investigates the variation in isotopic composition between coastal and inland areas further.

The osteological analysis recovered little evidence for dietary deficiency amongst the Auldhame population. For example, there was no evidence for vitamin C deficiency scurvy, which can be caused by limited consumption of fresh fruit and vegetables. Similarly, no skeletal evidence for scurvy was found in the collection from Wharram Percy (Mays 2007, 182) and low levels have been identified in general from the medieval period (as reviewed in Roberts & Cox 2003). While medieval historical records of dietary composition seldom refer to vegetables or fruits consumed, Roberts and Cox (2003, 247–8) have suggested that this could indicate that these were frequent dietary staples, too common to document in texts.

Two sub-adults showed cribra orbitalia, a condition that results in pitting or porosity in the bone surface in the roof of the orbit. These lesions may represent nutritional deficiencies, possibly of specific factors such as vitamin B12 or vitamin C, or may be caused by general dietary imbalances due to gastro-intestinal diseases, especially where linked to insanitary conditions, although the range of causative factors are not completely understood (see Walker et al 2009). The low levels of this condition in the Auldhame assemblage suggest that there is little evidence for dietary deficiency in the juvenile diets. It can also be suggested that there is little evidence for the detrimental nutritional effects of diarrhoeal conditions that are frequently associated with the transition to weaning foods in infants. The absence of evidence for these conditions cannot be attributed to high numbers of infant deaths prior to, or at, weaning age and prior to the development of the skeletal lesions, because the data indicate that a peak in mortality occurred in post-infant ages and into older childhood (6–11 years).

In general, it appears that there was little skeletal evidence of disease amongst the juveniles from Auldhame. This interpretation is further supported by the low prevalence of dental enamel hypoplasia at Auldhame (CPR 4.4%), which was considerably lower than at the comparative medieval site of The Hirsel (CPR 25.1%). These lesions are formed by a pathogen or illness temporarily stopping the formation of dental enamel during foetal and childhood growth up to approximately 6 years of age (excluding the third molar: Reid & Dean 2000). The data therefore indicate that there were few episodes of childhood 'stress' or illness of enough significant or long-standing periods to disrupt enamel formation.

In comparison to Auldhame, there is more evidence for childhood illness in the form of cribra obitalia (18.5%), dental enamel hypoplasia (25.1%) and skeletal cases of rickets in other Scottish assemblages, such as The Hirsel site, as well as high rates of cribra and examples of rickets (12.5%) at the Isle of May. There was more evidence for cribra orbitalia at Inchmarnock with 22 individuals affected, including adults and children (Henderson 2008, 216). The nature of this pathology is complex to interpret but could indicate that more parasitic disease or gastro-intestinal infection occurred at sites other than Auldhame. The findings further suggest that childhood health was relatively good at Auldhame compared to other sites.

Adult stature is attained following the cessation of juvenile growth. A range of processes can influence juvenile bone growth, such as chronic illness or malnutrition, which may contribute to a small individual stature (Humphrey 2000). The mean stature for the males and females from Auldhame are broadly comparable, if not better than a range of regional comparative sites, as shown in Table A4.39). The mean statures from Auldhame are comparable with The Hirsel and St Helen's assemblages. Although the women were comparable at the Fishergate, the men were slightly taller than those at Auldhame. The stature from the Isle of May groups is slightly higher than other comparable sites. The tall stature of females at the Isle of May has been attributed to the fact the females may have been of high status (James & Yeoman 2008). The male stature at the comparable rural site of Inchmarnock (Henderson 2008, 215) was very similar to that derived from Auldhame, although the females from Auldhame were marginally smaller than those from Inchmarnock (Table A4.39). Overall, the results indicate that long bone growth was not significantly stunted due to chronic ill-health or dietary deficiency during childhood growth in comparison to other medieval skeletal assemblages.

The mean statures from Auldhame are relatively comparable with modern populations. The Renfrew/Paisley study was a general population study of 15,402 middle-aged men and women living in the West of Scotland. The mean heights of males aged 45–49 years and 60–64 years were 171cm and 168cm respectively and the females 159cm and 156cm respectively (MacLennan 2003). There appears to have been little change in adult height between the medieval and modern periods. Waldron (2001) has shown that there is no consistent trend in height over the centuries with the exception of the last decade or so where there has been a considerable increase in height. This exaggerates the difference in height between past and modern populations, and which has probably contributed to the popular misconception that our ancestors were considerably shorter than today (Waldron 2001).

There was very little evidence for vitamin D deficiency in the assemblage from Auldhame. Only one adult female (SK611) showed skeletal changes of residual rickets (femoral bending), which are likely to have occurred during childhood rather than being due to the adult form of the condition (osteomalacia). This matches the identification of only one adult case of residual rickets from an adult female from burials at the contemporary rural site at Inchmarnock (Henderson 2008, 217). These findings support the general interpretation of the low prevalence of this disease from a survey of health during the medieval period (Roberts & Cox 2003, 247), although more recent advances in the recording of rickets may increase the prevalence in future investigations (Ortner & Mays 1998; Mays et al 2006).

A range of factors can contribute to the onset of this disease. For example, its presence in the post-medieval period has been attributed to a lack of sunlight in increasingly urbanised settlements, which created narrow and shadowed streets (Mays et al 2006; Roberts & Cox 2003, 189). The settlements around Auldhame during the medieval period were unlikely to have been as densely populated and built up as urban centres like contemporaneous York or London. The paucity of evidence at Auldhame for other diseases such as tuberculosis and leprosy that tend to occur in highly populated areas, also lends some support to this interpretation.

It is possible that other factors may have contributed to the presence of vitamin D deficiency. Ortner and Mays (1998) found a high prevalence of rickets cases (*n.* 8) in very young infants (aged 3–18 months) from medieval Wharram Percy in Yorkshire. These authors suggested that severe childhood illnesses may have necessitated keeping the individuals indoors for prolonged periods, which resulted in the lack of vitamin D production (Ortner & Mays 1998). There was no other skeletal evidence on the affected individual from Auldhame that indicated additional childhood illness had occurred together with the rickets. In many instances, however, if the illness was not capable of contributing to the premature death of the child, any skeletal evidence of it may have become remodelled during adult life, removing the evidence for previous episodes of poor health. Only a fraction of illnesses may actually involve the skeleton or result in the chronic or long-standing periods of disease that are necessary to create an identifiable skeletal response. These factors can complicate our interpretations of health from skeletal remains.

Where lack of sunlight exposure occurs, there is an increased reliance on attaining vitamin D from food sources such as oily fish (salmon, tuna, mackerel) and eggs. During the medieval period, it is likely that farming practices would have enabled relatively good supplies of produce such as eggs. As outlined above, the adoption of some marine fish protein in the medieval diet at Auldhame as indicated by the chemical analysis may have contributed to the low levels of vitamin D deficiency at this site.

*Interpersonal violence and accidental injury*

In the skeletal assemblage from Auldhame, the majority of evidence for injury derives from accidental trauma like fractures or dislocations, with, in some instances, evidence for associated soft tissue involvement. Weapon-related trauma is frequently documented in medieval skeletal assemblages, although in a recent survey of health across Britain few Scottish sites presented skeletal evidence indicative of interpersonal violence (Roberts & Cox 2003, 168). There is, however, some skeletal evidence for weapon-related trauma and injury from Auldhame. The osteological analysis identified two cases of severe wounding with sharp weapons in adult males from Auldhame with very different age-at-death characteristics; one young adult (18–25 years) and one older adult (46+ years).

Evidence for cut marks on the skeleton from British medieval sites has indicated that males were more affected by this type of injury than females, by a ratio of 6:1 (Roberts & Cox 2003, 169). Patterns of broader skeletal trauma including all types of weapon injury rather than just by bladed weapons also demonstrate that males were more frequently injured compared to females (32 males compared to four females affected, as reported by Roberts & Cox 2003, 169).

At Auldhame, both males had experienced cranial injuries, with cuts to the top, bottom and sides of the head as well as to the face (Figures 78 and 79). The cuts were linear and were made by a sharp-edged weapon (Boylston 2000, 361). The location and direction of blows indicates the individuals who inflicted the injuries were right-handed. There was no evidence of bone healing, which demonstrates that the injuries were fatal. The number of individuals affected by weapon trauma at Auldhame is 2/242 (0.8%), and is 1.2% when only considered for the adult assemblage (2/161). The rate of weapon-related injuries evident at Auldhame is quite small but is likely to underestimate the true occurrence, as many injuries would have affected the soft tissues only and would not be visible on the skeleton. Data from comparative assemblages indicate the adult prevalence at Auldhame for this type of injury is low; the rate of injury at The Hirsel site is 1.5% and at the Isle of May, 1.8%. As at Auldhame, all of the injured individuals from these sites were men and all injuries were to the skull. The data from Auldhame lend support to the trends indicated in the survey of evidence for weapon trauma undertaken by Roberts and Cox (2003, 169) discussed above. The data contrast, however, with two incidents of weapon-related injury identified at Inchmarnock. At this site, a juvenile aged 14–15 years suffered blade injuries to the left arm, resulting in the complete severing of the limb from midway through the humerus, together with wounds to the scapulae and vertebrae, pelvis and skull (Henderson 2008, 217–18). There was also a middle-adult female who had suffered from five separate blade wounds to the skull. This variation clearly illustrates the severity of the conflicts that occurred throughout the medieval and early historic period.

Evidence for interpersonal violence during the early medieval period is sometimes linked with Viking raids or fighting between migrants and the native population (Roberts & Cox 2003, 168). Documentary references allude to the destruction of the church of St Baldred and the nearby village of Tyninghame in AD 941 by Olaf Godfreyson, which may have had significant implications for the safety of residents of Auldhame (Chapter 7.2.1). One of the adult burials with evidence of weapon-related injury (SK216) is dated to cal AD 860–1020 (Table 1; SUERC-15600). While this date range does span the spoiling at Tyninghame, it is not possible to relate this individual specifically to this event.

SK216 was identified by stable isotope analyses as a resident of the Lothian area but SK868, dated to cal AD 1270–1400 (Table 1; SUERC-15607), and which had comparable injuries, was identified by the strontium isotope analysis as a possible outsider who may have spent his childhood elsewhere. The oxygen isotope results do not, however, suggest this individual was local to Lothian, but it is possible that this individual may have migrated to the district from quite a local region.

One adult female from Auldhame displayed evidence for a fracture of the mandibular condyle with subsequent pathology to the joint articulations. Fractures at this location frequently occur in the modern population due to vehicle accidents, although a recent review by Tawfilis et al (2006) highlighted the role that interpersonal assaults can have in causing fractures at this location. There was no other evidence on the female skeleton from Auldhame to indicate interpersonal violence, although any associated soft tissue lesions would not be identifiable from the skeletal remains. Falls and sporting accidents have also caused fractures of the mandible. It is likely, however, that the range of causative factors for such fractures may have differed across past populations.

Two individuals were identified with multiple fractures. The fractures in these cases are likely to have resulted from accidents, although one individual (SK293) may have had an underlying osteoporosis or severe loss of bone that would have increased the risk of fractures occurring in accidental falls.

The osteological investigation has identified quite a varied range of fractures and soft tissue injuries on the skeletons from Auldhame. While there are not high numbers of individuals affected by trauma in this collection, the types of injury do collectively add to what is known of fractures from this period. Many studies that specifically aim to investigate trauma from skeletal remains do so through examination of the long bones only, as illustrated by a detailed study into trauma evidence from the urban medieval population of St Helens-on-the-Walls, York (Grauer & Roberts 1996). The current study has demonstrated evidence for long bone fracture affecting the humerus and clavicles, as well as evidence for injuries to the kneecaps, hands and feet. Soft tissue injury was indicated by ossified haematomas caused by muscle tears (myositis ossificans traumatica). Evidence for this condition was observed on arm and leg bones in individuals from Auldhame, and is likely to have been caused by accidental injury, possibly related to the agricultural lifestyle. Skeletal and soft tissue trauma to the lower legs, together with crushing injuries of the hands and feet were also observed in the comparable assemblage from Inchmarnock, as described by Henderson (2008, 218–19) and are most likely attributable to agricultural activities and accidental falls.

Two individuals were identified with multiple fractures. The fractures in these cases are likely to have resulted from accidents, although one individual (SK293) may have had an underlying osteoporosis or severe loss of bone that would have increased the risk of fractures occurring in accidental falls.

The incidence of fractures was higher in the Isle of May assemblage (CPR 17.9%) than at Auldhame (CPR 6.7%). The frequency was more closely comparable with the Newbattle Abbey assemblage (CPR 6.3%) and that from The Hirsel (CPR 5.4%). The incidence was even lower at St Andrews (CPR 4.6%), which is probably indicative of the nature of the population at a religious and monastic centre. With Auldhame, the fact that fractures were seen in males and females suggests that the types of fracture and their incidence do not indicate a high level of interpersonal violence.

*Pathological fractures*

Evidence of traumatic lesions within the Auldhame collection provides indirect evidence for another group of diseases, the metabolic bone diseases. These conditions can be mediated by factors within a lifestyle, such as diet and physical activity, as well as by age and sex (Brickley & Ives 2008). Three adult individuals presented evidence indicative of age-related osteoporosis from Auldhame with associated compression fractures of the vertebrae.

In the modern population, osteoporosis is a condition frequently identified in post-menopausal females and old adults. Osteoporosis is caused by various hormonal and age-related imbalances that affect the manner in which the bone tissue in the skeleton is maintained during adult life. The net effect of the changes in osteoporosis is a loss of bone tissue together with qualitative changes in the remaining bone. In consequence, individuals with osteoporosis have an increased susceptibility to bone fracture following relatively simple accidents such as falls. Three skeletal areas are frequently fractured due to an underlying osteoporosis: the distal radius (Colles' fractures); the vertebrae; and the hip (femoral neck). It can be difficult to differentiate between fractures that occurred in a past population due to an accidental fall and those fractures that occurred during a simple accident but which were caused by an underlying pathology such as osteoporosis. While frequently perceived to be a condition that only affects older females in the modern population, recent clinical research has demonstrated the extent to which older males are also affected by pathological fractures in this condition (as reviewed in Brickley & Ives 2008). The aetiology of osteoporosis is multifactorial as it can be affected by lifestyle, physical activity, ethnicity and genetic factors, as well as other diseases. The risk of this condition can also be exacerbated by the dietary supply of minerals such as calcium, as well as vitamin D, or by prolonged malnutrition or eating disorders (Brickley & Ives 2008).

The demographic composition of the Auldhame sample indicated that adults were surviving into older ages (46+ years). All three adults affected by osteoporosis from Auldhame were assigned to this age category and it is likely that increased age was a significant factor in the two probable males affected and increased age and/or hormonal changes following the menopause were causative factors for the female affected. All three adults manifested vertebral compression fractures, either of the whole body or by anterior wedging. Such fractures in the vertebrae often cause anterior bending or kyphosis.

One individual had a fracture to the left radius. Fractures to the distal radius are frequent in osteoporosis and several osteoporosis-related fractures may occur at different locations in an affected individual owing to the nature of increased skeletal fragility. It is also possible for individuals to have sustained a fracture at a previous episode during their life, which will remain identifiable on the skeleton. As outlined above, the radius fracture on the individual with vertebral fractures from Auldhame was not a typical Colles' fracture, a type that usually occurs in osteoporosis. As the fracture was well healed with smooth lamellar bone, it is probable that the radius fracture occurred earlier in the individual's lifetime than the trauma that resulted in the vertebral compressions exacerbated by osteoporosis. There was no evidence for femoral neck fractures or distal radius Colles' fractures in the sample from Auldhame, which is similar to the results of an investigation into osteoporosis-related fractures from the medieval assemblage from Wharram Percy (Mays 1996; 2007, 181). At Wharram Percy, three out of 44 old adult females (6.8%) were affected by vertebral fractures. At Auldhame, the prevalence of this type of fracture for old adult females is 1/7 (14.2%) and for old adult males 2/14 (14.2%).

*Infections and consequences*

There was little evidence of infection in the sample from Auldhame and such as there was pointed towards non-specific conditions. Two severe cases of osteomyelitis were identified, providing an incidence of 0.8% at Auldhame; comparable with the evidence from The Hirsel (CPR 0.9%). The crude prevalence in the Isle of May was higher at 1.8%. The prevalence of periostitis was considerably lower at Auldhame (CPR 1.7%) than at The Hirsel (CPR 7.3%) and the Isle of May (10.7%).

The knee region, followed by the distal third of the tibia and proximal third of the femur, are the most common sites for osteomyelitis to occur (Aufderheide & Rodríguez-Martín 1998). One case from Auldhame presented involvement of the lower leg. In a second individual, however, the infectious condition resulting in osteomyelitis was systemic throughout the legs, which would have been extremely painful. The presence of cloacae in these individuals indicates that pus would have drained from abscesses formed in the internal aspect of the infected bone to the external bone surfaces and into the surrounding soft tissues. Osteomyelitis can arrive in the skeleton as a result of a long-standing bacterial infection initiated from areas of the body such as a throat, ear, sinus or a chest infection, from which bacteria pass through the bloodstream into the bone (Roberts & Manchester 2005, 168–9). Bacteria present on the outside of the body can also be forced internally into the blood system and into bones via penetrating injuries including compound fractures, but there was no evidence of bone fracture on either of the Auldhame individuals affected by osteomyelitis. It is likely that a bacterial infection arising from a source within the body was the origin of the bone infection in these cases. Severe pathological conditions, such as the osteomyelitis cases, would have been chronic, painful and potentially crippling. This would imply that such cases would have required some level of care within the medieval community during this period.

*Joint degeneration and activity-related changes*

The skeletal evidence from Auldhame reveals the most common degenerative joint changes were the articulations between the sternum and the clavicles, as well as the shoulder joints. There were no clear differences in the pattern of joints affected by generative changes and osteoarthritis between the sexes. While inferring patterns of occupation from skeletal remains can be challenging (Larsen 1999; Jurmain 1999), these patterns indicate that there was no obvious division of occupational trends leading to different rates of degenerative joint changes between the males and females at Auldhame.

A number of adults were also identified with rotator cuff disease, in which damage to the soft tissues of the shoulder joint occurs, frequently as a result of injury or repetitive motions of the shoulder. The frequency of osteoarthritis in the acromioclavicular joints from the medieval population sample from the Isle of May (Group A: left TPR 35%, right 30%) is similar to the pattern identified in the Auldhame assemblage. Battley et al (2008) tentatively suggested that the pattern of joint degeneration evident at the Isle of May site may have been caused by rowing. Given Auldhame's location and the excavated evidence for fishing, this is not an improbable suggestion for the skeletons similarly affected there.

*Dental health*

The Auldhame sample presented evidence for increasing amounts of calculus deposits with age, from 18 to 45 years. Adults aged 46+ years did not demonstrate higher rates of dental calculus when compared to young adults, although it is possible that this relationship may be influenced by increased rates of ante-mortem tooth loss in older age. Trends in modern populations often indicate increasing amounts of calculus with age (Hillson 1996, 260), likely linked to the duration of exposure to micro-organisms and proteins from the diet and the formation of mineralised deposits. Modern studies also indicate a trend for males to have more deposits of calculus than females (Hillson 1996, 260). The results indicate a tendency for males to be affected more by calculus deposits than females, although the differences were not proven statistically. A review of 18 early medieval sites studied for evidence of dental calculus by Roberts and Cox (2003, 193–4) identified 10 sites (55.5%) that showed evidence for males to be affected by calculus more than females. Whether these trends are influenced by differences in dietary composition or oral hygiene practices is not entirely clear.

The results demonstrated that the majority of individuals in the sample were not affected by periodontal disease. Of those affected, most presented only mild degrees of alveolar bone resorption. There was no evidence for an age-related increase in alveolar disease in the sample. These interpretations can be complicated by increasing levels of ante-mortem tooth loss with age, either as a result of conditions such as caries or due to severe periodontal disease causing loosening of the periodontal ligaments and soft tissues securing teeth in the sockets. Adults aged 26–35 years showed the highest frequency of alveolar resorption in individuals with evidence of this condition. While causative inferences are difficult to draw and many aspects of dental disease are multifactorial, the data do suggest there may be a link between higher levels of calculus deposits in adults aged 26–35 years and the occurrence of alveolar disease. The raw data indicated that males were more affected by alveolar disease than females at Auldhame, which could also be reflective of the trends identified for dental calculus. Statistical analysis indicates that the differences in prevalence between the sexes do not reach a significant level.

The true prevalence rate (TPR) for ante-mortem tooth loss at Auldhame was 5.4%. This is relatively comparable with The Hirsel (6.9%). For Fishergate, the prevalence for the earlier assemblage was 3.2% and for the later assemblage, 11.4%. At St Helen's this was much higher at 17.5%, which may be a reflection of differences in food availability in more urbanised areas during this period.

It has been documented in previous studies of both modern and archaeological populations that females tend to be affected more by caries than are males (Larsen 1999, 72–6; Hillson 2001; Roberts & Manchester 2005, 66). While the causes of dental caries are multifactorial (Powell 1985), it is likely that dietary differences between the sexes may have contributed to this trend with males consuming more meat and females more carbohydrates (Larsen 1999, 72). This trend was demonstrable in the current investigation of dental caries from the medieval skeletons from Auldhame, with statistically more caries in females than in males. In the modern population the sex differences in caries are multifactorial but this condition is strongly linked to dietary composition. The difference identified at Auldhame is likely to reflect dietary differences. Caries occurs most commonly in teeth that are difficult to clean, and often become manifest in the fissures of the molars and the approximal contact areas (Hillson 1986). Dental caries is uncommon in prehistoric material but increases in frequency in later periods, reaching its peak in modern times according to Waldron (2001), who noted that, 'parallel to the increase in frequency, the number of teeth affected per individual has increased and so has the number of children with the disease'.

At Auldhame the TPR for dental caries was 3.9%. The prevalence was higher at St Helen's (6.1%) and Fishergate (4.3% and 12.1%). Again, the TPR at The Hirsel was lower (0.2%). A survey of caries prevalence in Scottish populations from the 'Dark Ages' by Lunt (1974), reported on by Roberts and Cox (2003, 189), presents a frequency of 4.3% (45/1941). For Auldhame, dental abscesses were present in 1.3% of individuals. This is comparable with St Helen's (1.2%) and the early Fishergate sample (1.9%). The TPR at The Hirsel was quite low in comparison (0.2%).

## 5.5 CONCLUSIONS

The results of the osteological analysis of the 242 burials from Auldhame have presented a large corpus of evidence for a local population group from this Scottish community, spanning approximately 1,000 years. While the results do reflect on an incomplete representation of the graveyard as a whole, the health of the skeletal sample analysed is similar in many ways to assemblages known from this period. The results highlight trends of disease pattern more in line with the rural setting of the graveyard, however, rather than patterns indicative of high density urban or crowded locales. In contrast to many medieval urban centres, health during childhood appears to have been relatively good. The coastal location and agricultural lifestyle were likely to have played an important role in both the activities of the adults and the dietary composition of the sample. The lifestyle is also likely to have contributed to the range of accidental injuries evidenced in several of the adults. While interpersonal violence was a factor affecting many throughout the spread of the medieval period, the individuals at Auldhame present very little skeletal evidence for this, suggesting it was not a frequent occurrence for individuals represented in the graveyard.

# CHAPTER 6

# THE ECOFACT ASSEMBLAGE

Small assemblages of animal bone, carbonised plant remains and marine shells were recovered during the excavation and subsequent sample processing. The analyses of these assemblages are presented in this section. The results of the micromorphological analysis of the buried soil [002] are also presented here.

## 6.1 THE FAUNAL REMAINS

JACKALINE ROBERTSON

### 6.1.1 Introduction

An assemblage of 884 animal bone fragments was recovered. The overall preservation of the bone ranged from mainly poor, to adequate. The species and minimum numbers present are presented in Table 10. The level of bone fragmentation was recorded, as was any evidence relating to mortality profiles, economic strategies, pathologies and butchery.

All bone was, as far as possible, identified to element and species using the AOC mammal and bird bone reference collection. In cases where species could not be identified they were described as either large or small mammal. All complete bones were measured according to the criteria as used by Von den Driesch (1976). Evidence for pathology, butchery, size, animal gnawing and post-depositional damage was observed and recorded. The presence of bird and fish bone was noted but given the very small numbers present they were not identified as to species.

### 6.1.2 Discussion

The faunal remains identified as bovine consisted mainly of loose molars, skull fragments, long and short bones. Given the high level of fragmentation it was not possible to identify the sex of the animals. The proximal epiphysis of one ulna, the distal end of two tibias and the distal end of one metatarsal remained unfused at time of death, which gives an approximate age at death of between two to three years (Silver 1969).

The sheep remains consisted of loose teeth, skull fragments, pelvis, long bones and phalanges. Given the high level of fragmentation it was not possible to identify sex. Fusion rates and tooth wear were used in an effort to identify specific mortality profiles and economic practices.

The PM4, M1 and M2 were present in one recovered mandible and were all worn. The absence of the third molar made it difficult to establish a precise age for this animal, although the wear on the first two molars suggest it died between 8 and 18 months (Payne 1973). The dpm4, M1 and M2 were identified in a second mandible, which all displayed signs of wear. This gives an age of death of between 1 to 8 months (Payne 1973). The distal epiphysis of one radius remained unfused, giving an age of death of before 3 years. The remaining tibias were fused at both the proximal and distal epiphysis, which gave age at death as 3 years or over (Silver 1969).

Few pig remains were recovered, with only skull, atlas and tooth fragments represented in the assemblage.

Table 10
The chipped stone assemblage by type

|  | *Flint* | *Quartz* |
|---|---|---|
| Flakes | 1 | 0 |
| Retouched blade | 1 | 0 |
| Amorphous core | 0 | 1 |
| Bipolar remnant | 0 | 1 |
| Chunk | 1 | 0 |
| Pebbles | 0 | 12 |

A tusk was recovered, indicating that this animal was male. The tooth wear was minimal, suggesting this animal was slaughtered as soon as it had reached its prime meat-bearing size.

*Butchery and pathology*

One pathology was identified on the adult sheep mandible. Part of the bone surrounding the first and second molars had receded and exposed the lower part of the teeth and the roots. This would have exposed the animal to oral infections and possible pain while eating. There were also cut marks made by a metal blade along several ribs and phalanges.

*Taphonomy*

The bone assemblage had suffered from significant post-depositional damage in the form of ploughing. There are large volumes of loose teeth, badly fragmented horn cores, skull fragments and badly damaged long and short bones. All of the recovered long bones had suffered chop marks associated with modern ploughing rather than ancient butchery techniques. Ploughing was also responsible for disturbing and mixing grave and refuse contexts, which has resulted in disarticulated human and animal remains becoming mixed within the same feature. There is also evidence of weathering. However, as there is no obvious evidence of animal gnawing it is likely that the weathering is due to plough disturbance. The rabbit bones were much better preserved than the other animal bones and are likely to be intrusive in all the contexts in which they occurred.

### 6.1.3 Summary

The evidence of fusion and tooth wear suggests that the animals were primarily exploited for resources such as meat and milk. The lack of pathologies associated with extreme age and traction suggests that these animals were culled as they reached their optimal weight. However, given the small number of identifiable elements and the high level of fragmentation, little more can be said about the nature of the pastoral economy that these animals represent.

## 6.2 THE CHARRED MACROPLANT REMAINS

JACKALINE ROBERTSON

### 6.2.1 Introduction

The analysis comprised examination of 16 samples collected from ditches, pits and grave cuts. Samples were processed in laboratory conditions using a standard floatation method (cf Kenward et al 1980). The samples were easily disaggregated and required no pre-treatment. The light floating material (flot) was collected in a 1mm and 300 micron sieve. The heavy residue was collected in a 1mm mesh and allowed to air dry before further processing. The flots were analysed using a microscope at ×10 and up to ×100 where necessary to aid identification. Identifications were confirmed using the AOC modern reference material, keys and texts (Cappers et al 2006; Jacomet 2006). The retents were scanned by eye.

### 6.2.2 Results (Table 11)

A small assemblage consisting of 98 cereal grains and 119 weed seeds was recovered. The cereal grains are poorly preserved with several displaying extreme signs of distortion in the form of tar excretions. This can be attributed to prolonged exposure to heat during the original charring process. The weed seeds are slightly better preserved, although their number is too small to permit a valid interpretation.

Of the cereal grains only 50 were identifiable to species, poor preservation preventing the

**Table 11**
**Species and minimum number of individuals present**

| Species | Fragment count | MNI |
|---|---|---|
| Bovine | 43 | 2 |
| Ovis | 59 | 4 |
| Sus | 5 | 1 |
| Bird | 27 | – |
| Fish | 4 | – |
| Rabbit | 50 | – |
| Large mammal | 672 | – |
| Small mammal | 24 | – |
| Unidentified | – | – |
| Total | 884 | 5 |

identification of the remainder. *Hordeum* sp. (barley) was the dominant cereal, followed by *Triticum aestivum/compactum* (bread/club wheat). Two barley grains displayed morphological characteristics similar to the hulled variety (Renfrew 1973). A few *Avena* sp. (oat) grains were present. It was not possible to establish whether the oats had been deliberately cultivated or were a wild variety that had contaminated the main crop. The absence of chaff and the relatively small number of weed seeds recovered indicates that this material is waste produce from domestic activities such as cooking, baking and cleaning, as opposed to residue from threshing and winnowing. Several seeds of *Linum usitatissimum* L. (flax) were also identified.

The charred weed seeds consisted of *Chenopodium album* L. (fat hen), *Polygonum aviculare* L. (common knotweed) *Bilderdykia convolvulus* L. (black bindweed) and *Polygonum persicaria* L. (lady's thumb).

### 6.2.3 Summary

The charred macroplant assemblage contains a mixture of domestic cereal grains representative of agriculture and wild weed seeds that are common contaminants of cultivated fields. The presence of *Linum usitatissimum* L (flax) could suggest either local cultivation or trade. However, as only two seeds were recovered, little useful information can be derived concerning its economic importance and role, if any, within this economy. The size and poor condition of the assemblage limits any further useful information that can be obtained concerning the agricultural economy practised in and around this site.

## 6.3 MARINE MOLLUSCS

Ruby Ceron-Carrasco

### 6.3.1 Introduction

Marine molluscs were retrieved from seven contexts, although only two contexts contained more than five fragments (Table 12). The apical fragments of shell were identified to species using standard guides (Campbell 1989; Moreno-Nuño 1994a). Frequency was estimated by counting shell apices for gastropods and valve umbos for bivalve species (Moreno-Nuño 1994b). Broken fragments were scanned; an approximate quantification to give a general idea of the presence and importance of the different species found in the assemblage is shown in Table 12. The fragments identified to species were then quantified in terms of their relative frequency within each sample.

### 6.3.2 Results

*Littorina littorea* (periwinkles) and *Nucella lapillus* (the dog-whelk) were the most abundant marine molluscs recovered at Auldhame. Both these species of gastropod have quite sturdy shells and survive well in archaeological deposits. Virtually all the periwinkles came from [91], a layer within Ditch 1 interpreted as midden debris; in fact, [91] was almost entirely composed of periwinkles. *Littorina littorea* is known as the edible periwinkle; the meat is high in protein and low in fat. Periwinkles are still collected for consumption in vast quantities in Scotland (more than 2,000 tonnes annually), although mainly for export to the Continent. Periwinkles can also be used as fishing bait but the purity of the [91] deposit suggests that at Auldhame they were being collected as a foodstuff.

The richest context in terms of marine molluscs was [259], which contained all but one of the dog-whelks collected from the site. The presence of the dog-whelk is intriguing because, unlike the other species present, these molluscs have not generally been used for human consumption, although some argue that it was used as food by Mesolithic hunter-gatherers along the western seaboard of Scotland (Russel et al 1995). However, a purple dye can be extracted from the dog-whelk (Biggam 2006) and it will be argued in Chapter 7.2.2 that dye/pigment extraction was the reason for their collection at Auldhame.

The other species present include *Ostrea edulis* (oyster), *Cerasoderma edule* (cockle), *Ensis ensis* (razor shell) and *Patella vulgata* (limpet). The remains of these species consisted of mainly broken shell fragments. Also present in the assemblage were *Littorina littoralis* (the flat periwinkle) and *Littorina saxatilis* (the rough periwinkle).

Most of the mollusca found at Auldhame could have been used originally as a source of food (eg oyster, razor shell, periwinkle, cockles) or as fishing bait (eg cockle, periwinkle, limpet). The variety of marine shell recovered indicates a wide-ranging use of the shoreline. The beaches around Auldhame would have provided an easily accessible resource; most of the contexts contained species that could have been collected from these beaches.

**Table 12**
The charred macroplant assemblage. All plant remains were recorded using a four point semi-quantitative scale of abundance. Taxonomic order and nomenclature for plants follow Tutin *et al* (1964–80)

| Context | | | 32 | 87 | 96 | 124 | 259 | 419 | 420 | 456 |
|---|---|---|---|---|---|---|---|---|---|---|
| Flot (ml) | | | 10 | 10 | 50 | 10 | 10 | 10 | 20 | 10 |
| **Vernacular species** | **Common name** | **Plant part** | | | | | | | | |
| *Hordeum* sp(p). | Barley | caryopsis/es | + | + | | | + | + | + | |
| *Triticum aestivum/compactum* sp(p). | Bread/Club wheat | caryopsis/es | + | + | | | | | + | |
| *Avena* sp(p). | Oat | caryopsis/es | + | + | | | | | | |
| *Cerealia* indet | Cereals | caryopsis/es | ++ | + | + | + | + | | + | |
| *Linum usitatissimum* L. | Cultivated flax | seed(s) | | | | | | | | |
| *Polygonum aviculare* agg. | Knotgrass | fruit(s) | | + | | + | | + | | |
| *Persicaria lapathifolium* L. | Pale Persicaria | fruit(s) | | + | | | | | | |
| *Bilderdykia convolvulus* L. | Black bindweed | fruit(s) | | | | | + | | | |
| *Persicaria* sp(p). | Smartweeds | fruit(s) | | | | | | | | |
| *Chenopodium album* L. | Fat hen | seed(s) | + | | + | + | + | | | + |
| indet plant material | | seed(s)/fruits(s) | | + | | + | | + | + | + |
| *Cenococcum* spherical fungal | | | | | | | | + | | |
| Context | | | 534 | 538 | 540 | 542 | 560 | 565 | 567 | 570 |
| Flot (ml) | | | 10 | 60 | 10 | 10 | 10 | 10 | 10 | 10 |
| **Vernacular species** | **Common name** | **Plant part** | | | | | | | | |
| *Hordeum* sp(p). | Barley | caryopsis/es | | | | | + | | + | |
| *Triticum aestivum/compactum* sp(p). | Bread/Club wheat | caryopsis/es | | | | | | | | |
| *Avena* sp(p). | Oat | caryopsis/es | | | | | | | | |
| *Cerealia* indet | Cereals | caryopsis/es | + | + | + | + | + | + | + | |
| *Linum usitatissimum* L. | Cultivated flax | seed(s) | + | | + | | | | | |
| *Polygonum aviculare* agg. | Knotgrass | fruit(s) | | | | | | | | |
| *Persicaria lapathifolium* L. | Pale Persicaria | fruit(s) | | | | | + | | | |
| *Bilderdykia convolvulus* L. | Black bindweed | fruit(s) | | | | | | | | |
| *Persicaria* sp(p). | Smartweeds | fruit(s) | | | | | + | | | |
| *Chenopodium album* L. | Fat hen | seed(s) | + | + | + | | ++ | + | + | + |
| indet plant material | | seed(s)/fruits(s) | | + | | + | ++ | | | + |
| *Cenococcum* spherical fungal | | | | + | + | | + | | | |

Key: + = infrequent, ++ = Occasional, +++ = Frequent, ++++ = Abundant

# THE ECOFACT ASSEMBLAGE

## 6.4 MICROMORPHOLOGICAL ANALYSIS OF THE BURIED SOIL [002]

Lynne Roy

### 6.4.1 Introduction

Three undisturbed kubiena samples were removed from [002], a buried soil thought to represent a possible *plaggen* soil present across the north of the site at Auldhame. The buried soil underlay an undeveloped AP horizon and overlay the natural subsoil [550]. The buried soil was identified in the field as an improved soil, dark brown in colour and of clay silt texture. The buried soil was approximately 1m deep across the northern area with local variations in depth. Three samples (79, 80 and 82) were subject to full analysis (see Appendix 6), the summary results of which are given below.

Micromorphology is an analytical technique by which soils and sediments are made into thin transparent glass mounted slides (usually 30μm thick) which can then be examined using a petrographic microscope. The dynamics of sedimentary processes, in situ physio-chemical soil processes and processes related to the impact of humans upon soils and sediments can all be studied using micromorphology.

Micromorphological indicators of manuring practices include the identification of fuel residues, indicated by colour, indicative of iron immobilisation when heated (Courty et al 1989): charcoal material (February 1991; Umbanhower & McGrath 1998); calcite crystals (Goldberg 1979; Wattez & Courty 1987); and silica phytoliths and diatoms (Courty et al 1989). Highly active invertebrate faunas, in particular large earthworm populations, are a widely reported characteristic of man-made deep soils, a reflection of their high nutrient status (Davidson & Carter 1998, 837).

The main aim of micromorphological analysis of [002] was:

- to determine the nature of the buried soil and materials added;
- to determine the nature of the relationship between the buried soil and lower subsoil;
- to determine if the buried soil is a *plaggen* soil.

### 6.4.2 Summary description

Each thin section sample consisted of two main units:

(1) the buried soil, [002];
(2) the natural subsoil, [550].

[002] originated as a moderately to poorly sorted coarse sand with larger grit-sized mineral grains; the coarse mineral component accounts for approximately 40% of [002] and is dominated by quartz with occasional calcite, common weathered rock fragments and rare plagioclase feldspars.

The porosity of [002] is up to 10% with moderately linear voids and vughs. The fine fraction is dark reddish-brown in plane polarised light (PPL) with an undifferentiated birefringence fabric. The high organic content of [002] is responsible for the domination of the brown, dark brown, dark reddish-brown and black matrix colours and for its isotropic nature in cross polarised light (CPL). [002] has been moderately reworked in an aerobic environment by a variety of pedogenic processes and all but the merest trace of the original fabric has been destroyed.

Exotic components contribute to approximately 10% of Samples 79 and 82. Sample 80 contained over 20% exotic materials due to a higher concentration of large coal and charcoal fragments. All three samples were rich in fragmentary charcoal and small charcoal fragments within the matrix at various stages of decomposition. Some of the charcoal retained cellular structure but was not identifiable to species level. Other organic matter is well decomposed, which hinders its identification, although the presence of rare and fragmentary phytoliths indicates that grasses contributed to the source.

The unit has been subject to intensive and extensive bioturbation, which has resulted in the fragmentation of the organic matter and the mixing of the mineral material. The bioturbation is evident in the form of faecal pellets, most commonly located within pseudomorphic voids and the by-product of small arthropods (Dawod & Fitzpatrick 1992). Pseudomorphic voids stained with bright orange organic matter are identifiable in all three samples, although there was a greater incidence of these at the top of Sample 79.

The boundary between Units 1 and 2 in Samples 79 and 80 is diffuse. The basic composition of the fine fraction of Unit 2 [550] in Samples 79 and 80 is similar to the upper soil, but with some variation in the relative abundance of components. The lower organic content and higher coarse mineral content give the unit a yellowish-brown colour in PPL. Sample 82 consists of a single unit [002].

### 6.4.3 Discussion and interpretation

It was hypothesised that [002] represented an artificially enriched *plaggen* soil and the samples under discussion were taken to verify the nature of the development of this soil and determine whether the sample had been artificially deepened by the addition of exotic manuring materials.

The boundary between Units 1 and 2 in Samples 79 and 80 is diffuse and the similarity in mineral composition between the units in both samples suggests that the soils developed gradually from the underlying natural subsoil. Extensive bioturbation of both samples prevents any further analysis of the relationship between the buried soil and the underlying subsoil.

The soil profiles surrounding the excavation area consist of sandy brown calcareous soils and are part of the Fraserburgh series (Ragg & Futty 1967). The natural organic content of the lower profile of Fraserburgh soils is generally low to none. Sandy soils such as those found at Auldhame are prone to drought and would have been unsuitable for cultivation without careful maintenance of their fertility. Manuring of the soils at Auldhame would have provided the nutrients necessary for plant growth, and the organic matter would have retained water, providing cohesion to the sandy soil. Organic material also provides food for earthworms, which aerate the soil, increase aggregate stability and enhance the availability of plant nutrients.

Whether the extensive deepened and heavily manured top-soils of Auldhame are *plaggen* soils in the strictest sense in which the term was originally coined remains a matter for debate. The term *plaggen* was used in the Netherlands to describe the medieval practice of mixing byre floor material and soil for spreading on fields but the use of the term is imprecise and is now widely applied to describe cultivation soils that have been deepened by the deliberate addition of organic material as manure. Turf is the most commonly identified input to *plaggen* soils and depths in excess of 1m are widely reported (Pape 1970). In Britain, *plaggen* soils are well known from sub-Roman (MacPhail 1983), Early Historic (Barber 1981; Davidson & Simpson 1994, 68–71) and medieval (Romans & Robertson, 1983, 63) contexts. In the Roman period, animal manure was used extensively to improve soil fertility; the classical authors wrote in great detail on the best types of animal manure and which parts of the farm ought to be manured (Fenton 1981). The agricultural texts written by classical authors remained in use until the 18th century (Woodward 1994). Indeed, *plaggen* soils are often associated with medieval/ecclesiastical contexts, where it is argued (Barber 1981) that educated Christians like monks or priests had access to Roman texts that described how to improve ground for agriculture by the addition of manuring material.

The frequency of the exotic components identified within the Auldhame samples suggest that the soils around Auldhame have been the subject of heavy and extensive manuring, probably in an attempt to improve the fertility of the land by the addition of missing nutrients in the form of domestic refuse or fuel. However, given the recent wider applicability of the term, the soils at Auldhame can be described as *plaggen* soils only insofar as they are an artefact of human intervention without which it is unlikely that sustained cultivation and occupation of Auldhame would have been possible.

## 6.5 SUMMARY OF THE ECOFACTUAL EVIDENCE

The presence of food residues, in the form of animal bone, charred cereals and shellfish, is seemingly at odds with the ecclesiastical nature of the site but, in fact, the bulk of these residues were recovered from non-grave contexts, from the fills of ditches, pits, post-holes and other deposits. Animal bone was found in only two grave fills and charred plant remains in three grave fills, and in all cases the amounts were so small as to represent accidental inclusion in the fill.

With one exception, all the dated animal bone is from Phase 1 (Chapter 3), the exception being bone from one of the grave fills, which is 13th–14th-century in date (Figure 41). None of the plant remains have been dated but they mainly derive from the same contexts that have produced Phase 1 dates, and we would argue that all the food residues probably represent the same discard events. The presence of food residues implies the existence of a settlement on the headland and in Chapter 3 we suggested that this was monastic in nature, a proposition that will be more fully developed in Chapter 7.

Although the ecofact assemblage is very limited it is still possible to make some comment on the agricultural economy it represents. Barley was the main cultivar, with some wheat and possibly oats. The absence of chaff and minimal weed assemblage suggests that processing did not take place in the excavated portion of the site, although it could have taken place elsewhere on

# THE ECOFACT ASSEMBLAGE

the headland (see Chapter 7.2.2). The dominance of barley may be due to the poor nature of the sandy soils on the headland but the monastic community sought to improve their condition by manuring. Cattle, sheep and pigs were raised, primarily for meat and milk production; butchery marks were observed and there is no evidence that older animals were retained for traction. Bird bones were also recovered, suggesting that these may have been sources of food, too; butchery marks on bird bones from the Isle of May indicate that they were an important food resource there during the early medieval period (Smith 2008). They could also have been hunted for their eggs, feathers and fat. Marine resources were also, unsurprisingly, exploited; periwinkles and other shellfish were collected and fish were caught.

# CHAPTER 7

# LIVING AND DYING AT AULDHAME

## 7.1 INTRODUCTION

The radiocarbon dates distinguish up to four phases of activity on the site, each defined by clear breaks in burial activity (Chapter 3). However, the nature of that activity is such that it is perhaps more useful to discuss the evidence in terms of two major episodes: that relating to a monastic settlement some time between *c* AD 650 and *c* AD 1000; and the later use of the site as a parish church and graveyard, from *c* AD 1000 until *c* AD 1650 when the graveyard finally goes out of use. Although burial activity appears to be continuous throughout Phase 1 (Figure 39) it has been split into two, 1a relating to the monastic settlement and 1b relating to the distinct pulse of activity towards the very end of the phase, which, we will argue, relates to Viking activity in the graveyard.

### 7.1.1 Later prehistoric activity

Before moving on to discuss these major episodes we must consider the slight evidence for earlier activity on the headland. Before the excavations, the headland was considered to be an Iron Age promontory fort on account of the large ditch-like cropmark that cut across the neck of the headland (Figure 3). However, there are no radiocarbon dates to indicate any activity on the headland prior to the late 7th century AD and the only possible evidence for later prehistoric activity uncovered during the excavations amounts to a few sherds of undiagnostic pottery and some flints. There is some slight evidence that Ditch 1 may be the recut of an earlier ditch; it cuts through a deposit, [291], that looks like redeposited natural (Chapter 2.5.1) but the dating evidence for Ditch 1 is, unfortunately, inconclusive as it was never fully excavated. All that is certain is that it was backfilled some time after the 9th century AD (see below) so was clearly dug out before then. There is evidence of later prehistoric activity in the immediate environs of the site, including a cluster of cist burials (with crouched inhumations) along the shore beyond Seacliff, stone-paved roundhouses of the type found at Broxmouth hillfort, and the curious stone building on the Ghegan Rock from which artefacts of Roman provenance were found (see Chapter 1.3). Furthermore, the headland is an ideal location for a promontory fort and there are a string of such sites along this stretch of the North Sea coast (Kinghorn 1934). The possibility therefore remains that the ditch could have been a later prehistoric construction that was subsequently remodelled as the *vallum* ditch for the monastic settlement.

## 7.2 EPISODE 1: THE MONASTIC SETTLEMENT AD 650–1000

### 7.2.1 Anglian Lothian; the historical and archaeological context

*The historical context*

The context for this episode of activity at Auldhame is the Anglian occupation and settlement of the Lothians and the establishment of their brand of Christianity throughout the region. The period is roughly defined by two documented historical events; it begins with the siege of Edinburgh by Oswald, king of Northumbria in AD 638 and ends in AD 973 when Edgar of Wessex ceded Lothian to the Scottish king, Kenneth II. Anglian expansion into the Lothians had begun in the reign of Ethelfrith (AD 592–616). He had defeated the Gododdin at Catterick, in North Yorkshire *c* AD 600 and a few years later in AD 603 he defeated their ally, the Dalriadic king Aedan at *Degsastan*, an unidentified battleground probably in either the lower Tweed basin or in Liddesdale (Smyth 1984, 30). These defeats, and particularly the loss of the strategically important site of Catterick, will have seriously weakened the position of the northern British chieftains and it is probable that by the time of Ethelfrith's death in AD 616, Lothian was already a tributary state. Certainly, by the time of the siege of Edinburgh in AD 638 we can assume that at least those parts of Lothian to the south and east of Edinburgh had been effectively annexed by the Angles, even if we cannot assume that Edinburgh definitely fell into Anglian hands in that year (Smyth 1984, 31). However, excavation of a *Grübenhaus* atop a low hill at Ratho, Midlothian has produced radiocarbon dates indicating activity possibly as early as the late 6th century AD, so Anglian settlement of West Lothian may have been well advanced before the siege of Edinburgh (Smith 1995). That aside, the presence of early English place-names in East Lothian and Berwickshire, such as the *-ingaham* element in Whittinghame, Tyninghame and Coldingham, as well as the *-ham* element in Auldhame and Oldhamstocks, supports a mid-7th-century date for the settlement of Lothian (Smyth 1984, 31).

We have used words like battle, siege, defeat, annexation, all of which suggest an aggressive takeover, but the manner in which Lothian became part of the Northumbrian kingdom is moot. Rollason (2003, 65) has evaluated several models for the development of Northumbria and concludes that none are overwhelmingly plausible; *the following discussion is based primarily on his evaluation.* Some evidence points to a relatively peaceful transition from British to English rule, for instance the British names of known Anglian power centres Bamburgh (*Din Guoaroy*), Lindisfarne (*Broninis*), Dunbar (*Dynbaer*), Yeavering (*Ad Gefrin*), Milfield (*Maelmin*) and Coldingham (*Coludi urbs*). This is adduced as evidence that a Northumbrian elite took over these British centres, but left their associated administrative, political and social functions in place (Alcock 2003, 45), presumably allowing the British population to continue as before. The archaeological evidence from some of these sites (ie Yeavering, Milfield and Dunbar) tends to support this model (and see Doon Hill and Eldbotle below), indicating as it does supposed 'British' structures immediately prior to Northumbrian development of the site (Hope-Taylor 1977, 205–13; Perry 2000, 312–16). If the transition was a peaceful one, Rollason (2003, 89) argues that we should see the survival of native British land organisation, and in parts of Northumbria this may be adduced (ibid; and see Proudfoot & Aliaga-Kelly 1997).

However, this evidence has to be set against the written sources, in which relations between English and British are frequently portrayed as hostile (Rollason 2003, 100–3). Bede, in particular, appears to display an almost personal hatred of the British; however, this may simply reflect his personal hostility to the British as heretics (Alcock 2003, 45) rather than reflecting a real ethnic antagonism, or it could be seen as part of the process of defining ethnic identities that probably began in Bede's time (Rollason 2003, 103). Certainly, the archaeological evidence for violent conquest and subsequent decimation of the British population is ambiguous; the evidence for continuity of British settlement at some sites is slight and the pagan burial evidence can be interpreted to suit whatever model is favoured (ibid 93–9). By contrast, the use of the long-cist cemeteries, surely a British rite, into the 7th and 8th centuries implies the continued presence of a large British population in the Lothians (see below), while the survival of some place-name components also suggests that both the British language and British customs continued in this region, at the very least in small pockets (Rollason 2003, 61).

What constituted the Lothians in Anglian times? The most important site in the region in terms of secular status was probably that of Dunbar. Eddius Stephanus, in his *Life of Wilfrid* described the place as '*urbs sua Dynbaer*' – 'his (the Northumbrian king, Ecgfrith's) town of Dynbaer' – implying that it was a royal stronghold where Ecgfrith was able to imprison Wilfred, Bishop of York in AD 680 (Webb 1986). Furthermore, Eddius says that Dunbar was in the charge of a *praefectus*, interpreted as a royal official who may have had administrative responsibility for a region centred on Dunbar (Alcock 1988, 33). Proudfoot and Aliaga-Kelly (1997, 38) suggest that this region may have been that subsequently defined in the *Historia de Sancto Cuthberto* as 'all the land that pertains to the monastery of Saint Balthere which is called Tynningham, from the Lammermuir Hills to the mouth of the Esk'. The Lammermuirs form a natural southern boundary, while the Roman road, Dere Street, ends at the mouth of the Esk and will always have formed a significant mental and physical boundary in the post-Roman world (ibid 39). Ecgfrith is recorded as giving these lands to St Cuthbert and Lindisfarne but, as Proudfoot and Aliaga-Kelly point out, this is historically impossible as Ecgfrith died before Balthere's time. Rather, they suggest that the confusion may have arisen because Ecgfrith had granted lands with the same boundaries to Dunbar, and thus the association between Ecgfrith and these particular lands arose.

*The archaeological context; the evidence for settlement*

Place-name and documentary evidence notwithstanding, the physical evidence for Northumbrian activity in Lothian is not extensive. Excavations at Castle Park, Dunbar have revealed evidence that this was a fortified British tribal centre taken over by the Northumbrians (Perry 2000). There were many buildings of Northumbrian date and character (Perry 2000), rectangular earthfast timber buildings, including a *Grübenhaus*, which were later replaced by stone-footed timber buildings, many with semi-industrial functions. None of these buildings was of sufficient size and character to constitute the royal hall that one might expect to find in an *urbs regis* but this might lie outwith the excavated area. Perry (2000, 319) chose to interpret the only mortared stone structure found during the excavation as a royal hall, but Alcock (2003, 216) preferred to see this building as a church. Nonetheless, Dunbar's royal status, as implied by Eddius Stephanus' description, has been confirmed by the discovery of a mortar-mixer, a structure only associated with high-status sites elsewhere in Britain and on the Continent (Perry 2000, 319).

Northumbrian settlement archaeology has tended to be dominated by the identification of large earthfast timber buildings, traditionally referred to as halls, probably because of resonances with *Heorot*, the great feasting hall of the Beowulf epic (Alcock 2003, 245); hence the desire to find such a hall at Dunbar. These buildings are exemplified by the excavated examples at Yeavering (Hope-Taylor 1977) and have been identified as cropmarks at Milfield, Thirlings and Sprouston (Alcock 2003, 245–8). Within Lothian, timber halls have been identified at Doon Hill (Reynolds 1980), Whitekirk (Brown 1983) and Aberlady (Neighbour et al 1995; Tulloch & Davies 1998). Hope-Taylor (1977, 233) had argued that his 'Yeavering-style' halls (ie those of continuous trench construction) were insular developments, influenced by native, Romano-British construction techniques, and his excavations at Doon Hill, just inland from Dunbar tended to support that thesis. Here, a timber hall of continuous trench construction (B) had replaced an earlier post-built hall (A) which had been destroyed by fire, the footprint of (B) lying neatly within that of (A), and thus the argument followed that this represented Anglian destruction of a British building and its replacement with an Anglian hall (Hope-Taylor 1980; Reynolds 1980, 52). This argument has since been undermined by the subsequent dating of post-built timber buildings at Balbridie and Crathes, Aberdeenshire and Claish, Perthshire, which are identical in plan to Hall A at Doon Hill, to the Neolithic period (for summary see Murray et al 2009, 50–4). Nonetheless, the striking similarity between Hall B and the Yeavering trench-built halls remains and many writers prefer to accept its Northumbrian date (Smith 1991, 267), Alcock (2003, 263) suggesting that Doon Hill is a lesser royal centre in the Northumbrian settlement pattern of Lothian.

The hall on Doon Hill sits within a polygonal palisaded enclosure, and large enclosures are a distinctive characteristic of other high status Northumbrian sites, such as Milfield, Yeavering and Sprouston (Alcock 2003, 234–5). The other known hall sites in Lothian, at Aberlady and Whitekirk, are not enclosed. The cropmark evidence at Whitekirk shows two large halls and a row of small rectangular enclosures, within which are what may be small buildings (Brown 1983). Smith (1991, 286) has suggested that the absence of enclosure at Whitekirk implies a lesser status, and that it could have been a *vill*, a township subordinate to the royal centre at Dunbar. Lowe (1999, 33), on the other hand, has suggested that the Whitekirk settlement could be a small farmstead attached to the monastery at Tyninghame (but see below). At Aberlady, radiometer and resistivity survey around Kilspindie Castle has also revealed two timber halls, one overlying the other, and a series of ditch-defined enclosures (Neighbour et al 1995; Tulloch & Davies 1998).

Only two other sites in the Lothians have yielded evidence of Northumbrian settlement, at Eldbotle, near North Berwick, and Ratho, in Midlothian. The place-name Eldbotle is Northumbrian in origin; *Eld-bōtl* means 'old hall or building' (Nicolaisen 1976, 77), so an Anglian settlement at Eldbotle was always anticipated (Proudfoot & Aliaga-Kelly 1997). Excavations there have revealed a first phase of curvilinear cut features with associated radiocarbon dates spanning the 5th to 7th centuries AD, followed by a second phase of more cut features with radiocarbon dates spanning the 9th to 11th centuries AD (Morrison et al 2008). The features were only investigated in a narrow trench so their full extent was not exposed, but their profile and fill suggest that they are probably the remains of post-in-trench timber buildings, one of which appears to be sub-rectangular in plan (ibid fig. 4). The place-name component *bōtl* went out of use by the end of the 9th century so it must have been applied to the site between *c* AD 600 and *c* AD 900, while the use of *Eld*, old, in the place-name implies the existence of an earlier settlement (ibid). The excavators have therefore suggested that the excavated features represent a British settlement that was subsequently taken over by Northumbrian settlers.

The evidence for Anglian settlement at Ratho consisted of a palisade enclosing a sunken-featured building, a *Grübenhaus* interpreted as a weaving workshop on account of the assemblage of clay loomweights found within it, situated on a low hill with commanding views (Smith 1995). Two small rectilinear, post-in-trench buildings that lie outside the palisade may also belong to the Anglian settlement. Radiocarbon dates from the sunken-featured building indicate activity from the 6th to 9th centuries AD (ibid 111).

*The archaeological context; the artefactual evidence*

The 'personal archaeology' of Anglian expansion and settlement into southern Scotland, in the form of weapons, jewellery and the like, is hard to trace (Lowe 1999, 30), due largely to the absence of pagan Anglian unfurnished graves in southern Scotland. While Anglo-Saxon artefacts remain scarce, the number is increasing. Laing (1973) and Proudfoot and Aliaga-Kelly (1996) are still the standard works, but these lists are being augmented by re-analysis of old finds and by recent discoveries, largely from metal detecting (eg Blackwell 2004). Taking East Lothian and the Borders as a convenient study area, there are now over 20 findspots of Anglo-Saxon material. In East Lothian, recent finds include the Aberlady assemblage, which is the largest collection of finds from the area and includes various pins, a sword pommel, coins and strap ends (Hunter 2001; 2002; Sheils 2001). The equally impressive gold and garnet circular domed sword button from Markle (Proudfoot & Aliaga-Kelly 1996, 4), with its similarities to those found with the sword at Sutton Hoo, is another welcome addition to the East Lothian corpus.

Interpreting these finds is problematic. Some commentators (eg Proudfoot & Aliaga-Kelly 1996; Cessford 1999) view such finds as indicative of Anglo-Saxon presence within the landscape. While this may be valid, it does not necessarily follow that there is an automatic relationship between specific material cultures and the presence of an ethnic group. As Blackwell (2004, 53) reminds us, we cannot simply equate the presence of Northumbrian material culture with the presence of Anglo-Saxons in south-east Scotland. While such a presence is likely, we cannot say that every Northumbrian artefact belonged to a Northumbrian person. It is, perhaps, safer to suggest that the finds reveal Northumbrian influence in the area.

The Auldhame assemblage is a significant contribution to the expanding corpus of Anglo-Saxon material from northern Northumbria (see Chapter 4.1.1).

*Early Christianity in Lothian*

The period of Anglian annexation of Lothian coincides with the conversion of the Angles to Christianity, although secular conquest probably preceded ecclesiastical expansion (Thomas 1984, 327). However, there were already Christian communities in the lands they annexed. These communities are represented in the archaeological record by the numerous long-cist cemeteries that have been found, predominantly in the Lothians, Fife and Angus (Proudfoot 1996, illus 28; Rees 2002, illus 40). Excavated examples in Lothian include Thornybank (Rees 2002) and Parkburn (Henshall 1956), both near Dalkeith; the Catstane, near Edinburgh (Cowie 1978); and Kingston Common, North Berwick (Suddaby 2009). These cemeteries can contain as many as 200 burials, although estimates of up to 500 burials have been made for some (Henshall 1956, 267; and see below). They are characterised by burial in either stone-lined graves or simple dug graves, which are generally aligned east–west but with considerable variation to north and south of those cardinal points. The graves tend to be loosely organised in rows and there is rarely evidence of intercutting, suggesting either the use of grave markers and/or the presence of a custodian (Rees 2002, 350). The east–west alignment, the absence of grave goods and, in the case of the Catstane, the association of cemetery with a stone with Christian inscription, all point to a Christian burial rite. There are sizeable assemblages of radiocarbon dates from Thornybank and from Hallow Hill, in Fife (Proudfoot 1996) and these indicate burial activity from the mid-5th to 9th centuries AD. At Thornybank, Rees (2002, 349) infers a peak in burial activity between the mid-5th century and the mid-6th century, while at Hallow Hill, Proudfoot (1996, 423) identifies a floruit of activity in the 7th century AD.

Clearly, then, there were thriving Christian communities in the Lothians by the time the Northumbrians arrived. Rees (2002, 347) suggests that the concentration of long-cist cemeteries on the Lothian plain reflects a large, settled, organised population, amongst whom Christianity was widespread and who rapidly adopted an egalitarian

# LIVING AND DYING AT AULDHAME

mainland Scotland there are examples from Caithness, Sutherland, Galloway, Elgin, Moray and Perth. To date, Auldhame is the most southerly example known from Scotland.

However, it is more appropriate to consider the Auldhame grave within the ever expanding corpus from northern England, particularly Cumbria, which lies only 120 miles from Auldhame (see Richards 2004; Speed & Walton Rogers 2004; Redmond 2007; Griffiths 2010; Paterson et al 2014; McCarthy 2014). Importantly, like the Auldhame example, many of the graves from this area were furnished with weapons (including spearheads) and with horse spurs and associated fittings, the various graves at Cumwhitton, Aspatria and Hesket-in-the Forest being excellent examples (see Wilson 2008, 52–3; Griffiths 2010, 89–96; Paterson et al 2014, 161–70; figs 123–4 for recent overviews). Further, the excavations at Carlisle Cathedral revealed a collection of Viking Age metalwork, including a copper alloy buckle-set; the closest parallels are from Cnip and Auldhame (Paterson & Tweddle 2014, 217–18, illus 19). There can be little doubt then that the Auldhame grave should best be viewed within this wider Cumbrian corpus.

Indeed, as well as looking south to understand the wider cultural affiliations of the Auldhame assemblage, we also need to look west. As many argue (eg Richards 2004, 190) graves found in the north-west should be viewed as part of a distribution of Norse burials in the areas bordering the Irish Sea with many reflecting a similar culture in those graves known from, for example, the Isle of Man (see also Paterson et al 2014, 166–7 for a useful summary). As stressed in Chapter 4, links with the Irish Sea, Isle of Man and Auldhame are clear. As Walton Rogers (Chapter 4.2.1) outlines, the two belt fittings from the furnished grave belong to a distinctive group of metalwork found in Viking Age sites around the Irish Sea and in the Scottish Islands (Grieg 1940, 48–58, 67–9; Bersu & Wilson 1966, 19–26, Pls V–VI; Graham-Campbell 1973; Laing 1993, 38–9, 84–8; Thomas 2001, 45–6; 2004, 4–5; Paterson 2001, 127–9). Indeed, buckles, strap ends, and bridle and harness fittings have all been found within this corpus, for example at Kiloran Bay and Balladoole, Isle of Man. As noted earlier, the Auldhame prick spurs are comparable to examples known from Balladoole, Isle of Man (Bersu & Wilson 1966, 35–6, fig. 25) but we should also remember that some of the Auldhame artefacts find parallels slightly farther south in England, particularly in York (see Chapter 4, above).

In summary, the Viking Age grave at Auldhame could be more usefully seen as part of a corpus with strong links to groups in and around the Irish Sea, the Isle of Man and northern England in particular. As Walton Rogers has argued, it is possible that the buckle and strap end from the Auldhame grave had been made for horse bridles or harnesses somewhere in the Irish Sea region, possibly even in Dublin, in the late 9th or 10th century. If so, the Auldhame example lies on the north-eastern edge of this group's distribution. With this in mind we should reflect on Paterson et al's (2014, 172) comment that 'the evidence would suggest that the people buried at Cumwhitton were clearly influenced in their cultural choices by association with Viking settlements in Scotland, and probably also Man ... it might be possible to speculate that the original settlers came from the north, but were open to influence from the south and east through the conduit of the Eden Valley'.

*Interpreting the furnished grave within its immediate context*

Above, the discussion focused on the broader geographical context of the Auldhame grave. But what does it also tell us about the Viking presence in East Lothian? Walton Rogers (Chapter 4.2.1) has suggested that the belt set may have reached East Lothian with a traveller, as merchandise, or by down-the-line exchange. In considering the meagre and sporadic archaeological evidence for Viking activity from south-east Scotland, Graham-Campbell and Batey (1998, 105) suggest that there is certainly nothing to indicate large-scale land-taking, and suggest two possibilities. First, the meagre evidence is indicative of refugees. Second, and based largely on the 9th/10th-century Hiberno-Viking arm-ring from the Gordon hoard, which may point to an Irish Sea connection, it is possible that some of the evidence is due to the activities of Ragnall, a member of the Scandinavian dynasty of Dublin, who raided and fought in the lowlands during the second decade of the 10th century, before he took the throne in York.

Perhaps one of the most interesting aspects of the Auldhame assemblage is its recovery from a site that was recently a thriving monastic settlement. The Scottish Norse settlers do not seem to have had any obvious desire to bury their dead in existing Christian cemeteries. Although the axe from St Olaf's Churchyard, Whiteness and the recent finds from Mail, Shetland may represent such activity, Viking graves in Scottish Christian cemeteries are rarely found (see

143

Graham-Campbell & Batey 1998, 144). However, the practice is well documented, for example, in the Isle of Man (eg Bersu & Wilson 1966, xiii–xiv; Wilson 2008, 51) and Ireland (Harrison 2001). Similar occurrences have been noted in Denmark and in other parts of Scandinavia (Krogh & Voss 1961) and in England (see below). Taking a wider view, there does appear to have been a tradition by some incoming Viking groups to bury their dead in existing Christian cemeteries. So what does this mean?

Richards (2003; 2004) has recently discussed this theme and highlighted the often contradictory interpretations. On the one hand, some scholars still uphold the Viking warrior image whereby they worshipped violent and unforgiving gods and had a complete disregard for Christian ethics. This is often the interpretation for many of the burials found during the early to mid-20th century. For example, violent, marauding pagan behaviour has been the explanation for the Viking burial inserted into the pre-existing Christian cemetery at Balladoole (for a summary, see Tarlow 1997, 139–40; and Wilson 2008, 38–46). In publishing the original report some 30 years previous, the excavator states:

> I still feel inclined to suggest, therefore, that the pagan Viking was buried intentionally above the slightly earlier burials of the Christians who lived in the island before the advent of the Vikings. The Vikings may have wished to demonstrate that they were now masters in the island and, for that reason, deliberately slighted the Christian community with this pagan burial of a personality of high rank (Bersu & Wilson 1966, 13)

Wilson (2008, 46) has recently toned down these earlier suggestions, suggesting that the grave 'represents at least an acceptance … of the sacred nature of the site, while following the pagan-burial rite of Scandinavia. At the same time it symbolised the power and status of the new settler – a wealthy landowner with a background as a warrior. The weapons and horse trappings found … show that they were burials of mean of wealth and status'.

This movement away from explanations centred solely on violence and desecration have become more widespread over the last two decades. Some scholars now argue for peaceful immigrants and traders eager to take on all the trappings of the host society, including its religion. In Anglo-Saxon England, within the space of a single generation, pagan warriors had become Christian farmers and Christian burial was rapidly adopted, with many choosing to be buried in churchyards (Graham-Campbell 1980). As Richards (2003, 383) comments, 'the rapid conversion of Scandinavian settlers, so we are led to believe, demonstrates the weakness of their own pagan religions in the face of an all-embracing Christianity, and provides another example of their eagerness to become assimilated'. Wilson (2008, 56) argues that perhaps Christianity was the agent that ultimately helped to solve the tensions between the incomers and the natives – a tension that was often released fairly quickly.

However, as recent studies have shown (eg Hadley 2000; 2001; Halsall 2000; Richards 2003; 2004), there is great variety in burial practices in late Anglo-Saxon England, which defies simple classification into pagan and Christian. Different approaches were adopted in different situations. In other words, when considering Viking graves, pagan or otherwise, we would do well to look at the specifics of the immediate region and locale in which they have been found.

*Desecration and domination?*

The Auldhame individuals were interred in an existing graveyard. One view could be that, as argued for Balladoole (*sensu* Tarlow 1997), this represents a dominant Viking presence wishing to demonstrate their social and political control over the new order. As outlined in Chapter 3.2.1, radiocarbon dates suggest that midden accumulation, and by implication the monastic settlement, had ceased *c* AD 850–900. We know that during this period Viking attacks were taking place along the North Sea littoral, and in the Northumbrian heartlands. Did they prompt the abandonment of monastic settlement at Auldhame at about this time, with the community moving to Tyninghame, perhaps considered a safer location, taking with them St Balthere's relics? (The relics were reportedly at Tyninghame in the early 11th century when Aelfred, a priest from Durham, dug them up and removed them to Durham for display and veneration; Woolf 2007, 235.) Auldhame may have gone into abeyance after this, although the chapel probably continued to function, as witnessed by the late burials in the graveyard, while Tyninghame became pre-eminent as the location of Balthere's relics. This may thus explain the dual nature of the attack in AD 941, on St Balthere's chapel *and* Tyninghame (see above). The wounds on one of the Auldhame dead also suggest some form of conflict. The strategic position of the site should also not be overlooked. Auldhame sits on a prominent clifftop, with views over the entrance to the Firth of Forth (Figure 89).

*Symbolism and legitimisation?*

But this interpretation may be too simplistic. The recovery of Viking artefacts and graves from churchyards in northern Britain, Isle of Man and Ireland gives some support to the idea that some pagan Vikings chose to associate themselves with churchyard sites and that many Scandinavian settlers were using established cemeteries (Richards 2004, 202, 205; Griffiths 2010, 96–9). We have seen that by the late 8th century the monastic settlement at Auldhame was well established, a principal ecclesiastical centre, and linked to important individuals, saints and groups. Scores of individuals were buried in the graveyard. The Vikings could not have failed to understand the symbolic as well as tactical significance of seizing a significant holy place of Christendom. Perhaps its continuing use by the new group suggests a desire to gain authority by association.

It could be argued that the Vikings invested effort in maintaining the legitimacy of the site. None of the five graves cut, disturb or desecrate the earlier burials in the manner of, say, Balladoole. It may be significant that the graves encircle the chapel (Figure 40). Indeed, although difficult to prove, the monastic building may also have been remodelled during this period. Perhaps the burials were placed around the existing building and within the graveyard boundaries because of the powerful associations of burial next to saintly relics. Indeed, there is a strong suggestion that the individuals who were burying the dead (at least the individual in the furnished burial) were keeping their options open. This is not a new phenomenon; the same practice is suggested at, for example, Kiloran Bay, Colonsay. The five unfurnished burials may suggest that full conversion to archetypal Christian burial practices may have happened in a few generations.

In other words, although the Vikings may have had a strong hand to play in the cessation and abandonment of the Anglo-Saxon monastic graveyard at Auldhame, it can be argued that the site itself still had a significant, continuing socio-political role to play in the lives of those who came to inhabit the surrounding landscape, intermittently or otherwise. There appears to have been a continuity of purpose and a degree of accommodation of existing practices and establishments. Indeed, one could argue that those Vikings buried at Auldhame were seeking to legitimise themselves by their association with a principal ecclesiastical centre, and while some maintained some pagan trappings, others found it expedient to allow themselves to be converted to Christianity. This is not unparalleled; as has been suggested for Repton, in Derbyshire (Richards 2003), perhaps Auldhame provided the perfect location for the demonstration of new spiritual convictions combined with political/military subjugation. It was expedient for newcomers to align themselves with existing elite practices. From the burial evidence it appears that the new identity frequently included the adoption of Christianity. Scandinavian settlers were particularly adaptable to local circumstance, and so was their religion (see Richards 2004, 211–12; and also Wilson 2008, 56).

## 7.3 EPISODE 2: THE PARISH CHURCH AND GRAVEYARD AD 1000–1650

### 7.3.1 A documentary history of Auldhame from AD 1000 to c AD 1830

MORAG CROSS

There are two immediately notable features of the site of Auldhame Church, the first being that the view is dominated by the Bass Rock, which is 1.5 miles (2.5km) due north (Figure 1). Auldhame was built above the nearest accessible landing place to the island, and they share strong historical ties. Secondly, the boundaries of the medieval parish follow those of the modern estate of Seacliff, which covers only 750 acres (T Dale pers comm). This makes it smaller than Morham and Bara in East Lothian, and must make it one of the smallest parishes in mainland Scotland (Martine 1883, 291; B Patterson pers comm).

Churches were once considered as accessory to, or appurtenances of, the ground on which they stood, conveyed with the land but incidental to it (Cowan 1995b 5–6; Morgan 1947, 136–7). Auldhame has been overlooked in the same way. It is impossible to discuss this parish without also considering its larger parochial neighbours, Whitekirk and Tyninghame, to which Auldhame was an adjunct. Diminutive Auldhame was first annexed to Tyninghame parish in July 1618 (St A, SM110/SB25/13), and that conjoined entity then united with Whitekirk in August 1761 (Ritchie 1880, 22; NAS, CH2/371/4/4), to form the modern tripartite unit of 'Whitekirk and Tyninghame' (Figure 1).

George Chalmers, an early authority, wrongly linked Auldhame with Whitekirk, and this error has since been continuously reproduced (Chalmers 1889, IV, 547; *Fasti* I, 422; NAS, Online Public Catalogue (Opac) entry for CH2/371, Administrative History; NMRS, NT68SW 17). Auldhame was part of Tyninghame first, not Whitekirk. The date of union had previously been given as 1619, but this too has now been revised by new research (Ritchie 1880, 22; St A, SM110/SB25/13).

There seems to have been a gradual change to a possibly pre-/semi-parochial or minster-centred burial system by the 10th–11th centuries (Owen 2003, 250; Proudfoot 1998, 57, 61, 66; 2011, pers comm). The early emergence of proto-parishes may support the apparent antiquity of Auldhame's survival as a complete land unit of some sort, whether it was originally a *vill*, an entire estate or some form of parish. Indeed, the early establishment of embryonic or proto-parishes around Lothian, under Northumbrian influence has already been suggested (Cowan 1995b 2, 3–4; Crowe 2003, 201, 204–5; Morgan 1947 135, 144–5; Rogers 1997, 70, 73).

The case for the great age of Auldhame's territorial integrity is also supported by two early sources once credited to Symeon of Durham (d. *c* 1130): his *History of the Kings of England*, as well as the anonymous *Historia de Sancto Cuthberto (HSC)*. HSC has been characterised as a 'cartulary ... in a narrative form', probably engrossing parts of charters, which were otherwise lost during the Viking attacks of the 9th century (Hinde 1868, xxxvi). At this period, the bishopric of Lindisfarne's territories stretched 'beyond the Tweed ... and all the land which lies between ... [the] Blackadder and ... Leader ... and all the land that pertains to the monastery of Saint Balthere which is called Tynningham, from the Lammermuir Hills [to Inveresk]' (*HSC* 4, text given in Johnson South 2002, 47). In the *History of the Kings*, the same area of Lothian is described as if in a confirmation charter. 'These manors ... the two Jedburghs ... Melrose ... Edinburgh, and Pefferham, and Aldham, and Tiningham', according to Symeon, all belong to the church by AD 854 (Stevenson 1858, 72).

As Pefferham is unidentified (Proudfoot & Aliaga-Kelly 1995, 21, 23), if the three 'ham' settlements were 'manors', this might explain why they were allegedly gifted to Lindisfarne. The otherwise anomalous size of Auldhame parish may fossilise the form of an early estate component.

Rollason notes the compound, and hence possibly dateable, form of these names, 'peffer' being an existing British and (Tyn)'ingaham' an early Anglian form. This might suggest a settlement, if not a monastic community, at Tyninghame, during or even predating Baldred's floruit of the mid-8th century.

The ceremonial consecration of graveyards like Auldhame was a later medieval concern, as initially it was believed that it was actual proximity to the saint's shrine itself, or burial 'at the saint' (*ad sanctos*) that conferred the benefits of sanctity (Zadora-Rio 2003, 11–13; Aries 1981, 32–3). St Baldred was apparently miraculously buried, simultaneously, at Tyninghame, Whitekirk and Auldhame. If Auldhame was initially a burial place *ad sanctos*, as was the case on the nearby, and intervisible, Isle of May, the body of the tutelary saint has not yet been identified. However, his supposed presence might account for the longevity of the site, as later burials were also attracted to the cells of St Marnock on Inchmarnock, and St Ethernan on the May, which likewise continued as places of minor pilgrimage into the medieval period (James & Yeoman 2008, 5, 182; Yeoman 1999, 63–4, 106; Ernan, Inchmarnock – Oram 2008, 48–9; Butter 2008, 53–4; Lowe 2008, 267–9; Dawson 2007, 70).

In Lothian, the fate of the lands and churches of St Baldred appears obscure from 941 until 1094 (Lawrie 1905, 242), when the first Scottish written evidence appears. However, the story of the relic 'pilferer' Aelfred at Auldhame may reveal the extent of 'the province of the Northumbrians', in the 1020s (Woolf 2007, 240). Aelfred, an assiduously pious priest of Durham, 'raised from the earth the bones ... of those saints ... and enshrined them above ground, so that they might be ... venerated ... [including] the bones ... [of] Balthere and Bilfrith ...' (Rollason 2000, 163–5). Woolf (2007, 235–6) suggests the relics' findspots are all within a single polity, the earldom of Northumbria, which would have to have included Tyninghame at this late date, if he is correct.

A charter of 1094, by King Duncan II, eldest son of Malcolm Canmore and Ingibjorg, can be interpreted contrary to Woolf's suggestions. This document has generated lengthy discussions as to whether it is genuine or an anachronistic forgery to buttress Durham's traditional claims to 'holy suzerainty' over Lothian (Duncan 1958; 1999;

Donnelly 1989). If spurious, the charter may tell us little about Auldhame in 1094, but it is worth assuming its authenticity for the present, if only for its circumstantial value.

Duncan was raised in England, and accepted as king in Scotland only if he introduced no more Norman followers or customs (Barrow 2003a, 250; Duncan 1958, 125; Oram 2006, 58). Although king for only a few months, he granted Scottish land to a Norman Benedictine monastery in Northumbria, perhaps acknowledging his fealty to the king of England, and in fulfilment of his own father's promised benefactions (Duncan 1958, 120; 1996, 125; 1999, 4, 34).

Firstly, Duncan felt able to grant this territory (apparently not royal demesne), despite it previously being held by the bishop of St Andrews, Fothad (d. 1093; Angus 1926, 6, 9; Donnelly 1989, 6; Lawrie 1905, 242). This may betoken a lack of regard for the 'Celtic' church at Kilrimond, and a premium placed on the 'reformed' church of Durham (Rollason 2003, 280). The charter mentions what may be vills constituting parts of a single estate, namely 'Tiningeham Aldeham Scuchale Cnolle Hatheruuich et de Broccesmuthe' (Duncan 1958, 119; Lawrie 1905, No. 12). Alternatively, these may each be self-contained manors in their own rights because until the 17th century, Auldhame and Scoughall estates, at least, formed separate properties, although they were both in the same parish (ie Auldhame). Equally, these may be the lands associated in folk memory with the presumably defunct Tyninghame monastery (Donnelly 1989, 22).

Secondly, the charter concedes that the bishop of St Andrews had rights (characterised by its Durham writers, at least, as if they were using feudal formulae; Duncan 1999, 12) and that he received customary service from around Tyninghame (Barrow 2003a, 29, n140). It acknowledges Fothad's privileges, rather than just stating baldly that his rivals in Durham had prior and superior claims on the same territory (Duncan 1958, 119; 1999, 3, 4). This acknowledgement may suggest authenticity – its inclusion adds little to Durham's case (Duncan 1958, 120). Duncan (1999, 3–4) sees the charter as the culmination of a long-term strategy to recover St Cuthbert's 'ancestral' lands.

The grant was never operational, however; it was made while Duncan II was still a mere claimant to the throne and may have been regarded as void by his death soon after (Duncan 1958, 120; Lawrie 1905, 241–2; Donnelly 1989, 3–4). His successor had policies hostile to Duncan, and the see of St Andrews remained empty (Duncan 1996, 125, 127–8) so that there was neither need nor pressure for St Andrews (or the Pope; Donnelly 1989, 18) to ratify the grant (even if such a thing had been common practice at the time; Morgan 1947, 137–8).

*Auldhame parish and land division in Lothian*

Commentators on the lists of Lindisfarne's possessions have missed the fact that Auldhame formed its own pre-Reformation parish, and have annexed it to Tyninghame, which did not happen until 1618 (St A, SM110/SB25/13; Craster 1954, 179; Johnson South 2002, 80). As has been noted above, Auldhame is unusually small compared to the surrounding medieval parishes, and is now farmed as a single unit. Other such 'reduced' or 'anomalous' ecclesiastical territories tended to become amalgamated with their neighbours, for example Altermunin (Antermony now in Campsie parish), which ceased separate mention by 1221 (Cowan 1967, 6; *Kelso Liber* No. 226, 230–1; No. II, 386). Others 'failed' and never attained parochial status, such as Birgham, a chaplainry of Eccles (Barrow 2003a, 23). Cowan (1995a, 13) states that 98 parishes vanished before the Reformation; others such as Snow in Aberdeen did not survive it Cowan 1967, 2) and the status of others seems uncertain, including Haliburton, Berwickshire (Hamilton 2007, 31–2 and n; Cowan 1967, 80).

Much has been written about the land division in the Lothian part of the diocese of Lindisfarne and St Andrews, before the reign of David I in 1124 (Barrow 2003a, 233–9; Craster 1954; Proudfoot & Aliaga-Kelly 1997; Johnson South 2002, 79–80, 124–9). Barrow (2003a, 304) stresses 'the fact that . . . the royal sheriff or vicecomes seems to have simply evolved from the older pre-feudal scir-gerefa or officer in charge of a multiple [or composite] estate only serves to emphasize the conservatism and continuity of Northumbria whether English or Scots'. The endurance of Auldhame, as a fossilised unit of defunct land division, may be due to precisely this Northumbrian traditionalism in land management.

There would seem to be various possibilities as to what Auldhame's survival represents, and whether as an area it is complete in itself or only part of a larger pre-feudal British or Anglian whole. Johnson South (2002, 124–9) has analysed the various vills, or constituents, of Durham's pre-conquest composite estates on the ground and found congruent parcels of land, each adjoining, containing 6 or 12 vills or townships (Johnson South 2002, 113–15, 126–7). If the list in Duncan II's charter is mapped, a line of six littoral properties running from the northernmost, Auldhame, to the southern, Broxmouth, emerges (Figure 1), viz 'Tiningeham Aldeham Scuchale (Scoughall) Cnolle (Knowes) Hatheruuich (Hedderwick) ... [and] Broccesmuthe (Broxmouth)' (Lawrie 1905, No. 12). It is suggested that the initial property, here Tyninghame, indicates by its position on the list that it is the caput, or centre of the estate (Johnson South 2002, 128; Proudfoot & Aliaga-Kelly 1997, 38).

In this scenario, Auldhame and Scoughall would be *appendici* (Johnson South 2002, 128), remnants of a once more believable and economically viable multiple estate, such as has been proposed by Proudfoot and Aliaga-Kelly (1997, 35–6, 38–42) around Manor Valley, Peeblesshire, at Hownam Law, Roxburghshire and at Inveresk. Lawrie (1905, 242) breaks the 1094 list into two estates, Broxmouth and Hedderwick forming one, and the other four names forming the other. Barrow (2003a, 29) follows a similar line: 'Tyninghame in East Lothian was clearly a shire in 1094, even if a reduced one; it had four dependencies and tribute from a fifth, and was held with sake and soke.' There was a thane at Haddington, a neighbouring district, and the shire's 'characteristic features of fee-farm ... money rents, seasonal ploughing ... carrying duties [and] tribute [in kind]' are also readily found in the surrounding area (Barrow 2003a, 29).

It has been generally agreed that many churches predate the formal parish creations of the reign of David I, often starting as proprietary churches, built by landowners on estates whose boundaries are mirrored by the later parishes (Clancy 1995, 104–5; Cowan 1995b, 4–8; Lynch 1992, 81–2; Rogers 1997, 69–72). Many parishes were then 'appropriated', or gifted by their patron to a bishopric or monastic body, accompanied by endowments such as land, the right to appoint priests (advowson) and the right to collect teind and other dues (Cowan 1995a; Duncan 1996, 296–300). Neighbouring Tyninghame Church 'was reputedly granted to the priory of St Andrews ... in 1144 [but] the lands of Tyninghame belonged to the bishop ... from an early date' (Cowan 1967, 203).

If it is a pre-feudal survival, Auldhame may preserve the outline of a unit of lordship that owed some duty to the bishops of St Andrews. The episcopal demesne, or 'mensal' lands (for the personal support of the bishop) in Lothian included baronies based on Stow and Tyninghame, 'ancient ecclesiastical sites ... [that] could have come into the [mensa] before 1000 ... [bishop] Fothad enjoyed *servitiium* from Broxmouth, a few miles from Tyninghame' (Anderson 1976, 7–8; Duncan 1999, 14, n147). The inclusion of similar rights in 1094 would appear to be of no advantage if Duncan II's charter was a forgery. Such dues or privileges 'built up in an undocumented period' can survive, fossilising an otherwise defunct connection between church bodies (Barrell 2000, 44–5). Although it was formally unappropriated (ie a self-governing parsonage), Auldhame nonetheless had some enduring and personal connection with the bishops of St Andrews, the nature of which is unclear (discussed below).

Auldhame was one of only 14% of medieval churches that were 'free parsonages', which alone makes Auldhame unusual (Cowan 1995a, 13–14). Auldhame's proprietors, before the 16th century, are unknown, but it may have been someone sufficiently influential to retain the parish for themselves. Alternatively, as two of the first documented owners are closely connected with the hierarchy of St Andrews archdiocese, it may have been an 'unofficial' mensal property, used to sustain the clergy's family or other followers (as compared with the official mensal estate of Tyninghame; Barrow 1994, 2).

The miracle of Baldred's triplicated corpses, whereby each of three squabbling parishes, Tyninghame, Whitekirk and Auldhame, could bury an equal and complete share of his remains, may preserve some memory of the astute resolution of a dispute over relics between three pre-existing foundations or landowners. A similar such compromise can be seen in 12th-century Dunsyre and Thankerton, 'where the lands were divided, difficulties were avoided by the two lords jointly bestowing the churches on Kelso, in language which implies that each lord gave the whole church' (Morgan 1947, 142).

Whether secular or ecclesiastical, church patrons placed great importance on control of lucrative holy relics. The excavation did not discover whether there is a focal burial in the church, but it may have been too late anyway. As discussed above, Aelfred, a priest of Durham, allegedly removed the saint's body in the 1020s (Woolf 2007, 235, 240; Rollason 2000, 163–5), though it would be interesting to know whether he went to each of Baldred's three graves, and how many corpses he retrieved. As with the multiple burials, Aelfred's story may be a vague recollection of various competing claims to Baldred's relics (or appreciation of their income-generating potential).

The requirements for a parish church during the 12th century became formalised to include the right of baptism, the celebration of Easter Mass and the collection of the teind or tax in cash and kind, on the produce of the parish (Barrow 2003b, 82–3; Cowan 1995b, 8, 10). The enforcement of teind by royal command helped to consolidate the concept of the parish as the 'tribute-area' of the church, which would provide the clerical living (Duncan 1996, 298–9; Barrow 1960, 65–6; 1971, 73). By this standard, Auldhame looks surprisingly small, and to try and support even one non-labouring rector (let alone a vicar as well), from agricultural land of just eight ploughgates (as reckoned in 1798; NAS, CH2/371/7/33) must have seemed rather ambitious, even when the boundaries were first perambulated (Donnelly 1997, 65–6; Duncan 1996, 298, 301–2). A ploughgate was traditionally the area ploughed by an eight-oxen team in a year, which varied by soil type but is nominally reckoned at 104 acres today (Duncan 1996, 311–13). The situation at Inchmarnock, counted as a parish at 660 acres, is different because that is of self-limiting extent, being an island, whereas Auldhame has been artificially delineated, ending on the south at the Pilmure Burn (Oram 2008, 49; Ritchie 1880, 22). The fact that Auldhame is so small, whether spiritual or temporal purposes are being considered, further suggests that its form antedates the parish, and reflects some older pre-existing, and possibly secular, arrangement.

*Auldhame, the Bass and the sea*

The longevity of Auldhame as a territorial unit may have been partly due to its economic resources, which look to the sea. The discovery of dog-whelks in large quantities has raised the possibility that the site was being used as a collection or processing plant for the manufacture of purple dye/pigment (Chapter 7.2.2). Fraser (2009, 171–2) suggests that the Bernician expansion into Lothian by the 650s was motivated partly to control traffic between and access to the holy sites of Iona and Lindisfarne, and for the movement of luxury goods imported via the Irish Sea.

The continuity of the church corporation, and its permanent, indivisible and inalienable (in theory) land-tenure, enabled 'long-term strategies of [economic] exploitation [to] be developed' (Woolf 2007, 34, 35).

The production of dye/pigment may have been one reason for the continuing interest of the bishops of St Andrews in Auldhame, despite its small size and seeming poverty. The myriad uses of sulan geese from the Bass, and the harvesting of 'seaware' or seaweed on Scoughall beach may also have added to Auldhame's economic potential.

The physical and spiritual qualities of littoral sites were not lost on early observers. As well as the panorama of the even earlier Christian Isle of May and the Bass offshore, seemingly aligned with Auldhame, the symbolic value of a liminal burial had obvious appeal, representing the boundary of life and death. This had pagan origins: 'Beowulf's barrow was deliberately constructed on a cliff overlooking the sea' (Daniell 1997, 100). Martin Carver (2004, 26, 28) notes the significance of the degrees of intervisibility of the early Christian sculptures at Portmahomack, on promontories adjacent to their churches, and the sea: 'The corollary is that travellers on the sea could likewise see one of them, and so be guided to a landing place and an official reception' (Carver 2004, 26). This may be paralleled by Auldhame in relation to the Isle of May and the Bass Rock, where Seacliff beach was long used as a landing place. The Viking raiders of 941 would also have taken advantage of this. Such 'kidnap by sea' is given a human face in a church record of 1757, relating to the infamous naval recruitment by 'press gangs' who seized men working on beaches: 'To Helen Norwall, spouse of Robert Mason, fisher at Scougal, [parish donation] ... her husband being latly press'd into His Majestie's Service ... £2' (NAS, CH2/359/6/93, 28 July 1757).

Auldhame's geographical, and conceptual, position in relation to the Bass Rock is emphasised in a charter by the bishop of St Andrews to Robert Lauder of Bass in 1316 (McCrie 1848, Appendix, 41–2). In this, William Lamberton confirms to Lauder possession of 'the Island in the sea which is called the Bass, near to Aldham in Lothian' (McCrie 1848, Appendix, 41). The rock's location is specified by reference not to Tantallon (possibly not yet under construction) or Traprain Law (used for sightings on later maritime charts) or North Berwick (in whose parish it lay), but to Auldhame, the spiritual and physical 'shore station' above the landing place at Seacliff.

The difficulties caused by foul weather and its maritime location are a recurrent thread in Auldhame's history. In about 1491, a later Lauder of Bass petitioned the Pope to be allowed to erect the existing chapel on the island into a parish church. Innocent VIII's reply is worth quoting at length, despite the fact that 'supplications are notoriously unreliable' (Cowan 1995a, 25), because ulterior motives are not hard to spot behind the fine words:

> 8 June 1491 ... The recent petition of Robert Landar [sic] ... lord of the island of Bas ... stated that since there is no parish church on the said island, which is distant two miles ... from the mainland, and since its inhabitants are parishioners of the parish churches of St Andrew ... [North Berwick] and St Baldred ... Alden [sic] ... which are on the mainland, it often happens that at certain times of the year, particularly when the sea is swollen, they cannot conveniently receive the sacraments from the rectors of the said churches, with the frequent result that many of them die without the sacraments. It was also stated that if a certain chapel ... on the island were erected as a parish church ... and if the tithes of fruits growing there, which [are currently paid to] the said churches, were ... assigned for the sustenance of the rector of the proposed parish church, and if [Robert became patron, he would further endow the new parish] (*CPL* XV, No. 719).

The rectors of Auldhame and North Berwick were amply provided for, and would not lose by 'the subtraction of the said tithes', as they would no longer endure physical danger, 'on account of the perils of the sea which they must undergo to administer the sacraments' on the Bass (*CPL* XV, No. 719).

Apart from implying that St Baldred's charge entailed a travelling ministry, this suggests another link between Auldhame and the Bass. No one could be buried at the existing chapel of ease there (insufficient subsoil notwithstanding) because it had not been specifically granted the right of burial (Dr C Pamela Graves pers comm), so Auldhame (and for the Lauders, St Andrews at North Berwick) was used instead. Now the island would have 'a cemetery, baptismal font and other markers of a parish church' (*CPL* XV, No. 719).

Lauder was not being altruistic; he would have the patronage and, as the rock was so isolated, total influence over the destination of 'the teinds of the solan geese which he apparently obtained thereafter' (Cowan 1995d, 177; by Act of Privy Council, McCrie 1848, 43–6). An English traveller records his visit to the laird of Auldhame in 1618, where he ate 'the soleand goose, a most delicate fowle, which breeds in great abundance in ... the Basse ... The lord or owner of the Basse doth profit at the least two hundred pound yearly by those geese' (Ferrier 1980, 46).

The coast continued to be a danger to shipping – the laird of Scoughall was told in 1531 to see to the 'keiping and saiffing of the guidis cumin on land furtht of the Franche ship that brak on that cost' (*Treas Acc* VI, 56). The obituary of farmer John Dale, in 1872, recalled he was 'highly honoured by the unfortunate mariners [rescued by him] wrecked upon the iron-bound coast of Auldhame and Scoughall' (*Scotsman* 1872, 6). The coal found both at the Isle of May and Auldhame may have been used to fuel warning beacons for passing ships (James & Yeoman 2008, 5; and see Chapter 2.3.5).

'The burial of corpses washed ashore in consecrated graveyards only became common practice after [legislation passed in] 1808' (Pollard 1991, 37) but this was not the case at Scoughall beach. Local shipwreck victims were interred at Tyninghame Kirk before this date, as burial on the seashore itself was rare (Daniell 1997, 100), and probably undesirable due to erosion. The expense of disposing of such drowned bodies is a constant theme in the surviving Tyninghame Kirk Session minutes, which date to after 1615. They give a good picture of the (probably identical) situation at Auldhame before the early 17th century, when Auldhame churchyard was still in use. The entries include: 24 September 1620, 'for ane winding sheitt to ane deid corpis qlk [which] came in on the sands of Aldhame ...' (Ritchie 1880, 189); 15 November 1628, 'ane man of Rotardame buryit, his ship being cast away besyd Skugall ... about ane in the morning' (Ritchie 1880, 216); 6 January 1746, 'for digging a grave to one thrown up on the sands after a shipwreck' (NAS, CH2/359/5/250).

*The history of Auldhame church in the 13th–16th centuries*

Building 3 may be the church dedicated by David de Bernham, bishop of St Andrews, on 23 April 1243, the sixtieth of 140 churches so honoured by the bishop (Lockhart 1892, 53). Bernham arrived at Auldhame from Hutton, in Berwickshire, and continued on to Smailholm (Lockhart 1892, 53); unless he returned to St Andrews, it is likely that he spent time at his mensal property at Tyninghame. These runs of consecrations, spread over the 1240s, were '"conditional" dedications, where knowledge of the original ceremony ... was uncertain or lost' (Ash 1976, 35). The antiquity and obscurity of Auldhame would make it a candidate for this treatment. Bernham seems to have been instituting the statutes of the Legatine Council held in Edinburgh in 1239, which stated 'that all churches were to be properly consecrated' (Ash 1976, 35).

Another of de Bernham's projects was the canonisation of St Margaret, ancestress of his patron Alexander II, and the promotion of her cult at Dunfermline. As a former vicar of Haddington and native of Berwickshire (Ash 1976, 33–4; Lockhart 1892, 19–20), he would have also been familiar with the local cult centres of St Mary at Whitekirk, and St Baldred at Tyninghame, neither of which was felt to need additional confirmation of their dedications (but St Baldred's at Prestonkirk was consecrated, in 1241; Lockhart 1892, 47).

The pontifical in which the dedications are recorded also contains offices for the consecration of cemeteries, but it is not clear if this would be reflected in any change in burial practice, as the cemetery would already have been assumed to be sacred ground (Anderson 1990, 520). However, Bernham's statutes for the exercise of Christianity do survive, dated to 1242 (Patrick 1907, 57). One that may have affected Auldhame began, 'Churchyards (shall) be suitably enclosed all the way round, so that no access be open to unclean and brutish beasts, for sacred places should be kept clean' (Patrick 1907, 57). A diocesan visitation such as Bernham's also acted to implement clerical and doctrinal discipline, although there are no comments on what he found in each parish.

The *Antiqua Taxatio*, or 'Old Extent', assumed to date from the early 13th century, was a land valuation that has been set against later tax returns (Gemmill & Mayhew 1995, 363–4). Of the six contiguous parishes of Dunbar, Tyninghame, Whitekirk, Linton, North Berwick and Auldhame, the latter is the least valuable at £4, compared to Whitekirk's £6/13/4d, and Tyninghame's £26/13/4d. Linton and North Berwick are ten times more valuable than Auldhame, and this difference would persist for centuries (Gemmill & Mayhew 1995, 366, Table 76).

Auldhame appears next in 'Bagimond's Roll' of 1275–6 (Watt 2001, 4–5): 'On 20th September 1274, Pope Gregory X appointed Master Baiamundus de Vitia Collector-General in Scotland … to collect the tenth which had been authorised by the General Council of Lyons for the relief of the Holy Land' (Dunlop 1939, 6; Watt 2001, 2). This tax assessment, some of which was promised to Edward I's crusading ventures, caused great controversy (Watt 2001, 4–5), but it provides a comparative list of the actual tithe collected from Auldhame and other parishes in the archdeaconry of Lothian (Watt 2001, 6–13). The usual arrangement when an absentee rector divided the living with his locum, or vicar, was that the garbal and lesser teinds were split unequally, usually in proportions varying between 4:1 and 2:1, which greatly favoured the rector (Cowan 1995c, 49–54). By a statute of 1224, 'the stipend of a vicar net and free, after all burdens have been deducted, shall amount at least to the value of ten merks' (Patrick 1907, 11; Cowan 1995c, 53).

The diversion of revenues away from congregations and pastoral care, towards distant, impersonal corporate bodies, was more extensive in Scotland than any other European country (except Switzerland; Cowan 1995a, 12). Obviously open to abuse, it was frequently administered inadequately or corruptly, and deprived money from the curate in situ, who was frequently an underpaid vicar, without security of tenure, and hence without much incentive to care about his particular parish (Cowan 1995c; Duncan 1996, 299–302).

Auldhame appears to be served by a resident rctor, the living too meagre to split, and its teind is the smallest of any rectory in Lothian (save Slamanan) at only 4/- (Dunlop 1939, 33–4). The following year, as part of the deanery of Haddington, Auldhame appears equally pitiful although its taxation has increased to 6/-. Tyninghame, by contrast, remits 60/-, and North Berwick, despite being a vicarage, sends 13/4d, or 1 merk (Dunlop 1939, 58).

After an inglorious career as a tax collector, Bagimond was replaced by John Halton, who was bishop of Carlisle in 1292 (Donnelly 1999, 9–11; 1997, 48–9). Halton's assessments survive only for Lothian (Donnelly 1997, 48; *Cold Corr*, cviii–cxvii). The confidence that can be placed upon the 'true' valuations and tithes therein is discussed elsewhere (Gemmill & Mayhew 1995, 363–8; Donnelly 1997, 48–50) but, as expected, Auldhame comes bottom of the list of rectories, and below several vicarages in the deanery of Haddington (*Cold Corr*, cix). Tyninghame's 'true value' is £53/6/8d, Linton or Prestonkirk's is £93/6/8d and the vicarage (usually a less valuable benefice) of North Berwick is £13/6/8d. Auldhame musters only £9/4/2d, and teind of 18/5d, again the lowest (non-vicarage) tenth out of the 29 assessments in the deanery (*Cold Corr*, cix). It is difficult to see Auldhame as a sought-after post for the priest concerned.

During the wars of the Scottish succession, Edward I had captured Berwick in 1296, and subdued Scotland in a few months, forcing forced John Balliol to abdicate. 'When [Edward] held parliament at

Berwick [in] August 1296 further submissions [of fealty] were received … names of hundreds of Scots, nobles, prelates and even men of lesser standing filled … the Ragman Roll' (Nicholson 1978, 50–1). Those of 'lesser standing' included William, parson of Auldhame, his colleagues the parsons of Logie and Chirnside, and episcopal tenants from Tyninghame (*Inst Pub* 147, 151, 154, 167). Auldhame was too close to the English border to escape the realities of international politics.

As suggested by the Halton and Bagimond taxations, the rector of Auldhame soon felt it necessary to acquire multiple benefices, and so accumulate an appropriate stipend. In 1325 John Harkars, the second incumbent known by name, applied to the Pope for provision to a canonry of Aberdeen Cathedral, 'notwithstanding that he is rector of Aldam, in the diocese of St Andrews, value 10 marks' (*CPL* II, 245). As mentioned above, this was the minimum stipend for a vicarage over a century earlier, since when inflation had eroded its value (Gemmill & Mayhew 1995, 362, 364).

Harkars was successful but his income was still inadequate as, five years later in 1329, he again petitions the Pope for a prebend in Moray, 'notwithstanding that he has a canonry and prebend of Aberdeen' (*CPL* II, 313). The collection of benefices, or pluralism, became a well-known abuse of the church (Duncan 1996, 305), giving 'sinecure' its now-derogatory sense, but it was probably the only option open to the holder of low-yielding Auldhame. It is not known whether there was a vicar or chaplain, or where Harkars himself resided.

During the intermittent struggles of the second War of Independence (1332–57; Barrow 2003a, 308; Shead 1996, 104), David II was captured by the English at Neville's Cross in 1346, and during his 11 years of imprisonment, his supporters and rivals in Scotland argued among themselves (Brown 2004, 247–9; Nicholson 1978, 147, 149–50). Edward III wanted to be acknowledged as overlord of Scotland, which in turn wished to preserve its own rights and privileges (Brown 2004, 254; Grant 1984, 35–7). The war directly affected Whitekirk, two miles from Auldhame, during the 'Burnt Candlemas' in 1356, when Edward 'burned a swathe through Lothian on his 10-day march, destroying Haddington and Edinburgh … local inhabitants had been forced to hide in caves, woods and bogs' (Brown 2004, 316).

A storm forced Edward's supplies to land at or near Tyninghame, allowing his sailors to ransack Whitekirk. John of Fordun describes the incident: 'Sons of Belial, had, shortly before, disembarked, and fallen upon the white kirk of the Virgin, which stands by the sea-side. There … they … stripped the image of the Virgin … which was decked with gold rings, necklaces, and armlets … [with which] the faithful had becomingly loaded it; and two canons of … Holyrood [they kidnapped] … after having carried off all the property … in the chapel … the ship which had wrought the heinous robbery' sank in a storm' (Skene 1872, 364–5).

Fordun demonstrates that Whitekirk possessed votive images, which could be very elaborate (Marks 2004, 172, 186–7, 246–7), and to which parishioners and supplicants bequeathed personal effects. A statue of the patron saint was customary furnishing for every parish church, and Auldhame should have possessed, at the least, a (modest) figure of St Baldred (McRoberts 1976, 70–1; Marks 2004, 73, 77–8). Home of Dunglass, in 1423, left money that a mass would be celebrated for his soul in 'the church of the blessed Mary which is called Whitekirk' (Rankin 1914, 14). It is not known if Auldhame and St Baldred's churches and holy wells were included as part of a pious circuit in visits to the more famous Marian shrine and well, or indeed visited by Whitekirk pilgrims as additional destinations in their own right.

In 1427, a 'poor hermit', who had been a pilgrims' 'aide' at Whitekirk, 'desire(d) to live a hermit's life in the hermitage and chapel' of Whitekirk, which has been unconvincingly identified with Seacliff tower (*CSSR* II, 172). This suggests that the area around Whitekirk (and thereby around Auldhame) was considered sufficiently secluded for an anchoritic existence, at least away from its church. The visit in 1435 of Andreas Piccolimini to Whitekirk, in thanksgiving for surviving a storm off Dunbar, is well known (Nicholson 1978, 297) as he became Pope Pius II but, as always, any mention of Auldhame is just out of sight.

The academic and theologian John Mair was born at Gleghornie, between Auldhame and Whitekirk, about 1467, and studied and taught at Paris, St Andrews and Glasgow (among his students was John Knox; Broadie 2004–11). The local legend of the saint's triplicate burials appears in his writings, 'where, in treating of the Holy Eucharist, he seeks to prove, by the example of the body of S Baldred, that the same body can be in diverse places, *simul et semel*' (Forbes 1872, 274; Mackinlay 1894, 80–1).

The parson of Auldhame in 1485 may have been Mr William Lindsay, who appears with Patrick Scougall, owner of the lands of Scoughall in this parish, as a witness to an act of sasine in Edinburgh (*Prot Bk Young*, No. 8). In 1498, Lindsay appeared before the Lords of Council, under pressure from chaplain Andrew Bassindean to resign Auldhame to the latter, who otherwise accused Lindsay of being 'our ... soverane Lordis rebel' (*ADC* II, 81, 281). Presumably Lindsay won, because in 1502, as 'rectore de Auldhame notario publico' he witnessed a charter in Edinburgh (*RMS* II, No. 2711) along with two other lawyers, and was again in Edinburgh the following year (*Prot Bk Foular* I, No. 192). Bassindean, perhaps fortunately considering his methods of personal advancement, was still just a chaplain in 1502 (*Prot Bk Young*, No. 1226).

The most famous owner of Auldhame first appears in connection with the parish in 1504. Patrick Scougall of that Ilk, and rising young lawyer Adam Otterburn, both witnessed a sasine in Edinburgh, and two days later Patrick was in Beil, to see to business concerning Auldhame (*Prot Bk Young*, Nos 1467–8). Beil belonged to Robert Lauder of Bass (*RMS* II, No. 1894), who was also present. Scougall had leased a quarter of Auldhame from George Hume of Spott, at an unspecified date, for 10 years, and agreed to consider feuing it later (*Prot Bk Young*, No. 1468). The parties were once again before the Lords of Council in 1506, when Scougall apparently purchased the land outright (Inglis 1935, 12 n3). As Scougall was already the owner of the lands of Scoughall in the parish of Auldhame, it was natural that he would seek to consolidate his holdings. If Scougall did not possess the other three-quarters of 'the lands of Auldhame' already, this would still leave the ownership of that portion unaccounted for.

*Auldhame and the Archbishops of St Andrews*

The earlier landownership, superiority and church patronage of Auldhame are unclear and frequently undocumented. Chalmers (1889 IV, 429–30, 544 note g, 546) asserts, without citing any authorities, that 'the bishops of St Andrews ... were patrons of the church of Aldham from the earliest times'. They were certainly feudal superiors; as a 1594 grant relates, 'the kirklands were once held of the rector of Auldhame, the rest were held of the archbishop' (*RMS* VI, No. 86). The first female commentator claims Auldhame 'formed part of the estate of the Lauders of the Bass for many years', but gives no dates (Smith 1898, 206), and Chalmers (1889 IV, 546) names the Scougalls of that Ilk, as landowners of Scoughall estate, which is securely recorded elsewhere (see Black 1949, 715).

The bishops may originally have cherished the site due to the production of the purple dye/pigment (Chapters 6.3 and 7.2.2) but over time, this interest mutated. There is considerable circumstantial evidence that points to the parish being treated like a private family fief by successive high-ranking clergy of the St Andrews diocese. William Schevez, the second archbishop (1476–97; *Fasti 2*, 383–4) had begun leasing his demesne lands, including Tyninghame, to raise money to improve the cathedral (*CPL* XIV, 7–8). The rector of Tyninghame, as part of a general trend towards feuing church property (Wormald 1981, 51–2) feued his glebe in 1498 to one John Schevez of Greenspott (in the vicinity; *RSS* I, No. 198). Given the locality, it would not seem unreasonable to suspect some link between the two Schevez men. In 1513, one John Schevez became macer, or peripatetic court official, to the Lords of Council (*ADCP*, 14). A 'John Schevez', either a namesake or possibly actually the same individual, already held another similar office (*RMS* II, Nos 2932, 3137, 3756). Again, some familial connection seems probable, given that in 1518, heirs of the late 'Scheves, masser' held one-quarter of Auldhame, near Tyninghame, as security for a loan (*Prot Bk Foular* II, No. 113).

The archdeacon of St Andrews from 1480–96, and second in the hierarchy, was Alexander Inglis, uncle of George Inglis of Lochend near Dunbar (*Fasti 2*, 397–8; *RMS* II, No. 2618, 1281–2). George, who had previously been pardoned for assault and mutilation (*RSS* I, No. 686) had come into possession of one fourth of the lands of Auldhame by 1518. It is not clear if this was the quarter previously owned by Hume of Spott, or if it was another part. He had used the annual rent of the property as security, or to guarantee a loan of 40 merks from John Schevez, which debt was redeemed by Adam Otterburn, along with the land (*Prot Bk Foular* II, No. 113). Most of these families appear in the same charter, dated 1477, holding neighbouring land in Berwick upon Tweed (the Inglis brothers, Archdeacon Schevez, and Robert Lauder of Bass (*RMS* II, Nos 1281–2)). A final thread tying the Inglis and Schevez families may be that they were themselves related. Archbishop Schevez describes his archdeacon William Inglis as 'his kinsman', when writing to the Pope in 1481 (*CPL* XIII, Pt 2, 105).

According to his biographer, Otterburn bought Auldhame in instalments (Inglis 1935, 11–12) and he seems to have received the 'terris sectariis vocat lie sutelands', from George Inglis in 1518/19 (NAS, GD100/63). Another sign of the episcopal links to the site is that Andrew Forman, archbishop 1514–21, acted as feudal superior in the transactions, and calls Otterburn his 'dilecto consanguineo et familiari servitori', although whether they were actual blood relations is unknown (NAS, GD100/63). St Andrews University archives, despite having many of the archiepiscopal muniments, appear, oddly enough, to have no pre-Reformation documents relating to Auldhame itself, which only confirms its ambiguous and 'twilight' status relative to official mensal properties.

Finally, among the shadowy and obscure connections between Auldhame and the archdiocese, two suggestive documents appear in the *St Andrews Formulare*, or legal style-book, of John Lauder (fl. 1517–51), who collected examples of deeds for future reference (Herkless & Hannay 1909 II, 226–30; *St A Form* I, vii–viii; *Fasti 2*, 202, 231). Archbishop Forman, in the formulare, grants lands to 'J . . . , filio . . . magistri A . . . O . . . de A . . .', surely an alias of John, son of Adam Otterburn of Auldhame. The land had been acquired in parcels, and was erected 'into one holding for his heir' (*St A Form* I, No. 246). The key item is 'the Soytorlands . . . with three suits at Tynyghame' barony court per year (Herkless & Hannay 1909 II, 257, No. 5, with Adam 'O' wrongly transcribed as Adam 'D'). The meaning of the name is discussed below, but the only suitor's lands in the barony (as distinct from the parish) of Tyninghame are those at Auldhame. This identification is strengthened when the pseudonymous 'A O' purchases the lands of 'R' from 'W C' and his wife 'K B', which Adam Otterburn did when he bought Reidhall, near Edinburgh from William Cunninghame and Katherine Borthwick in 1527 (Inglis 1935, 32; *St A Form* I, No. 317).

'Souterlands' (from 'soutar' or cobbler) are recorded elsewhere (eg at Wemyss; Taylor & Markus 2006, 597), as well as in a series of documents for Auldhame. The latter include 'terris sectariis vocat lie sutelands', and 'le sutlandis', in 1519 (NAS, GD100/63; *St A Form* I, No. 246), 'Soyttourland' and 'Soutterland' in 1594, and 'Soyterlandis', in 1618 (*RMS* VI, No. 86; *RMS* VII, No. 1906). 'Terra sectabilis' is 'land subject to suit', whose tenant (the 'suitor') owes suit of court, and must attend on certain days (Latham 1965, 428). In Scots, 'sutour', or 'soytour', refers to the person so obligated (*DSL (DOST)*, Entry for Sut(o)ur, Suito(u)r, soyto(ur), use from *c* 1290 onwards). At Auldhame, within the supporting documentary context, it is likely to mean 'the lands of the tenant who pays suit of court' rather than 'shoemaker's lands' (S Taylor, B Patterson 2009 pers comm). Auldhame lay within the jurisdiction of Tyninghame for such feudal court service (discussed above; see also Herkless & Hannay 1909 II, 257; *St A Form* I, No. 246). Little and Meikle Auldhame are also mentioned, along with the kirklands of Auldhame, but their locations are never specified, as they would once have been self-evident.

*Adam Otterburn and his heirs*

The origin of another local place-name has also been clarified during the present research. The field containing the excavation site is known as 'Old Adam' and was taken to refer to Adam Otterburn, king's advocate to James V, and owner of Auldhame from 1518 (T Dale pers comm). However, the phrase 'Old Auldhame' recorded on the 1854 Ordnance Survey map, appears a more likely origin (OS 1854, 3). The local pronunciation of 'Auldhame' is recorded as 'Adam' in 1618 (seven times) and 'Addum' in 1952, which in folk etymology would easily transmute to referring to the king's lawyer, rather than to a forgotten fermtoun.

Adam Otterburn (d. 1548) rose to the highest legal offices in the land, being successively Edinburgh burgh clerk, a lord of council in 1517, receiver of the queen's rents and, in 1524, sheriff-depute of Stirling (Finlay 2004). Otterburn served four terms as provost of Edinburgh between 1521 and 1548, as well as serving as king's advocate, diplomat and ambassador to England. Despite periods of royal disfavour, he also acted as parliamentary commissioner for Edinburgh and accumulated considerable landholdings, which included Orchardfield and Dirleton (Finlay 2004).

Otterburn 'did not favour the reformed religion' and was a political ally of Cardinal Beaton, as well as intermittently supporting Archibald Douglas, 6th earl of Angus and second husband of Margaret Tudor (Finlay 2004). In the constantly changing alliances between the major parties of Albany, Arran and Angus during the minority of James V, Otterburn favoured his neighbour Angus, who inherited Tantallon Castle in 1513 (Dawson 2007, 89–113; Donaldson 1965, 31–42; Inglis 1935, 6–22).

Partisanship aside, Otterburn the lawyer was careful to exact compensation for damage sustained by his Auldhame farm, at the time the duke of Albany besieged Tantallon in January 1522 (Inglis 1935, 15–16; Exch Rolls XIV, 473). His compensation of £100 for loss of grain, burning and destruction, presumably covered the burning of his barn or granary, as crops would have been ingathered over winter. Otterburn continued to work as an advocate for private clients and had plenty of disposable income, having acquired at least five estates around Edinburgh by the late 1530s (Finlay 2004; *RMS* III, Nos 572, 772, 767, 1487), including Gorgie and Redheugh.

A recent, closely dateable discovery in Edinburgh may strengthen the case for Otterburn's willingness to spend money on building and decoration. Rare and high status floor tiles found off North Gray's Close in 2008 had been imported from Flanders around the early 1530s, and among their scarce British parallels are examples in Whitehall Palace, London (J Franklin pers comm). Among the few candidates for their ownership is Otterburn, who owned a house neighbouring North Gray's Close and visited Henry VIII in London in 1533 and 1534 (Franklin forthcoming; Inglis 1935, 47–59).

Otterburn also showed his interest in religion – he endowed memorial masses in St Giles in 1525 for his own and his first and second wives' souls, which he hugely augmented in 1535–6, with more ceremony and alms for the poor (*Prot Bk Foular* III, Nos 540–1; *St Giles Reg* No. 135). This latter gift also lists his considerable Edinburgh property holdings. Endowing chantries and collegiate churches, with their emphasis on the salvation of the individual, was very popular among the propertied classes of the early 16th century, and may provide a context for the elaboration of the east end of the chapel at Auldhame, represented by Building 4 (Figure 10).

Building 4 could have formed a family burial aisle or mortuary chapel in its own right, fitting into the late medieval Scottish chantry tradition. It would have stood as a self-contained building of the 1520s or 1530s, that is, before Otterburn got into serious financial difficulty in 1538–9 (Finlay 2004). It could have provided a suitable setting for Otterburn's burial, which seems to be unrecorded, along with his two wives, or his son, lying beside the relics of St Baldred. Building 3 may have been ruinous (Chapter 3.2.5), or even storm-damaged and required to be replaced or extended by Otterburn, although there was arguably still a functioning church there in the early 16th century. The contemporary Auldhame clergy are on record, although this is not definitive proof that they were actually resident and ministering to their congregation. During this period, the church does not seem to have received any ongoing maintenance that is archaeologically traceable, so at best, it was still working but in poor repair around the time of Otterburn's purchase in 1518.

The desire to be buried within the protective aumbra of the saint (and later *apud ecclesiam*, with its divine service) has always made church burial prestigious (Aries 1981, 71–3, 82; Dinn 1995, 244, 247; Daniell 1997, 95; Spicer 2000, 151, 153–5). Burial at the altar became the most sought after in the hierarchy of sacred spaces because of the celebration of the mass (Marks 2004, 173–4; Graves 1989, 308; Daniell 1997, 95–101; Dinn 1995, 247–9; Aries 1981, 71–3, 79–80). This seems likely to have appealed to an individual such as Otterburn, status-conscious in death, as in life.

Otterburn had the classic requisites to be the probable builder of Building 4; that is, he had the motive, means and opportunity. He was wealthy, a self-made man with serious social ambitions – his own son married the daughter of an earl, and his daughters married very wealthy landowners (Inglis 1935, 120; *RSS* V, 2, No. 2634). Although Otterburn's own testament is not in the National Archives of Scotland, those of his sons-in-law are, and indicate his family's social connections. Their inventories only contain the 'moveable' family property (ie excluding land), but Sir John Wemyss was still extremely rich. In 1571, he had 86 'drawand oxin' and other assets worth £34, 695/12/9d (Scots, after tax; NAS, CC8/8/3/156–7). The Scougall family, the only other landowners in the parish, in 1566 had only four oxen, and moveables totalling £260/-/8d (Scots money; NAS, CC8/8/1/35-6). It would seem that the Scougalls are less likely candidates for the building programme, if only for financial reasons. One is tempted to wonder about the state of Wemyss's marriage, however, in which he openly leaves money to his two natural sons and natural daughter, and 'to ilk ane of his uth(e)r bastard dochteris' (NAS, CC8/8/3/158).

According to the *St Andrews Formulare*, Otterburn intended Auldhame as the future 'ancestral' home, and he resigned it to his son, but '[Adam] holds the lands for life, and her third is reserved for 'E M', [alias Eupham Mowbray] his spouse' (Herkless & Hannay 1909, 257; *St A Form* I, No. 246, 292). This indicates forethought, and the expectation that Eupham would benefit from Auldhame estate specifically, if she outlived Adam (which she did). Otterburn is also the probable builder of Auldhame Castle, or the L-plan laird's dwelling called 'St Baldred's House', just south of the church, which appears to be 16th century and later (T Addyman pers comm).

The cliffs beside Tantallon offered an ideal opportunity for conspicuous display, being readily visible by land and sea. Being a colleague of the earl of Angus, who was forced to rebuild and 'improve' Tantallon after the siege of 1521, and seeing the later alterations by James V after another siege in 1528, may have provided additional impetus for Otterburn to improve his estate (Tabraham 2007, 7, 23–4; Richardson 1980, 17–20). Auldhame Castle, in direct contrast to Tantallon, was built more for comfort than defence, but would still have provided an impressive suite of buildings if seen in conjunction with the extended church, against the blank background of the sea (if viewed from the land) or the sky (from the sea).

*Clergy, the Reformation and the 'extra-parochial' period 1560–1618*

The continuing presence of priests at Auldhame throughout the mid-16th century suggests that it did not stop being a functioning church until the Reformation. After William Lindsay, David Swinton, son of Swinton of that Ilk, is recorded as rector in 1519, fulfilling the traditional destiny of younger sons by entering the church (NAS, GD12/89). He was followed by two brothers, Archibald Hay, who died before October 1547, and John Hay, who succeeded Archibald (*RSS* III, 2503–4).

Archibald had been simultaneously rector of both Auldhame and Melville, and principal of the New or St Mary's College in St Andrews (*RSS* III, Nos 1738, 2503–4, 2457). New College was founded in 1538 by Archbishop James Beaton, uncle of Otterburn's patron Cardinal David Beaton (Cowan & Easson 1976, 233). The link between the Hay rectors of Auldhame and St Mary's may be the reason that the college presumed to collect the teinds of Auldhame after the Reformation, although it had ceased to be a working parish.

The other appointments, before and after the Reformation, are more tentative. A Coldingham monk, William Learmonth, may have served the church (Durkan, cited in Haws 1972, 9) but this would be unusual, as Auldhame was unappropriated. Patrick Alexander, apparently the last priest, had leased the parsonage to Jean Stewart, John Otterburn's wife, in 1573 (Kirk 1995b, 117 n89, 118 and n92–4, 179).

The 19th-century minister believed that 'from 1560 to 1618, Auldhame belonged to no parish' (Ritchie 1880, 22, 24) and the list of ministers' stipends for 1576 says 'Bass and Auldhame neidis na reidaris' (Macdonald 1830, 74). But there was no escaping the tax system, as St Mary's or New College, at St Andrews had annexed the teinds (eg for Scougall, St A, SM110/SB25/4). According to two contemporary 'wills' in 1585 and 1595/6, the parishioners were paying for the support of a minister who did not actually exist – the College never actually supplied any clergy in return for the tithe (NAS, CC8/8/12/343; CC8/8/28/731). The minister of North Berwick may possibly have had nominal charge of the parish (*Fasti* I, 380; MacDonald 1830, 9–10). However, he seemed lax about undertaking the parochial duties – he witnessed a testament in Castleton in 1586, but did not travel that little bit farther to Scoughall in 1582 when an Auldhame parishioner died (NAS, CC8/8/20/494, 496; CC8/8/12/342, 344). He left that to the minister of Tyninghame, who apparently acted as the *de facto* curate of Auldhame, whether he was paid for it or not (NAS, CC8/8/12/342, 344).

The kirk session minutes for Tyninghame do not survive before 1615, so Auldhame's condition is undocumented, but the church probably went unused, as there was no recognised mechanism to repair and maintain it (ie, no official collection of teinds). The records for the teinds of Tyninghame, gifted to New College in 1538 (St A, SM110, B1/P1/3 and 4) remain at St Andrews University, where the college still teaches divinity but, to date, only one brief mention of Auldhame has been found in uncatalogued archive documents examined for this project (St A, SM110/SB25/13; L Smith, R Hart pers comm).

It has been suggested that Auldhame was a 'chapel of ease [for Tantallon], an accessible church building that saved the residents from having to walk to … North Berwick' (Tabraham 2007, 16) but there is no evidence either for or against this. Certainly the graveyard continued in use after the church, possibly because kirkyards required less maintenance than upstanding buildings. It became traditional for some rural graveyards to look unkempt, although efforts were made to keep animals out (Gordon 1984, 85–7, 164–5; Love 1989 40; Patrick 1907, 40, 56, 57 and n). A folk superstition is recorded whereby 'to cut the churchyard vegetation was thought to be disrespectful to the dead' (Gordon 1984, 85; Grant 1961, 367).

Residents of Tantallon may have been buried there, or soldiers killed during military actions, although again there is nothing written down. John Douglas was the captain of Tantallon, who died in 1613 (although his testament was unregistered until 1638). In his latterwill, which contains his wishes for his burial, he says, 'he leives his sauell to god almytie and ordeines his bodie to be buried in the kirk of north beruik' (NAS, CC8/8/58/601–03). Tantallon was in North Berwick parish, rather than in Auldhame, and when the due proprieties could be observed, North Berwick seems to have been used for burials from the castle.

The Otterburns sold Auldhame sometime after 1599 (when they were still dating charters there) to the Auchmuthie family, who also purchased Scoughall, uniting the parish under single ownership by 1615 (St A, SM110/SB25/13; *RMS* VI, No. 983; VII, Nos 1823, 1906). The 'fortalice and buildings of Scoughall were burnt by a sudden fire 26 years ago [ie before 1607, so *c* 1581], in which the charters and writings were burned', which may account for the lack of documentation for the current estate of Seacliff, including Auldhame (*RMS* VII, 669). John Auchmuthie was one of James VI's gentlemen of the bedchamber, and became master of the king's wardrobe in Scotland (*RMS* VII, No. 1823; VIII, No. 1600). He acquired the right of presentation to the church of Auldhame (useless if there was no church), as well as the right to the parson's and vicar's teinds (which meant actual income; *RMS* VII, No. 1945).

John Lauder, the minister of Tyninghame from 1613 to 1662, was the last nominal recipient of the parsonage monies of Auldhame in 1618 (*Fasti* I, 425; Ritchie 1880, 22). It may be that the church of Auldhame was deliberately kept vacant, for financial reasons. The parsonage and vicarage teinds of adjacent Tyninghame went to the New College, not to the incumbent minister (St A, SM110/SB25/4 and 9). The (admittedly modest) Auldhame teinds may have been seen as a sop, or compensation to augment the minister's stipend at Tyninghame, as he was doing the actual parochial work for Auldhame in any case.

Lauder was painfully conscientious in recording all baptisms, burials and immorality, and the extra problems posed by the unfilled church at Auldhame. Where should the parishioners of Auldhame have their banns proclaimed, or children christened – in Whitekirk or Tyninghame (Ritchie 1880, 24–5)? In 1615, James Kirkwood, from Scoughall, and Archibald Hutton from Auldhame witnessed the baptism of Kirkwood's son in Tyninghame church (NAS, CH2/359/1/3). Before 1616, some of the inhabitants of the non-parish also used Whitekirk, as recorded: 'Aldhame … the pe(o)pll of q(uhi)lk bounds [within the boundaries of which] for some yeiris befor [1616] war in uss to resort to [went to] the quhytkirk [Whitekirk]' (NAS, CH2/359/1, f9). When the new Auchmuthie laird wanted to marry in 1615, the question of where to wed was referred to a higher church court, the presbytery of Dunbar – who chose Tyninghame (NAS, CH2/359/1/1, Ritchie 1880, 24–5).

The 19th-century minister only had one, 200-year-old list of documents (the originals all being lost), to help him guess at the missing 17th-century history of Auldhame (Ritchie 1880, 22). However, a new chronology can now be constructed, using a legal opinion of 1671, which cites vanished sources (St A, SM110/SB25/13). New College, acting in their capacity as parsons and vicars of Tyninghame, in 1615 leased the teinds of Scougall, in Auldhame parish, to John Auchmuthie (St A, SM110/SB25/4). The College were careful never to claim any legal entitlement to be parsons of Auldhame, but obviously felt entitled to act as though they were such, and so proceeded to make several other rulings concerning the parishioners of Auldhame (Ritchie 1880, 155). Revd John Lauder listed the parishioners of Tyninghame as including those of Scougall (which was in Auldhame) in February 1618, and then asked both them and New College for a larger stipend for serving Tyninghame (Ritchie 1880, 168).

This was probably the impetus to officially resolve the problem, and on 20 July 1618 Lauder was formally appointed as the first rector and vicar of Auldhame since the Reformation (Ritchie 1880, 22). Auldhame was actually incorporated into Tyninghame by the Commissioners of Surrender on 28 July 1618 (St A, SM110/SB25/13). 'The teinds of the parishes of Tyninghame and Adam [were] for the said decreit united in one parish (the kirk and parish of Adam being by the said decreit annexed to Tyninghame)' (St A, SM110/SB25/13).

The 19th-century historian had wrongly dated the union to 20 June 1619, mistaking a brief aside in the Session minutes to refer to that date (Ritchie 1880, 22, 176, 180). Chalmers, the RCAHMS, NMRS and Scott's *Fasti* all inaccurately unite Auldhame to Whitekirk instead, as previously discussed (Chalmers 1889, IV, 547; *Fasti* I, 422; NAS, Opac catalogue entry NA12977; NMRS, NT68SW 17).

*Auldhame joined to Tyninghame Parish – 1619 and after*

The last two known burials in the kirkyard of Auldhame are noted by Lauder, but further study of his minutes may reveal more. In April 1619, after the union with Tyninghame, Lauder was absent when the infant son of laird John Auchmuthie died. 'Jhone, being half year ald or thairby was buryed in aldhame.

Item the said day hugo foster in tynynghame was buryit' so presumably there was a personal reason to want the baby interred in Auldhame rather than the usual and operational Tynynghame kirk (NAS, CH2/359/1/26). There may have been an unrecorded, folk tradition of using Auldhame as an informal, or customary infants' cemetery after the Reformation, although all the other documented child burials are at Tynynghame.

In 1637, 'Margaret Gib the laird of skugall [John Auchmuthie] his mother buryet at Aldhame Kirk' (NAS, CH2/359/1, f98v). In neither entry does it say there was a standing building, or even a ruin. The only unambiguous information is that the churchyard was still recognisable as a burial place. The church had repeatedly, but ineffectually, forbidden intra-mural or indoors 'kirk burial' in 1581, 1588, 1597, 1638 and 1643 (a mark of its popularity; Todd 2002, 333 and n65, 334–5; Spicer 2000, 150–3). Revd John Lauder was angry in 1629 when this ordinance was broken and parishioners were illicitly buried under the church floor at Tynynghame, 'sore against the minister his will' (Ritchie 1880, 217–18). Margaret Gib may have wanted burial at Auldhame as an uncontroversial and inexpensive way (no fines) to be buried inside a church, although she may also have seen it as the rightful burial place of the lairds of Scoughall (ie the Otterburns and now the Auchmuthies).

There is another intriguing possibility for Gib's choice of graveyard: 'The belief that the spirit of the last person buried had to keep watch until another interment took place seems to have been fairly general' (Grant 1961, 367). As the grandmother of the last noted infant burial, she may have wanted to watch over her grandson, but such intangible desires are now beyond all proof.

Each year several bodies were 'cast ashore at Oldham', from shipwrecks off Scoughall, which was also a landing place for herring boats (Ritchie 1880, 140, 211, 242, 253). To keep the fishing grounds clear, such corpses may also have been occasionally disposed of at Auldhame, although Tynynghame was officially used (Ritchie 1880, 189, 215, 216).

It seems unlikely that a ready source of worked stone such as that in Building 4 would sit unnoticed, considering the intensive effort of quarrying and transporting new material. Chalmers (1889 IV, 546–7) states that 'the ruins of the ancient church of Aldham on the sea-cliff were apparent in 1770, but were soon after removed for some domestic purpose'. This demolition is recorded at the same time as the abandonment of Auldhame Castle, and the erection of Seacliff House, both around 1770–80.

The church may also link with the interdict applied against 'Mr Colt', the 18th-century estate owner, to prevent him 'from tearing down the (Auldhame kirkyard) wall, or in any way interfering with the ground' (Ritchie 1880, 18). Unfortunately, the reference is frustratingly vague, and no trace of any court judgement, secular or ecclesiastical, has been found, or of who brought the action. The upkeep of the physical boundary of 'God's real estate' was written into the *First Book of Discipline*, and continued to exercise committees of heritors for centuries after the Reformation (Cameron 1972, 201–3). They took the maintenance of this Presbyterian 'vallum', seriously even when, as at Bara, the site was unused (but a new wall was still erected; Martine 1883, 287–8).

The L-plan laird's house at Auldhame was subject to erosion and subsidence (NLS, Acc. No. 12527/2) although the Colts had been living there during the 1760s (when family births at Auldhame were recorded by the Colt ministers of Inveresk; NLS, Acc No. 12527/1, ff94r, 96r). Robert Colt, MP and his wife Grizel, daughter of the famous Lord Dundas, President of the Court of Session, were wealthy enough to commission portraits from Henry Raeburn, and a new house at Scoughall (NLS, Acc. No. 12527/2; Raeburn portrait in Carnegie Museum, Pittsburgh). Seacliff House (*c* 1783) was 'picturesque' and fanciful, overlooking the North Sea and incorporating a bastion for cannon, though the potential enemy's identity is obscure (Colt 1887, 154).

The old laird's house, built by Otterburn, soon became known as 'St Baldred's Priory', which seems to be fashionably Romantic conceit rather than a serious reference to history (discussed in Colt 1887, 153; Waddell 1893, 3). Colt well knew that it was not a priory, or a church, as it had been his own mother's dower house and his uncle had died there in 1751 (Colt 1887, 168; NLS, Acc. No. 12527/3, f59v). In common with other late 18th-century 'improving' landowners, he dressed up the ruinous old estate house with an instant but bogus ancestry, and antiquarian confusion soon followed. An inscription 'carved ... over the chimney-piece in the great hall ... state(d) that "St Baldred built this house"' (Colt 1887, 153). Robert Colt also seems to be the likely culprit for removing the last remains of St Baldred's Church, and probably reusing the stone on his domestic building projects at Seacliff. The existence of the church was never lost or forgotten in the legal deeds and grants concerning the estate. Instead, it is explicitly mentioned, and the Colt family would have known this (eg in 1782, *SAH*, No. 72, To the widow of 'Oliver Coult of Auldhame … Patronage of Kirk of Auldhame'; *SAH* 1783, No. 73; NAS, GD110/337, 3, 11). While they developed their other estate at Gartsherrie using the profits from their ironworks in Lanarkshire, they sold Auldhame to George Sligo in 1816 (*SAH* 1816, Nos 1985, 1991, 2010–11).

Sligo was the amateur archaeologist who uncovered St Baldred's Cave, and may have given it the name, which is of recent, antiquarian origin (B Patterson pers comm; Sligo 1857). In 1831, he offered the unlikely, and Gothick interpretation of the cave (NMRS, NT68SW 7) as the site of human sacrifice. He found two children's skeletons, bloodstains and 'the remains of Pagan worship in nearly the same state of preservation as when the last victim was offered upon the altar' (Sligo 1857, 353). This sensibility would also suit 'St Baldred's House', or priory, which could be redesignated as fashion dictated. The house featured in two popular works of fiction, *The White Cockade*, by J Grant (1868, 52; he also quotes the fireplace inscription, and may have invented it) and R L Stevenson's *The Wreckers*.

### 7.3.2 Phase 2; AD 1000–1200

This phase begins after a short hiatus in burial activity on the headland. The political events around the hiatus between Episode 1 and the beginning of Episode 2 are the loss of Lothian by the Angles. This was probably a gradual process beginning in the mid-10th century, involving conquest by the Scots and the relinquishing of territories by the earl of Northumbria.

A roughly contemporary hiatus has been observed at nearby Kingston Common between the abandonment of the long-cist cemetery in the late first millennium AD and the re-use of the site sometime between the late 10th and mid-12th centuries AD when the burial rite changes to dug graves, possibly with an associated chapel (Suddaby 2009, 18). This may reflect the same socio-political processes and influences as those affecting Auldhame.

In the 11th century, churches and chapels were often built 'by laymen as private property' (Cruden 1986, 126). Such early ecclesiastical buildings might serve estates. Medieval churches often had monastic origins, as is likely at Auldhame, but over time it was common for monks to be replaced by priests (Fawcett 1985, 24). The formal system of parishes was developed between the late 11th and 13th century, notably in the 12th century, under David I. Commonly there was continuity between the earlier churches and the new parish system; existing estates and parish boundaries were on occasion identical (Cruden 1986, 126).

The historical evidence suggests that Auldhame was by the 12th century a parish unit of worship, albeit one of the smallest and poorest in the archdeaconry of Lothian. Such a small land area would have struggled to support the normal requirements of parochial clergy, implying, perhaps, that the parish boundaries reflect a pre-existing land unit, perhaps associated with the monastic settlement, for which its area was not a constraint. It is possible that it was not until the consecration of the church by Bishop Bernham of St Andrews in 1243 (see above), that Auldhame was established formally as a parish. We hypothesise that this corresponds with the apparent reconstruction of the chapel at Auldhame at the beginning of Phase 3.

*The form of the chapel*

Building 2, the Phase 1 chapel that we have argued was a timber construction over a drystone foundation, was retained for use in Phase 2 but was enlarged by the addition of a timber nave at its western end, or the extension of an undifferentiated unicameral church westward. The evidence for this lies in Ditch 6, a trench that does not extend beyond the width of Building 2 and that is rectangular in transverse cross-sectional profile (Figure 10), like timber foundation trenches at Yeavering, for example (Hope-Taylor 1977, eg figs 14.3 and 4). It is possible that the timber superstructure of Building 2 had fallen into disrepair after the end of the monastic settlement and that this extension was built as part of a general renovation at the beginning of Phase 2. Although significantly earlier in date, the construction of the church at Yeavering (Building B built Phase IV, AD 547–616; ibid 73, 164, 319) provides a comparable situation, in that a western annexe was added at a later date (in Phase V, AD 616–32; ibid 166, 320).

Although there are examples of more complex forms, early Scottish parish church buildings, at least from the 12th century onwards, were commonly rectangular structures with the chancel (to house the altar and clergy) to the east and the nave (for the lay congregation), the larger component, to the west (Fawcett 1985, 27). The form of early Saxon and Anglo-Saxon churches in the south of Britain emulated Roman architecture and comprised rectangular naves, often without apparent side aisles, and with apsidal chancels. The surviving early masonry churches of the northern Anglo Saxon church like Escomb, Co. Durham (c AD 670–675) have long narrow naves and small, square (as at Escomb) or rectangular chancels. It is notable, however, that surviving early Norman church sites in east central Scotland, such as Dalmeny and Leuchars (Cruden 1986, 128–32; Fawcett 1985, 27), are rather more complex. St Cuthbert's Parish Church, Dalmeny dates to AD 1130 and is composed of a nave, a chancel with a D-shaped apse. This is a European form, identified in Norway, Denmark, North France and the Danish-influenced areas of England (Fawcett 1985, 27; Hume 2005, 18–19). It is not impossible that the Norman Romanesque churches simply fused the southern semicircular apse to the square or rectangular chancel of northern church plans to provide the pleasing stepped appearance of the east end of churches like Dalmeny.

Early Scottish masonry churches from Abernethy, Brechin, Egilsay, Restennet, Edinburgh Castle and St Andrews have traditionally been assigned dates ranging from the 8th to 10th centuries and from the 11th to the early 12th. Fernie contends that all of these structures belong between c AD 1090 and c AD 1130, a period marked by the diversity of its building types and decorative forms (Fernie 1986, 393). Furthermore, Fernie looks to the south Baltic littoral and northern Germany for the antecedents to the bicameral churches with western towers, arguing that, for example, St Magnus church on Egilsay belongs to 'a far-flung group of buildings set around the North Sea in a way which suggests that they were connected by water rather than by land' (ibid).

We have noted above (Chapter 7.2.2) the Irish and Anglian ancestry of the earliest wooden churches in the region, such as Whithorn (c AD 800) and Ardwall (mid-7th century AD) and, of course, the churches on and associated with Lindisfarne, referred to by Bede. Indeed, Bede describes the sending of masons from his home monastery to build masonry churches for Nechtan, in or about AD 717, after the expulsion of the monks connected to Iona. This of course implies that the churches built in Scotland before that date were uniformly not masonry-built and it is a reasonable inference to imagine that they were in fact wooden churches. Tomas O'Carragain has noted the use in Ireland of churches built of other organic and ephemeral materials including turves, clay with wattle and wood (O'Carragain 2010). This evidence and inference, taken together with less securely dated examples, for example the church from Yeavering (Hope-Taylor 1977, 73, 166; it should be noted that the dates quoted above are based on Hope-Taylor's application of the Anglo-Saxon regnal chronology to the phases at Yeavering), and less secure interpretations, attest to the continuous and continuing use of wooden churches into the 9th century, at least. The earliest surviving British wooden church is that at Greensted, Essex, which has been dated by dendrochronological analysis, the balance of the evidence suggesting construction at some date between c AD 1063 and c AD 1100 (Tyers 1996).

It has been suggested above that the Phase 2 church at Auldhame had a wooden superstructure, although the latest known wooden examples elsewhere in the region are earlier than Phase 2 by perhaps three centuries or more. Certainly wooden churches have always been built when construction was urgently required even in Northumbria, and despite Bede's dismissal of wooden churches as somehow apostate or symbolic of Celtic apostasy, he, Bede, noted the use of churches made from branches, when need arose. However, the formality of arrangements at Auldhame and the pre-existing and succeeding ecclesiastical structures on the site taken as a whole imply that the Phase 2 structures are unlikely to have been adventitious, *ad hoc* or temporary arrangements.

Clear evidence for wooden structures of late first millennium date in central and southern Scotland is lacking but the tradition of wooden church building continued into the high medieval and beyond in Scandinavia, and across the Baltic in Karelia. The dated Norwegian Stavkirken were built in the early 12th century (eg AD 1129–31 for Urnes [but note a date of AD 950 for a displaced sill-beam at the site] and AD 1143 for a Stavkirk in Hallingdal; Thun 2002, 103, 127). The long form of stave-built church was still being built in Norway after AD 1200 and in Denmark, where no stave-built church now survives, they were being built a century or more later. In Russian Karelia, wooden churches have been built from the 14th century to early Soviet times (see for example the Church of the Transfiguration, Kizhi Island, a World Heritage Site).

Thus, while we lack clear evidence for local antecedents to the Phase 2 church at Auldhame, there is abundant evidence for a very active building programme in wooden churches across the North Sea. Bearing in mind the evidence already described for influences from that source on the construction of masonry churches farther north at this date and the evidence for widespread trade between Scotland and the Baltic, we need not dismiss the possibility of timber-built churches at this date for want of accessible exemplars, skills and influences. Whether these came directly or via an Anglian or Anglo-Saxon filter is immaterial.

*The graveyard*

The ruinous structures of the old monastic settlement were probably demolished at the beginning of this phase and the ditches backfilled with the debris of the settlement. However, the lines of Ditch 1 and Ditch 3 clearly continued to define the graveyard throughout the medieval period (Figure 40). The stone revetment [442] may have been part of the *vallum* construction but it would still have been visible during Phase 2 and would have continued to form a distinct boundary along the outer edge of the ditch for some time (Figures 31 and 32). This boundary may have been enhanced by an ephemeral structure that has not survived, such as a fence or hedgerow, which may have lain along the middle or outer edge of the ditch as Phase 2 graves began to encroach over the inner edge (Figure 40). That these early boundaries retained their significance throughout the lifetime of the graveyard may relate to the cult that sprang up around St Balthere (see above).

It is not impossible that there were other discrete burial areas on the headland, not identified during the excavation. The 1854 Ordnance Survey map of Haddingtonshire marks the site of a graveyard amongst trees north of 'St Baldred's House', to the east of the present excavation area (Figure 7). O'Sullivan (1994) has noted that early sites like Iona had several burial grounds, including some exclusively for women. The bipartite graveyard at St Blane's on Bute (Laing et al 1998, 562–3; Hewison 1893 I, 188–91), exemplifies burial in separate enclosed areas, explained as either areas associated with shrines to different saints or, according to common tradition, separate male and female burial. At Auldhame there is only slightly greater prevalence of male over female burials, which is not statistically significant and does not support conclusions on gender separation within the graveyard.

During Phase 2 the alignments of graves became more uniform (Figure 42), although paradoxically, this phase also witnessed the greatest variety in burial types, with coffins and cists, as well as simple graves in use (Figure 44). Two of the cist burials may represent a high status family plot in close proximity to the chapel. It seems unlikely that these cist burials are a continuation of the early Christian long-cist tradition seen throughout Lothian, Fife and Angus, as radiocarbon dates suggest they had gone out of use by the 9th century AD (see above). However, the longevity of the practice of cist burial is remarkable; Henshall (1956, 269) records other medieval instances of this burial custom, while their construction within living memory is described by various 19th-century writers: 'Unhewn slabs were set on their edges against the sides and ends of the graves … one or more flat stones were laid … for a lid' (Edgar 1886, 250). This form was used at St Blane's, Bute, as recently as 1892, according to the minister of Rothesay (Hewison 1893 I, 214).

Patterns in the density of distribution of inhumations at Auldhame demonstrate the relative importance of the south side of the church, in particular in the period prior to the end of the 12th century (Figure 40). The burials of neonates and infants were concentrated in close proximity to the chapel building, especially along its south wall; these commonly dated between the mid-7th and the mid-12th century (Figure 29). The south side of the church was believed to be propitious, being associated with light and resurrection, and the concentration of burials there may reflect this belief (Gordon 1984, 88; Dinn 1995, 249). In the liturgy of the mass, the south was privileged over the north, which 'was associated with evil, darkness, the Jews and the crucifixion' (Graves 1989, 306–7). John of Fordun quotes a saying, 'evil will come from the north', reinforcing this popular belief (Skene 1872, 364). Special infant burial areas are also a recognised phenomenon (Binski 1996, 56; Lowe 2008, 95, 272; Daniell 1997, 124, 127–8).

### 7.3.3 Phase 3; AD 1200–1500

Burials around the chapel continued intermittently throughout the medieval period, with gaps in the depositional sequence, defined by the radiocarbon evidence, around the early to mid-13th century and the early to mid-15th century. These gaps chronologically define Phase 3. The chapel is renovated during this period, and this activity may be related to its formal consecration by David de Bernham, bishop of St Andrews, on 23 April 1243 (Chapter 7.3.1).

It is possible that the renovation of the chapel building, the apparent diminution in burial at Auldhame and concomitant decay of the chapel towards the end of this phase, around the early 1400s, are related to economic and population factors.

Oram (in Hindmarch & Oram 2012) has studied the environmental factors affecting south-east Scotland and East Lothian during this period. He notes that during the late 12th and early 13th centuries there was a growth in population levels in south-east Scotland, a local manifestation of an economic boom in Europe following the end of the 11th century. This was followed by a severe drop in population levels in this area from the early 1300s onwards, which would have had a significant impact by the early 1400s. Causes of this demographic collapse include the end of the medieval 'warm period' around 1300, crop failures, epidemics (including the recurrent bubonic plague) and epizootics (including the great cattle epizootic of 1318–25). On top of this, the population of southern Scotland also suffered from the effects of Edward I's military campaigns of the late 13th/early 14th century onwards.

*Development of the chapel*

Building 3 represents the renovation and development of the chapel in this phase. The evidence for Building 3 consists of a mortared wall built just behind the eastern wall of Building 2 in the middle of which is an entrance (Figure 10). The nature and chronology of this structure remain unclear but two possible interpretations present themselves. Building 3 may represent the construction of a new east wall for Building 2, with a more robust, masonry build, perhaps due to the poor condition of the existing chapel. A parallel for this development sequence can be found on the Isle of May, albeit of slightly earlier date, viz, 10th–11th centuries AD (James & Yeoman 2008, 38). Here, the first drystone-built church was extended by the construction of a new mortared wall, only 1.8m to the east. Perhaps more plausibly, given the entrance in the wall, Building 3 at Auldhame may represent an extension eastwards to create a new chancel, following the loss or removal of the Phase 2 timber nave to the west. The remains of this chancel may still survive under Building 4, or may have been removed by it. The wall may have supported no more than a low altar rail, with the cross-base to one side of the entrance into the chancel. Speculation about the nature of the putative extension remains weak because of the limited scope of the excavations but, such as they are, the excavated remains indicate that the extension would have been at least as wide as the existing chapel building.

At least some of the nails and the small assemblage of folded lead strips and sheet fragments (Chapter 4.3.5) may relate to the fittings of Building 3. A single window came and a floor tile were also recovered (Chapter 4.3.9).

The construction of one of the walls comprising Building 3 was quite distinctive; the foundation trench of wall [64] had been lined with edge-set stones (Figure 10 and Chapter 2.3.4). Walls [944] and [945] both displayed a similar style of construction (Figure 37; and see Chapter 2.5.6) so it is possible that the building they represent is of similar date.

SK714, interred during the 14th/early 15th century over the western entrance to the chapel, demonstrates that the chapel must have been derelict by this time. Interestingly, statistical analysis indicates that SK714 is distinct from the Phase 3 burials and must represent a separate event (Figure 39; Table 1), so it was probably an isolated burial after the formal use of the graveyard ceased at the end of this phase. Although documentary evidence indicates that there was a rector at Auldhame until the Reformation (Chapter 7.3.1), this may have been a nominal position, not associated with a functioning chapel structure.

*Burial*

The line of the old Ditch 1 must have become totally obscured during this phase, as deposit [441], which contained SWGW pottery, covered both the residual remnants of the stone revetment [442] and the slumped hollow along the centre of the ditch (Figure 32). Nonetheless, while burials continue to encroach over the line of the inner edge they do not spread beyond the centre line of the ditch, implying that there may have been a more ephemeral boundary feature such as a hedgerow or fence line defining the graveyard boundary.

A range of burial rites and customs was identified during the later medieval period at Auldhame. Cist burial was most common during Phase 2, but one individual, SK742, was buried in a cist in Phase 3 (Figure 44). The majority of the iron objects recovered during the excavation were associated with wooden coffin furniture and fittings (Chapter 4.3.4) but finds such as these were recovered from only 16 graves, so burial in wooden coffins was not the norm. Gilchrist and Sloane (2005, 111) note that although wooden coffins were the most common container for burials between the 11th and 16th centuries, most medieval burials were not furnished with a substantial container, and this appears to have been the case at Auldhame. The presence of hinged brackets suggests that other *ad hoc* containers such as domestic boxes and caskets may also have been used for burial (Chapter 4.3.4).

Grave goods were not commonly found. A copper alloy buckle was recovered from one of the dated Phase 3 graves. It was found under the wrist of SK074, and its location near the thigh and the presence of traces of textile preserved on its rear, suggest that this was from a low-slung belt fastening. This suggests that the deceased was interred fully clothed rather than being buried in a simple shroud. A complete knife with wooden handle was found in G716; knives and tools in general are very rarely found, as grave goods within medieval burials and their significance is unclear. It is not improbable that it was simply lost by a gravedigger.

Quartz pebbles were observed in the majority of grave fills and their recovery from the ploughsoil was at odds with the apparent lack of quartz in the surrounding fields. Quartz pebbles within Christian graves may have been burial 'talismans' or tickets of admission to the afterlife. This may also provide a context for the three possible gaming pieces recovered from grave fills. Another possible ritual deposit was the oval-shaped lump of fired clay found within the left hand of an adult skeleton, SK112. This artefact may have been deliberately placed in the hand of the deceased or placed within the hand of the dying man as a 'worry bead' as he awaited death.

*Non-burial activity on the headland*

The area outside the graveyard boundary, to the south-west of the old Ditch 1, appears to have been the focus of non-burial activity during this phase (Figure 34). Spreads of stone [968] and [070], from which a medieval wood-working axe, SF 292, was recovered, had been laid down over the old ditch (Figure 31), and layer [441], which contained SWGW, built up over this area, covering [968]. Ditch 7 cut through [441] and was in turn cut by two of a group of three pits; pit [954] contained fragments of medieval metalwork, an iron collar ring (SF 1281) which might have bound a tool handle (Chapter 4.3.4), and SF 1022a and b, a fragment of copper alloy sheet and paperclip rivet which were used to repair a sheet vessel (Chapter 4.3.2). The nature of the activity represented by these features and deposits is unclear but is unlikely to have been directly related to the use of the graveyard. Other unstratified finds of probable medieval date from the site hint at a range of agricultural and semi-industrial activities taking place in and around the headland; these include a reaping hook (SF 1149), the spindle whorl (BE618), and iron punches (SF 291 and SF 1163), which might have been used in leather- or metalworking. Hearth bottom fragments and slag indicate that smithing and iron-working probably also have taken place in the vicinity (Chapter 4.3.6).

*Late medieval population and society*

The limited number of dated burials and the 1,000-year duration of use of the graveyard limits the possibilities for specific statements about the population represented. Isotopic analysis has, however, identified that the population was of largely local origin. The few possible exceptions include SK158, an individual probably belonging to Phase 2, who may come from an upland environment, such as the nearby Southern Uplands or areas of Perthshire or Aberdeenshire. Isotopic analysis also indicates that the medieval diet was relatively high in fish protein, an interpretation that is consistent with the coastal location of the site. The coastal location is a possible factor in the high prevalence of rotator cuff disease amongst the adult population, which is associated with damage to the soft tissues of the shoulder joint. A similar pattern of joint degeneration identified at the Isle of May by James and Yeoman (2008) has been interpreted as indicative of damage due to rowing associated with coastal fishing.

### 7.3.4 Phase 4; AD *1500–1700*

The Auldhame estate was purchased by Adam Otterburn at the turn of the 16th century and he is credited with building St Baldred's House, the ruins of which lie to the south of the site (Figure 4). As noted above, he provided for memorial masses for himself and his two wives at St Giles's Cathedral in Edinburgh in 1525, and further endowed chantries and collegiate churches. It seems most likely that it was he who commissioned the construction of Building 4 and stimulated the renewal of burial activity in the graveyard.

Building 4 is a curious structure. It has very thick walls in relation to its overall size, which suggests a strong, tower-like construction (Figure 10). Two 19th-century engravings depict a tower on the headland. On George Cooke's engraving of *c* 1825, a ruinous tower is depicted on a cliff edge opposite the Bass Rock (Figure 90); we cannot be certain of the exact position from which the engraving was done but the topography of the Bass Rock depicted in the engraving is comparable to that in the recent photograph of the Bass Rock from Auldhame (Figure 89). However, we can be more certain that the buildings on the *c* 1849 engraving of Tantallon Castle (Figure 91) are on the headland at Auldhame. These could be the ruinous remains of 'Oldham' village, which appears on contemporary maps (Figure 6 and Chapter 1.3), although they should lie farther south, but what is distinctive is the roofed tower. Allowing for some artistic license in these romantic scenes it is hard to avoid the conclusion that Building 4 must be the tower depicted here. It may also be the square building depicted on Roy's map lying north of St Baldred's House (Figure 5b). With its bright red dressed sandstone walls, Building 4 would certainly have been a prominent landmark on the East Lothian coast; Cross (Chapter 7.5) has drawn attention to the relationship between Auldhame and the Bass Rock, and Building 4 may have been designed partly to act as a navigational aid, as well as to display Otterburn's wealth and power.

Nonetheless, whatever its other functions, Building 4 must first and foremost have been an ecclesiastical building. The Phase 3 chapel would probably have been completely derelict by the early 16th century; indeed, the interment of SK714 across the line of the west gable wall of that building implies that it was already in that state by the early 15th century. Building 4 was built at the east end of Building 3, possibly over the old chancel (see above), and on the same alignment, surely a clear demonstration of its intended association with the ancient church. One could argue that Otterburn simply took advantage of existing foundations to build his tower but the presence of what appear to be high status burials within the building, represented by three large, raised sandstone slabs, highlights its sacred nature. These

*Figure 90*
Engraving of the Bass Rock – by George Cooke *c* 1825 (© Hulton Archive, Getty Images). Note the prominent ruins of a tower on the headland opposite the Bass

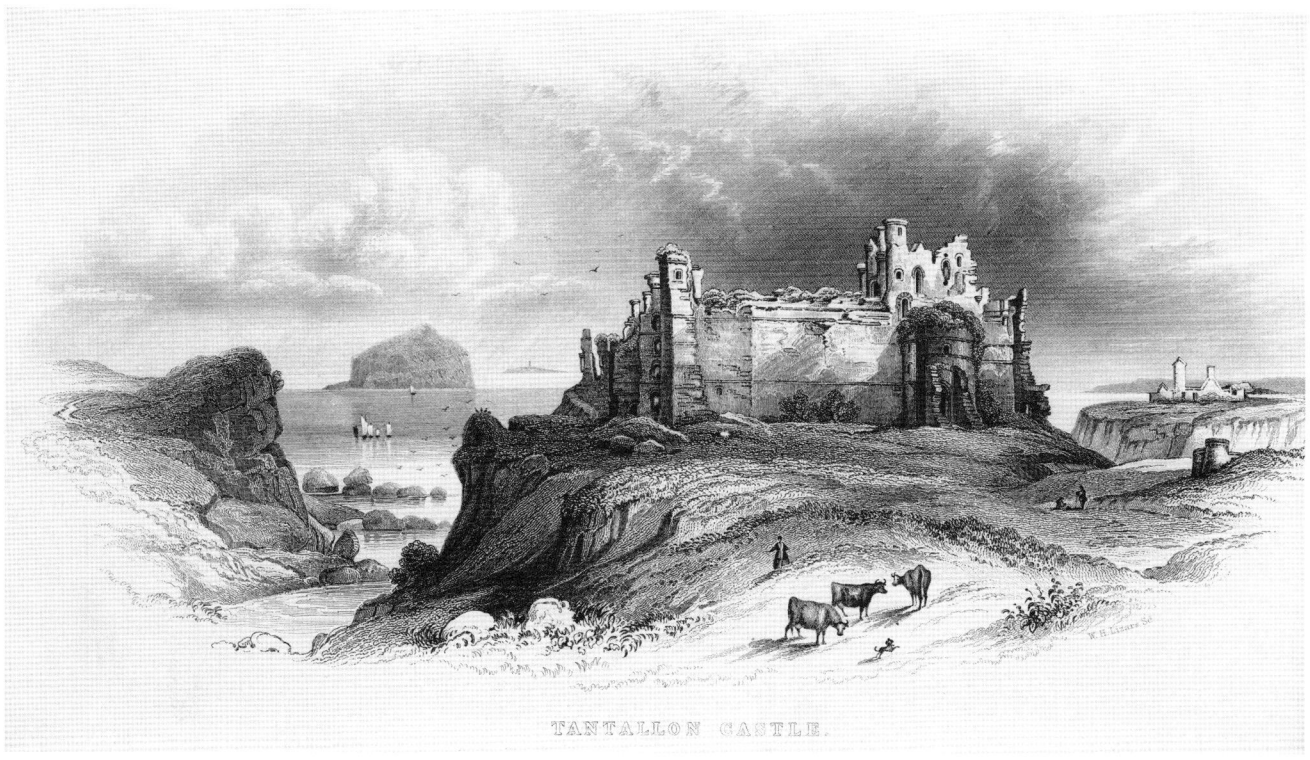

*Figure 91*
Engraving of Tantallon Castle by W H Lizars c 1849 (© Courtesy of RCAHMS. Licensor www.rcahms.gov.uk). Note the ruins of buildings on the headland at Auldhame including a tower-like structure

suggest that Building 4 may have been constructed initially as a family burial aisle or a mortuary chapel, in the late medieval Scottish chantry tradition. Space within the building was limited; the interior was only 4 × 4m and the burials would have further restricted the area available for rituals associated with burial. Nonetheless, the 16th-century Lindsay burial aisle at Edzell Church which is similarly restricted in internal size, being only c 3 × 3m, was originally a chantry chapel (RCAHMS 1984, 8), so we cannot define its character on size alone. Furthermore, there were priests at Auldhame until the Reformation (see above) who probably had a chapel in which to celebrate mass and the sacraments. If it was a tower-like construction, as its footprint suggests, then it is reminiscent of the defensible towers built onto many churches throughout the Anglo-Scottish borders in the 14th to 16th centuries (Brooke 2000). That said, it is far from clear where the associated church may have been at Auldhame and there is no evidence from the excavated area that a contemporaneous church existed separately on the site.

If Adam Otterburn did indeed erect Building 4 then we might conjecture that the sandstone slabs cover the graves of Otterburn and mark the final resting places of his wives, or descendants. Lying adjacent to, and over the footprint of the chancel of the earlier chapel, it would have provided a suitably auspicious setting for their burials. However, this must have happened prior to the Reformation, as conspicuous intra-mural burial within a functioning chapel was frowned upon in the years following the Reformation of 1560. However, rank hath its privilege and on occasion the nobility continued to have lavish burials (Raeburn 2009, 182–3). *The First Book of Discipline* (Cameron 1972, 71) states that burial should not take place within the church but rather 'some other secret and convenient place, lying in the most free aire, be appointed for that use, which place ought to be walled and fenced about, and kept for that use onely'. In some parts of Scotland, burial within the church was permitted only on payment of a fine (Raeburn 2009, 184–5). Following the first flush of the Reformation it became possible again for the wealthy to use a burial aisle, either an existing or a new structure usually located on the side of an extant church building, and therefore with extra-mural status; such structures also served the purpose of demonstrating the status of the family (Raeburn 2009, 186).

Burial started afresh in the graveyard in Phase 4, though this may have been limited to members of the laird's family. There are only four dated burials from Phase 4, one of which is the infant burial, SK474, inserted into the walls of Building 4. The others lay either to the east of the building or to the north (Figure 40), presumably because by this late date these were the only areas with space available for burials. Significantly, all the Phase 4 burials are juveniles (Figure 43). Several late burials at Auldhame are recorded (see above) including another juvenile, the infant son of the laird, John Auchmuthie, who was interred there in 1619. Later, in 1638, Margaret Gib, the mother of the laird, and hence the grandmother of this infant, was also buried there.

Shortly after the Reformation the parish was without its own clergy, a situation that continued into the 17th century. It is unlikely that Building 4 would have fallen into disrepair during the lifetimes of Otterburn or his direct descendents. The Otterburns sold Auldhame to the Auchmuthie family in 1599 and the chapel may have been abandoned after this. Without clergy there would have been no official collection of teinds, and thus no money for repairing and maintaining the structure. The chapel was no longer in use when Auldhame was incorporated with Tyninghame Parish in 1619. It was certainly derelict by the time the infant burial, SK474 (cal AD 1470–1650) was inserted into the walls. Oram (in Hindmarch & Oram 2012) notes that population levels in south-east Scotland took several centuries to recover from the environmental and economic stresses of the late medieval period (see above). The abandonment of Auldhame around the Reformation as a functioning parish entity, with its ultimate consolidation with Tyninghame, may have been due in large part to the small parish not having population sufficient to maintain its existence.

## 7.4 A HISTORIAN'S VIEW OF THE EVIDENCE FROM AULDHAME

Alex Woolf

The excavations around the site of the former Auldhame parish kirk revealed a cemetery in use from *c* AD 650 to 1650 with hiatuses in the decades around AD 1000 and around AD 1200. The headland on which the cemetery is located was surrounded by a ditch, which was filled in by the 10th century, presumably forming some sort of *vallum* though possibly pre-dating the cemetery. The present section seeks to present a historical context for the early medieval material recovered from the site and considers the significance of the 'Viking' burial.

### 7.4.1 Auldhame and Tyninghame

The earliest surviving textual reference to Auldhame appears to be contained within the Northumbrian annals preserved in *Historia Regum Anglorum* (formerly attributed to Simeon of Durham) in the entry under the year AD 854 (Arnold 1882, II, 101, discussed in Woolf 2007, 82 and 235), which lists an apparent circuit of ecclesiastical settlements claimed by the Church of 'Lindisfarne' including Norham, *Carnham, Culterham*, the two Jedworths (ie Jedburgh and Old Jedburgh), Melrose, *Tigbrethingham*, Abercorn, Edinburgh, Pefferham, Auldhame, Tyninghame, Coldinghame, Tillmouth and back to Norham. The sequence here makes it fairly clear that Auldhame in East Lothian is intended and Pefferham is probably the original English name for the Anglo-Saxon ecclesiastical site at Aberlady, which lies on the left bank of the estuary of the Peffer Burn. This may reflect the mid-9th-century date attributed to it since the *Historia de Sancto Cuthberto* of the 11th century repeats the list but omits *Tigbrethingham*, Abercorn and Edinburgh, and elsewhere marks Inveresk as the limit of Cuthbertine claims, presumably reflecting the Scottish annexation of the Edinburgh region in the mid-10th century. We should not, however, take this for granted. What is perhaps most interesting about Auldhame's appearance in this list is that it is already 'auld'. Alan James (2010) has thoroughly surveyed the use of *-ham* and *-ingaham* in the place-names of Anglo-Saxon Scotland and made a good case for them primarily indicating ecclesiastical centres, with 'ham' representing the estate dependent upon a minster and 'ingaham' the estate of the people dependent upon a minster. Auldhame was thus, it seems, already the 'old minster-estate' by the mid-9th century. Taken together with the evidence from *Historia De Sancto Cuthberto* that by the 11th century all the lands between Lammermuir and the Esk were dependent upon the Church of St Balthere at Tyninghame and the statement in the 16th-century Aberdeen Breviary that, along with Tyninghame and Preston, Auldhame was dedicated to St Baldred (as Balthere had become known by then), the easiest interpretation would be to assume that Auldhame was, in some sense, a precursor to Tyninghame.

That Auldhame was Balthere's 'original church' is perhaps supported by the tradition that Balthere spent some of his life as a hermit on the Bass Rock. This tradition is supported by the near-contemporary account of Balthere contained in Alcuin's poem *On the Bishops, Kings and Saints of York* (Godman 1982, ll, 1319–87), which describes his life as a hermit on a cliff-girt island surrounded by sea. Balthere's death is recorded in the Northumbrian annals, which form a continuation of Bede's history, under the year AD 756, which link him with Tyninghame. The Bass would have provided for Balthere, and perhaps for others of his house, a place for retreat and reflection similar to that provided for the community of Lindisfarne by Inner Farne or the community of Iona by Hinba. The Forth in the late pre-Viking Age may have hosted numerous pairings of island retreats with mainland ecclesiastical houses, May and Kilrenny (connected with Ethernan) and Inchcolm and Aberdour (for the Columbans). St Serf's Isle in Loch Leven may originally have performed this service for the community of Serf (whether this was based principally at Dunning or Culross).

Associating Auldhame with Balthere, however, raises a number of questions. Firstly, his obituary clearly links him with Tyninghame. It might be tempting to think of Auldhame as 'Old Tyninghame' and to suggest that the centre of the community moved to present day Tyninghame at a later date but its location is almost certainly too far from the Tyne for that to be the case. Although cropmarks at Whitekirk have tentatively been identified as the monastic community at Tyninghame there has, to date, been no excavation and so we have no sense of the chronology of the site. Secondly, the dates retrieved from Auldhame could push back the beginning of the sequence almost a century before Balthere's time. The radiocarbon dates, of course, give only an approximate range and if Balthere was very old at the time of his death he might still be counted the founder of the community interred at Auldhame.

We should not, however, assume too readily that Balthere, celebrated as the chief saint of the community by the 11th century, was necessarily its founder. Cuthbert, it will be remembered, was in fact the sixth bishop of Lindisfarne, a house that had been founded at about the time of his birth, and did not even join the community until it had been in existence for about 30 years. Yet Cuthbert is widely regarded as the saint of Lindisfarne and when that community abandoned the island in the 9th century and sought a new home they were known as the Congregation of Cuthbert. In the case of Lindisfarne this may have been in part because the actual founder bishop, the Iona monk Aidan (d. AD 651), was, by Cuthbert's time regarded as having been potentially schismatic on account of the Easter controversy, which had come to a head in Northumbria after his death in AD 664. Cuthbert, however, was the third bishop to follow the 'correct' method of calculating Easter. His immediate predecessor, Eata, however, was translated to the see of Hexham before his death (and thus his body lay there and was not available as a relic for the community on Lindisfarne to revere locally) and the first 'orthodox' bishop, the Irishman Tuda, died within a year of his consecration so presumably had little opportunity to make an impression. Cuthbert thus may have been regarded as the first orthodox bishop whose reputation and relics lent themselves easily to the formation of a cult, though it should be recalled that the physical, wooden, church built by Aidan was also one of Lindisfarne's chief relics and was carried to Norham as such in the 9th century.

By analogy, then, we might hypothesise that, while Balthere was eventually to become regarded as the premier saint and patron of Tyninghame and its dependent territories and churches, we are not compelled to imagine him to be the founder of the community. If the indications of the inception of the cemetery are correct, then it would be natural to assume that the early community at Auldhame would have followed the 84-year cycle *computus* in order to calculate the date of Easter and early abbots may even have been Irish (or perhaps even British). Alternatively, like Eata, who was abbot of Melrose and Ripon before becoming first bishop of Lindisfarne and then finally of Hexham, it is also possible that early abbots of Auldhame, and/or Tyninghame, had been promoted to more prestigious posts before their deaths and thus left their corporeal relics to other churches. A lack of corporeal relics from the age of foundation may also explain the continued importance of the site at Auldhame after the rise of Tyninghame, if the place itself, like Aidan's wooden church, was regarded as the locus of sanctity rather than a body that could be translated.

The relocation of the community from a circumscribed clifftop promontory site to a fertile and more spacious lowland site, as it grew in size and importance, reflects a transformation found elsewhere in the Northumbrian Church; compare, for example, the apparent shift in focus from *Urbs Coludi* (\*Coludesburh) on St Abbs Head to Coldingham. Bede describes Lindisfarne in AD 664, at the time that Colmán and the Iona clergy were expelled, thus (*HE* III.2) 6:

> There were very few buildings there except the church, in fact only those without which the life of the community was impossible. They had no wealth (*pecunia*) except for livestock, if they received *pecunia* from the rich they promptly gave it to the poor; for they had no need to amass wealth or to provide dwellings for the reception of worldly and powerful men, since these only came to the church to pray and to hear the word of God. The king himself used to come, when the opportunity allowed, with only five or six thegns, and when he had finished his prayers in the church he went away. If they happened to take a meal there, they were content with the simple daily fair of the brothers and asked for nothing more.

Large ecclesiastical endowments extending into scores of hides seem only to have begun during the reign of king Ecgfrith in the 670s, with his foundations of Hexham, Jarrow and Ripon, and it is from his time onwards that Northumbrian church settlements began to evolve into the major centres of production and consumption that produced most of the material culture we tend to associate with it; sculpture, display manuscripts, metalwork and so forth. This change in the practice of church endowment, from the land that a community of a head of house and 12 companions could farm themselves to extensive estates from which they might draw renders and services of an apparently secular community, seems to have occurred across the English-speaking kingdoms at this time and may reflect the reforms of the English church undertaken under the direction of Archbishop Theodore (AD 668–690). It seems likely that, while the site at Auldhame would have suited a small monastic community of perhaps a dozen brothers in the days of Kings Oswald (AD 634–642) and Oswiu (AD 642–671), the increasing complexity of such communities and settlements in the time of Oswiu's sons and their successors, which is doubtless connected to the rise of the North Sea *emporia* network, probably prompted a relocation of the complex to the more spacious and accessible site of Tyninghame across the estuary of the Tyne from the royal *burh* at Dunbar.

This interpretation of the relationship between Auldhame and Tyninghame, that they were in effect one establishment that was relocated in the decades around AD 700, is complicated by the continued survival of the former as a burial site and settlement, as a named place in the list from *HRA*, and eventually as a parish kirk. A possible explanation for the continued existence of Auldhame after the growth of Tyninghame may be that the site itself functioned in some ways as an associative (non-corporeal) relic. When Bishop Ecgred (AD 830–845) abandoned Lindisfarne in the second quarter of the 7th century, presumably out of fear of further Viking attacks, and relocated his see initially to Norham on the Tweed, he took with him not only the corporeal relics of Saint Cuthbert and King Ceolwulf (who had spent nearly 30 years in retirement on Lindisfarne) but also, we are told in *Historia de Sancto Cuthberto* (§9), a certain church built by Bishop Aidan. Here we see the original church building of Lindisfarne being regarded as a relic in its own right. In our corner of East Lothian, the distance between the original and the new site was not so great as to require the actual movement of the church (which might have been difficult if the building itself was not a timber frame building) but it may have become curated as part of a ritual and hagiological landscape. The presence nearby, in modern times, of a St Baldred's Well, Cave and Boat, together with the place-name Scoughall, in which the first element is Old English *scucca*, a devil or demon, suggests that the narrative of Balthere's saintly existence could be relived in the physical environment of Auldhame, which also, of course, retained a view of the Bass Rock that was not shared by Tyninghame. Thus both the brothers from the community at Tyninghame and pilgrims and visitors from farther afield could encounter the very landscape the saint had inhabited and reflect upon famous instances in his life and spiritual struggles.

The pre-Reformation parish of Auldhame seems to have comprised only 750 acres and encompassed two settlements; the hamlet of Auldhame and that of Scoughall. This must have been one of the geographically smallest parishes in Scotland. The parish system emerged in the course of the central Middle Ages, primarily it seems in the 12th century, but often adapted pre-existing structures. The small size and peculiar nature of Auldhame parish suggests that it emerged from an attempt to rationalise an existing unit into the new universalising model. It seems likely that Auldhame hamlet and the land that became the parish originated as provision for the residence and maintenance of the curatorial staff of the hagiological landscape described in the last paragraph. This staff would, presumably, have included at least one priest and his household. Indeed, it would be unsurprising if the peasantry of later medieval Auldhame were largely the descendants of a hereditary priestly family. The identity of the community at Auldhame for most of Phase 1, as the household of a secular priest or priests, would be consistent with the demographic make-up of the cemetery, which shows no segregation on the basis of gender as one would expect were this the cemetery of a coenobitic community. The absence of adolescent and young adult male skeletons, in contrast to the full range of female skeletons, might suggest that this was the cemetery of a family group whose sons were regularly sent away for education and training, presumably, in this case, either at Tyninghame or at the episcopal household on Lindisfarne (or both). A selected individual may have been returned to the household when it became time to take over from the incumbent at the time of the latter's death or retirement. This kind of hereditary caste of secular clergy seems to have been widespread in the Insular world, and beyond, prior to the Gregorian reforms of the 11th to 13th centuries.

The model outlined above of a secular priestly household intimately connected, as satellite, with a more significant monastic establishment, would explain the mixed signals given off by the archaeological material recovered from the site. Auldhame, I would suggest, was a farming community supported by about five hides of land (a flexible unit but conventionally *c* 600 acres of arable together with associated rough grazing, woodland etc), in which householders were educated clerics, at least one of whom at any time would have been a priest capable of performing mass in the church, which remained the focus of the cemetery. The bulk of the population might be regarded as what Colmán Etchingham has described as 'para-monastic', individuals and groups who lived lives largely indistinguishable from those of the mass of the laity, and who are sometimes described as 'monastic tenants' by modern scholars, but who regarded themselves, and were regarded by the Church authorities, as in some sense belonging to the monastic community. We should expect Auldhame to have been in a symbiotic relationship with Tyninghame with items of economic significance travelling in both directions. The rocky coastline at Auldhame, in contrast to that nearer Tyninghame, may have made it the obvious place to collect and process the whelks, even if the scriptorium or gynaecium which utilised the dye was located at the coenobitic centre.

A number of questions remain regarding the broader context of Auldhame in this period. Some of these remain unanswerable given the limited nature of the surviving evidence, textual and archaeological. The first of these relates to the perennial issue of the early Christian history of the region. Was the church established by the Bernicians inserted into a pre-existing ecclesiastical landscape occupied by British Christians and their churches or not? The evidence is hard to interpret since the date of English settlement is not established, and we cannot be certain that Christianity had necessarily penetrated the region in the pre-English period. Evidence for British Christianity in Scotland south of the Forth is mostly located farther west, ie the early Christian monuments at the Catstane (Edinburgh airport), Peebles and on the Yarrow water (Forsyth 2005). The British place-name Aberlady appears to be secondary to the name Pefferhame appearing in English texts and may, in origin, simply reflect the name of the location used by the inhabitants of Fife. This is, of course negative evidence, so the jury must remain out in this instance, but it is noticeable that the toponymy of East Lothian remains very English. An exception to this general rule is Dunbar itself, OE Dynbær, the nearest *villa regalis* that appears to have a British name. Our knowledge of this location as a royal centre comes from the Life of St Wilfrid (*VW* 38), which states that King Ecgfrith had Bishop Wilfrid imprisoned in his *urbs* there, in the charge of his prefect Tydlin. Tydlin's name may be an Anglo-Saxon spelling of a British or Gaelic name (in *Tud-* or *Tuath-*) but we cannot be certain of this, and even if it were it would not necessarily indicate that the bearer was not English. The continuity of the British name for this *urbs* may suggest continuity of occupation and perhaps relatively early occupation but although archaeological fieldwork has confirmed Anglo-Saxon occupation of the headland, precise chronology and evidence for pre-English settlement is lacking, at present. The royal centre may originally have drawn tribute from across East Lothian but it is quite likely that after the endowment of Tyninghame the river Tyne marked the boundary between two tributary districts, one supplying the *urbs* and one the monastery. The respective secular and ecclesiastical authority of the two sites, however, may have been coterminous. The large territory ascribed to the monastery of St Balthere in *HSC* (§4) is perhaps some of the best evidence for the existence of mother churches with shire-sized *parochia* in Anglo-Saxon England. There is no suggestion that this was not considered part of the diocese administered first from Lindisfarne and later from Norham and other places, but Tyninghame clearly had a special place amongst the churches of East Lothian, analogous perhaps to that of Coldingham in Berwickshire.

### 7.4.2 The 'Viking' burial

One of the latest burials in Phase 1 of the site, G751, containing SK752, caused some stir following the initial excavations and has become labelled the 'Viking' burial. This was a burial of a young adult male wearing a belt set reminiscent of those found in the Irish Sea region in the 9th and 10th centuries, prick spurs, and accompanied by a spearhead, apparently from a spear laid parallel to the body with the head pointed towards the feet (Chapter 4.2). It has to be emphasised that an extended inhumation in a churchyard strongly suggests a Christian burial and it should be noted that there is nothing explicitly non-Christian about dressed bodies or grave goods. The richest Merovingian burials come from within churches. Nonetheless, in the context of Northumbrian ecclesiastical graveyards of this period this is unusual. *Historia Regum Anglorum* records the sacking of Tyninghame by Olaf Guthfrithson, king of Dublin and Northumbria, shortly before his death in AD 941. It is tempting to associate this burial with that expedition, indeed even to speculate that it may be the body of King Olaf himself. This is not impossible but it is hard to see how it could be established beyond doubt. Olaf was probably still young when he died (his father had died as recently as AD 934) but since we have no idea where he was born or raised and have no secure DNA comparanda we are unlikely to be able to confirm or exclude this identification. What we can say is that the equipment accompanying the burial probably signals that the body was that of a man who spent time in the household or retinue of the kings of the Uí Ímar dynasty, which dominated both sides of the Irish Sea from about AD 917 until at least the middle of the 10th century. The belt, spurs and spear may represent part of an equipment set issued to royal retainers and thus regarded, on one level, as marks of status and honour, which their families may have liked to remind neighbours of at the time of burial. The major question regarding this burial at Auldhame is whether we should imagine the body to be that of a local boy who spent time in service with the kings of Northumbria and Dublin or whether it was a king's man, or even a king (?), who happened to die locally and was buried in the burial site most closely associated with Balthere as an act of piety by his companions. Unless the isotope analysis can be refined it is hard to know how we should answer this question.

## 7.5 SUMMARY

Excavation on the headland at Auldhame has revealed 1,000 years of burial activity and liturgical practice, the nature of which changed over the course of the millennium. It has charted the birth and death of a church, from a monastic settlement established in the 7th century AD, which became a parish church in the 12th century and ended its life in the 17th century AD as the burial aisle/mortuary chapel for its wealthy landowners.

That a parish church and graveyard existed at Auldhame from at least the 12th century is documented; Morag Cross has painstakingly identified every reference to Auldhame in existing records to construct a fascinating narrative of one of the smallest parishes in Scotland. The cartographic evidence placed the 'kirktown of Aldham' to the south of the headland so it was assumed that this was also the locus of the church, both village and church having long since disappeared. The excavation has now identified the actual position of the church but, more significantly, the subsequent post-excavation programme has established the early date at which it was founded and the nature of that early foundation. The body of evidence presented in this volume suggests that there was a monastic settlement on the headland, which flourished between the mid-7th and mid-9th centuries AD. Alex Woolf has proposed that this was a 'para-monastic' community, a secular but clerical household whose composition would explain the mixed genders and ages displayed by the occupants of the graveyard. The local cult of the Anglian St Balthere and the contemporary descriptions of his life make an association with the monastic settlement at Auldhame compelling but whether it was his foundation is another matter. Alex Woolf explores other contemporary examples to show how Balthere may have become the premier saint of the religious community without necessarily being its founder.

The monastic settlement ceased to exist some time towards the end of the 9th century AD, an event that may or may not have been influenced by Viking activity around the coast. The burial in the graveyard of a young man, fully dressed and accompanied by horse equipment and weaponry, has engendered much attention, not least because his date spans a known Viking raid in the area. Whether or not he was Olaf Guthfrithson, king of Dublin and Northumbria or just a member of his retinue, this brief Viking interlude in south-east Scotland is a reminder that the boundaries of the Viking sphere of influence centred on the Irish Sea, the Isle of Man and northern England extended north into Scotland as well.

After its abandonment as a monastic settlement, Auldhame continued to function as a church and graveyard, presumably because of the sanctity conveyed by its association with Balthere. It served as the parish church for Auldhame for nigh on seven centuries, albeit with periods of disuse. The archaeological evidence consists primarily of the skeletal remains, the hiatuses in burial reflecting political and socio/economic events in the wider world, the conquest of the Lothians by the Scots in the mid-10th century AD, and the demographic collapse in the 14th century caused by crop failure, epidemics and epizootics, not to mention the effects of Edward I's armies rampaging through the region. The daily activities of the medieval population are briefly glimpsed in the small assemblage of ceramics and metalwork found just outside the graveyard boundary. The enduring nature of this boundary throughout the history of the graveyard is notable, burial never extending beyond the line demarcated by the Anglian ditches. The evolution of the church buildings throughout this period are poorly understood and in retrospect, the decision not to fully excavate them was misguided, not only because so few churches of this early date have been investigated but also because the opportunity to trace the development of church architecture over a millennium has been missed.

Without doubt, the most significant element of the evidence from Auldhame is that covering the Anglian period. This is a major contribution to our relatively sparse understanding of Anglian activity in the Lothians, albeit that it is primarily religious and not secular activity. Nonetheless, the political and social landscape of the Lothians is now populated by another site, another focus around which British and Anglian interests must have circled, alongside Tyninghame, Dunbar and Doon Hill. The context of Auldhame would be much enriched by investigation of the cropmarks at Whitekirk and Aberlady, and by full excavation of the church buildings that still survive on the headland, but we are moving nearer to being able to write an Anglian archaeology of the Lothians.

# BIBLIOGRAPHY

## PUBLISHED SOURCES

Acsádi, G & Nemeskeri, J 1970 *History of Human Lifespan and Mortality*. Budapest: Akademai Kiado.

*ADC* II = Neilson, G & Paton, H (eds) 1918 *Acts of the Lords of Council in Civil Causes*, Vol. II, *1496–1501*. Edinburgh.

*ADCP* = Hannay, R K (ed) 1932 *Acts of the Lords of Council in Public Affairs, 1501–1554*. Edinburgh.

Alcock, L 1988 'The activities of potentates in Celtic Britain, AD 500–800: a positivist approach', *in* Driscoll, S T & Nieke, M R (eds) *Power and Politics in Early Medieval Britain and Ireland*, 22–39. Edinburgh: Edinburgh University Press.

Alcock, L 2003 *Kings and Warriors, Craftsmen and Priests in Northern Britain AD 550–850*. Edinburgh: Soc Antiq Scot Monog Ser.

Alcock, L, Alcock, E & Foster, S 1986 'Reconnaissance excavations on Early Historic fortifications and other royal sites in Scotland, 1974–84:1, excavations near St Abbs's Head, Berwickshire, 1980', *Proc Soc Antiq Scot* 116, 255–79.

Anderson, A O 1908 *Scottish Annals from English Chroniclers AD 500 to 1286*. London: David Nutt.

Anderson, A O 1990 *Early Sources of Scottish history, AD 500 to 1286*, Vol. 2. Stamford.

Anderson, M O 1976 'The Celtic Church in Kinrimund', *in* McRoberts, D (ed) *The Medieval Church of St Andrews*, 1–10. Glasgow.

Anderson, S 1994 *The Human Skeletal Remains from The Hirsel, Coldstream*. Unpubl archive report.

Angus, W 1926 'Two early East Lothian Charters', *Trans E Loth Antiq and Fld Natur Soc*, 5–11.

Aries, P (transl Weaver, H) 1981 *The Hour of our Death*. Oxford.

Arnold, T 1882 (ed.) *Symeonis Monachi Opera Omnia*. 2 vols, Rolls Series 75. London.

Arrhenius, B 1985 *Merovingian Garnet Jewellery*. Stockholm: Almqvist & Wiksell.

Ash, M 1976 'David Bernham, Bishop of St Andrews, 1239–1253', *in* McRoberts, D (ed.) *The Medieval Church of St Andrews*, 33–44. Glasgow.

Aufderheide, A C & Rodríguez-Martín, C 1998 *The Cambridge Encyclopaedia of Human Paleopathology*. Cambridge: Cambridge University Press.

Barber, J W 1981 'Excavations on Iona', *Proc Soc Antiq Scot* 111, 282–380.

Barber, J 2003 *Bronze Age Farms and Iron Age Farm Mounds of the Outer Hebrides*. Scot Archaeol Internet Reps 3.

Barrell, A Dm 2000 *Medieval Scotland*. Cambridge.

Barrow, G W S 1960 'Introduction: analysis of the Acts of Malcolm IV', *in Regesta Regum Scottorum I: The Acts of Malcolm IV, 1153–1165*, 57–89. Edinburgh.

Barrow, G W S 1971 'Introduction: analysis of the Acts of William I', *in Regesta Regum Scottorum I: The Acts of William I, 1165–1214*, 68–95. Edinburgh.

Barrow, G 1994 'The medieval diocese of St Andrew', *in* Higgitt, J (ed.), *Medieval Art and Architecture in the Medieval Diocese of St Andrews*, 1–6. London.

Barrow, G W S 2003a *The Kingdom of the Scot*. Edinburgh.

Barrow, G W S 2003b *Kingship and Unity*. Edinburgh.

Bateson, J D & Holmes, N M McQ 2003 'Roman and medieval coins in Scotland, 1996–2000', *Proc Soc Antiq Scot* 133, 245–76.

Batey, C & Paterson, C 2013 'A Viking burial at Balnakeil, Sutherland', *in* Reynolds, A & Webster, L (eds) *Early Medieval Art and Archaeology in the Northern World: Studies in honour of James Graham-Campbell*, Leiden, 631–61

Battley, N, Roberts, J & King, S 2008 'Human remains', *in* James, H F & Yeoman, P, 83–91.

Bayley, J, 1992 *Non-ferrous Metalworking from Coppergate. The Archaeology of York 17/7*. London: CBA.

Beckett, A, MacGregor, G, Maguire, D & Sneddon, D forthcoming 'Living and dying on the bonniebanks: ten thousand years at the Carrick, Midross, Loch Lomond', *Proc Soc Antiq Scot*.

Bender Jørgensen, L 1987 'The textile remains', *in* Welander, R D E, Batey, C & Cowie, T G 'A Viking burial from Kneep, Uig, Isle of Lewis', *Proc Soc Antiq Scot* 117, 164–8.

Bender Jørgensen, L 1992 *North European Textiles until AD 1000*. Aarhus: Aarhus University Press.

Berry, A C & Berry, R J 1967 'Epigenetic variation in the human cranium', *J Anatomy* 101, 361–79.

Bersu, G & Wilson, Dm 1966 *Three Viking Graves in the Isle of Man*. Soc Med Archaeol Monog Ser 1.

Biddle, M & Hinton, D A 1990 'Annular and other brooches', *in* Biddle, M *Object and Economy in Medieval Winchester:*

*Volume II*, 639–43. Oxford: Clarendon (Winchester studies 7ii).

Biggam, C P 2006 'Knowledge of whelk dyes and pigments in Anglo-Saxon England', *Anglo-Saxon England* 35, 23–55.

Bimson, M & Freestone, I 2000 'Analysis of some glass from Anglo-Saxon jewellery', *in* Price, J (ed.) *Glass in Britain and Ireland AD 350–1100*, 131–5. London: Trustees of the British Museum.

Binski, P 1996 *Medieval Death, Ritual and Representation*. London.

Birck, J L 1986 'Precision K-Rb-Sr isotopic analysis – application to Rb-Sr chronology', *Chemical Geology* 56, 73–83.

Black, G F 1949 *The Surnames of Scotland, Their Origin, Meaning and History*. Edinburgh: Birlinn (repr. 1999).

Blackwell, A 2004 *An alternative approach to Northumbrian-period Scotland: the stray finds material from East Lothian and the Scottish Borders*. Univ Glasgow: unpub MPhil thesis.

Bøe, J 1940 'Norse antiquities in Ireland', *in* Shetelig, H (ed.) *Viking Antiquities in Great Britain and Ireland* Part III. Oslo.

Boece, H 1821 *The History and Chronicles of Scotland, Written in Latin by Hector Boece, translated by John Bellenden, Vol. I*. Edinburgh.

Bogaard, A, Heaton, T H E, Oulton, P & Merbach, I 2007 'The impact of manuring on nitrogen isotope ratios in cereals: archaeological implications for the reconstruction of diet and crop management practices', *J Archaeol Sci* 34, 335–43.

Borland, J, Fraser, I & Sherriff, J 2007 'Eight socketed stones from Eastern Scotland', *Tayside & Fife Archaeol J* 13, 100–11.

Bowler, D & Cachart, R 1994 'Tay Street, Perth: the excavation of an early harbour site', *Proc Soc Antiq Scot* 124, 467–89.

Boyd, W E 1989 'Perth: the wooden coffins', *in* Stones, J A (ed.) *Three Scottish Carmelite Friaries: Aberdeen, Linlithgow and Perth*, 117–8. Edinburgh: Soc Antiq Scot Monog Ser No. 6.

Boylston, A 2000 'Evidence for weapon-related trauma in British archaeological samples', *in* Cox, M & Mays, S (eds) *Human Osteology in Archaeology and Forensic Science*, 357–80. London: Greenwich Medical Media Ltd.

Brickley, M & Ives, R 2008 *The Bioarchaeology of Metabolic Bone Disease*. Oxford: Academic Press.

Brickley, M & McKinley, J I (eds) 2004 *Guidelines to the Standards for Recording Human Remains*. Institute of Field Archaeologists Paper No. 7. BABAO, IFA.

Brooke, C 2000 *Safe Sanctuaries: Security and Defence in Anglo-Scottish border churches, 1296–1603*. Edinburgh: John Donald.

Brooks, S T & Suchey, Jm 1990 'Skeletal age determination based on the os pubis: a comparison of the Acsadi-Nemeskeri and Suchey-Brooks methods', *Human Evolution* 5, 227–38.

Brothwell, D R 1981 *Digging up Bones*, 3rd edn. British Museum Nat. Hist./OUP. London

Brown, C J & Shipley, B M 1982 *South-East Scotland: Soil Survey of Scotland*. Aberdeen: AUP & Macaulay Institute for Soil Research.

Brown, M 1983 'New evidence for Anglian settlement in East Lothian', *Scottish Archaeol Rev*, 2, 156–63.

Brown, M 2004 *The Wars of Scotland 1214–1371*. Edinburgh.

Brown, T A, Nelson, D E M Vogel, J S & Southon, J R 1988 'Improved collagen extraction by modified Longin method', *Radiocarbon* 30, 171–7.

Bruce-Mitford, R L S 1956 'The pectoral cross', *in* Battiscombe, C F (ed.) *The Relics of Saint Cuthbert*, 308–25. Oxford: OUP.

Bruce-Mitford, R L S 1978 *The Sutton Hoo Ship Burial. Volume II: Arms, Armour and Regalia*. London: Trustees of the British Museum.

Buikstra, J & Ubelaker, D H 1994 *Standards for Data Collection from Human Skeletal Remains*. Arkansas Archaeol Survey Ser 44.

Butter, R 2008 'Inchmarnock and Kildavanan: The place name evidence', *in* Lowe, C (ed.) *Inchmarnock: An Early Historic Island Monastery and its Archaeological Landscape*, 53–4. Edinburgh: Soc Antiq Scot Monog Ser.

Caldwell, D H 1995a 'Bone and iron', *in* Lewis & Ewart 1995, 82–3.

Caldwell, D H 1995b 'The iron objects', *in* Lewis & Ewart 1995, 91–3.

Callander, J G 1924 'Fourteenth-century brooches and other ornaments in the National Museum of Antiquities of Scotland', *Proc Soc Antiq Scot* 58, 160–84.

Cameron, E 2000 *Sheaths and Scabbards in England AD 400–1100*. BAR Brit Ser 301, Oxford: British Archaeological Reports.

Cameron, E 2007 *Scabbards and Sheaths from Viking and Medieval Dublin*. Dublin: National Museum of Ireland.

Cameron, J K (ed.) 1972 *The First Book of Discipline*. Glasgow (repr. 2005).

Campbell, A C 1989 *Seashores and Shallow Seas of Britain and Europe*. London: Hamlyn.

Campbell, E 1998 'Spearhead', *in* Sharples, N *Scalloway. A Broch, Late Iron Age Settlement and Medieval Cemetery in Shetland*, 159. Oxford: Oxbow Books.

Campbell, E 2010 'The archaeology of writing in the time of Adomnán', *in* Wooding, J with Aist, R, Clancy, T & O'Loughlin, T (eds) *Adomnán of Iona: Theologian, Lawmaker, Peacemaker*, 139–44. Dublin: Four Courts Press.

Cappers, R T J, Bekker, R M & Jans, J E A 2006 *Digital Seed Atlas of the Netherlands*. Eelde: Barkhuis Publishing.

Carter, S 1990 'Seacliff (Whitekirk and Tyninghame parish), burials and associated enclosure', *Disc Excav Scot*, 31.

Carver, M 2004 'An Iona of the East: the early medieval monastery at Portmahomack, Tarbat Ness', *Medieval Archaeol* 48, 1–30.

Carver, M 2008 *Portmahomack – Monastery of the Picts*. Edinburgh: Edinburgh University Press.

# BIBLIOGRAPHY

Carver, M 2009 'Early Scottish monasteries and prehistory; a preliminary dialogue', *Scottish Historical Review* 226, 332–51.

Ceron-Carrasco, R 2005 'The fish remains and marine shell from Geodha Smoo Caves', *in* Pollard, T 'The excavation of four caves in Geodha Smoo near Durness, Sutherland', *Scottish Archaeol Internet Reps* 18, 32–5.

Cessford, C 1999 'Relations between the Britons of Southern Scotland and Anglo-Saxon Northumbria', *in* Hawkes, J & Mills, S (eds) *Northumbria's Golden Age*, 150–60. Stroud: Sutton.

Chadburn, R & Hill, P 1997 'Exotic, imported and transformed stones', *in* Hill, P *Whithorn and St Ninian: The Excavations of a Monastic Town 1984–91*, 468–74. Stroud: Sutton Publishing & The Whithorn Trust.

Chalmers, G 1889 *Caledonia: or, a historical . . . account of North Britain*, Vol. IV (new edn). Paisley.

Chenery, C, Muldner, G, Evans, J, Eckardt, H & Lewis, M 2010 'Strontium and stable isotope evidence for diet and mobility in Roman Gloucester, UK', *J Archaeol Sci* 37.1, 150–63.

Clancy, T O 1995 'Annat in Scotland and the origins of the parish', *Innes Rev* 46, 91–115.

Clark, J 1997a 'The medieval bonework', *in* Driscoll, S T & Yeoman, P A 1997 *Excavations within Edinburgh Castle in 1988–91*, 146–9. Edinburgh: Soc Antiq Scot monog ser 12.

Cohen, M N 1994 'The osteological paradox reconsidered', *Current Anthropology* 35, 629–31.

*Cold Corr* = *The correspondence, inventories, account rolls and law proceedings of the priory of Coldingham*, Surtees Soc, 1841.

Colgrave, B & Mynors, R A B (eds) 1991 *Bede's Ecclesiastical History of the English People*. Oxford: Clarendon Press.

Colt, G F R 1887 *History and Genealogy of the Colts of that ilk and Gartsherrie*. Edinburgh.

Connell, B & Rauxloh, P 2003 *A rapid method for recording human skeletal data*. Oracle Manual. Unpubl Rep by the Museum of London.

Cormack, W F 1995 'Barhobble, Mochrum – excavation of a forgotten church site in Galloway', *Trans Dumfries & Galloway Natur Hist & Antiq Soc* 70, 5–106.

Coughlan, J & Holst, M 2000 'Health status', *in* Fiorato, V, Boylston, A & Knüsel, C (eds), *Blood Red Roses. The Archaeology of a Mass Grave from the Battle of Towton AD 1461*, 61–76. Oxford: Oxbow Books.

Courty, M A, Goldberg, P & Macphail, R 1989 *Soils and Micromorphology in Archaeology*. Cambridge: Cambridge University Press.

Cowan, I B 1967 *The Parishes of medieval Scotland*. Edinburgh.

Cowan, I B 1995a 'The appropriation of parish churches', *in* Kirk, J (ed.) 1995a, 12–29.

Cowan, I B 1995b 'The development of the parochial system', *in* Kirk, J (ed.) 1995a, 1–11.

Cowan, I B 1995c 'Vicarages and the cure of souls', *in* Kirk, J (ed.) 1995a, 46–61.

Cowan, I B 1995d 'Church and society in the fifteenth century', *in* Kirk, J (ed.) 1995a, 170–92.

Cowan, I B & Easson, D E 1976 *Medieval Religious Houses Scotland*. London.

Cowgill, J, de Neergaard, M & Griffiths, N 1987 *Knives and Scabbards. Medieval Finds from Excavations in London: 1*. London: Museum of London.

Cowie, T G 1978 'Excavations at the Catstane, Midlothian 1977', *Proc Soc Antiq Scot* 109, 166–201.

Cox, A 1996 'Backland activities in medieval Perth; excavations at Meal Vennel & Scott Street', *Proc Soc Antiq Scot* 126, 733–821.

Cox, A 2000 'The artefacts', *in* Perry, D *Castle Park, Dunbar. Two Thousand Years on a Fortified Headland*, 113–67. Edinburgh: Soc Antiq Scot Monog Ser 16.

*CPL II* = Bliss, W H (ed.) 1895 *Calendar of entries in the Papal Registers relating to Great Britain and Ireland: Papal Letters* Vol. II, AD *1305–1342*. London.

*CPL XIII, Pt 2* = Twemlow, J A (ed.) 1955 *Calendar of entries in the Papal Registers relating to Great Britain and Ireland, Papal Letters* Vol. XIII, Pt 2, *1471–1484*. London.

*CPL XIV* = Twemlow, J A (ed.) 1960 *Calendar of entries in the Papal Registers relating to Great Britain and Ireland: Papal Letters Vol. 14: 1484–92*. Dublin.

*CPL XV* = Haren, M J (ed.) 1978 *Calendar of entries in the Papal Registers relating to Great Britain and Ireland*, Vol. XV: *Innocent BIII: Lateran Registers 1484–1492*. Dublin.

Craig, D 2006 'The later carved stone assemblage', *in* Lowe, C *Excavations at Hoddom, Dumfriesshire*, 123–32. Edinburgh: Soc Antiq Scot Monog Ser.

Cramp, R & Douglas-Home, C 1980 'New discoveries at The Hirsel, Coldstream, Berwickshire', *Proc Soc Antiq Scot* 109, 223–321.

Craster, E 1954 'The Patrimony of St Cuthbert', *Eng Hist Rev* 69, 178–99.

Crawford, J H 1987 *Outline of Fractures*. London: Churchill.

Crowe, C 1982 'A note on white quartz pebbles found in Early Christian contexts on the Isle of Man', *Isle of Man Natur Hist Antiq Soc* 7.4, 413–15.

Crowe, C 2003 'Early medieval parish formation in Dumfries and Galloway', *in* Carver, M (ed.) *The Cross goes North: Processes of Conversion in Northern Europe*, AD *300–1300*, 195–206. Boydell Press.

Cruden, S 1986 *Scottish Medieval Churches*. Edinburgh.

*CSSR* II = Dunlop, A I (ed.) 1956 *Calendar of Scottish Supplications to Rome*, Vol. II *1423–28*. Scott Hist Soc.

Cunnington, C W, Cunnington, P E & Beard, C 1960 *A Dictionary of English Costume, 900–1900*. London: Black.

Daniell, C 1997 *Death and Burial in Medieval England, 1066–1550*. London.

Daniels, R 1988 'The Anglo-Saxon monastery at Church Close, Hartlepool, Cleveland', *Archaeol J* 145, 158–210.

Daux, V, Lecuyer, C, Heran, M A, Amiot, R, Simon, L, Fourel, F, Martineau, F, Lynnerup, N, Reychler, H & Escarguel, G 2008 'Oxygen isotope fractionation between human phosphate and water revisited', *J Human Evolution* 55, 1138–47.

Davidson, D A & Carter, S P 1998 'Micromorphological evidence of past agricultural practices in cultivated soils: the impact of a traditional agricultural system on soils at Papa Stour, Shetland', *J Archaeol Sci* 25, 827–38.

Davidson, D & Simpson, I 1994 'Soils and landscape history: cast studies from the Northern Isles of Scotland', in Smout, T C & Foster, S (eds) *The History of Soils and Field Systems*, 66–73. Dalkeith: Scottish Cultural Press.

Dawes J 1980 'The human bones', in Dawes, J & Magilton, J *The Cemetery of St Helen-on-the-Walls, Aldwark*. The Archaeology of York Vol. 12, Fasicule 2. London: CBA.

Dawod, V & FitzPatrick, E A 1992 'Some population sizes and effects of the Enchytraeidae (Oligochaeta) on soil structure in a selection of Scottish soils', *Geoderma* 56, 173–8.

Dawson, J E 2007 *Scotland Re-formed 1488–1587*. Edinburgh.

DeNiro, M J 1985 'Postmortem preservation and alteration of in vivo bone collagen isotope ratios in relation to paleodietary reconstruction', *Nature* 317, 806–9.

Dinn, R 1995 'Monuments answerable to men's worth': burial patterns, social status and gender in late medieval Bury St Edmunds', *J Eccles Hist* 46, 237–55.

Donaldson, G 1965 *Scotland: James V to James VII*. Edinburgh.

Donnelly, J 1989 'The earliest Scottish charters?', *Scott Hist Rev* 68, 1–22.

Donnelly, J 1997 'Spiritual estates: the Durham monks in Scotland, 1094–1293', *Rec Scott Church Hist Soc* 27, 43–67.

Donnelly, J 1999 'Skinned to the bone: Durham evidence for taxations of the church in Scotland, 1254–1366', *Innes Rev* 50, 1–24.

Duncan, A A M 1958 'The Earliest Scottish charters', *Scott Hist Rev* 37, 103–35.

Duncan, A A M 1996 *Scotland: The Making of the Kingdom*. Edinburgh.

Duncan, A A M 1999 'Yes, the earliest Scottish charters', *Scott Hist Rev* 78, 1–38.

Dunlop, A I 1939 'Bagimond's Roll: statement of the tenths of the Kingdom of Scotland', *Misc Scott Hist Soc* 6, 3–80.

Edgar, A 1886 *Old Church Life in Scotland*. Paisley.

Egan, G & Pritchard, F 1991 *Medieval Finds from Excavations in London 3: Dress Accessories c. 1150–1450*. London: Museum of London.

Ellis, B M A 2002 *Prick Spurs 700–1700*. Finds Research Group AD 700–1700. Datasheet 30.

English Heritage 2002 *Centre for Archaeology Guidelines. Human Bones from Archaeological Sites. Guidelines for Producing Assessment Documents and Analytical Reports*.

Evans, J A, Montgomery, J, Wildman, G & Boulton, N 2010 'Spatial variations in biosphere Sr-87/Sr-86 in Britain', *J Geological Society* 167, 1–4.

Evison, V I 1982 'Bichrome vessels of the seventh and eighth centuries', *Studien zur Sachsenforschung* 3, 7–21.

Evison, V I 2000 'Glass vessels in England AD 400–1100', in Price, J (ed.) 2000 *Glass in Britain and Ireland, AD 350–1100*, 47–104. Brit Museum Occ Pap 127. London: British Museum Press.

Ewing, T 2006 *Viking Clothing*. Stroud: Tempus.

*Exch Rolls XIV* = *Exchequer Rolls of Scotland, Rotuli Scacarii Regum Scotorum*, Vol. XIV *(1513–22)*, Edinburgh.

*Fasti 1* = Scott, H et al (eds) 1915–81 *Fasti Ecclesiae Scoticanae: The Succession of Ministers in the Church of Scotland*. Edinburgh (10 vols).

*Fasti 2* = Watt, D E R & Murray, A L (eds) 2003 *Fasti Ecclesiae Scoticanae Medii Aevi Ad Annum 1638*. Edinburgh.

Fawcett, R 1985 *Scottish Medieval Churches*. Edinburgh.

February, E 1991 'Archaeological charcoals as indicators of vegetation change and human fuel choice in the late Holocene at Elands Bay, South Africa', *J Archaeol Sci* 19, 347–54.

Fellows-Jensen, G 2007 'Place-names as evidence of Scandinavian influence', reported in Heald, A (rapporteur) *The Vikings and Scotland – Impact and Influence*, 15–17. Edinburgh: Royal Soc Edinburgh.

Fenton, A 1981 'Early manuring techniques', in Mercer, R (ed.) *Farming Practice in British Prehistory*, 210–17. Edinburgh: Edinburgh University Press.

Fernie, E 1983 *The Architecture of the Anglo-Saxons*. London.

Fernie, E 1986 'Early church architecture in Scotland', *Proc Soc Antiq Scot* 116, 393–411.

Ferrier, W M 1980 *The North Berwick story*. North Berwick.

Finlay, J 2004 'Otterburn, Sir Adam (d. 1548)', in *Oxford Dictionary of National Biography*. www.oxforddnb.com/view/article/20938, accessed 29 April 2011.

Finnigan, M 1978 'Non metric variation in the infra-cranial skeleton', *J Anatomy* 125, 23–37.

Fiorato, V, Boylston, A & Knüsel, C (eds) 2000 *Blood red roses. The archaeology of a mass grave from the Battle of Towton AD 1461*. Oxford: Oxbow Books.

Fisher, I 2001 *Early Medieval Sculpture in the West Highlands and Islands*. Edinburgh: RCAHMS Monog Ser 1.

Forbes, A P 1872 *Kalendars of Scottish Saints*. Edinburgh.

Ford, B 1987 'The copper alloy objects', in Holdsworth, P (ed.) *Excavations in the Medieval Burgh of Perth 1979–1981*, 121–30, Edinburgh: Soc Antiq Scot Monog Ser No. 5.

Forsyth, K 2005 '*Hic memoria perpetua*: the early inscribed stones of southern Scotland in context', in Foster, S M & Cross, M (ed.) *Able Hands and Practiced Minds. Scotland's Early Medieval Sculpture in the 21st Century*, 113–34. Edinburgh: Historic Scotland.

Franklin, J (forthcoming) 'The finds', in Masser, P 'Excavations at Jeffrey Street, Edinburgh: the development of closes and tenements north of the Royal Mile during the 16th–18th centuries', *Scottish Archaeological Internet Reports*.

Franklin, J & Collard, M 2006 'The other finds', in Collard, M, Lawson, J A & Holmes, N *Archaeological Excavations in St Giles' Cathedral, Edinburgh, 1981–93*, Scot Archaeol Internet Reps 22, 54–6.

# BIBLIOGRAPHY

Fraser, J E 2009 *From Caledonia to Pictland: Scotland to 795*. Edinburgh.

Freestone, I, Hughes, M J & Stapleton, C P 2008 'The composition and production of Anglo-Saxon glass', *Catalogue of Anglo-Saxon Glass in the British Museum*, 29–46. London: Trustees of the British Museum.

Gabra-Sanders, T 1999a 'The textiles from Scar: a summary', in Owen, O & Dalland, M 1999 *Scar: A Viking Boat Burial on Sanday, Orkney*, 133–5. East Linton: Tuckwell.

Gabra-Sanders, T 1999b 'Appendix 2: catalogue of textiles', in Owen, O & Dalland, M 1999 *Scar: A Viking Boat Burial on Sanday, Orkney*, 198–200. East Linton: Tuckwell.

Gemmill, E & Mayhew, N 1995 *Changing Values in Medieval Scotland: A Study of Prices, Money and Weights and Measures*. Cambridge.

Giesler, U 1974 'Datierung und Herleitung der Vogelförmigen Riemenzungen', in Kossack, G & Ulbert, G (eds) *Studien zur vor- und frühgeschichtlichen Archäologie*, Teil II Frühmittelalter, 521–43, München.

Gilchrist, R & Sloane, B 2005 *Requiem. The Medieval Monastic Cemetery in Britain*. London: Museum of London Archaeology Service.

Godman, P 1982 'Introduction, iv: the political and ecclesiastical background', in Godman, P (ed.) *Alcuin: The Bishops, Kings, and Saints of York*, xlvii–xlvi. Oxford.

Goldberg, P 1979 'Micromorphology of sediments from Hayonim cave, Israel', *Catena* 6, 167–81.

Gooder, J 2004 'Excavation at Newbattle Abbey College Annexe, Dalkeith. Midlothian', *Proc Soc Antiq Scot* 134, 371–401.

Goodall, I H 1979 'The iron objects', in Williams, J H *St Peter's Northampton. Excavations 1973–1976*, 268–77. Northampton Development Corporation.

Goodall, I H 1984 'The metalwork', in Allan, J *Medieval and Post-medieval Finds from Exeter, 1971–80*, 337–48. Exeter: Exeter City Council & the University of Exeter (= Exeter Archeological Reports: Volume 3).

Goodman, A H 1993 'On the interpretation of health from skeletal remains', *Current Anthropology* 34, 281–8.

Gordon, A 1984 *Death is for the Living*. Edinburgh.

Graham-Campbell, J 1973 'A fragmentary bronze strap-end of the Viking period from The Udal, North Uist, Inverness-shire', *Med Archaeol* 17, 128–31.

Graham-Campbell, J 1980 *Viking Artefacts: A Select Catalogue*. London: British Museum Publications.

Graham-Campbell, J 1995 *The Viking-Age Gold and Silver of Scotland (AD 850–1100)*. Edinburgh: NMS.

Graham-Campbell, J 2004 '"Danes … in this country": discovering the Vikings in Scotland', *Proc Soc Antiq Scot* 134, 201–39.

Graham-Campbell, J & Batey, C 1998 *Vikings in Scotland: An Archaeological Survey*. Edinburgh: Edinburgh University Press.

Graham-Campbell, J & Paterson, C forthcoming *The Viking Graves of Scotland*.

Grant, A 1984 *Independence and Nationhood: Scotland 1306–1469*. London.

Grant, I F 1961 *Highland Folk Ways*. London.

Grant, J 1868 *The White Cockade; or, Faith and Fortitude*. London.

Graves, C P 1989 'Social space in the English medieval parish church', *Economy and Society* xviii, 297–322.

Grauer, A L & Roberts C A 1996 'Paleoepidemiology, healing, and possible treatment of trauma in the medieval cemetery population of St Helen-on-the-Walls, York, England', *American J Physical Anthropology* 100, 531–44.

Grieg, S 1940 *Viking Antiquities in Great Britain and Ireland*, II: *Viking Antiquities in Scotland*. Oslo: Aschehoug.

Griffiths, D 2010 *Vikings of the Irish Sea*. Stroud.

Hadley, D M 2000 'Burial practices in the northern Danelaw, c. 650–1100', *Northern History* 36, 199–216.

Hadley, D M 2001 *Death in Medieval England*. Stroud: Tempus.

Hall, D W 1996 'The pottery', in Bowler, D, Cox, A & Smith, C (eds) 'Four excavations in Perth 1980–1984', *Proc Soc Antiq Scot* 125, 952–9.

Hall, D W 2007 'Excavations at the pottery production centre of Colstoun, East Lothian', *Medieval Ceramics* 28, 35–76.

Halsall, G 2000 'The Viking presence in England? The burial evidence reconsidered', in Hadley, D M & Richards, J D (eds), *Cultures in Contact: Scandinavian Settlement in England in the 9th and 10th Centuries*, 259–76. Turnhout: Brepols.

Hamilton, E C 2007 'The earls of Dunbar and the church in Lothian and the Merse', *Innes Rev* 58, 1–34.

Harrison, S H 2001 'Viking graves and grave-goods in Ireland', in Larsen, A C (ed.) *The Vikings in Ireland*, 61–75. Roskilde.

Hatherley, C 2009 'Into the west: excavation of an early Christian cemetery at Montfode, Ardrossan, North Ayrshire', *Proc Soc Antiq Scot* 139, 195–211.

Haws, C H 1972 *Scottish Parish Clergy at the Reformation*. Edinburgh.

Henderson, D 2008 'The human remains from the church and graveyard (site 4)', in Lowe, C *Inchmarnock: An Early Historic Island Monastery and its Archaeological Landscape*, 209–21. Edinburgh: Soc Antiq Scot Monog Ser.

Henderson, J 1991 'The glass', in Armstrong, D, Tomlison, D & Evans, D H *Excavations at Lurk Lane, Beverley 1979–82*, 124–30. Sheffield Excavation Reports 1.

Henry, F 1952 'A wooden hut on Inishkea North, Co. Mayo (Site 3, House A)', *J Roy Soc Antiq Ireland* 82.2, 163–78.

Henshall, A S 1956 'A long cist cemetery at Parkburn Sand Pit, Lasswade, Midlothian', *Proc Soc Antiq Scot* 89, 252–83.

Herkless, J & Hannay, R K 1909 *The Archbishops of St Andrews*, Vol. II. Edinburgh.

Hewison, J K 1893 *The Isle of Bute in the Olden Time*. Edinburgh, 2 vols.

Hill, P H 1982 'Broxmouth Hill-fort excavations, 1977–8: an interim report', in Harding, D W *Later Prehistoric Settlement in South-East Scotland*. Univ Edinburgh, Dept Archaeol, Occ Paper 8.

Hill, P 1997 *Whithorn and St Ninian. The Excavation of a Monastic Town, 1984–91*. Stroud: Sutton.

Hillson, S 1986 *Teeth*. Cambridge: Cambridge University Press.

Hillson, S 1996 *Dental Anthropology*. Cambridge: Cambridge University Press.

Hillson, S 2001 'Recording dental caries in archaeological human remains', *Int J Osteoarchaeology* 11, 249–89.

Hinde, J H (ed.) 1868 'Preface', in *Symeonis Dunelmensis Opera et Collectanea*, Vol. I, Surtees Soc Vol. 51, iv–lxvi.

Hindmarch, E & Melikian, M 2006 'Baldred's Auldhame: a medieval chapel and cemetery in East Lothian', *The Archaeologist* 60, 37–9.

Hindmarch, E & Oram, R 2012 'Eldbotle; the archaeology and environmental history of a medieval rural settlement in East Lothian', *Proc Soc Antiq Scot* 142, 245–99.

Hinton, D 1996 *Southampton Finds Vol. 2. The Gold, Silver and other Non-ferrous Metalworking Evidence*. Stroud: Alan Sutton.

Historic Scotland 1997 *The Treatment of Human Remains in Archaeology*. Historic Scotland Operational Policy Paper 5.

Hope-Taylor, B 1977 *Yeavering. An Anglo-British Centre of early Northumbria*. London: HMSO.

Hope-Taylor, B 1980 'Balbridie … and Doon Hill', *Current Archaeol*, 72, 18–19.

Howells, W W 1973 'Cranial variation and multivariate analysis', *Papers of the Peabody Museum* 7, 95–105.

Hume, J R 2005 *Scotland's Best Churches*. Edinburgh University Press.

Humphrey, L 2000 'Growth studies of past populations: an overview and an example', *in* Cox, M & Mays, S (eds) 2000 *Human Osteology in Archaeology and Forensic science*, 23–38. London: Greenwich Medical Media Ltd.

Hunter, F 1994 'Dowalton Loch reconsidered', *Trans Dumfries & Galloway Nat Hist & Antiq Soc* 69, 53–71.

Hunter, F 2001 'Aberlady Anglo-Saxon pin', *Disc Excav Scot*, 30.

Hunter, F 2002 'Aberlady Anglo-Saxon lobed sword pommel and early historic mount', *Disc Excav Scot*, 34.

Hunter, J & Heyworth, M 1998 *The Hamwic Glass*. York: Council for British Archaeology (Research Report 116).

Inglis, J A 1935 *Sir Adam Otterburn of Redhall, King's Advocate, 1524–1538*. Glasgow.

*Inst Pub* = *Instrumenta Publica sive processus super Fidelitatibus et Hamagiis Scotorum Domino Regi Angliae Factis 1291–1296*, Bannatyne Club 1834.

Jacomet, S 2006 *Identification of Cereal Remains from Archaeological Sites*. Basel: Archaeobotany Lab IPAS.

James, A G 2010 'Scotland's -ham and -ingaham names: a reconsideration', *J Scottish Names Studies* 4, 103–30.

James, H 1996 *Coastal Assessment Survey: The Firth of Forth from Dunbar to the Border of Fife*. GUARD Rep 224.

James, H F & Yeoman, P 2008 *Excavations at St Ethernan's Monastery, Isle of May, Fife, 1992–97*. Perth: TAFAC Monog 6.

Jay, M & Richards, M P 2007 'Diet in the Iron Age cemetery population at Wetwang Slack, East Yorkshire, UK: carbon and nitrogen stable isotope evidence', *J Archaeol Sci* 33, 653–62.

Jennings, S 1992 *Medieval Pottery in the Yorkshire Museum*. York: Yorkshire Museum.

Johnson South, T (ed.) 2002 *Historia de Sancto Cuthberto: A History of St Cuthbert and a Record of his Patrimony*. Cambridge: Boydell & Brewer.

Jones, R, Haggarty, G, Hall, D W & Will, R 2006 'Sourcing Scottish white gritty ware', *Medieval Ceramics* 26 & 27, 45–84.

Jurmain, R 1999 *Stories from the Skeleton: Behavioural Reconstruction in Human Osteology*. Amsterdam: Gordon & Breach Science Publishers.

*Kelso Liber* = Innes, C (ed.) 1846 *Liber S Marie de Calchou*. Bannatyne Club.

Kenward, H K, Hall, A R & Jones, A K G 1980 'A tested set of techniques for the extraction of plant and animal macrofossils from waterlogged archaeological deposits', *Science and Archaeology* 22, 3–15.

Kilmurray, K 1980 *The Pottery Industry of Stamford, Lincolnshire*. Oxford: British Archaeological Reports, British Series 84.

Kinghorn, R 1934 'Unrecoded Berwickshire antiquities, being the Charmers-Jervise prize essay for 1933', *Proc Soc Antiq Scot*, 69, 157–67.

Kinsella, J 2010 'A new Irish early medieval site type? Exploring the 'recent' archaeological evidence for non-circular enclosed settlement and burial sites', *Proc Royal Irish Academy* 110C, 89–132.

Kirk, J (ed.) 1995a *The Medieval Church in Scotland (Papers by I Cowan)*. Edinburgh: Scottish Academic Press

Kirk, J (ed.) 1995b *The Books of Assumption of the Thirds of Benefices*. Oxford.

Knüsel, C 2000 'Activity-related skeletal change', *in* Fiorato, V, Boylston, A & Knüsel, C (eds) *Blood Red Roses. The Archaeology of a Mass Grave from the Battle of Towton AD 1461*, 103–18. Oxford: Oxbow Books.

Krogh, K J & Voss, O 1961 'Fra hedenskab tilkristendom i Hørning. En vikingetids kammergrav og en trækirke fra 1000-tallet under Hørning kirke', *Nationalmuseets Arbejdsmark* 1961, 5–34.

Laidlaw, J W 1871 'Notice of an ancient structure and remains from a kitchen midden, on "The Gegan", an isolated rock near Seacliff', *Proc Soc Antiq Scot* 8, 372–7.

Laing, L 1973 'The Angles in Scotland and the Mote of Mark', *Trans Dumfr Gallow Nat His Antiq Soc* 1, 37–52.

Laing, L 1993 *A Catalogue of Celtic Ornamental Metalwork in the British Isles c. AD 400–1200*. BAR British Series 229, Nottingham Monographs in Archaeology 5.

Laing, L, Laing, J & Longley, D 1998 'The early Christian and later medieval ecclesiastical site at St Blane's, Kingarth, Bute', *Proc Soc Antiq Scot* 128, 551–65.

Lamb, A, Melikian, M, Ives R & Evans J 2012 'Multi-isotope analysis of the population of the lost medieval village of

Auldhame, East Lothian, Scotland', *J Analytical Atomic Spectrometry* 27.5, 765–77.

Lang, J T 1974 'Hogback monuments in Scotland', *Proc Soc Antiq Scot* 105, 206–35.

Larsen, C S 1999 *Bioarchaeology. Interpreting Behaviour from the Human Skeleton*. Cambridge: Cambridge University Press.

Latham, R E 1965 *Revised Medieval Latin Word List*. Oxford (repr. 1989).

Lawrie, A C 1905 *Early Scottish Charters prior to AD 115*. Glasgow.

Leahy, K 2000 'Catalogue of finds from South Newbald', in Geake, H & Kenny, J (eds) *Early Deira: Archaeological Studies of the East Riding in the Fourth to Ninth Centuries*, 51–82. Oxford: Oxbow.

Levinson, A A, Luz, B & Kolodny, Y 1987 'Variations in oxygen isotope compositions of human teeth and urinary stones', *Applied Geochemistry* 2, 367–71.

Lewis, J & Ewart, G 1995 *Jedburgh Abbey: The Archaeology and Architecture of a Border Abbey*. Edinburgh: Soc Monog Ser 10.

LMCC 1940 *London Museum Medieval Catalogue*. London.

Lockhart, W 1892 *The Church of Scotland in the Thirteenth Century: The Life and Times of David de Bernham of St Andrews (Bishop) AD 1239 to 1253*. Edinburgh.

Løken, T 1987 'The correlation between the shape of grave monuments and sex in the Iron Age, based on material from Østfold and Vestfold', in Bertelsen, R, Lillehammer, A & Naess, J R (eds) *Were they all men? : an examination of sex roles in prehistoric society : acts from a workshop held at Utstein kloster, Rogaland 2.-4. November 1979*, 53–64. Stavanger: Archaeological Museum.

Long, A & Rippeteau, B 1974 'Testing contemporaneity and averaging radiocarbon dates', *American Antiquity* 39.2, 205–15.

Love, D 1989 *Scottish Kirkyards*. London.

Lovejoy, C O, Meindl, R S, Pryzbeck, T R & Mensforth, R P 1985 'Chronological metamorphosis of the auricular surface of the ilium: a new method for the determination of adult skeletal age at death', *American J Physical Anthropology* 68, 15–28.

Lowe, C 1999 *Angels, Fools and Tyrants*. Edinburgh: Canongate.

Lowe, C 2006 *Excavations at Hoddom, Dumfriesshire*. Edinburgh: Soc Antiq Scot Monog Ser.

Lowe, C 2008 *Inchmarnock: An Early Historic Island Monastery and its Archaeological Landscape*. Edinburgh: Soc Antiq Scot Monog Ser.

Lunt, D A 1974 'The prevalence of dental caries in the permanent dentition of Scottish prehistoric and mediaeval populations', *Archives of Oral Biology* 19, 431–7.

Lynch, M 1992 *A New History of Scotland*. London.

Macdonald, A 1830 *Register of Ministers, Exhorters and Readers, and of their Stipends, after the Period of the Reformation*. Edinburgh.

MacGregor, M 1976 *Early Celtic Art in North Britain: A Study of Decorative Metalwork from the Third Century BC to the Third Century AD*. Leicester: Leicester University Press.

MacKinlay, J M 1894 'Some notes on Baldred's country', *Proc Soc Antiq Scot* 28, 78–83.

MacLennan, W J 2003 'Stature in Scotland over the centuries', *J Royal College of Edinburgh* 33, 46–53.

Macphail, R I 1983 'The micromorphology of dark earth from Gloucester, London and Norfolk: an analysis of urban anthropogenic deposits from the late Roman to early medieval periods', in Bullock, P & Murphy, C P *Soil micromorphology*, 245–53. Berkhampstead: A B Academic Publishers.

Mainman, A J 2000 *Craft, Industry and Everyday Life: Finds from Anglo-Scandinavian York 17/14*. York: Council for British Archaeology for York Archaeological Trust.

Manning, W F 1985a 'The iron objects', in Pitts, L F & St Joseph, J K 1985 *Inchtuthil. The Roman Legionary Fortress Excavations 1952–65*, 289–99. London: Society for the Promotion of Roman Studies (Britannia Monograph Series 6).

Manning, W H 1985b *Catalogue of the Romano-British Iron Tools, Fittings and Weapons in the British Museum*. London: British Museum Press.

Marks, R 2004 *Image and Devotion in Late Medieval England*. Stroud.

Martine, J 1883 *Reminiscences of the Royal Burgh of Haddington and Old East Lothian*. Edinburgh.

Mays, S 1996 'Age-dependent cortical bone loss in a Mediaeval population', *Int J Osteoarchaeology* 6, 144–54.

Mays, S 2007 'The human remains', in Mays, S, Harding, C & Heighway, C *Wharram Percy: A Study of Settlement on the Yorkshire Wolds. The Churchyard*, 77–192. York: York Univ Archaeol Pub 13.

Mays, S, Brickley, M & Ives, R 2006 'Skeletal manifestations of rickets in infants and young children in an historic population from England', *American J Physical Anthropology* 129, 362–74.

McCarthy, M 2014 'A post-Roman sequence at Carlisle Cathedral', *Archaeol J* 171, 185–257.

McCrie, T 1848 'Civil and ecclesiastical history of the Bass', in McCrie, T (ed.), *The Bass Rock: Its Civil and Ecclesiastic History, Geology, Martyrology*, 1–48. Edinburgh.

McDonnell, G 1994 'The slag report', in Ballin-Smith, B (ed.) *Howe: Four Millennia of Orkney Prehistory. Excavations 1978–82*, 228–34. Edinburgh (= Soc Antiq Scot Monogr Ser, 9).

McKinley, J 2004 'Compiling a skeletal inventory: disarticulated and co-mingled remains', in Brickley, M & McKinley, J (eds) *Guidelines to the Standards for Recording Human Remains*, 13–17. IFA Technical Paper 7.

McRoberts, D 1976 'The glorious house of St Andrew', in McRoberts, D (ed.) *The Medieval Church of St Andrews*, 63–120. Glasgow.

Moreno-Nuñom R 1994a *Arqueomalacologia: identificación de moluscos*. Informe No. 1994/18. Laboratorio de Arqueozoologia. Informe técnico. Universidad Autónoma. Madrid.

Moreno-Nuñom R 1994b *Arqueomalacologia: cuantificación de moluscos*. Informe No. 1994/19. Laboratorio de Arqueozoologia. Informe técnico. Universidad Autónoma. Madrid.

Morgan, M 1947 'The organisation of the Scottish Church in the twelfth century', *Trans Roy Hist Soc*, 4th Ser, 19, 135–49.

Morris, C D & Emery, N 1986 'The chapel and enclosure on the Brough of Deerness, Orkney: survey and excavations, 1975–1977', *Proc Soc Antiq Scot* 116, 301–74.

Morrison, J, Oram, R & Oliver, F 2008 'Ancient Eldbotle unearthed: archaeological and historical evidence for a long-lost early medieval village', *Trans E Lothian Antiq Fld Natur Soc* 27, 21–45.

Mould, Q 2011 'Dress accessories', in Rodwell, W & Atkins, C, *St Peter's, Barton-upon-Humber, Lincolnshire: A Parish Church and its Community. Volume 1: History, Archaeology and Architecture*. Oxford: Oxbow Books.

Mould, Q, Carlisle, I & Cameron, E 2003, *Leather and Leatherworking in Anglo-Scandinavian and Medieval York*, The Archaeology of York, 17/16. York: CBA.

Müldner, G & Richards, M P 2005 'Fast or feast: reconstructing diet in later Medieval England by stable isotope analysis', *J Archaeol Sci* 32, 39–48.

Müldner, G & Richards, M P 2007a 'Stable isotope evidence for 1,500 years of human diet at the city of York, UK', *American J Physical Anthropology* 133, 682–97.

Müldner, G & Richards, M P 2007b 'Diet and diversity at later medieval Fishergate: the isotopic evidence', *American J Physical Anthropology* 134, 162–74.

Murray, H K, Murray, J C & Fraser, Sm 2009 *A Tale of the Unknown Unknowns. A Mesolithic Pit Alignment and a Neolithic Timber Hall at Warren Field, Crathes, Aberdeenshire*. Oxford: Oxbow.

Murray, J C 1982 'The pottery', in Murray, J C (ed.) *Excavations in the Medieval Burgh of Aberdeen, 1973–81*, 116–76. Edinburgh: Soc Antiq Scot Monog.

Neighbour, T, Shaw, W & Cavanagh, E 1995 'Kilspindie Castle, Aberlady', *Discovery & Excavation Scotland 1995*, 48–9.

Nicolaisen, W F H 1976 *Scottish Place-names*. London.

Nicholson, A 1997a 'The copper alloy', in Hill, P *Whithorn and St Ninian. The Excavation of a Monastic Town, 1984–91*, 360–89. Stroud: Sutton.

Nicholson, A 1997b 'The iron', in Hill, P 1997 *Whithorn and St Ninian. The Excavation of a Monastic Town, 1984–91*, 404–33. Stroud: Sutton.

Nicholson, A & Hill, P 1997 'The non-ferrous metals', in Hill, P *Whithorn and St Ninian. The Excavation of a Monastic Town, 1984–91*, 360–404. Stroud: Sutton.

Nicholson, R 1978 *Scotland: The Later Middle Ages*. Edinburgh.

Nisbet, H C 1975 'Seacliff, pavings, kitchen midden, human remains', *Disc Excav Scot*, 23.

Noddle, B & Stallibrass, S 2006 'The animal bones and marine shells from Jarrow', in Cramp, R *Wearmouth and Jarrow Monastic Sites Vol. 2*, 552–75. Swindon: English Heritage.

Nolan, J, Harbottle, B & Vaughan, J 2011 'The early medieval cemetery at the Castle, Newcastle upon Tyne', *Archaeologia Aeliana* 39, 147–287.

Nowakowski, J & Thomas, C 1992 'Grave news from Tintagel; an account of a second season of archaeological excavation at Tintagel churchyard, Cornwall, 1991', *Cornish Archaeology* 31, 131–4.

NSA 1845 *New Statistical Account of Scotland 1834–45 Vol. 2 Whitekirk & Tynninghame, County of Haddington*. http://stat-acc-scot.edina.ac.uk/link/1834-45/Haddington/Whitekirk%20and%20Tynninghame/

O'Carragain, 2009 'New light on early Insular monasteries', *Antiquity* 83, 1182–6.

O'Carragain, 2010 *Churches in Early Medieval Ireland*. New Haven & London: Yale Univ Press.

Oram, R 2006 *The Kings and Queens of Scotland*. Stroud.

Oram, R 2008 'Medieval Inchmarnock to c. 1600', in Lowe, C (ed.) *Inchmarnock: An Early Historic Island Monastery and its Archaeological Landscape*, 35–52. Edinburgh: Soc Antiq Scot Monog Ser.

Ortner, D J 2003 *Identification of Pathological Conditions in Human Skeletal Remains*. Washington DC: Smithsonian Institution Press.

Ortner, D J & Mays, S 1998 'Dry-bone manifestations of rickets in infancy and early childhood', *International Journal of Osteoarchaeology* 8, 45–55.

O'Sullivan, J 1994 'Excavation of a church and cemetery at St Ronan's, Iona', *Proc Soc Antiq Scot* 124, 327–65.

Ottaway, P 1992 *Anglo-Scandinavian Ironwork from 16–22 Coppergate*. York: CBA.

Owen, O 2003 'The archaeology of the county, 1945–2000', in Baker, S (ed.) *East Lothian Fourth Statistical Account 1945–2000*, 247–51. Haddington.

Pape, J C 1970 'Plaggen soils in the Netherlands', *Geoderma* 4 229–55.

Paterson, C 2001 'Insular belt-fittings from the pagan Norse graves of Scotland: a reappraisal in the light of scientific and stylistic analysis', in Redknap *et al* (eds), 125–39.

Paterson, C, Parsons, A J, Newman, R M, Johnson, M & Howard Davis, C 2014 *Shadows in the Sand. Excavation of a Viking-age Cemetery at Cumwhitton, Cumbria*. Lancaster: Lancaster Imprints 22.

Paterson, C & Tweddle, D 2014 'Copper alloy', in McCarthy, M 'A post-Roman sequence at Carlisle Cathedral', *Archaeol J* 171, 211–22.

Paterson, I B & McAdam, A D 2005 *Provenance of the building stone used at Auldhame*. Unpublished note for AOC Archaeology Group.

Patrick, D (ed.) 1907 *Statutes of the Scottish Church, 1225–1559, being a translation of Concilia Scotiae*. Edinburgh.

Payne, S 1973 'Kill-off patterns in sheep and goats. The mandibles from Asvan Kale', *Anatolian Studies* 23, 281–303.

Perry, D R 2000 *Castle Park Dunbar: Two Thousand Years on a Fortified Headland*. Soc Antiq Scot Monog Ser 16.

Petersen, J 1919 *De Norske Vikingesverd*. Kristiania.

# BIBLIOGRAPHY

Phenice, T W 1969 'A newly developed visual method of sexing the os pubis', *American J Physical Anthropology* 30, 297–302.

Pinder, M 1995 'Anglo-Saxon garnet cloisonné composite disc brooches: some aspects of their construction', *Journal of British Archaeological Association* 148, 6–28.

Pollard, T 1999 'The Drowned and the Saved: archaeological perspectives on the sea as a grave', in Downes, J & Pollard, T (eds) *The Loved Body's Corruption: Archaeological Contributions to the Study of Human Mortality*, 30–51. Glasgow: Cruithne Press.

Powell, M L 1985 'The analysis of dental wear and caries for dietary reconstruction', in Gilbert, R I & Mielke, M L (eds) *Analysis of Prehistoric Diets*, 307–38. London: Academic Press.

Powers, N 2007 *A rapid method for recording human skeletal data*. Oracle Manual, 2nd edition. Unpubl Rep by the Museum of London.

*Prot Bk Foular* I = Macleod, W & Wood, M (eds) 1930 *Protocol Book of John Foular, 9 March 1500–01 to 18 September 1503*. Edinburgh.

*Prot Bk Foular* II = Wood, M (ed.) 1953 *Protocol Book of John Foular II, 1514–1518*. Scott Rec Soc, Edinburgh.

*Prot Bk Foular* III = Wood, M (ed.) 1953 *Protocol Book of John Foular III, 1519–1528*. Scott Rec Soc, Edinburgh.

*Prot Bk Young* = Donaldson, G (ed.) 1952 *Protocol Book of James Young, 1485–1515*. Edinburgh.

Proudfoot, E 1996 'Excavations at the long cist cemetery on the Hallow Hill, St Andrews, Fife, 1975–7', *Proc Soc Antiq Scot* 126, 387–454.

Proudfoot, E 1998 'The Hallow Hill and the origins of Christianity in eastern Scotland', in Crawford, B E (ed.) *Conversion and Christianity in the North Sea World*, 57–73. St Andrews.

Proudfoot, E & Aliaga-Kelly, C 1995 'Place-names and other evidence for Anglian settlement in south-east Scotland', *Landscape Hist* 17, 17–26.

Proudfoot, E & Aliaga-Kelly, C 1996 'Towards an interpretation of anomalous finds and placenames of Anglo-Saxon origin in Scotland', *Anglo-Saxon Studies in Archaeology and History*, 9, 1–13. Oxford: Oxford University Committee for Archaeology.

Proudfoot, E & Aliaga-Kelly, C 1997 'Aspects of settlement and territorial arrangements in south-east Scotland in the late prehistoric and early medieval periods', *Med Archaeol* 41, 33–50.

Raeburn, G D 2009 'The changing face of Scottish burial practices, 1560–1645', *Reformation and Renaissance Review* 11.2, 181–201.

Ragg, J M & Futty, D W 1967 *The Soils of the Country round Haddington and Eyemouth*. Edinburgh: The Macaulay Institute for Soil Research.

Rahtz, P 1976 'The building plan of the Anglo-Saxon monastery at Whitby Abbey', in Wilson, D (ed.) *The Archaeology of Anglo-Saxon England*, 459–62. London.

Rains, M J & Hall, D 1997 *Excavations in St Andrews 1980–9. A Decade of Archaeology in a Historic Scottish Burgh*. Tayside & Fife Archaeological Committee Monog 1.

Rankin, E R 1914 *Saint Mary's Whitekirk 1356–1914*. Edinburgh.

RCAHMS 1924 *The Royal Commission on the Ancient and Historical Monuments and Constructions of Scotland. Eighth Report with Inventory of Monuments and Constructions in the County of East Lothian*. Edinburgh.

RCAHMS 1984 *The Archaeological Sites and Monuments of Central Angus (Medieval and Later), Angus District, Tayside Region*. Edinburgh: RCAHMS.

Redmond, A Z 2007 *Viking Burial in the north of England*. Oxford: British Archaeol Rep 429.

Redknap, M, Edwards, N, Youngs, S, Lane, A & Knight, J 2001 *Pattern and Purpose in Insular Art. Proceedings of the Fourth International Conference on Insular Art held at the National Museum and Gallery, Cardiff, 3–6 September 1998*. Oxford: Oxbow Books.

Rees, A R 2002 'A first millennium AD cemetery, rectangular Bronze Age structure and later prehistoric settlement at Thornybank, Midlothian', *Proc Soc Antiq Scot* 132, 313–55.

Reid, D J & Dean, M C 2000 'Brief communication: the timing of linear enamel hypoplasias on human anterior teeth', *American J Physical Anthropology* 113, 135–9.

Reimer, P J, Baillie, M G L, Bard, E, Bayliss, A, Beck, J W, Blackwell, P G, Bronk Ramsey, C, Buck, C E, Burr, G S, Edwards, R L, Friedrich, M, Grootes, P M, Guilderson, T P, Hajdas, I, Heaton, T J, Hogg, A G, Hughen, K A, Kaiser, K F, Kromer, B, McCormac, F G, Manning, S W, Reimer, R W, Richards, D A, Southon, J R, Talamo, S, Turney, C S M, van der Plicht, J & Weyhenmeyer, C E 2009 'IntCal09 and Marine09 radiocarbon age calibration curves, 0–50,000 years cal BP', *Radiocarbon* 51.4, 1111–50.

Renfrew, J M 1973 *Paleoethnobotany*. Methuen & Co Ltd.

Reynolds, N 1980 'Dark Age timber halls and the background to excavation at Balbridie', in Thoms, L M (ed.) *Settlements in Scotland 1000 BC – AD 1000*, 41–60. Scottish Archaeol Forum 10.

Richards, J 2003 'Pagans and Christians at the frontier: Viking burial in the Danelaw', in Carver, M O H (ed.) *The Cross goes North: Processes of Conversion in Northern Europe, AD 300–1300*, 383–95. York: York Medieval Press.

Richards, J 2004 *Viking Age England*. Stroud: Tempus Publishing Ltd.

Richards, M P, Fuller, B T & Molleson, T I 2006 'Stable isotope paleodietary study of humans and fauna from the multi-period (Iron Age, Viking, late medieval) site of Newark Bay, Orkney', *J Archaeol Sci* 33, 122–31.

Richards, M P, Mays, S & Fuller, B T 2002 'Stable carbon and nitrogen isotope values of bone and teeth reflect weaning age at the medieval Wharram Percy site, Yorkshire, UK', *American J Physical Anthropology* 119, 205–10.

Richardson, J S 1980 *Tantallon Castle: Official Guide Book*, 3rd edn. Edinburgh.

Ritchie, A I 1880 *The Churches of St Baldred: Auldhame, Whitekirk, Tyninghame, Prestonkir*. Edinburgh.

*RMS* II = Paul, J B & Thomson, J M (eds) 1883–1914 *Registrum Magnum Sigillum, The Register of the Great Seal of Scotland, 1424–1513* Vol. II. Edinburgh (repr. 1984).

*RMS* III = Paul, J B & Thomson, J M (eds) 1883–1914 *Registrum Magnum Sigillum, The Register of the Great Seal of Scotland, 1513–1546* Vol. III. Edinburgh (repr. 1984).

*RMS* VI = Paul, J B & Thomson, J M (eds), 1883–1914 *Registrum Magnum Sigillum, The Register of the Great Seal of Scotland, 1593–1608* Vol. VI. Edinburgh (repr. 1984).

*RMS* VII = Paul, J B & Thomson, J M (eds) 1883–1914 *Registrum Magnum Sigillum, The Register of the Great Seal of Scotland, 1609–1620* Vol. VII. Edinburgh (repr. 1984).

Roberts, C & Cox, M 2003 *Health and Disease in Britain*. Stroud: Sutton Pub.

Roberts, C & Manchester, K 2005 *The Archaeology of Disease*, 3rd edn. Stroud: Sutton Pub.

Robertson, A S 1970 'Roman finds from non-Roman sites in Scotland', *Britannia* 1, 198–226.

Rodwell, W 1981 *The Archaeology of the English Church*. London.

Rogers, J M 1997 'The formation of parishes in twelfth-century Perthshire', *Rec Scott Church Hist Soc* 27, 68–96.

Rogers, J & Waldron, T 1995 *A Field Guide to Joint Disease in Archaeology*. Chichester; John Wiley & Sons.

Rogers, J, Waldron, T, Dieppe, P & Watt, I 1987 'Arthropathies in paleopathology: the basis of classification according to most probable cause', *J Archaeol Sci* 14, 179–83.

Rogers, N S H 1993 *Anglian and other Finds from 46–54 Fishergate*. London: CBA (= The Archaeology of York. Volume 17/9: the small finds).

Rollason, D (ed.) 2000 *Symeon of Durham: Libellus de Exordio atque procursus istius, hoc est Dunhelmensis, Ecclesie*. Oxford: Oxford Med Texts.

Rollason, D 2003 *Northumbria, 500–1100: Creation and Destruction of a Kingdom*. Cambridge.

Rollason, D, Piper, A J & Harvey, M (eds) 2004 *The Durham Liber Vitae and its Context*. Woodbridge: Boydell & Brewer.

Romans, J C C & Robertson, L 1983 'The environment of North Britain – soils', *in* Chapman, J C & Mytum, H C (eds) *Settlement in North Britain 1000 BC – AD 1000* 55–80. Brit Archaeol Rep 118.

Ross, S 1991 *Dress pins from Anglo-Saxon England: their production and typo-chronological development*. Unpubl PhD thesis Oxford University.

Roy, M forthcoming *A Matter of Life and Death: Trade and Burial around St Giles' Cathedral: Archaeological Investigations at Parliament House, Edinburgh*.

*RSS* I = Livingstone, M (ed.) 1908 *Registrum Secreti Sigilli Regum Scotorum: Register of the Privy Seal of Scotland, 1488–1529*, Vol. I. Edinburgh.

*RSS* III = Fleming, D H & Beveridge, J (eds) 1936 *Registrum Secreti Sigilli Regum Scotorum: Register of the Privy Seal of Scotland 1542–1548*, Vol. III. Edinburgh.

*RSS* V = Beveridge, J & Donaldson, G (eds) 1957 *Registrum Secreti Sigilli Regum Scotorum: Register of the Privy Seal of Scotland 1565–7*, Vol. V, Pt 2. Edinburgh.

Russel, N J, Bonsall C & Sutherland, D G 1995 'The exploitation of marine molluscs in the Mesolithic of western Scotland: evidence from Ulva Cave, Inner Hebrides', *in* Fischer A (ed.) *Man and Sea in the Mesolithic*. Oxford: Oxbow.

Russell-Smith, F 1956 'The medieval "brygyrdyl"', *Antiquaries J* 36, 218–21.

*SAH* = *Abridgements of Sasines, County of Haddington 1781–1820*. Edinburgh: HMSO.

Scheuer, L & Black, S 2000 *Developmental Juvenile Osteology*. London: Academic Press.

*Scotsman* 1872 'Death of Mr John Dale of Auldhame', *The Scotsman*, 1 June 1872, 6.

Shead, N 1996 'Anglo–Scottish relations 1329–1422', *in* McNeill, P G B & MacQueen, H L (eds) *Atlas of Scottish History to 1707*, 104–9. Edinburgh.

Sheils, J 2001 'Aberlady zoomorphic buckle', *Disc Excav Scot*, 30.

Shortt, H de S 1959 'A provincial Roman spur from Longstock, Hants, and other spurs from Roman Britain', *Antiq J* 39, 61–76.

Silver, I A 1969 'The ageing of domestic animals', *in* Brothwell, D R & Higgs, E S (eds) *Science and Archaeology*, 283–302. London: Thames & Hudson.

Skene, W F (ed.) 1872 *John of Fordun's Chronicle of the Scottish Nation*. Edinburgh (Historians of Scotland, Vol. IV) .

Sligo, G 1857 'Notes on an ancient cave, etc, discovered at Aldham, now called Seacliff, in East Lothian, in 1831', *Archaeol Scotica* 4, 353–61.

Smith, A N 1995 'The excavation of Neolithic, Bronze Age and early historic features near Ratho, Edinburgh', *Proc Soc Antiq Scot* 125, 69–138.

Smith, C 2008 'The bird bone', *in* James, H F & Yeoman, P *Excavations at St Ethernan's Monastery, Isle of May, Fife, 1992–97*, 93–7. Perth: TAFAC Monog 6.

Smith, I M 1991 'Sprouston, Roxburghshire: an early Anglian centre of the eastern Tweed basin', *Proc Soc Antiqs Scot* 121, 261–94.

Smith, J S 1898 *The Grange of St Giles, the Bass and . . . the Dick Lauder Family*. Edinburgh.

Smyth, A P 1984 *Warlords and Holy Men. Scotland AD 80–1000*. Edinburgh: Edinburgh University Press.

Speed, G & Walton Rogers, P 2004 'A burial of a Viking woman at Aldwick-le-Street, South Yorkshire', *Med Archaeol*, 48, 51–90.

Spicer, A 2000 '"Defyle not Christ's kirk with your carrion": burial and the development of burial aisles in post-Reformation Scotland', *in* Gordon, B & Marshall, P (eds) *The Place of the Dead: Death and Remembrance in Late Medieval and Early Modern Europe*, 149–69. Cambridge.

SPP 2010 *Scottish Planning Policy*. Scottish Government.

Starley, D 2000 'Metalworking debris', *in* Buxton, K & Howard-Davis, C (eds) *Bremetenacum: Excavations at Roman Ribchester 1980, 1989–1990,* 337–47. Lancaster (=Lancaster Imprints Ser No. 9).

*St A Form*=Donaldson, G & Macrae, C 1942–44 *St Andrews Formulare 1514–46.* Edinburgh (2 vols).

*St Giles Reg*=Laing, D (ed.) 1859 *Registrum Cartarum Ecclesie Sancti Egidii de Edinburgh 1344–1567.* Edinburgh.

Stevens, T, Melikian, M & Grieve, S J 2005 'Excavations at an early medieval cemetery at Stromness, Orkney', *Proc Soc Antiq Scot* 135, 371–93.

Stevenson, J (trans) 1858 *Symeon of Durham, a History of the kings of England.* Church Historians of England (repr. Llanerch, 1987).

Stevenson, R B K 1959 'The Inchyra stone and some other unpublished Early Christian monuments', *Proc Soc Antiq Scot* 92, 33–55.

Stirland, A 2000 *Raising the Dead: The Skeleton Crew of King Henry VIII's Great Ship the* Mary Rose. Chichester: John Wiley & Sons Ltd.

Stones, J A (ed.) 1989 *Three Scottish Carmelite Friaries. Excavations at Aberdeen, Linlithgow and Perth, 1980–86.* Edinburgh: Soc Antiq Scot Monog Ser 6.

Stroud, G 1993 'The human bones', *in* Stroud, G & Kemp, R L *Cemeteries of the Church and Priory of St Andrew, Fishergate,* 160–260. The Archaeology of York, Vol. 12 Fascicule 2, CBA.

Strutt, J 1796 (reprinted in facsimile of the updated 1842 edition in 1970) *The Dress and Habits of the People of England* (2 vols). London: Tabard.

Stuart, J 1867 *Sculptured Stones of Scotland.* Edinburgh.

Suddaby, I 2009 'Two prehistoric short-cists and an early medieval long-cist cemetery with dug graves on Kingston Common, North Berwick, East Lothian', *Scottish Archaeol Internet Reps* 34.

Sundick, R I 1978 'Human skeletal growth and age determination', *Homo* 29, 228–49.

Swanton, M J 1973 *The Spearheads of the Anglo-Saxon Settlements.* Leeds: The Royal Archaeological Institute.

Tabraham, C J 2007 *Tantallon Castle: Official Souvenir Guide.* Edinburgh: HMSO.

TAR 2004 *Treasure Annual Report 2004.* Dept Culture, Media and Sport http://finds.org.uk/documents/treasurereports/2004.pdf.

Tarlow, S 1997 'The dread of something after death; violation and desecration in the Isle of Man in the tenth century', *in* Carman, J (ed.) *Material Harm. Archaeological Studies of War and Violence,* 133–42. Glasgow.

Tate, J, Troalen, L & Blackwell, A 2010 *Technological Study of the Gold Cloisonné Stud.* Unpubl report for AOC Archaeology.

Taylor, S & Markus, G 2006 *The Place-names of Fife, Vol. 1: West Fife between Leven and Forth.* Donington.

Thomas, A C 1967 'An early Christian cemetery and chapel on Ardwall Isle, Kirkcudbright', *Med Archaeol* 11, 127–88.

Thomas, A C 1981 *Christianity in Roman Britain to AD 500.* London: Batsford.

Thomas, A C 1984 'Abercorn and the Provincia Pictorum', *in* Miket, R & Burgess, C *Between and Beyond the Walls: Essays on the Prehistory and History of North Britain in Honour of George Jobey,* 324–7. Edinburgh.

Thomas, G 2001 'Strap-ends and the identification of regional patterns in the production and circulation of ornamental metalwork in Late Anglo-Saxon and Viking-Age Britain', *in* Redknap et al 2001, 39–48.

Thomas, G, 2004 *Late Anglo-Saxon and Viking-Age Strap-Ends, 750–1100, Part 2, Finds Research Group AD 700–1700 Datasheet 33.*

Thomas, G 2012 'Carolingian culture in the North Sea World: Rethinking the cultural dynamics of personal adornment in Viking-age England', *European Journal of Archaeology* 15.3, 486–518.

Thordeman, B 1939 *Armour from the Battle of Wisby 1361,* 1. Stockholm (Kungl.Vitterhets Historie och Antikvitets Akademien).

Thun, T 2002 *Dendrochronological constructions of Norwegian conifer chronologies providing dating of historical material.* Trondheim: Norwegian Univ Science & Technology.

Todd, M 2002 *The Culture of Protestantism in Early Modern Scotland.* London.

*Treas Acc* VI=Paul, J B et al (eds) 1906 *Accounts of the Lord High Treasurer of Scotland 1531–38,* Vol. VI. Edinburgh.

Trotter, M 1970 'Estimation of stature from intact limb bones', *in* Stewart, T D (ed.) *Personal Identification in Mass Disasters,* 71–83. Washington DC: Smithsonian Institution Press.

Trotter, M & Gleser, G 1952 'Estimation of stature from long bones of American whites and negroes', *American J Physical Anthropology* 10, 463–514.

Trotter, M & Gleser, G 1958 'A re-evaluation of estimation of stature based on measurements of stature taken during life and long bones after death', *American J Physical Anthropology* 16, 79–123.

Trotter, M & Gleser, G 1977 'Corrigenda to "Estimation of stature from long bones of American whites and negroes"', *American J Physical Anthropology* 47, 355–6.

Tulloch, W & Davies, C 1998 'Kilspindie Castle', *Discovery & Excavation Scotland 1998,* 32.

Tyers, I, 1996 *Tree-ring Analysis of Timbers from the Stave Church at Greensted, Essex.* Ancient Monuments Lab Rep 14/96.

Tyrrell, A 2000 'Non-metric traits and the assessment of inter- and intra-population diversity: past populations and future potential', *in* Cox, M & Mays, S (eds) *Human Osteology in Archaeology and Forensic Science,* 289–306. London: Greenwich Medical Media Ltd.

Tyson, R 2000 *Medieval Glass Vessels found in England c. AD 1200–1500.* York: CBA Res Rep 121.

Ubelaker, D H 1989 *Human Skeletal Remains.* Washington: Taraxacum.

Umbanhower, C E & McGrath, M 1998 'Experimental production and analysis of microscopic charcoal from wood, leaves and grasses', *The Holocene* 8, 341–6.

Van Klinken, G J, Richards, M P & Hedges, R E M 2000 'An overview of causes for stable isotope variations in past European human populations. Environmental, ecophysiological and cultural effects', *in* Ambrose, S H & Katzenberg, M A (eds) *Biogeochemical Approaches to Paleodietary Analysis*, 39–63. New York: Kluwer Academic/Plenum Publishing.

Von den Driesch, A 1976 *A Guide to the Measurement of Animal Bones from Archaeological Sites*. Harvard University: Peabody Museum Bulletin 1.

Waddell, P H 1893 *An Old Kirk Chronicle being a History of Auldhame, Tyninghame and Whitekirk in East Lothian from Session Records 1615–1850*. Edinburgh.

Waldron, T 2001 *Shadows in the Soil. Human Bones and Archaeology*. Tempus.

Walker, P, Bathurst, R, Richman, R, Gjerdrum, T & Andrushko, V 2009 'The causes of porotic hyperostosis and cribra orbitalia: a reappraisal of the iron-deficiency-anemia hypothesis', *American J Physical Anthropology* 139, 109–25.

Walton Rogers, P 2007 *Cloth and Clothing in Early Anglo-Saxon England, AD 450–700*. York: CBA.

Wamers, E 1998 'Insular finds in Viking age Scandinavia and the state formation of Norway', *in* Clarke, H B, Ní Mhaonaigh, M & Ó'Floinn, R (eds) *Ireland and Scandinavia in the Early Viking Age*, 37–72. Dublin: Four Courts Press.

Watt, D E R 2001 'Bagimond di Vezza and his "Roll"', *Scott Hist Rev* 80, 1–23.

Wattez, J & Courty, M A 1987 'Morphology of ash of some plant materials', *in* Federoff, N, Bresson, L M & Courty, M A (eds) *Micromorphologie des sols – Soil micromorphology*, 677–83. Plaiser: AES.

Watts, V 1994 'The place-name Hexham: a mainly philological approach', *Nomina* 17, 119–36.

Weatherhead, R 1993 'Anglian cross fragments found in East Lothian', *Trans E Lothian Antiq Fld Natur Soc* 22, 53–61.

Weatherhead, R 2000 'Baldred – the recorded facts, and his "miracles" told in Alcuin's York poem', *Trans E Lothian Antiq Fld Natur Soc* 24, 27–8.

Webb, J F 1986 'Eddius Stephanus: life of Wilfred', *in* Farmer, D H (ed.) *The Age of Bede*, 105–82. London: Harmondsworth.

Webster, L & Backhouse, J 1991 *The Making of England. Anglo-Saxon Art and Culture, AD 600–900*. London: British Museum Press.

Welander, R D E, Batey, C & Cowie, T G 1987 'A Viking burial from Kneep, Uig, Isle of Lewis', *Proc Soc Antiq Scot* 117, 149–74.

West, S 1998 *A Corpus of Anglo-Saxon Material from Suffolk*. Ipswich: Suffolk County Council (East Anglian Archaeology Report 84).

Wheeler, R E M (ed.) 1954 *Medieval Catalogue*. London: London Museum.

White, C, Longstaffe, F J & Law, K R 2004 'Exploring the effects of environment, physiology and diet oxygen isotope ratios in ancient Nubian bones and teeth', *J Archaeol Sci* 31, 233–50.

Whitehead, R 1996 *Buckles 1250–1800*. Essex: Greenlight Publishing.

Whitfield, N 2007 'Motifs and techniques in early medieval Celtic filigree: their ultimate origins', *in* Moss, R (ed.) *Making and Meaning in Insular Art*, 18–39. Dublin: Four Courts Press.

Wilson, D M 2008 *The Vikings in the Isle of Man*. Aarhus.

Wise, P J & Seaby, W A 1995 'Finds from a new "productive site" at Bidford-on-Avon, Warwickshire', *TransBirmingham and Warwickshire Archaeol Soc* 99, 57–64.

Wood, J W, Milner, G R, Harpending, H C & Weiss, K M 1992 'The osteological paradox: problems in inferring prehistoric health from skeletal samples', *Current Anthropology* 33, 343–58.

Woodward, D 1994 'Gooding the earth', *in* Foster, S & Smout, T C (eds) *The History of Soils and Field Systems*, 101–9. Aberdeen: Scottish Cultural Press

Woolf, A 2007 *From Pictland to Alba 789–1070*. Edinburgh.

Wormald, J 1981 *Court, Kirk and Community: New History of Scotland*. London.

Wright, L E & Yoder, C J 2003 'Recent progress in bioarchaeology: approaches to the osteological paradox', *J Archaeol Res* 11, 43–70.

Yeoman, P 1999 *Pilgrimage in Medieval Scotland*. London.

Zadora-Rio, E 2003 'The making of churchyards and parish territories in the early-medieval landscape of France and England in the 7th–12th centuries: a reconsideration', *Med Archaeol* 47, 1–19.

## UNPUBLISHED SOURCES

*National Archives of Scotland*

CC8/8/1/35-6 Scowgall, Jhone, testament dative and inventory, 27 Nov 1567

CC8/8/3/156-8 Wemis, Johne, testament testamentary and inventory, 27 May 1574

CC8/8/12/342-4 George Scowgale in Skowgall (d. 14 Aug 1582), testament testamentary and inventory, 24 June 1583

CC8/8/20/494-6 Walter Webster, Castletoun (d. 1586), testament testamentary and inventory, 13 Nov 1589

CC8/8/28/730-1 Johnne Scowgall of Scowgall (d. Feb 1594/5), Testament Dative, 27 January 1595/6

CC8/8/58/601-03, Johne Douglas (d. Feb 1613), Captaine of Tantallane, testament testamentary and inventory, 4 April 1638

CH2/359/1 Minutes of Tyninghame Kirk Session 1615–50

CH2/359/5 Minutes of Tyninghame Kirk Session 1717–49

CH2/359/6 Minutes of Tyninghame Kirk Session 1747–62

CH2/371/4 Kirk Session Minutes, Whitekirk and Tyninghame, 1760–1823

CH2/371/6 Kirk Session Minutes, Whitekirk and Tyninghame, 1759–84

# BIBLIOGRAPHY

CH2/371/7 Heritors' Minutes and Accounts, Whitekirk and Tyninghame, 1786–1822

GD12/89 Letters of procutory by John Swinton of Swinton resigning lands in favour of his son, John, 1 May 1519

GD100/63 Archbishop Andrew Foreman, charter to Adam Otterburn of quarter of the lands of Auldhame

GD110/337 Antenuptial contract of marriage between James Suttie of Balgone and Elizabeth Dalrymple, 1715

*St Andrews University Archives*

SM110 = Archives of St Mary's College, Special Collections Dept, St Andrews University

SM110, B1/P1/3 Papal bull of Paul III confirming foundation of St Mary's College and annexation of churches of Tyninghame and Tannadice, 12 Feb 1537–8

SM110, B1/P1/4 Notarial instrument confirming institution of revenue, rents and crop of Tyninghame to St Mary's College, 25 Feb 1538–9

SM110/SB25/4 = UY-SM110, Supplementary Bundle 25, No. 4, Tack between masters of St Mary's College and John Auchmuthie, of teinds of Scoughall, parish of Tyninghame [actually in Auldhame], 1615, reg 12 June 1629

SM110/SB25/9 = UY-SM110, Supplementary Bundle 25, No. 9, Tack between masters of St Mary's College and Sir John Auchmuthie of Scoughall, of teinds of Scoughall, 29 Dec 1636 and 3 Jan 1637

SM110/SB25/13 Information for the Masters of the New College against the minister of Tynignhame (re teinds), 1671 (partly illeg – possibly 1670)

*National Library of Scotland*

Acc 12527/1 Scrapbook of research material, 1870s–80s, for G F Russell Colt's 1887 family history, 'The Colts of that Ilk'

Acc 12527/2 Notes, unpaginated ms, by G R Russell Colt, 19th cent, on Robert Colt MP, of Auldhame

Acc 12527/3 Handwritten draft text of G F Russell Colt's 'Colts of that Ilk (pub 1887)', 1880s

Online Public Access Catalogue (OPAC) entry, for CH2/371, Records of Whitekirk (Later Whitekirk and Tyninghame) Kirk Session, 1691–1978, Administrative History, at http://www.nas.gov.uk/catalogues/, accessed on 7 May 2011.

*Cartographic sources*

Adair, J 1682 *East Lothian/authore Johanne Adair*

Adair, J 1736 *A map of East Lothian/Survey'd by J Adair*

Ainslie, J 1821 *Map of the southern part of Scotland*, Edinburgh

Blaeu, 1654 *Lothian and Linlitquo/Joh. Et Cornelius Blaeu exc.* Amsterdam

Forrest, W 1802 *Map of Haddingtonshire*, Edinburgh

Ordnance Survey 1854 *Six inch 1st Edition, Scotland Sheet 3, Whitkirk and Tynninghame*

Ordnance Survey 1857 *One inch to the mile maps of Scotland, Sheet 41, North Berwick*

Ordnance Survey 1898 *One inch 2nd Edition, Scotland, 1898–1904, Sheet 33 Haddington*

Ordnance Survey 1899 *One inch 2nd Edition, Scotland, 1898–1904, Sheet 41 North Berwick*

Ordnance Survey of Scotland 1976, *Soil Survey of Scotland, 1976, Haddington, Eyemouth and North Berwick Sheets 33, 34 and part 41*

Roy, W 1747–55 *Military survey of Scotland*

Sharp, T, Greenwood, C & Fowler, W 1825 *Map of the county of Haddington*

Sharp, T, Greenwood, C & Fowler, W 1844 *Map of the county of Haddington*

Thomson, J 1820 *Haddington*, Edinburgh

*Web pages*

Broadie, A 2004–11 'Mair, John (c. 1467–1550)', in *Oxford Dictionary of National Biography,* Oxford www.oxforddnb.com/view/article/17843, accessed 6 Feb 2009.

DSL (DOST) = Dictionary of the Scots Language (Dictionary of the Older Scottish Tongue), at www.dsl.ac.uk, accessed 3 Feb 2009.

Online Public Access Catalogue (OPAC) entry, for CH2/371, Records of Whitekirk (Later Whitekirk and Tyninghame) Kirk Session, 1691–1978, Administrative History, at http://www.nas.gov.uk/catalogues/, accessed 7 May 2011

Tawfilis, A R, Byrne, P & Kim, D W 2006 'Facial trauma, mandibular fractures', *Emedicine* www.emedicine.com/plastic/topic227.htm, accessed August 2008.

# APPENDICES

## APPENDIX 1: THE HAMILTON ARCHIVE

The following has been transcribed word for word from the rediscovered notes and correspondence relating to archaeological works carried out in 1948–49 by JRC Hamilton at Auldhame. Dr James Marple found the originals in the National Archive of Scotland (West Search Room) after a long search.

### Document 1

A. S. Scotland 3.

*Having been familiar all my life with the coast area in the vicinity of Tantallon Castle, I should like to point out that Canty Bay is a particular line of the coast between Ragged Rock on the west and Taling Head on the east, and that the sandy area covered with turf at the base of the steep banks has produced in the past evidence of early occupation. The site in question lies three hundred yards eastwards from the limit of Canty Bay, and at the present time part of the area is covered by constructions which contend with the amenity of Tantallon Castle. This monument being about 250 yards as the crow flies south-west of the Admiralty buildings. I do think that the ministry should have some indication of the nature of the buildings which the Admiralty propose to retain as storage accommodation.*

*Some time ago I dealt with an Admiralty paper which concerned the setting up of some erection on an area of ground to the south-east of Tantallon Castle and to the north of the old ruined castle at Auldhame, this site was of particular interest as from the relics picked up on the area, and the many human burials it was clearly the place where the old mediaeval village and Kirk of Auldhame once stood. From the day I forwarded my memorandum I have heard nothing further, but I do know that a pylon now stands on the site.*

James Richardson
I.A.M.
16th March 1948.

Handwritten notes on bottom of page:

*Illegible signature*

*To see the forgoing*
*Patterson AS (Scot) 3*
*18/3/48*

*B. S. (Scotland) 3 Seen and thank you.*
*From a perusal of these papers it would appear that the Department of Health will approach us for clearance in the usual way and I assume you will not desire any (illegible word)*

This first document would appear to be showing the concerns of Richardson regarding the Admiralty's development of a known site. He clearly states that the site is a known graveyard and indicates the possibility that it is Auldhame. He also mentions that many relics have been found in the area but their whereabouts now are unknown.

### Document 2

| | Minute sheet |
| --- | --- |
| | (Stamped *Office of works* |
| 2 | – *P.M. 25March 1949* |
| | *190204//*) |
| 1. | Mr Watson – A. S. Scot. 3. |
| 2. | Mr Turner – A. D. L. A. |

Service land requirements – Admiralty.
Sites at Canty Bay – East Lothian

Mr. MacCusker's report was not available at the Canty Bay site until Thursday 5th August 1948 when he accompanied me along with a Me. Cameron of the Admiralty Office at Rosyth to these places. At the Gin Head Station I met Mr. Exeter the officer in charge of the station.

1). Area North-west of Canty Bay Hotel.
This site has already been taken over and a Radar pylon erected thereon, and the setting for the high tension pole places in position.

*2). Gin Head Site.*
*I saw the area which has been stripped of surface soil at Gin Head. Naturally one could not now establish any archaeological interest as whatever there might have existed of this kind has been swept away. Mr. Exeter stated that two spoons which had been found and which appeared to him to be of recent date, had been passed to the officer at Rosyth for submission to a museum authority. Mr. Exeter did not know whether this had been done, and suggested tracing up the history of the spoons since they left his hands some time ago.*

*3). Cliff hut site.*
*A brick hut of moderate size has been erected on the site since I reported that a Radar Pylon had been established there. They have also set the anchoring for a high tension pole. By an unusual coincidence, workmen had just previous to our coming on the site, dug twenty five pits 2ft. 6 inches deep for the reception of the boundary concrete posts. These pits are spaced at 8ft. centres and each presented evidence of human burial disposed in the ground approximately just below a plough's depth from the surface. The skeletons were all lying east and west and it would appear that on the line of the boundary the burial area extended for some 80 feet. The depth however, cannot be established until the field outwith the admiralty area has been cropped.*

*I have arranged for Mr. Hamilton the Assistant Inspector of Ancient monuments to make a sketch investigation of the site, as I anticipate that there might still exist evidence of an early church within the Admiralty area. Mr. Exeter is going to supply the labour necessary. Mr Hamilton's report will be forwarded in due course, but in the mean time we can discharge by our official clearance the three sites mentioned. So far as the site known as 'B' Beach Head is concerned Mr. Exeter informed me that this area was not now to be taken over by the Admiralty.*

*From what I gather from Mr. Exeter and Mr. McCusker they had no knowledge of my original report on sites No's 2 and 3. Apparently the movements of officers from place to place upset the continuity of action so far as commitments with other government departments are concerned.*

*Copies of the report will be passed in due course to the Royal Commission on Ancient Monuments, the Ordnance Survey and the Society of Antiquaries of Scotland for noting.*

*James Richardson*
*I.A.M.*
*6th August 1948*

This document appears to be reporting on a site visit following the Admiralty's development of the site and the initiation of works in retrospect of the development. It appears that works were not carried out prior to development due to a breakdown in communications. Although concerned with a number of sites along the coast, it is the Cliff Hut site that concerns us here, as it is the same as the excavations reported on here.

**Document 3**
*A. S. Scotland, 3.*
*Mr. White, Architect's Division.*
*Admiralty site at Canty Bay, East Lothian*

*Cliff Hut site.*

*This site acquired by the Admiralty (see previous memo dated 6th August 1948) occupies a headland half mile east of Tantallion Castle. During the digging of foundation pits for concrete boundary posts across the neck of the promontory several burials came to light. Human bones with fragments of mediaeval pottery.*

*It was conjectured that a mediaeval church had once existed on the headland and it was arranged that I should make further instigations to locate the position of such a building. In addition to excavating a cist burial discovered in a cable trench, I have succeeded in tracing the foundation of a section of one wall of the church. This lies within the Admiralty area as indicated on the following sketch* (Figure 8).

*So far the work has been confined to digging a small exploratory trench with the aid of workmen engaged by the Admiralty.*

*As the Admiralty intend to erect additional buildings within the area involved it is important that we should trace the foundation walls and excavate at least part of the interior. The site is of considerable archaeological interest, and important finds may come to light.*

*Could arrangements be made for a foreman supervisor to be present on the site in order to direct the operations of three or four workmen? As regards the latter it might be possible to come to some arrangement with the Supt. of works at Rosyth for the labourers employed by the admiralty to undertake the work.*

A page from the document may be missing but it continues:

*/work. The earliest possible date should be fixed.*

*I have spoken to Mr. White about this matter and we are arranging to visit the site with a view to determining the length of time involved by the excavation. It should be possible judging from present indications to carry out the work in a period of two–three weeks.*

*J. R. C. Hamilton*
*Asst. I. A. M.*
*24th March 1949*

There follows a series of handwritten notes at the bottom of the document:

A. S. (Scot) 3.
To see correspondence with admiralty phone.

Excavation work commenced the 20th April and is proceeding satisfactorily.

It is estimated that a sum of £60 will be required for this service and a 'blue Estimate' for this amount is being submitted for your approval

Illegible White
25/4/49

Note: Blue estimate for £60 approved today
Patterson
A S (Scot) 3
27/4/49

Illegible 27/6/49 for report
Patterson A S (Scot) 3. 27 4 49

This document would seem to outline the results of an evaluation carried out on the Cliff Hut site and outlining the need for further excavation. The handwritten notes indicate that further works have been started.

### Document 4

*Cliff Hut Site*

*An examination of the foundation pits for the boundary fence was made with the assistance of labour supplied by Mr. Exeter.*

*In the majority of cases the burials had been disturbed by ploughing and the bones scattered. In one pit however, an extension was made and a skeleton revealed enclosed in a stone slab coffin. There was no cover slab or base, only the sides being formed of upright stones approximately 1 ft. to 1ft. 6 ins. in length, 1ft. high and ½ in. to 1 in. thick. The burial was orientated E/W and though no finds occurred in association the pottery sherds recovered from the site generally suggested a late 13th or 14th century date.*

*A series of trial trenches was dug within the area enclosed by the fence across the base of the promontory. These revealed that the area had been used as a graveyard in mediaeval times (in 13th and 14th century). Traces of a much decayed structure were discovered flanked by a paved path. Further excavation failed to reveal anything more of archaeological interest.*

*The gable foundation was drystone built and had no cement as would have been expected in the case of a medieval church. It would appear that this building was domestic in purpose. A certain amount of ash and midden refuse occurred round the paving and a spindle whirl recovered from its surface. Trenches cut across the floor of the building showed that it had been extensively robbed, only a scatter of stones remaining of the side walls. The width of the gable was approximately 25ft. The skeletal remains and pottery were removed to our technical laboratory at Castle Terrace*

*J. R. C. Hamilton*
*23rd July 1954*

This document, written some time after the works were carried out, summarises the results of the investigation. It is not known if a more formal illustrated report was ever produced.

## APPENDIX 2: BURIAL DATA

### (organised in order of Grave No.)

| Grave | Skeleton | Phase | Age | Gender | Type | Alignment | Comments |
|---|---|---|---|---|---|---|---|
| 5 | 4 | | MA | F? | coffin? | 134 | Single nail may be intrusive |
| 12 | 11 | 1–2 | MA | F | | 71 | |
| 15 | 14 | | adult | U | | 134 | |
| 18 | 17 | | MA | U | | 76 | |
| 23 | 120 | 2 | OA | M | | 76 | |
| 41 | 40 | | MA | U | | 101 | |
| 44 | 43 | | MA | M? | | 101 | |
| 79 | 78 | | adult | U | | 63 | |
| 81 | 82 | | adult | U | | 81 | |
| 84 | 85 | | MA | F? | | 102 | |
| 92 | 94 | | MA | U | | 90 | |
| 99 | 100 | | MA | M? | | | |
| 102 | 103 | | MA | F | | | |
| 106 | 104 | 1 | adult | U | | 71 | |
| 108 | 109 | | MA | M? | | 90 | |
| 111 | 112 | | MA | M? | | 83 | |
| 114 | 115 | | YA | F | | 90 | |
| 116 | 118 | | J | F? | | 90 | |
| 121 | 122 | 1 | YA | F? | | 90 | |
| 126 | 125 | 1–2 | N/I | U | | 79 | |
| 127 | 129 | | J | U | | 90 | |
| 132 | 133 | | N/I | U | | 113 | |
| 135 | 136 | | MA | I | | 90 | |
| 139 | 140 | | MA | M | | 80 | |
| 143 | 144 | | J | F? | | 94 | |
| 149 | 148 | | MA | F | | 73 | |
| 150 | 151 | | MA | M | Pillow stones | 90 | |
| 154 | 155 | | MA | F? | | 90 | |
| 157 | 158 | 2 | MA | M | coffin? | 82 | Single nail may be intrusive |
| 162 | 190 | | MA | I | Partial cist | 90 | |
| 163 | 164 | | OA | M? | | 80 | |
| 171 | 170 | | MA | F? | | 78 | |

# APPENDICES

| Grave | Skeleton | Phase | Age | Gender | Type | Alignment | Comments |
|---|---|---|---|---|---|---|---|
| 172 | 173 | | adult | U | | 81 | |
| 175 | 176 | 1–2 | OA | F? | Coffin | 63 | Coffin fittings |
| 178 | 179 | | MA | I | Partial cist | 93 | |
| 181 | 182 | | YA | M | | | |
| 186 | 185 | | J | U | | 74 | |
| 191 | 192 | | MA | F | Pillow stones | 80 | |
| 196 | 195 | | MA | U | | 80 | |
| 199 | 198 | | MA | M | | 86 | |
| 200 | 201 | | adult | U | | | |
| 209 | 210 | | OA | M | | 71 | |
| 212 | 213 | | N/I | U | | 90 | |
| 215 | 216 | 1 | OA | M | | 90 | |
| 218 | 219 | 1 | YA | F? | | 87 | |
| 224 | 225 | | OA | M | | 87 | |
| 227 | 228 | | N/I | U | | 119 | |
| 230 | 231 | | OA | M? | | 111 | |
| 235 | 234 | | MA | M | | 97 | |
| 241 | 242 | | OA | M | | 135 | |
| 246 | 245 | | J | U | | 103 | |
| 247 | 248 | 2 | N/I | U | Partial cist | 117 | |
| 251 | 252 | | | | | 213 | plough-disturbed – cut not discernible/not analysed |
| 254 | 255 | | MA | F | | 106 | |
| 260 | 261 | | MA | F | Coffin? | 90 | Single nail may be intrusive |
| 263 | 264 | | OA | M | | 112 | |
| 266 | 267 | | MA | M | Pillow stones | 81 | |
| 269 | 257 | | adult | U | | | |
| 271 | 258 | | adult | U | | | |
| 276 | 273 | 2 | MA | F | | 97 | |
| 276 | 274 | 3 | N/I | U | | 97 | overlying pelvis of SK273 |
| 276 | 965 | | N/I | U | | | earlier burial within fill of G276 |
| 279 | 278 | | adult | U | | 133 | |
| 280 | 281 | | OA | F? | | 112 | |
| 287 | 286 | | adult | U | | 110 | |

# LIVING AND DYING AT AULDHAME, EAST LOTHIAN

| Grave | Skeleton | Phase | Age | Gender | Type | Alignment | Comments |
|---|---|---|---|---|---|---|---|
| 290 | 289 | 1 | MA | F | | 112 | |
| 292 | 293 | 1 | OA | M? | | 96 | |
| 295 | 296 | | adult | U | | 134 | |
| 300 | 299 | | MA | I | | 84 | |
| 304 | 303 | | MA | M | | 71 | |
| 307 | 306 | | J | U | | 90 | |
| 310 | 309 | | J | U | | 95 | |
| 311 | 312 | | MA | M | | 103 | |
| 316 | 315 | 1–2 | MA | U | | 86 | |
| 317 | 318 | 2 | MA | I | | 96 | |
| 320 | 321 | 1 | MA | I | | 131 | |
| 323 | 324 | | N/I | U | | 92 | |
| 326 | 327 | 3 | YA | M | | 92 | |
| 329 | 330 | | N/I | U | | 83 | |
| 332 | 333 | | YA | U | Partial cist | 102 | |
| 337 | 336 | | adult | U | | 115 | |
| 340 | 339 | 2–3 | MA | M | | 118 | |
| 343 | 342 | | YA | U | | 112 | |
| 346 | 345 | 2–3 | MA | F | | | |
| 349 | 348 | | OA | F | | 78 | |
| 353 | 352 | 1 | J | F? | | 113 | |
| 356 | 355 | | MA | U | | 86 | |
| 359 | 358 | | adult | U | | 93 | |
| 360 | 361 | | YA | I | | 89 | |
| 365 | 364 | | MA | M | | 123 | |
| 368 | 367 | 2–3 | J | U | | 90 | |
| 371 | 370 | | YA | M | | 86 | |
| 374 | 373 | | adult | U | | 113 | |
| 377 | 376 | | N/I | U | | 103 | |
| 380 | 379 | | J | U | | 86 | |
| 383 | 382 | | MA | M? | | 80 | |
| 386 | 385 | | N/I | U | | 98 | |
| 389 | 388 | | N/I | U | Pillow stones | 83 | |
| 392 | 391 | | J | U | Pillow stones | 94 | |

# APPENDICES

| Grave | Skeleton | Phase | Age | Gender | Type | Alignment | Comments |
|---|---|---|---|---|---|---|---|
| 395 | 394 | 1 | MA | I | | | |
| 399 | 398 | | adult | U | | 90 | |
| 402 | 401 | | adult | U | | 90 | |
| 404 | 404 | 2–3 | MA | M | Coffin | 157 | Three nail fragments |
| 408 | 407 | | MA | M? | | 96 | |
| 411 | 410 | | OA | F | Pillow stones | 90 | |
| 417 | 416 | | J | U | | 99 | |
| 425 | 426 | 3 | MA | U | | 90 | |
| 430 | 429 | | MA | I | | 97 | |
| 433 | 432 | | J | U | | 97 | |
| 436 | 435 | | MA | F | | 81 | |
| 437 | 438 | | adult | M? | | 92 | |
| 447 | 446 | | adult | U | | 90 | |
| 448 | 449 | | J | U | | 90 | |
| 453 | 452 | | MA | F | | 98 | |
| 454 | 455 | 1 | YA | U | Flexed | 90 | |
| 459 | 458 | | adult | U | | 90 | |
| 462 | 461 | | YA | M? | | 90 | |
| 465 | 464 | | MA | M? | | 81 | |
| 468 | 467 | 2 | MA | M? | Coffin | 94 | |
| 475 | 474 | 4 | N/I | U | | | |
| 481 | 480 | | MA | F? | | 107 | |
| 484 | 483 | | MA | M? | | 75 | |
| 487 | 486 | | OA | M? | | 72 | |
| 490 | 489 | | adult | U | | 92 | |
| 493 | 492 | | OA | F? | | 88 | |
| 496 | 495 | | MA | F? | | 87 | |
| 499 | 498 | | MA | M? | | 100 | |
| 512 | 511 | 1–2 | N/I | U | Partial cist | 82 | |
| 515 | 514 | 2–3 | N/I | U | | 90 | |
| 518 | 517 | | YA | U | | 92 | |
| 521 | 520 | 2 | OA | M? | | 95 | |
| 526 | 525 | | J | U | | 91 | |
| 546 | 545 | | MA | U | | 71 | |

# LIVING AND DYING AT AULDHAME, EAST LOTHIAN

| Grave | Skeleton | Phase | Age | Gender | Type | Alignment | Comments |
|---|---|---|---|---|---|---|---|
| 549 | 548 | | MA | U | | 75 | |
| 554 | 555 | | adult | U | | 71 | |
| 559 | 558 | | OA | M? | | 106 | |
| 564 | 563 | | OA | M | | 92 | |
| 577 | 576 | | N/I | U | | 90 | |
| 580 | 579 | | J | U | | 81 | |
| 584 | 585 | 4 | J | U | Coffin | 87 | |
| 588 | 589 | | YA | M? | | 90 | |
| 591 | 592 | | MA | U | | 84 | |
| 599 | 598 | | J | U | | 101 | |
| 602 | 601 | | MA | M? | | 59 | |
| 605 | 604 | | J | U | | 67 | |
| 607 | 608 | | J | U | | 85 | |
| 612 | 611 | | MA | F | | 94 | |
| 618 | 617 | | J | F? | | 65 | |
| 620 | 621 | | J | U | | | |
| 627 | 626 | 1 | MA | M | Coffin? | 73 | Single Fe bar |
| 628 | 629 | | MA | F? | | 90 | |
| 637 | 638 | | MA | F? | Coffin | 90 | Coffin furniture |
| 640 | 641 | 1 | adult | U | | 95 | |
| 659 | 658 | | J | U | | 58 | |
| 662 | 663 | 2 | J | U | Pillow stones | 73 | |
| 665 | 666 | | J | U | | 56 | |
| 668 | 669 | 3 | N/I | U | | 75 | |
| 671 | 672 | | MA | F? | | 85 | |
| 676 | 675 | | J | U | | 61 | |
| 677 | 678 | | MA | M | | 90 | |
| 682 | 681 | | J | U | | 53 | |
| 683 | 684 | | adult | U | | 90 | |
| 688 | 687 | | YA | F? | | 106 | |
| 689 | 690 | | J | U | | 90 | |
| 692 | 693 | | N/I | U | | 90 | |
| 695 | 696 | | N/I | U | | 90 | |
| 700 | 699 | | MA | M? | Coffin? | 110 | Single hinge |

# APPENDICES

| Grave | Skeleton | Phase | Age | Gender | Type | Alignment | Comments |
|---|---|---|---|---|---|---|---|
| 701 | 702 |  | adult | U |  | 90 |  |
| 706 | 705 |  | adult | U |  | 75 |  |
| 707 | 708 | 3 | MA | M |  | 115 |  |
| 710 | 711 |  | MA | F |  | 76 |  |
| 713 | 714 | 3 | adult | F? |  | 90 |  |
| 716 | 717 |  | J | U |  | 90 |  |
| 723 | 720 |  | adult | U | Cist | 95 | later burial in G723 |
| 723 | 724 | 2 | YA | M | Cist | 95 | first burial in G723 |
| 726 | 727 |  | N/I | U |  | 85 |  |
| 729 | 730 |  | N/I | U |  | 92 |  |
| 732 | 733 | 2 | MA | F? | Pillow stones | 100 |  |
| 735 | 736 | 1–2 | OA | U |  | 102 |  |
| 738 | 739 |  | J | U |  | 78 |  |
| 743 | 742 | 3 | YA | M? | Partial cist | 94 |  |
| 746 | 745 |  | MA | I | Flexed | 94 |  |
| 747 | 748 |  | OA | F? | Coffin? | 94 | Single nail |
| 751 | 752 | 1 | MA | M |  |  |  |
| 756 | 755 | 1 | MA | U |  | 90 |  |
| 759 | 758 |  | N/I | U |  | 86 |  |
| 762 | 761 |  | N/I | U |  | 84 |  |
| 765 | 764 |  | N/I | U |  | 84 |  |
| 769 | 768 | 1–2 | adult | U |  | 96 |  |
| 772 | 771 |  | adult | M? |  | 90 |  |
| 775 | 774 |  | MA | F |  | 90 |  |
| 779 | 74 |  | MA | M? |  | 92 |  |
| 782 | 783 |  | MA | M? |  | 86 |  |
| 787 | 786 | 1–2 | MA | U |  |  |  |
| 790 | 789 |  | MA | F? |  | 97 |  |
| 791 | 792 |  | J | U |  | 82 |  |
| 796 | 794 |  |  |  |  | 82 | not analysed |
| 799 | 798 | 2 | N/I | U | Pillow stones | 93 |  |
| 800 | 801 |  | J | M |  | 87 |  |
| 805 | 804 |  | J | U |  | 97 |  |
| 808 | 807 |  | N/I | U |  | 135 |  |

# LIVING AND DYING AT AULDHAME, EAST LOTHIAN

| Grave | Skeleton | Phase | Age | Gender | Type | Alignment | Comments |
|---|---|---|---|---|---|---|---|
| 811 | 810 | 1–2 | N/I | U | | 91 | |
| 812 | 813 | 1–2 | OA | M | Coffin? | | Single nail fragment |
| 815 | 816 | 2–3 | OA | M? | | | |
| 818 | 819 | | adult | U | | 83 | |
| 821 | 822 | | MA | M | | 87 | |
| 826 | 825 | 1 | N/I | U | | 135 | |
| 827 | 828 | | J | U | | 85 | |
| 830 | 831 | | N/I | U | | 89 | |
| 835 | 834 | 1–2 | J | U | | | |
| 836 | 837 | | N/I | U | | 90 | |
| 839 | 840 | | N/I | U | | 90 | |
| 844 | 843 | 1 | OA | F? | | | |
| 845 | 846 | | N/I | U | | | |
| 848 | 849 | | N/I | U | | 81 | |
| 851 | 852 | 4 | J | I | Coffin | 95 | |
| 855 | 856 | | J | U | | 88 | |
| 858 | 859 | | MA | F | | 100 | |
| 861 | 862 | | MA | F | | 82 | |
| 864 | 865 | | MA | M | | 86 | |
| 867 | 868 | 3 | YA | M | | 92 | |
| 870 | 871 | 3–4 | MA | F? | | 90 | |
| 873 | 874 | 3–4 | MA | M | | 90 | |
| 878 | 877 | 2–3 | adult | U | | | |
| 882 | 883 | 3 | MA | M | | | |
| 885 | 886 | | MA | F | | | |
| 888 | 889 | | MA | U | | 84 | |
| 891 | 892 | | N/I | U | | 90 | |
| 896 | 897 | | YA | U | | 82 | |
| 899 | 900 | 4 | J | U | | 120 | |
| 902 | 903 | | J | U | | 90 | |
| 905 | 906 | | N/I | U | | 93 | |
| 908 | 909 | | N/I | U | | 107 | |
| 911 | 912 | | adult | U | | 93 | |
| 914 | 915 | 3 | adult | U | | 76 | |

# APPENDICES

| Grave | Skeleton | Phase | Age | Gender | Type | Alignment | Comments |
|---|---|---|---|---|---|---|---|
| 917 | 918 | | adult | U | | 113 | |
| 922 | 923 | | J | U | | 90 | |
| 925 | 926 | | J | U | | 85 | |
| 928 | 929 | | MA | F | | 82 | |
| 932 | 933 | | MA | U | | 90 | |
| / | 146 | | N/I | U | | | Cut not recorded |
| / | 795 | | N/I | U | | | Cut not recorded |
| / | 1040 | 1 | N/I | U | | N/A | plough-disturbed |
| / | 1042 | | N/I | U | | N/A | plough-disturbed |
| / | 1043 | 1 | N/I | U | | N/A | plough-disturbed |

KEY

Age; N/I = neonate/infant; J = juvenile 6 - 17 yrs; YA = young adult 18–25 yrs; MA = middle adult 26 – 45 yrs; OA = old adult 46+ yrs; A = adult

Gender; M = male; F = female; I = intermediate; U = undetermined

## APPENDIX 3: OSTEOARCHAEOLOGICAL STUDIES: METHODOLOGY

The articulated human bones were analysed in accordance with recommendations by English Heritage (2002), Historic Scotland (1997) and BABAO/IFA (Brickley & McKinley 2004). The methods for osteological analysis are presented in summary below. The methods are reported in detail in the site archive report.

### Inventory

A full inventory of the skeletal remains was created for each burial. A numerical recording system was utilised where remains are coded as present (1) or absent (0). Long bones and bones with multiple elements (eg the scapula) were coded with multiple digits in order to provide a more accurate gauge of the bones present in the collection. Each bone had to be at least 50% complete to be recorded as present.

### Preservation and completeness

Alterations to the surface preservation of each skeleton were assessed and classified according to the recording scheme of the Museum of London (Connell & Rauxloh 2003; Powers 2007) as follows:

- Grade 1 = Bone surface is in good condition with no erosion; fine surface detail such as coarse woven bone deposition would be clearly visible (if present) to the naked eye
- Grade 2 = Bone surface is in moderate condition with some post-mortem erosion on long bone shafts but the margins of articular surfaces are eroded and some prominences are eroded
- Grade 3 = Bone surface is in poor condition with extensive post-mortem erosion resulting in pitted and eroded cortical surfaces and long bones with articular surfaces missing or severely eroded.

The percentage completeness of each skeleton was also determined. This was calculated by assuming that the skull comprises up to 20% of the skeleton, the torso 40%, the upper limbs 20% and the lower limbs 20%.

### Osteological age determination

The rate of developmental or degenerative physiological changes in the skeleton can be determined and correlated with chronological age. Ageing sub-adults skeletons (those under 18 years) is based on the rate of mineralisation and eruption of the dentition, both deciduous and adult, as well as the growth rate of the skeleton. In this study, sub-adult age determination was classified according to dental eruption (Ubelaker 1989) and long bone diaphyseal length (Sundick 1978; Scheuer & Black 2000), as well as rates of epiphyseal fusion (Scheuer & Black 2000), which assigned the metaphysis and epiphysis as unfused, fusing (growth plate only partially closed or line still visible) or fused. Adult skeletons were aged according to the rate of degenerative changes at the pubic symphysis (Brooks & Suchey 1990), the auricular surface (Lovejoy et al 1985) and the rate of tooth wear (Brothwell 1981). An individual age estimate was derived from as many estimates as were applicable and was then assigned to an age category as outlined in Table A3.1.

### Sex determination

The osteological determination of sex is based on the development of secondary sex characteristics that follow puberty. Accordingly, juveniles that had not yet experienced puberty are difficult to sex accurately from skeletal morphology.

An adult female skeleton is generally gracile with a large pelvic cavity that is modified for childbirth. The male skeleton is generally more robust than a female's, with a narrower pelvic cavity. In the current study, the biological sex of the adult skeletons was recorded based on the morphology of the pelvis, following Phenice (1969) and Buikstra and Ubelaker (1994), and the skull (Acsádi & Nemeskeri 1970). Sex determination was derived from as many methods as possible for each adult individual and an overall sex estimation was assigned according to Table A3.2.

Where no skeletal indicators had survived, the skeleton was classified as of undetermined sex. Individuals that showed mixed or ambiguous features, with some male and some female characteristics, were classified as indeterminate.

### Metrical and non-metric trait recording (normal data)

Skeletal metric data are recorded for a number of reasons; to calculate stature, to aid sex determination and to identify secular trends and ethnicity. In the current study, measurements were adopted following the definitions of Howells (1973) and Brothwell (1981) as outlined in Table A3.3.

In this study, individual height or stature was calculated using the formulae of Trotter (1970) and Trotter and Gleser (1952; 1958; 1977). The bone present with the lowest standard error was used for the calculation. Where applicable, the following indexes were also calculated: cranial capacity; cephalic index; platymeric index; and platycnemic index.

Non-metric traits are minor, genetically determined variations that occur in the skeleton, such as the retention of a metopic suture into adulthood. Such traits may be able to identify the 'biodistance' of one population group to another, as well as indicating potential inter-relatedness of individuals within a population as has been reviewed by Tyrrell (2000). The traits were recorded following Berry and Berry (1967), Finnigan (1978) and Brothwell (1981). Only adults were included in the study of non-metric traits.

### Dental health

A dental inventory was compiled in order to count all of the individual teeth or tooth positions, determine how complete the dentition was and calculate the accurate prevalence of dental pathology. Each tooth or tooth position was assessed and scored according to Table A3.4.

The presence or absence of dental caries and the location of any lesions were recorded for each tooth, following Table A3.5. Where the majority of the tooth crown was destroyed by caries preventing determination of the site of initiation, the lesion was recorded as gross, following Hillson (1996).

The amount of dental calculus and degree of alveolar disease was recorded following Brothwell (1981), using a grading system of (0) no data, (1) none, (2) mild, (3) moderate or (4) severe for both conditions where applicable. The presence or absence of enamel hypoplastic defects was also recorded for the deciduous and permanent dentition.

### Pathology

Any gross skeletal pathology was identified, recorded and diagnosed on the basis of skeletal descriptions presented in paleopathology references (Aufderheide & Rodríguez-Martín 1998; Ortner 2003).

In addition, and where applicable, every joint of the skeleton was assessed for joint disease (osteoarthritis) following Rogers et al (1987) and Rogers and Waldron (1995). Osteoarthritis (OA) is a progressive joint disease characterised by the loss of joint cartilage and subsequent bone pitting and new bone formation as well as a polished or eburnated bone surface. It is the most common joint disease identified in archaeological assemblages. OA is multi-factorial in its aetiology; it is related to increasing age, genetic predisposition, obesity, activity/lifestyle and environmental factors (Roberts & Manchester 2005). OA can also be caused by secondary factors such as trauma or disease, for example following bending deformities of the limbs in vitamin D deficiency rickets. The prevalence of OA in the past seems to be lower than in the present day (Waldron 2001). However, OA appears slightly more common in women than in men, both archaeologically and clinically. The joints often affected by OA in archaeological collections are the spine and the acromio-clavicular joint of the shoulder (Waldron 2001). The distribution of joints affected may vary over time, however, and can serve as broad indicators of lifestyle and occupation.

The presence or absence of the following pathologies were recorded for each vertebra present, following Rogers et al (1987) and Rogers and Waldron (1995): OA; osteophyte formation; bone fusion; intervertebral disc disease; Schmorl's nodes; and ligamentum flavum. Osteophytes (OP) are extra spurs or growths of bone that project from a bone surface and are often age-related. Intervertebral disc disease (IVD) or degenerative disc disease is commonly seen in skeletal material and is often asymptomatic. It can be manifest as coarse pitting on the superior and inferior surfaces of vertebral bodies and is often accompanied by new bone formation at the vertebral body margins (Rogers & Waldron 1995, 27). The changes most likely derive from degeneration of the intervertebral discs.

Rupture or vertical herniation of the intervertebral disc can cause pressure defects that result from the compression of material from the disc into the trabecular bone of the vertebral body. This process produces recognisable defects in the bone surface. These lesions are indentations that are often oval and have a smooth surface, and are called Schmorl's nodes (Rogers & Waldron 1995, 27). They can often measure up to 5mm in diameter and 1–1.5cm in depth (Aufderheide & Rodríguez-Martín 1998, 97). Schmorl's nodes are stress and activity-related lesions. They often occur when the intervertebral disc is subject to stress during childhood or adolescence, particularly as the central nucleus of the disc is still soft. Schmorl's nodes can be an indicator of activities that exert pressure on the spine, especially compression forces such as those incurred during lifting. The ligamentum flavum is a posterior spinal ligament that attaches to the articular capsule of the apophyseal joints and laminae of the vertebrae. Calcification or ossification of this ligament frequently occurs and may be age-related.

Enthesopathies are extra bone growths that develop for a variety of reasons, including trauma, stress or muscle activity, and may also be age-related.

The following areas of the skeleton were examined for the presence of enthesopathies: rotator cuff; deltoid tubercle; medial and lateral epicondyles of the humerus; radial tuberosity; olecranon process; iliac crest; ischial tuberosity; greater trochanter; lesser trochanter; linea aspera; tibial tubercle; soleal line; fibula; patella; posterior and inferior surfaces of the calcaneus; finger flexors; and metatarsal shafts.

Table A3.1
Age categories

| Age category | Age range |
|---|---|
| 0 | No data |
| 1 | Foetal/neonate |
| 2 | 1–6 months |
| 3 | 7–11 months |
| 4 | 1–5 years |
| 5 | 6–11 years |
| 6 | 12–17 years |
| 7 | 18–25 years |
| 8 | 26–35 years |
| 9 | 36–45 years |
| 10 | 46+ years |
| 11 | Adult |
| 12 | Sub-adult |

Table A3.2
Sex categories

| Code | Sex |
|---|---|
| 0 | Undetermined sex |
| 1 | Male |
| 2 | Probable male |
| 3 | Indeterminate |
| 4 | Probable female |
| 5 | Female |

# APPENDICES

**Table A3.3**
**Metric data recorded**

| Howells code | Brothwell code | Other metrics | Description |
|---|---|---|---|
| GOL | – | – | Greatest cranial length |
| XCB | – | – | Maximum cranial breadth |
| BBH | – | – | Basion to bregma height |
| – | – | CIL1 | Maximum clavicle length |
| – | – | GIL1 | Maximum glenoid length |
| – | HuL1 | – | Maximum humeral length |
| – | HuD1 | – | Maximum diameter humeral shaft |
| – | RaL1 | – | Maximum radial length |
| – | UIL1 | – | Maximum ulna length |
| – | FeL1 | – | Maximum femoral length |
| – | FeD1 | – | Subtrochanteric antero-posterior diameter femur |
| – | FeD2 | – | Subtrochanteric transverse diameter of femur |
| – | – | FHD1 | Maximum femoral head diameter |
| – | TiL1 | – | Maximum tibial length |
| – | TiD1 | – | Maximum antero-posterior diameter of tibia |
| – | TiD2 | – | Projective transverse diameter of tibia |

**Table A3.4**
**Dental codes**

| Dental code | Definition |
|---|---|
| 0 | No data |
| 1 | Tooth present in socket |
| 2 | Tooth lost ante-mortem |
| 3 | Tooth lost post-mortem |
| 4 | Loose tooth present |
| 5 | Tooth erupting |
| 6 | Tooth present un-erupted |
| 7 | Tooth present with abscess cavity |
| 8 | Tooth lost ante-mortem with abscess cavity |
| 9 | Tooth lost post-mortem with abscess cavity |

**Table A3.5**
**Dental caries codes**

| Dental code | Definition |
|---|---|
| 0 | No data |
| 1 | Absent |
| 2 | Occlusal |
| 3 | Lingual |
| 4 | Buccal |
| 5 | Mesial |
| 6 | Distal |
| 7 | Gross |
| 8 | Root surface |

# APPENDIX 4: OSTEOARCHAEOLOGICAL STUDIES: TABLES

Table A4.1
Demographic profile of the assemblage of Auldhame skeletons

| Sex \ Age | 0 | 1 | 2 | 3 | 4 | 5 | 6 | 7 | 8 | 9 | 10 | 11 | 12 | Total |
|---|---|---|---|---|---|---|---|---|---|---|---|---|---|---|
| Male | 0 | 0 | 0 | 0 | 0 | 0 | 1 | 8 | 19 | 15 | 14 | 2 | 0 | 59 |
| Female | 0 | 0 | 0 | 0 | 0 | 0 | 4 | 4 | 13 | 17 | 7 | 1 | 0 | 46 |
| Intermediate | 0 | 0 | 0 | 0 | 0 | 0 | 1 | 1 | 4 | 5 | 0 | 0 | 0 | 11 |
| Undetermined | 0 | 11 | 8 | 8 | 13 | 20 | 7 | 5 | 6 | 8 | 1 | 31 | 8 | 126 |
| Total | 0 | 11 | 8 | 8 | 13 | 20 | 13 | 18 | 42 | 45 | 22 | 34 | 8 | 242 |

Table A4.2
Summary of stature for the sexed adults from Auldhame

| Sex | N | Mean (cm) | Range (cm) |
|---|---|---|---|
| Male | 46 | 169.6 | 153–82 |
| Female | 34 | 158.6 | 151–67 |

Table A4.3
Summary of indices for the Auldhame adults

| Index | Sex | N | Mean (mm) | Range (mm) |
|---|---|---|---|---|
| Platymeric | Male | 51 | 76.9 | 62.9–96.2 |
|  | Female | 34 | 73.9 | 56.4–83.9 |
| Platycnemic | Male | 36 | 73.9 | 62.5–93.8 |
|  | Female | 33 | 75.1 | 63.1–142.2 |

Table A4.4
Frequency of cranial and mandibular non-metric traits

| Trait | Present/observed (% prevalence) | |
|---|---|---|
| Metopism | 4/57 (7%) | |
| Coronal wormians | 14/60 (23.3%) | |
| Sagittal wormians | 10/63 (15.9%) | |
| Ossicle at lambda | 7/53 (13.2%) | |
| Os inca | 0/60 | |
|  | Right | Left |
| Lambdoid wormians | 20/56 (35.7%) | 23/57 (40.4%) |
| Maxillary torus | 0/49 | 0/50 |
| Mandibular torus | 1/70 (1.4%) | 1/72 (1.4%) |

Table A4.5
Frequency of post-cranial non-metric traits

| Trait | Present/observed (% prevalence) | |
|---|---|---|
|  | Right | Left |
| Os acromiale | 1/66 (1.5%) | 3/68 (4.4%) |
| Septal aperture | 6/82 (7.3%) | 8/88 (9.1%) |
| Supracondylar process | 0/83 | 0/94 |
| Vastus notch | 2/69 (2.9%) | 3/67 (4.5%) |
| Calcaneus – single large joint | 33/68 (48.5%) | 31/76 (40.8%) |
| Calcaneus – double joint | 33/68 (48.5%) | 43/76 (56.5%) |
| Calcaneus – single small joint | 3/68 (4.4%) | 3/76 (3.9%) |

## Table A4.6
### Calculus presence and severity in individuals with one or more teeth by age from Auldhame

| Calculus score | Age category | | | | | | | | | | | | | |
|---|---|---|---|---|---|---|---|---|---|---|---|---|---|---|
| | 0 | 1 | 2 | 3 | 4 | 5 | 6 | 7 | 8 | 9 | 10 | 11 | 12 | Total |
| 0 | 0 | 11 | 8 | 7 | 12 | 15 | 5 | 6 | 10 | 23 | 9 | 33 | 8 | 147 |
| 1 | 0 | 0 | 0 | 1 | 0 | 2 | 0 | 3 | 4 | 0 | 0 | 0 | 0 | 10 |
| 2 | 0 | 0 | 0 | 0 | 1 | 2 | 6 | 7 | 19 | 10 | 4 | 1 | 0 | 50 |
| 3 | 0 | 0 | 0 | 0 | 0 | 0 | 2 | 2 | 5 | 9 | 4 | 0 | 0 | 22 |
| 4 | 0 | 0 | 0 | 0 | 0 | 1 | 0 | 0 | 4 | 3 | 5 | 0 | 0 | 13 |

## Table A4.7
### Calculus presence and severity on one or more teeth by sex in individuals from Auldhame

| Calculus score | Sex | | | | |
|---|---|---|---|---|---|
| | Male | Female | Indeterminate | Undetermined | Total |
| 0 | 20 (13.6%) | 14 (9.5%) | 3 (2.0%) | 110 (74.8%) | 147 |
| 1 | 4 (40%) | 3 (30%) | 0 | 3 (30%) | 10 |
| 2 | 19 (38%) | 15 (30%) | 7 (14%) | 9 (18%) | 50 |
| 3 | 11 (50%) | 9 (40.9%) | 0 | 2 (9.1%) | 22 |
| 4 | 5 (38.5 %) | 5 (38.5%) | 1 (7.7%) | 2 (15.4%) | 13 |

## Table A4.8
### Alveolar disease scores from the Auldhame skeletons by age

| Alveolar disease score | Age category | | | | | | | | | | | | | |
|---|---|---|---|---|---|---|---|---|---|---|---|---|---|---|
| | 0 | 1 | 2 | 3 | 4 | 5 | 6 | 7 | 8 | 9 | 10 | 11 | 12 | Total |
| 0 | 0 | 11 | 8 | 8 | 13 | 16 | 5 | 7 | 13 | 24 | 11 | 33 | 8 | 157 |
| 1 | 0 | 0 | 0 | 0 | 0 | 3 | 6 | 10 | 18 | 9 | 1 | 0 | 0 | 47 |
| 2 | 0 | 0 | 0 | 0 | 0 | 1 | 2 | 1 | 11 | 7 | 5 | 1 | 0 | 28 |
| 3 | 0 | 0 | 0 | 0 | 0 | 0 | 0 | 0 | 0 | 4 | 3 | 0 | 0 | 7 |
| 4 | 0 | 0 | 0 | 0 | 0 | 0 | 0 | 0 | 0 | 1 | 2 | 0 | 0 | 3 |

## Table A4.9
### Alveolar disease score from the Auldhame skeletons by sex

| Alveolar disease score | Sex | | | | Total |
|---|---|---|---|---|---|
| | Male | Female | Intermediate | Undetermined | |
| 0 | 24 (15.2%) | 17 (10.8%) | 3 (1.9%) | 113 (71.9%) | 157 |
| 1 | 16 (34%) | 18 (38.2%) | 5 (10.6%) | 8 (17%) | 47 |
| 2 | 13 (46.4%) | 7 (25%) | 3 (10.7%) | 5 (17.9%) | 28 |
| 3 | 4 (57.1%) | 3 (42.9%) | 0 | 0 | 7 |
| 4 | 2 (66.6%) | 1 (33.3%) | 0 | 0 | 3 |

## Table A4.10
### Ante-mortem tooth loss in the adults

| Tooth position | Maxilla | | Mandible | |
|---|---|---|---|---|
| | Right (R) | Left (L) | Right (R) | Left (L) |
| 1 | 0/55 | 2/54 (3.7%) | 2/67 (2.9%) | 1/65 (1.5%) |
| 2 | 1/52 (1.9%) | 1/57 (1.7%) | 0/68 | 2/64 (3.1%) |
| 3 | 1/54 (1.9%) | 0/57 | 0/70 | 0/69 |
| 4 | 3/52 (5.8%) | 2/54 (3.7%) | 0/71 | 1/70 (1.4%) |
| 5 | 3/55 (5.5%) | 0/57 | 1/72 (1.4%) | 2/68 (2.9%) |
| 6 | 6/53 (11.3%) | 4/50 (8%) | 11/75 (14.7%) | 16/72 (22.2%) |
| 7 | 5/57 (8.8%) | 3/51 (5.9%) | 10/75 (13.3%) | 7/70 (10%) |
| 8 | 5/51 (9.8%) | 3/46 (6.5%) | 11/73 (15.1%) | 4/69 (5.8%) |
| Total | 24/429 (5.6%) | 15/426 (3.5%) | 35/571 (6.1%) | 33/547 (6%) |

# APPENDICES

**Table A4.11**
**Ante-mortem tooth loss in the maxilla by adult age category**

| Age | 7 | | 8 | | 9 | | 10 | | 11 | |
|---|---|---|---|---|---|---|---|---|---|---|
| Tooth | R | L | R | L | R | L | R | L | R | L |
| 1 | 0/8 | 0/9 | 0/23 | 0/22 | 0/15 | 0/15 | 0/8 | 2/7 (28.5%) | 0/1 | 0/1 |
| 2 | 0/6 | 0/8 | 0/23 | 1/24 (4.1%) | 0/15 | 0/15 | 1/7 (14.2%) | 1/9 (11.1%) | 0/1 | 0/1 |
| 3 | 0/7 | 0/8 | 0/24 | 0/23 | 1/15 (6/6%) | 0/16 | 0/7 | 0/9 | 0/1 | 0/1 |
| 4 | 0/6 | 0/8 | 0/23 | 0/21 | 0/15 | 0/15 | 2/7 (28.5%) | 2/9 (22.2%) | 0/1 | 0/1 |
| 5 | 0/8 | 0/9 | 0/24 | 0/23 | 0/15 | 0/16 | 2/7 (28.5%) | 2/8 (25%) | 0/1 | 0/1 |
| 6 | 0/8 | 0/8 | 2/22 (9.02%) | 1/20 (5%) | 2/14 (14.2%) | 0/13 0/13 | 2/8 (25%) | 1/8 | 0/1 | 1/1 |
| 7 | 0/8 | 0/9 | 1/24 (4.1%) | 1/21 (4.7%) | 1/14 (7.1%) | 1/14 (7.1%) | 3/10 (30%) | 1/6 (16.6%) | 0/1 0/1 | 0/1 0/1 |
| 8 | 0/8 | 0/9 | 0/21 | 0/20 | 1/12 (8.3%) | 1/12 (8.3%) | 4/9 (44.4%) | 1/4 (25%) | 0/1 0/1 | 1/1 (100%) |
| Total | 0/59 | 0/68 | 3/184 (1.6%) | 3/174 (1.7%) | 5/115 (4.3%) | 2/116 (1.7%) | 14/63 (22.2%) | 10/60 (16.6%) | 0/8 | 2/8 (25%) |

**Table A4.12**
**Adult ante-mortem tooth loss in the mandible by age category**

| Age | 7 | | 8 | | 9 | | 10 | | 11 | |
|---|---|---|---|---|---|---|---|---|---|---|
| Tooth | R | L | R | L | R | L | R | L | R | L |
| 1 | 1/8 (12.5%) | 0/7 | 0/29 | 0/29 | 0/18 | 0/18 | 1/11 (9.1%) | 1/10 (10%) | 0/1 | 0/1 |
| 2 | 0/8 | 0/7 | 0/30 | 1/28 (3.5%) | 0/18 | 0/18 | 0/11 | 1/10 (10%) | 0/1 0/1 | 0/1 0/1 |
| 3 | 0/9 | 0/9 | 0/30 | 0/30 | 0/19 | 0/19 | 0/11 | 0/10 | 0/1 | 0/1 |
| 4 | 0/11 | 0/11 | 0/30 | 1/29 (3.4%) | 0/18 | 0/19 | 0/11 | 0/10 | 0/1 | 0/1 |
| 5 | 0/11 | 0/10 | 0/30 | 0/30 | 0/19 | 1/18 (5.6%) | 1/11 (9.1%) | 1/9 (11.1%) | 0/1 | 0/1 |
| 6 | 1/10 (10%) | 1/10 (10%) | 3/32 (9.4%) | 4/30 (12.3%) | 3/21 (19%) | 6/20 (30%) | 4/11 (36.4%) | 4/11 (36.4%) | 0/1 | 1/1 (100%) |
| 7 | 0/10 | 0/9 | 3/32 (9.4%) | 2/30 (6.7%) | 4/21 (19%) | 1/19 (5.3%) | 2/11 (18.2%) | 3/10 (30%) | 1/1 (100%) | 1/2 (50%) |
| 8 | 0/10 | 0/10 | 3/31 (9.7%) | 1/28 (3.6%) | 5/20 (25%) | 1/19 (5.3%) | 2/11 (18.2%) | 2/10 (20%) | 1/1 (100%) | 0/2 |
| Total | 2/77 (2.5%) | 1/73 (1.3%) | 9/244 (3.7%) | 9/234 (3.8%) | 12/154 (7.7%) | 9/150 (6%) | 10/88 (11.4%) | 12/80 (15%) | 2/8 (25%) | 2/10 (20%) |

**Table A4.13**
**Prevalence of ante-mortem tooth loss of the adults by age category**

| Age | Present/observed | % prevalence |
|---|---|---|
| 7 | 2/278 | 0.7 |
| 8 | 28/836 | 3.3 |
| 9 | 29/535 | 5.4 |
| 10 | 45/291 | 15.5 |
| 11 | 5/34 | 14.7 |

# APPENDICES

**Table A4.14**
**Ante-mortem tooth loss of the maxilla in the adults by sex**

| Maxilla | Males | | Females | | Intermediates | |
|---|---|---|---|---|---|---|
| Tooth | R | L | R | L | R | L |
| 1 | 0/23 | 0/26 | 0/29 | 2/27 (7.4%) | 0/4 | 0/3 |
| 2 | 0/21 | 0/27 | 1/28 (3.6%) | 2/28 (7.1%) | 0/4 | 0/4 |
| 3 | 1/23 (4.3%) | 0/26 | 0/29 | 0/29 | 0/4 | 0/4 |
| 4 | 1/22 (4.5%) | 0/25 | 2/27 (7.4%) | 2/27 (7.4%) | 0/4 | 0/4 |
| 5 | 0/24 | 0/27 | 3/28 (10.7%) | 0/28 | 0/4 | 0/4 |
| 6 | 0/22 | 0/23 | 6/30 (20%) | 4/27 (14.8%) | 0/4 | 0/4 |
| 7 | 2/25 (8%) | 0/22 | 3/29 (10.3%) | 3/26 (11.5%) | 0/4 | 0/5 |
| 8 | 2/22 (9.1%) | 0/22 | 3/27 (11.1%) | 3/22 (13.6%) | 0/4 | 0/5 |
| Total | 6/182 (3.3%) | 0/198 | 18/227 (7.9%) | 16/214 (7.5%) | 0/32 | 0/33 |

**Table A4.15**
**Ante-mortem tooth loss of the mandible in the adults by sex**

| Mandible | Males | | Females | | Intermediates | |
|---|---|---|---|---|---|---|
| Tooth | R | L | R | L | R | L |
| 1 | 0/32 | 1/30 (3.3%) | 2/30 (6.7%) | 0/31 | 0/8 | 0/8 |
| 2 | 0/32 | 2/30 (6.7%) | 0/32 | 0/30 | 0/7 | 0/8 |
| 3 | 0/32 | 0/31 | 0/31 | 0/32 | 0/8 | 0/8 |
| 4 | 0/36 | 0/33 | 0/29 | 1/31 (3.2%) | 0/8 | 0/8 |
| 5 | 1/36 (2.8%) | 1/31 (3.2%) | 0/29 | 1/32 (3.1%) | 0/8 | 0/7 |
| 6 | 7/36 (19.4%) | 8/33 (24.2%) | 4/31 (12.9%) | 5/34 (14.7%) | 1/8 (12.5%) | 0/7 |
| 7 | 6/36 (16.7%) | 4/32 (12.5) | 4/32 (12.5%) | 3/32 (9.4%) | 0/8 | 0/7 |
| 8 | 7/35 (20%) | 2/32 (6.3%) | 3/32 (9.4%) | 2/32 (6.3%) | 1/8 (12.5%) | 0/7 |
| Total | 21/275 (7.6%) | 18/252 (7.1%) | 13/246 (5.3%) | 12/254 (4.7%) | 2/63 (3.2%) | 0/60 |

## Table A4.16
### Dental abscesses in the adults

| Tooth | Maxilla | | Mandible | |
|---|---|---|---|---|
| | R | L | R | L |
| 1 | 0/55 | 1/54 (1.9%) | 0/67 | 0/65 |
| 2 | 1/52 (1.9%) | 0/57 | 0/68 | 0/64 |
| 3 | 0/54 | 1/57 (1.8%) | 0/70 | 0/69 |
| 4 | 0/52 | 0/54 | 0/71 | 0/70 |
| 5 | 0/55 | 1/57 (1.8%) | 0/72 | 0/68 |
| 6 | 5/53 (9.4%) | 1/50 (2%) | 4/75 (5.3%) | 2/72 (2.8%) |
| 7 | 2/57 (3.5%) | 1/51 (2%) | 1/75 (1.3%) | 2/70 (2.9%) |
| 8 | 0/51 | 0/46 | 1/73 (1.4%) | 2/69 (2.9%) |
| Total | 8/429 (1.9%) | 5/426 (1.2%) | 6/571 (1.1%) | 6/547 (1.1%) |

## Table A4.17
### Dental abscesses in the maxilla by age category

| Age | 7 | | 8 | | 9 | | 10 | | 11 | |
|---|---|---|---|---|---|---|---|---|---|---|
| Tooth | R | L | R | L | R | L | R | L | R | L |
| 1 | 0/8 | 0/9 | 0/23 | 1/22 (4.5%) | 0/15 | 0/15 | 0/8 | 0/7 | 0/1 | 0/1 |
| 2 | 0/6 | 0/8 | 0/23 | 1/24 (4.2%) | 0/15 | 0/15 | 1/7 (14.3%) | 1/9 (11.0%) | 0/1 | 0/1 |
| 3 | 0/7 | 0/8 | 0/24 | 1/23 (4.3%) | 0/15 | 0/16 | 0/7 | 0/9 | 0/1 | 0/1 |
| 4 | 0/6 | 0/8 | 0/23 | 0/21 | 0/15 | 0/15 | 0/7 | 0/9 | 0/1 | 0/1 |
| 5 | 0/8 | 0/9 | 0/24 | 0/23 | 0/15 | 0/16 | 0/7 | 1/8 (12.5%) | 0/1 | 0/1 |
| 6 | 0/8 | 0/8 | 0/22 | 0/20 | 1/14 (7.1%) | 1/13 (7.7%) | 2/8 (25%) | 0/8 | 0/1 | 0/1 |
| 7 | 0/8 | 0/9 | 0/21 | 0/20 | 0/12 | 0/12 | 0/9 | 0/4 | 0/1 | 0/1 |
| 8 | 0/8 | 0/9 | 0/21 | 0/20 | 0/12 | 0/12 | 0/9 | 0/4 | 0/1 | 0/1 |
| Total | 0/59 | 0/68 | 0/184 | 3/174 (1.72%) | 2/115 (1.7%) | 2/116 (1.7%) | 4/63 (6.3%) | 2/60 (3.3%) | 0/8 | 0/8 |

# APPENDICES

**Table A4.18**
**Dental abscesses in the mandible by age category**

| Age | 7 | | 8 | | 9 | | 10 | | 11 | |
|---|---|---|---|---|---|---|---|---|---|---|
| Tooth | R | L | R | L | R | L | R | L | R | L |
| 1 | 0/8 | 0/8 | 0/29 | 0/29 | 0/18 | 0/18 | 0/11 | 0/10 | 0/1 | 0/1 |
| 2 | 0/8 | 0/7 | 0/30 | 0/28 | 0/18 | 0/18 | 0/11 | 0/10 | 0/1 | 0/1 |
| 3 | 0/9 | 0/9 | 0/30 | 0/30 | 0/19 | 0/19 | 0/11 | 0/10 | 0/1 | 0/1 |
| 4 | 0/11 | 0/11 | 0/30 | 0/29 | 0/18 | 0/19 | 0/11 | 0/10 | 0/1 | 0/1 |
| 5 | 0/11 | 0/10 | 0/30 | 0/30 | 0/19 | 0/18 | 0/11 | 0/9 | 0/1 | 0/1 |
| 6 | 0/10 | 0/10 | 0/32 | 0/30 | 3/21 (14.2%) | 1/20 (5%) | 0/11 | 1/11 (9.1%) | 1/1 (100%) | 0/1 |
| 7 | 0/10 | 0/9 | 0/32 | 0/30 | 1/21 (4.8%) | 2/19 (10.5%) | 0/11 | 0/10 | 0/1 | 0/2 |
| 8 | 0/10 | 0/10 | 1/31 (3.2%) | 0/28 | 0/20 | 2/19 (10.5%) | 0/11 | 0/10 | 0/1 | 0/2 |
| Total | 0/77 | 0/74 | 1/244 (0.4%) | 0/234 | 4/154 (2.6%) | 5/150 (3.3%) | 0/88 | 1/80 (1.3%) | 1/8 (12.5%) | 0/10 |

**Table A4.19**
**Prevalence of dental abscesses of the adults by age category**

| Age category | 7 | 8 | 9 | 10 | 11 |
|---|---|---|---|---|---|
| Number observable | 278 | 836 | 534 | 291 | 34 |
| Number present | 0 | 4 | 13 | 7 | 1 |
| Prevalence (%) | 0 | 0.5 | 2.4 | 2.4 | 2.9 |

**Table A4.20**
**Dental abscesses in maxilla in the adults by sex**

| Sex | Males | | Females | | Intermediates | |
|---|---|---|---|---|---|---|
| Tooth | R | L | R | L | R | L |
| 1 | 0/23 | 0/26 | 0/29 | 1/27 (3.7%) | 0/4 | 0/3 |
| 2 | 0/21 | 0/27 | 1/28 (3.6%) | 0/28 | 0/4 | 0/4 |
| 3 | 0/23 | 0/26 | 0/29 | 1/29 (3.4%) | 0/4 | 0/4 |
| 4 | 0/22 | 0/25 | 0/27 | 0/27 | 0/4 | 0/4 |
| 5 | 0/24 | 0/27 | 0/28 | 1/28 (3.6%) | 0/4 | 0/4 |
| 6 | 3/22 (13.6%) | 1/23 (4.4%) | 2/30 (6.7%) | 0/27 | 0/4 | 0/4 |
| 7 | 0/25 | 0/22 | 1/29 (3.4%) | 0/26 | 0/4 | 0/5 |
| 8 | 0/22 | 0/22 | 0/27 | 0/22 | 0/4 | 0/5 |
| Total | 3/182 (1.6%) | 1/198 (0.5%) | 4/227 (1.8%) | 3/214 (1.4%) | 0/32 | 0/33 |

**Table A4.21**
**Dental abscesses in mandible in the adults by sex**

| Sex | Males | | Females | | Intermediates | |
|---|---|---|---|---|---|---|
| Tooth | R | L | R | L | R | L |
| 1 | 0/32 | 0/30 | 0/30 | 0/31 | 0/8 | 0/8 |
| 2 | 0/32 | 0/30 | 0/32 | 0/30 | 0/7 | 0/8 |
| 3 | 0/32 | 0/31 | 0/31 | 0/32 | 0/8 | 0/8 |
| 4 | 0/36 | 0/33 | 0/29 | 0/31 | 0/8 | 0/8 |
| 5 | 0/36 | 0/31 | 0/29 | 0/32 | 0/8 | 0/7 |
| 6 | 2/36 (5.6%) | 0/33 | 1/31 (3.2%) | 2/34 (8.8%) | 0/8 | 0/7 |
| 7 | 1/36 (2.8%) | 1/32 (3.1%) | 0/32 | 1/32 (3.1%) | 0/8 | 0/7 |
| 8 | 0/35 | 1/32 (3.1%) | 1/32 (3.1%) | 1/32 (3.1%) | 0/8 | 0/7 |
| Total | 3/275 (1.1%) | 2/252 (0.8%) | 2/246 (0.8%) | 4/254 (1.6%) | 0/63 | 0/60 |

# APPENDICES

**Table A4.22**
**Dental caries in the adults**

| Tooth | Maxilla | | Mandible | |
|---|---|---|---|---|
| | R | L | R | L |
| 1 | 1/46 (2.1%) | 1/40 (2.5%) | 0/46 | 0/49 |
| 2 | 2/48 (4.2%) | 0/47 | 0/54 | 0/52 |
| 3 | 2/51 (3.9%) | 1/52 (1.9%) | 0/58 | 0/60 |
| 4 | 1/46 (2.2%) | 0/49 | 0/62 | 0/58 |
| 5 | 1/48 (2.1%) | 1/54 (1.9%) | 3/64 (4.6%) | 2/59 (3.4%) |
| 6 | 2/46 (4.3%) | 5/45 (11.1%) | 4/58 (6.9%) | 5/55 (9.1%) |
| 7 | 4/53 (7.5%) | 4/47 (8.5%) | 3/62 (4.8%) | 6/59 (10.1%) |
| 8 | 5/36 (13.9%) | 2/38 (5.3%) | 3/42 (7.1%) | 6/45 (13.3%) |
| Total | 18/374 (4.8%) | 14/372 (3.8%) | 13/446 (2.9%) | 19/437 (4.3%) |

**Table A4.23**
**Caries initiation site for the adults**

| Caries initiation site | Maxilla | Mandible |
|---|---|---|
| Occlusal | 4 | 10 |
| Lingual | 0 | 0 |
| Buccal | 0 | 2 |
| Mesial | 8 | 2 |
| Distal | 6 | 7 |
| Gross | 14 | 10 |
| Root | 0 | 1 |
| Total | 32 | 32 |

**Table A4.24**
**Prevalence of dental caries of the adults by age category**

| Age category | 7 | 8 | 9 | 10 | 11 |
|---|---|---|---|---|---|
| Number present | 1 | 20 | 30 | 11 | 2 |
| Number observable | 256 | 722 | 412 | 213 | 26 |
| Prevalence (%) | 0.4 | 4.2 | 7.3 | 5.2 | 11.5 |

**Table A4.25**
**Dental caries in the maxilla by age category**

| Age | 7 | | 8 | | 9 | | 10 | | 11 | |
|---|---|---|---|---|---|---|---|---|---|---|
| Tooth | R | L | R | L | R | L | R | L | R | L |
| 1 | 0/6 | 0/8 | 0/19 | 0/19 | 0/13 | 0/9 | 1/7 (14.2%) | 1/3 (33.3%) | 0/1 | 0/1 |
| 2 | 0/6 | 0/6 | 0/22 | 0/21 | 0/14 | 0/13 | 2/5 (40%) | 0/6 | 0/1 | 0/1 |
| 3 | 0/7 | 0/8 | 0/23 | 1/22 (4.5%) | 0/13 | 0/13 | 2/7 (28.6%) | 0/8 | 0/1 | 0/1 |
| 4 | 0/6 | 0/8 | 0/21 | 0/20 | 1/15 (6.7%) | 0/14 | 0/3 | 0/6 | 0/1 | 0/1 |
| 5 | 0/8 | 0/9 | 1/22 (4.5%) | 0/21 | 0/13 | 1/16 (6.3%) | 0/4 | 0/7 | 0/1 | 0/1 |
| 6 | 0/8 | 0/8 | 1/20 (5%) | 3/19 (15.7%) | 1/11 (9.1%) | 2/12 (16.7%) | 0/6 | 0/6 | 0/1 | 0 |
| 7 | 0/8 | 0/9 | 0/23 | 2/20 (10%) | 3/14 (21.4%) | 2/12 (16.7%) | 1/7 (14.3%) | 0/5 | 0/1 | 0/1 |
| 8 | 0/7 | 0/9 | 3/18 (16.7%) | 1/18 (5.6%) | 2/7 (28.6%) | 1/9 (11.1%) | 0/3 | 0/2 | 0/1 | 0 |
| Total | 0/56 | 0/65 | 5/168 (3%) | 7/160 (4.4%) | 7/100 (7%) | 6/98 6(6.1%) | 6/42 (14.3%) | 1/43 (2.3%) | 0/8 | 0/6 |

**Table A4.26**
**Dental caries in the mandible by age category**

| Age | 7 | | 8 | | 9 | | 10 | | 11 | |
|---|---|---|---|---|---|---|---|---|---|---|
| Tooth | R | L | R | L | R | L | R | L | R | L |
| 1 | 0/7 | 0/6 | 0/22 | 0/24 | 0/9 | 0/11 | 0/7 | 0/7 | 0/1 | 0/1 |
| 2 | 0/7 | 0/7 | 0/27 | 0/24 | 0/12 | 0/12 | 0/7 | 0/8 | 0/1 | 0/1 |
| 3 | 0/6 | 0/9 | 0/26 | 0/26 | 0/16 | 0/14 | 0/9 | 0/10 | 0/1 | 0/1 |
| 4 | 0/10 | 0/10 | 0/25 | 0/24 | 0/16 | 0/13 | 0/10 | 0/10 | 0/1 | 0/1 |
| 5 | 1/9 (11.1%) | 0/10 | 1/28 (3.6%) | 0/26 | 0/17 | 2/14 (14.3%) | 0/9 | 0/8 | 1/1 (100%) | 0/1 |
| 6 | 0/9 | 0/9 | 0/26 | 3/26 (11.5%) | 3/15 (20%) | 2/13 (15.4%) | 0/7 | 0/7 | 1/1 (100%) | 0 |
| 7 | 0/10 | 0/9 | 0/27 | 1/27 (3.7%) | 2/16 (12.5%) | 3/16 (18.8%) | 1/9 (11.1%) | 2/7 (42.9%) | 0 | 0 |
| 8 | 0/8 | 0/9 | 2/18 (11.1%) | 1/18 (5.6%) | 1/9 (11.1%) | 4/11 (36.4%) | 0/7 | 1/6 (16.7%) | 0 | 0/1 |
| Total | 1/66 (1.5%) | 0/69 | 3/199 (1.5%) | 5/195 (2.6%) | 6/110 (5.5%) | 11/104 6(10.6%) | 1/65 (1.5%) | 3/63 (4.8%) | 2/6 (33.3%) | 0/6 |

# APPENDICES

**Table A4.27**
**Dental caries in maxilla in the adults by sex**

| Sex | Males | | Females | | Intermediates | |
|---|---|---|---|---|---|---|
| Tooth | R | L | R | L | R | L |
| 1 | 0/15 | 0/17 | 1/25 (4%) | 1/19 (5.2%) | 0/3 | 0/3 |
| 2 | 1/18 (5.5%) | 0/19 | 1/24 (4.1%) | 0/22 | 0/3 | 0/3 |
| 3 | 1/21 (4.7%) | 0/24 | 1/25 (4%) | 1/22 (4.5%) | 0/3 | 0/3 |
| 4 | 0/20 | 0/22 | 1/20 (5%) | 0/21 | 0/3 | 0/3 |
| 5 | 0/20 | 0/25 | 1/22 (4.5%) | 1/23 (4.3%) | 0/3 | 0/3 |
| 6 | 2/21 (9.5%) | 2/23 (8.7%) | 0/21 | 1/20 (5%) | 0/3 | 2/2 (100%) |
| 7 | 1/22 (4.5%) | 1/21 (4.7%) | 2/25 (8%) | 0/19 | 0/3 | 2/4 (50%) |
| 8 | 2/16 (12.5%) | 1/18 (5.6%) | 2/15 (13.3%) | 1/15 (6.6%) | 0/3 | 0/4 |
| Total | 7/153 (4.5%) | 4/169 (2.3%) | 9/177 (5.0%) | 5/161 (3.1%) | 0/24 | 4/25 (16%) |

**Table A4.28**
**Dental caries in mandible in the adults by sex**

| Sex | Males | | Females | | Intermediates | |
|---|---|---|---|---|---|---|
| Tooth | R | L | R | L | R | L |
| 1 | 0/20 | 0/21 | 0/19 | 0/21 | 0/5 | 0/5 |
| 2 | 0/26 | 0/23 | 0/22 | 0/23 | 0/5 | 0/5 |
| 3 | 0/26 | 0/28 | 0/24 | 0/25 | 0/6 | 0/5 |
| 4 | 0/31 | 0/28 | 0/23 | 0/21 | 0/6 | 0/6 |
| 5 | 0/31 | 1/26 (3.8%) | 2/23 (8.6%) | 1/25 (4%) | 1/7 (14.3%) | 0/6 |
| 6 | 2/25 (8%) | 1/24 (4.1%) | 2/23 (8.6%) | 4/24 (16.6%) | 0/7 | 0/6 |
| 7 | 1/29 (3.4%) | 2/26 (7.6%) | 2/25 (8%) | 4/25 (16%) | 0/6 | 0/6 |
| 8 | 1/21 (4.7%) | 1/21 (4.7) | 2/17 (11.76%) | 5/21 (23.8%) | 0/2 | 0/2 |
| Total | 4/209 (1.9%) | 5/197 (2.5%) | 8/180 (4.4%) | 14/185 (7.5%) | 1/44 (2.3%) | 0/41 |

**Table A4.29**
**Osteoarthritis in the adult skeletons from Auldhame**

| Joint surface | Affected/observed (% prevalence) Right | A/O (%) Left | Joint surface | A/O (%) Right | A/O (%) Left |
|---|---|---|---|---|---|
| Cranium – temporomandibular | 0/62 | 1/62 (1.6%) | Scaphoid – radiocarpal | 1/59 (1.7%) | 0/63 |
| Mandible – temporomandibular | 2/55 (3.6%) | 2/56 (3.6%) | Lunate – radiocarpal | 1/49 (2%) | 2/55 (3.6%) |
| Manubrium – sternoclavicular | 3/47 (6.4%) | 3/41 (7.3%) | Os coxa – sacroiliac joint | 12/110 (10.9%) | 12/104 (11.5%) |
| Clavicle – sternoclavicular | 6/63 (9.5%) | 6/61 (9.8%) | Os coxa – acetabulum | 9/115 (7.8%) | 7/121 (5.8%) |
| Clavicle – acromioclavicular | 14/54 (25.9%) | 11/46 (23.9%) | Femur – head | 8/107 (7.8) | 8/101 (7.9%) |
| Scapula – acromioclavicular | 10/32 (31.2%) | 7/48 (14.6%) | Femur – femoropatellar – anterior | 4/92 (4.3%) | 2/98 (2%) |
| Scapula – glenoid cavity | 3/75 (4%) | 5/82 (6.1%) | Femur – femorotibial – medial | 3/95 (3.2%) | 4/101 (4%) |
| Humerus – glenohumeral | 7/74 (9.5%) | 4/78 (5.1%) | Femur – femorotibial – lateral | 5/97 (5.2%) | 3/100 (3%) |
| Humerus – humeroulnar – trochlea | 1/82 (1.2%) | 2/88 (2.3%) | Patella – femoropatella | 6/70 (8.6%) | 5/66 (7.6%) |
| Humerus – humeroradial – capitulum | 2/81 (2.5%) | 2/83 (2.4%) | Tibia – femorotibial – medial | 3/94 (3.2%) | 5/93 (5.4%) |
| Radius – humeroulnar – trochlea | 3/81 (3.7%) | 1/84 (1.2%) | Tibia – femorotibial – lateral | 4/94 (5.2%) | 3/87 (3.4%) |
| Radius – proximal radioulnar – head | 1/75 (1.3%) | 0/74 | Tibia – proximal tibiofibular | 1/87 (1.1%) | 1/81 (1.2%) |
| Radius – distal radioulnar | 1/81 (1.2%) | 2/79 (2.5%) | Tibia – talocrural | 2/85 (2.4%) | 3/88 (3.4%) |
| Radius – radiocarpal – scaphoid | 1/82 (1.2%) | 2/81 (2.5%) | Fibula – proximal tibiofibular | 2/58 (3.4%) | 1/56 (1.8%) |
| Radius – radiocarpal – lunate | 1/82 (1.2%) | 2/81 (2.5%) | Fibula – talofibular | 1/79 (1.3%) | 0/85 |
| Ulna – humeroulnar – trochlea notch | 5/86 (5.8%) | 5/90 (5.6%) | Talus – talocrural | 2/66 (3%) | 2/82 (2.4%) |
| Ulna – proximal radioulna – radial notch | 0/90 | 1/90 (1.1%) | Talus – talofibular | 0/66 | 1/83 (1.2%) |
| Ulna – distal radioulna | 1/69 (1.4%) | 4/63 (6.3%) | | | |

# APPENDICES

**Table A4.30**
**Prevalence of osteoarthritis per joint surface observed (excluding hands and feet) by age category**

| Age | Affected/observed (% prevalence) | Age | Affected/observed (% prevalence) |
|---|---|---|---|
| 1 | 0 | 7 | 2/752 (0.3%) |
| 2 | 0 | 8 | 40/1773 (2.3%) |
| 3 | 0/3 | 9 | 155/1770 (8.8%) |
| 4 | 0/42 | 10 | 34/813 (4.2%) |
| 5 | 0/369 | 11 | 12/332 (3.6%) |
| 6 | 3/359 (0.8%) | 12 | 0/29 |

## Table A4.31
### Osteoarthritis by sex

| Sex | Males | | Females | | Intermediate | |
|---|---|---|---|---|---|---|
| Joint surface | R | L | R | L | R | L |
| Cranium – temporomandibular | 0/31 | 0/33 | 0/26 | 0/28 | 0/5 | 0/4 |
| Mandible – temporomandibular | 0/25 | 0/25 | 1/16 (6.3%) | 2/25 (8%) | 0/6 | 0/5 |
| Manubrium – sternoclavicular | 1/26 (3.8%) | 1/21 (4.7%) | 1/18 (5.6%) | 1/18 (5.6%) | 1/5 (20%) | 1/3 (33.3%) |
| Clavicle – sternoclavicular | 3/28 (10.7%) | 1/23 (4.3%) | 1/25 (4%) | 1/28 (3.6%) | 2/4 (50%) | 3/5 (60%) |
| Clavicle – acromioclavicular | 5/23 (21.7%) | 4/21 (19%) | 5/23 (21.7%) | 0/20 | 3/8 (37.5%) | 2/6 (33.3%) |
| Scapula – acromioclavicular | 4/21 (19%) | 5/20 (25%) | 3/24 (12.5%) | 0/20 | 3/7 (42.9%) | 2/6 (33.3%) |
| Scapula – glenoid cavity | 1/36 (2.8%) | 1/36 (2.8%) | 1/28 (3.6%) | 2/36 (5.6%) | 1/8 (12.5%) | 3/7 (42.9%) |
| Humerus – glenohumeral | 1/33 (3%) | 1/34 (2.9%) | 5/29 (17.2 %) | 2/31 (6.4%) | 2/8 (25.%) | 2/8 (25%) |
| Humerus – trochlea | 0/41 | 0/38 | 1/28 (3.6%) | 1/36 (2.8%) | 0/7 | 1/8 (12.5%) |
| Humerus – capitulum | 0/41 | 0/36 | 1/29 (3.4%) | 1/35 (2.9%) | 0/7 | 1/8 (12.5%) |
| Radius – trochlea notch | 1/40 (2.5%) | 0/37 | 0/29 | 1/34 (2.9%) | 1/8 (12.5%) | 0/7 |
| Radius – head | 0/35 | 0/33 | 1/27 (3.7%) | 0/30 | 0/8 | 0/7 |
| Radius – distal radioulnar | 0/43 | 0/34 | 0/27 | 1/29 (3.4%) | 0/6 | 1/8 (12.5%) |
| Radius – scaphoid | 0/43 | 0/36 | 0/28 | 1/29 (3.4%) | 0/6 | 1/8 (12.5%) |
| Radius – lunate | 0/43 | 0/36 | 0/28 | 1/29 (3.4%) | 0/6 | 0/8 |
| Ulna – trochlea notch | 1/43 (2.3%) | 0/37 | 3/29 (103%) | 4/36 (11.1%) | 1/7 (14.3%) | 1/7 (14.3%) |
| Ulna – radial notch | 0/46 | 0/38 | 0/30 | 1/37 (2.7%) | 0/7 | 0/7 |
| Ulna – distal radioulnar | 0/35 | 0/31 | 1/24 (4.2%) | 3/23 (13%) | 0/4 | 1/7 (14.3%) |
| Scaphoid – radius | 0/33 | 0/29 | 0/18 | 0/22 | 0/4 | 0/7 |
| Lunate – radius | 0/25 | 1/24 (4.2%) | 1/18 (5.6%) | 1/20 (5%) | 0/4 | 0/7 |
| Os coxa – sacroiliac joint | 0/53 | 1/47 (2.1%) | 5/35 (14.3%) | 5/37 (13.5%) | 4/9 (44.4%) | 0/4 |
| Os coxa – acetabulum | 3/52 (5.8%) | 2/52 (3.8%) | 3/37 (8.1%) | 2/41 (4.9%) | 2/10 (20%) | 1/10 (10%) |
| Femoral head | 0/48 | 1/48 (2.1%) | 6/37 (16.2%) | 5/34 (14.7%) | 1/8 (12.5%) | 1/9 (11.1%) |
| Femur – patella | 1/43 (2.3%) | 1/44 (2.3%) | 2/34 (5.9%) | 1/34 (2.9%) | 0/7 | 0/6 |
| Femur – medial tibia | 1/45 (2.2%) | 2/43 (4.7%) | 1/32 (3.1%) | 1/33 (3%) | 1/8 (12.5%) | 0/7 |
| Femur – lateral tibia | 2/45 (4.4%) | 1/43 (2.3%) | 2/33 (6.1%) | 1/33 (3%) | 1/8 (12.5%) | 0/5 |
| Patella – femur | 2/34 (5.9%) | 1/28 (3.6%) | 2/27 (7.4%) | 2/30 (6.7%) | 2/5 (40%) | 1/4 (25%) |
| Tibia medial | 1/44 (2.3%) | 2/39 (5.1%) | 1/36 (2.8%) | 1/32 (3.1%) | 1/6 (16.7%) | 1/8 (12.5%) |
| Tibial lateral | 2/44 (4.5%) | 1/39 (2.6%) | 1/33 (3%) | 1/29 (3.4%) | 1/6 (16.7%) | 1/8 (12.5%) |
| Proximal tibiofibular | 0/41 | 0/35 | 1/30 (3.3%) | 0/28 | 0/6 | 0/6 |
| Tibia talocrural | 0/38 | 1/41 (2.4%) | 1/32 (3.1%) | 1/32 (3.1%) | 1/6 (16.7) | 0/7 |
| Fibula – tibiofibular | 0/28 | 0/24 | 1/22 (4.5%) | 1/19 (5.3%) | 0/5 | 0/6 |
| Fibula – talofibular | 0/37 | 0/36 | 1/25 (4%) | 0/30 | 0/6 | 0/7 |
| Talus – talocrural | 0/27 | 0/32 | 0/27 | 0/32 | 2/7 (28.6%) | 1/7 (14.3%) |
| Talus – talofibular | 0/28 | 0/33 | 0/27 | 0/32 | 0/7 | 0/7 |
| Totals | 29/1298 (2.2%) | 27/1206 (2.2%) | 52/971 (5.4%) | 44/1042 (4.2%) | 30/229 (13.1%) | 25/234 (10.7%) |

**Table A4.32**
**Osteoarthritis of the vertebrae in the adults**

| Vertebra | Affected/observed (% prevalence) | Vertebra | Affected/observed (% prevalence) |
|---|---|---|---|
| C1 | 5/68 (7.4%) | T7 | 15/76 (19.7%) |
| C2 | 6/69 (8.7%) | T8 | 19/80 (23.8%) |
| C3 | 13/65 (20%) | T9 | 12/81 (14.8%) |
| C4 | 12/75 (16%) | T10 | 9/84 (10.7%) |
| C5 | 11/73 (15.1%) | T11 | 13/86 (15.1%) |
| C6 | 9/71 (12.7%) | T12 | 7/87 (8%) |
| C7 | 6/70 (8.6%) | L1 | 2/96 (2.1%) |
| T1 | 6/82 (7.3%) | L2 | 4/101 (4%) |
| T2 | 7/76 (9.2%) | L3 | 7/105 (6.7%) |
| T3 | 6/76 (7.9%) | L4 | 12/104 (11.5%) |
| T4 | 11/75 (14.7%) | L5 | 15/102 (14.7%) |
| T5 | 14/81 (17.3%) | S1 | 14/98 (14.7%) |
| T6 | 13/77 (16.9%) | | |

**Table A4.33**
**Prevalence of osteoarthritis of the vertebrae for the adults by sex**

| Sex | Male | Female | Intermediate |
|---|---|---|---|
| Vertebra | Affected/observed (% prevalence) | A/O (%) | A/O (%) |
| C1 | 2/33 (6.1%) | 3/30 (10%) | 0/6 |
| C2 | 3/34 (8.8%) | 2/28 (7.1%) | 1/6 (16.7%) |
| C3 | 7/32 (21.9%) | 6/26 (23.1%) | 0/6 |
| C4 | 5/35 (14.3%) | 6/33 (18.2%) | 0/7 |
| C5 | 3/33 (9.1%) | 6/33 (18.2%) | 0/7 |
| C6 | 2/32 (6.3%) | 4/32 (12.5%) | 2/7 (28.6%) |
| C7 | 2/31 (6.5%) | 3/31 (9.7%) | 1/7 (14.3%) |
| T1 | 3/39 (7.7%) | 2/30 (6.7%) | 1/8 (12.5%) |
| T2 | 3/37 (8.1%) | 2/29 (6.9%) | 1/8 (12.5%) |
| T3 | 3/36 (8.3%) | 3/33 (9.1%) | 0/6 |
| T4 | 4/33 (12.1%) | 5/34 (14.7%) | 2/6 (33.3%) |
| T5 | 6/34 (17.6%) | 5/36 (13.9%) | 2/6 (33.3%) |
| T6 | 4/33 (12.1%) | 8/34 (23.5%) | 0/5 |
| T7 | 5/35 (14.3%) | 9/33 (27.2%) | 0/4 |
| T8 | 6/37 (16.2%) | 10/33 (30.3%) | 2/6 (33.3%) |
| T9 | 4/38 (10.5%) | 7/32 (21.9%) | 1/6 (16.7%) |
| T10 | 2/39 (5.1%) | 6/32 (18.8%) | 0/8 |
| T11 | 3/40 (7.5%) | 9/33 (27.3%) | 0/7 |
| T12 | 2/40 (5%) | 3/32 (9.4%) | 1/7 (14.3%) |
| L1 | 1/46 (2.2%) | 1/36 (2.8%) | 0/8 |
| L2 | 1/48 (2.1%) | 3/37 (8.1%) | 0/9 |
| L3 | 2/50 (4%) | 4/37 (10.8%) | 0/9 |
| L4 | 4/49 (8.2%) | 6/39 (15.4%) | 1/10 (10%) |
| L5 | 6/48 (12.5%) | 6/36 (16.7%) | 2/10 (20%) |
| S1 | 5/46 (10.9%) | 6/36 (16.7%) | 3/8 (37.5%) |
| Total | 88/958 (9.2%) | 125/825 (15.1%) | 20/177 (11.3%) |

# APPENDICES

**Table A4.34**
**Prevalence of IVD and Schmorl's nodes in the adults**

| Vertebra | IVD: affected/observed (% prevalence) | Schmorl's nodes: affected/observed (% prevalence) |
|---|---|---|
| C1 | 0/66 | 0/66 |
| C2 | 5/69 (7.2%) | 1/69 (1.4%) |
| C3 | 13/70 (18.6%) | 1/70 (1.4%) |
| C4 | 14/79 (17.7%) | 1/79 (1.3%) |
| C5 | 18/75 (24%) | 3/75 (4%) |
| C6 | 14/73 (19.2%) | 2/73 (2.7%) |
| C7 | 12/76 (15.8%) | 2/76 (2.6%) |
| T1 | 0/83 | 0/83 |
| T2 | 0/80 | 3/80 (3.8%) |
| T3 | 0/82 | 2/82 (2.4%) |
| T4 | 2/83 (2.4%) | 8/83 (9.6%) |
| T5 | 2/83 (2.4%) | 16/83 (19.3%) |
| T6 | 4/82 (4.8%) | 31/82 (37.8%) |
| T7 | 3/81 (3.7%) | 42/81 (51.8%) |
| T8 | 4/82 (4.8%) | 48/82 (58.5%) |
| T9 | 4/85 (4.7%) | 44/85 (51.8%) |
| T10 | 3/87 (3.4%) | 42/87 (48.3%) |
| T11 | 3/89 (3.4%) | 46/88 (52.3%) |
| T12 | 5/86 (5.8%) | 41/86 (47.7%) |
| L1 | 4/89 (4.5%) | 34/90 (37.8%) |
| L2 | 7/94 (7.4%) | 37/95 (38.9%) |
| L3 | 10/95 (10.5%) | 34/94 (36.2%) |
| L4 | 9/95 (9.5%) | 24/96 (25%) |
| L5 | 10/97 (10.3%) | 12/97 (12.4%) |
| S1 | 7/97 (7.2%) | 4/97 (4.1%) |

**Table A4.35**
**Prevalence of IVD by age**

| Age | 7 | 8 | 9 | 10 | 11 |
|---|---|---|---|---|---|
| Affected/observed | 11/286 | 38/671 | 44/671 | 51/354 | 3/95 |
| % prevalence | 3.8 | 5.7 | 6.6 | 14.4 | 3.2 |

### Table A4.36
### Prevalence of IVD by sex

| Sex | Male | Female | Intermediate |
|---|---|---|---|
| Affected/observed | 74/973 | 49/813 | 15/178 |
| % prevalence | 7.6 | 6 | 8.4 |

### Table A4.37
### Prevalence of Schmorl's nodes by age

| Age | 7 | 8 | 9 | 10 | 11 |
|---|---|---|---|---|---|
| Affected/observed | 86/286 | 123/673 | 143/669 | 100/357 | 24/95 |
| % prevalence | 30.1 | 18.3 | 21.4 | 28 | 25.3 |

### Table A4.38
### Prevalence of Schmorl's nodes by sex

| Sex | Male | Female | Intermediate |
|---|---|---|---|
| Affected/observed | 250/973 | 144/805 | 32/177 |
| % prevalence | 25.7 | 17.9 | 18.1 |

### Table A4.39
### Comparison of adult stature of Auldhame with other medieval sites

| Site | Males | | | Females | | |
|---|---|---|---|---|---|---|
| | N | Mean (cm) | Range (cm) | N | Mean (cm) | Range (cm) |
| Auldhame | 46 | 169.6 | 153–182 | 34 | 158.6 | 151–167 |
| The Hirsel | 61 | 168 | 155–177 | 58 | 158.6 | 147–169.7 |
| St Helen-on-the-Wall | 240 | 169 | – | 268 | 157.4 | – |
| Fishergate | 205 | 171.5 | 155–190 | 73 | 158.8 | 145.170 |
| Newbattle Abbey | 7 | 168.8 | 163–172 | 6 | 157.6 | 150–166 |
| Isle of May Group A | 29 | 170.4 | 164–173 | 2 | 159.1 | 159–160.5 |
| Isle of May Group B | 8 | 173.7 | 166.6–180 | 3 | 161.2 | 155–166.5 |
| Castle Park, Dunbar | – | 170 | – | – | 157 | – |
| Wharram Percy | 169 | 168.8 | 163.1–174.5 | 119 | 157.8 | 152.7–162.9 |

# APPENDICES

## APPENDIX 5: ISOTOPE ANALYSIS: METHODOLOGY

Jane Evans

A summary of the methods of chemical measurements is presented here. Full details of the methods of enamel sample preparation and collagen extraction for the chemical analyses are contained in the site archive report.

As isotopic analyses necessitate destructive processing of bone and teeth, full osteological analysis of the selected skeletons was undertaken prior to sampling. Fifty bone and 20 tooth enamel samples were submitted for chemical analysis. The samples manifested a range of preservation states. The majority of the teeth were in a satisfactory condition for analysis. Following cleaning, most of the enamel samples were hard and translucent, which is a sign of good preservation.

Strontium was collected using Dowex resin columns. Strontium was loaded onto a single Re Filament with TaF following the method of Birck (1986) and the isotope composition and concentrations were determined by thermal ionisation mass spectroscopy (TIMS) using a Finnigan Triton multi-collector mass spectrometer. The international standard for $^{87}Sr/^{86}Sr$, NBS987, gave a value of $0.710284 \pm 10$ ($n.$ 20, $2\sigma$) for static analysis. All strontium ratios have been corrected to a value for the standard of 0.710250. Blank values were in the region of 100pg.

Oxygen isotope measurements on each sample were analysed in triplicate by thermal conversion continuous flow isotope ratio mass spectrometry (TC/EA-CFIRMS). The reference material NBS120c, calibrated against certified reference material NBS127 (assuming $\delta^{18}O$ of NBS127 = +20.3‰ versus SMOW; IAEA 2004), has an accepted value of 21.70‰ (Chenery et al 2010). The reproducibility of NBS120c during this set of analyses was 21.64‰ $\pm$ 0.26 (1$\sigma$, n=54). Drinking water values are calculated using Levinson's equation (Levinson et al 1987), after correction for the difference between the average published values for NBS120c used at NIGL and the value for NBS120B used by Levinson. Chapter 5.3.2 presents the drinking water values calculated using equation 6 from Daux et al (2008).

Collagen was extracted following the method of Brown et al (1988) and M. Richards (pers comm). Analysis of carbon and nitrogen isotopes was by continuous flow isotope ratio mass spectrometry (CFIRMS). The instrumentation is comprised of an elemental analyser (Flash/EA) coupled to a ThermoFinnigan Delta Plus XL isotope ratio mass spectrometer via a ConFlo III interface. The 1$\sigma$ reproducibility for mass spectrometry controls in this batch of analysis were $\delta^{15}N = \pm 0.16$‰ and $\delta^{13}C = \pm 0.12$‰; and for the batch control (external reproducibility of the full chemical procedure) was $\delta^{15}N = \pm 0.14$‰ and $\delta^{13}C = \pm 0.21$‰. A discussion of the preservation of collagen in this study is presented in the archive report for this site.

## Table A5.1
### Isotope results

| SK | Age | Sex | $\delta^{13}C$ PDB | $\delta^{15}N$ AIR | C/N | Mean $D^{18}O‰$ | Sr ppm | $^{87}Sr/^{86}Sr_n$ |
|---|---|---|---|---|---|---|---|---|
| 11 | 36–45 | F | −20.4 | 10.7 | 3.3 | – | – | – |
| 74 | 36–45 | PM | −18.6 | 12.7 | 3.4 | 18.13 | 158 | 0.70993 |
| 104 | Adult | Indet | −20.6 | 10.9 | 3.7 | – | – | – |
| 120 | 46+ | M | −19.0 | 13.2 | 3.5 | – | – | – |
| 122 | 18–25 | PF | −20.2 | 10.7 | 3.6 | 17.06 | 143 | 0.70875 |
| 140 | 26–35 | M | −19.5 | 13.2 | 3.4 | – | – | – |
| 158 | 26–35 | M | −18.5 | 14.4 | 3.4 | 17.33 | 92 | 0.71354 |
| 182 | 18–25 | M | −19.3 | 11.7 | 3.5 | – | – | – |
| 190 | 36–45 | Indet | −19.5 | 12.5 | 3.3 | – | – | – |
| 216 | 46+ | M | −20.6 | 11.5 | 3.4 | 18.15 | 75 | 0.70934 |
| 219 | 18–25 | PF | −21.1 | 11.7 | 3.4 | 17.16 | 84 | 0.71021 |
| 273 | 26–35 | F | −19.2 | 11.4 | 3.4 | – | – | – |
| 289 | 26–35 | F | −20.1 | 13.5 | 3.3 | – | – | – |
| 293 | 46+ | PM | −19.7 | 11.8 | 3.4 | – | – | – |
| 299 | 36–45 | Indet | −19.5 | 11.8 | 3.4 | – | – | – |
| 318 | 26–35 | Indet | −19.4 | 13.6 | 3.5 | 16.54 | 85 | 0.70964 |
| 321 | 36–45 | Indet | −19.8 | 12.4 | 3.4 | – | – | – |
| 327 | 18–25 | M | −17.9 | 13.1 | 3.4 | 19.00 | 142 | 0.70948 |
| 345 | 26–35 | F | −19.6 | 11.8 | 3.4 | – | – | – |
| 352 | 12–17 | PF | −20.1 | 12.2 | 3.4 | 16.51 | 92 | 0.70890 |
| 394 | 26–35 | Indet | −20.1 | 11.8 | 3.3 | 17.29 | 140 | 0.70933 |
| 426 | 36–45 | Undet | −18.7 | 12.4 | 3.7 | – | – | – |
| 429 | 26–35 | Indet | −20.4 | 11.0 | 3.5 | – | – | – |
| 452 | 36–45 | F | −19.9 | 11.1 | 3.5 | – | – | – |
| 467 | 36–45 | PM | −18.9 | 12.8 | 3.3 | 16.90 | 178 | 0.70939 |
| 498 | 26–35 | PM | −19.5 | 11.7 | 3.4 | – | – | – |
| 520 | 46+ | PM | −19.3 | 14.4 | 3.4 | 16.92 | 99 | 0.71059 |
| 585 | 12–17 | Undet | −19.1 | 12.1 | 3.4 | – | – | – |
| 592 | 26–35 | Undet | −19.4 | 12.1 | 3.5 | – | – | – |
| 626 | 36–45 | M | −18.6 | 13.4 | 3.4 | – | 200 | 0.708647 |
| 629 | 26–35 | PM | −19.3 | 11.7 | 3.4 | – | – | – |
| 663 | 6–11 | Undet | −18.9 | 13.7 | 3.4 | – | 460 | 0.708012 |

# APPENDICES

| SK | Age | Sex | $\delta^{13}C$ PDB | $\delta^{15}N$ AIR | C/N | Mean $D^{18}O‰$ | Sr ppm | $^{87}Sr/^{86}Sr_n$ |
|---|---|---|---|---|---|---|---|---|
| 669 | 1–5 | Undet | −18.3 | 12.6 | 3.5 | – | 285 | 0.708189 |
| 684 | Adult | Undet | −20.8 | 11.4 | 3.3 | – | – | – |
| 708 | 26–35 | M | −18.8 | 13.0 | 3.4 | – | – | – |
| 714 | Adult | PF | −19.8 | 11.7 | 3.5 | 18.31 | 128 | 0.71031 |
| 717 | 6–11 | Undet | −19.3 | 14.1 | 3.4 | – | – | – |
| 724 | 18–25 | M | −19.2 | 12.5 | 3.4 | – | – | – |
| 733 | 36–45 | PF | −19.2 | 14.4 | 3.4 | 16.83 | 108 | 0.71084 |
| 736 | 46+ | Undet | −20.3 | 12.3 | 3.3 | – | – | – |
| 742 | 18–25 | PM | −19.6 | 11.1 | 3.3 | 17.74 | 137 | 0.71004 |
| 752 | 26–35 | M | −19.9 | 11.6 | 3.4 | 17.50 | 168 | 0.70924 |
| 755 | 26–35 | Undet | −20.3 | 10.7 | 3.4 | – | – | – |
| 816 | 46+ | PM | −20.0 | 11.8 | 3.4 | – | – | – |
| 825 | 1–6 months | Undet | −21.5 | 10.9 | 3.4 | – | – | – |
| 843 | 46+ | PF | −20.8 | 10.8 | 3.5 | – | – | – |
| 852 | 12–17 | Indet | −19.1 | 13.4 | 3.4 | – | – | – |
| 868 | 18–25 | M | −19.1 | 12.2 | 3.3 | 17.52 | 167 | 0.71116 |
| 883 | 26–35 | M | −19.0 | 12.8 | 3.5 | – | 203 | 0.708647 |
| 915 | Adult | Undet | −19.6 | 13.1 | 3.4 | – | – | – |

Age and sex estimation of the individuals sampled for isotopic analysis together with the results of chemical testing. This corrects previously published results by sex (Lamb et al 2012). Ages are given in years unless specified. Adult is specified where remains could not be accurately aged. Abbreviations: M, male; PM, probable male; F, female; PF, probable female; Indet, indeterminate sex; Undet, undetermined sex where of unsuitable age or preservation existed; C/N, carbon to nitrogen ratio in collagen extraction; − denotes data not available.

The tooth enamel from SK626, SK663, SK669 and SK883 was very poorly preserved, and the elevated Sr concentrations linked with the isotope values (highlighted in grey in Table A5.1) within the range of the estimates of the environmental burial environment (Table A5.2) means that these samples were not considered to record life signals for strontium isotopes.

# LIVING AND DYING AT AULDHAME, EAST LOTHIAN

Table A5.2
Environmental samples (see Figure 83)

| SK | Sr ppm | $^{87}Sr/^{86}Sr_n$ | |
|---|---|---|---|
| 032s | | 0.708246 | Soil |
| 216d | 351 | 0.708551 | Dentine |
| 883d | 370 | 0.708311 | Dentine |

Mean carbon and nitrogen isotope results from Auldhame are summarised by the demographic sample in Table A5.3. Previous publication of the results has the sexes transposed.

Table A5.3
Summary of isotope results

| | N | Mean $\delta^{13}C$ | Mean $\delta^{15}N$ |
|---|---|---|---|
| *Age groups* | | | |
| Less than 12 months | 1 | −21.5 | 10.9 |
| 1–5 years | 1 | −18.3 | 12.6 |
| 6–11 years | 2 | −19.1 | 13.9 |
| 12–17 years | 3 | −19.4 | 12.6 |
| 18–25 years | 6 | −19.4 | 12.1 |
| 26–35 years | 15 | −17.5 | 12.3 |
| 26–45 years | 10 | −19.3 | 12.4 |
| 46+ years | 7 | −20.0 | 12.3 |
| Sex groups | | | |
| Female | 11 | −20.0 | 11.9 |
| Males | 19 | −19.2 | 12.6 |

# APPENDICES

## APPENDIX 6: MICROMORPHOLOGICAL ANALYSES: THIN-SECTION DESCRIPTIONS

Lynne Roy

Full descriptions of the three samples, 79, 80 and 82, taken from the buried soil [002] are presented here.

### Sample 79

This sample was removed from the west baulk section of the excavation and is described as a buried soil [002]. The sample was removed at the base of the soil profile to include the boundary with the natural clay subsoil [550]. The boundary between the buried soil [002] and subsoil [550] is curved and diffuse.

*Microstructure*

Comprises two contexts. The lowermost [550] is a poorly sorted, coarse natural subsoil with a single grained microstructure. Complex packing voids. The uppermost sediment has a complex packing structure comprising a mixture of bridged grain, intergrain and spongy structure. The vughs and voids are randomly oriented and are generally moderately linear.

*Matrix*

The lower context is poorly sorted silt containing some quartz and calcite and rare feldspar fragments. The matrix is yellowish-brown in plane polarised light (PPL). The upper context [002] is a poorly sorted sand in a well-sorted silt. The matrix has an angular blocky structure with close poryphoric related distribution and is dominated by sand-sized quartz grains. The matrix also contains plagioclase feldspar and calcite, although many of the mineral grains are masked by amorphous organic material. The matrix is dark reddish/yellowish-brown in plain polarised light (PPL) and very dark reddish-brown in cross polarised light (CPL). The matrix comprises a largely undifferentiated birefringence fabric due to being composed of isotropic masking humus.

*Basic mineral component and rock fragments*

The basic mineral component and rock fragments comprise approximately 40% of Unit 1 and 65% of Unit 2. Quartz is the dominant mineral component in both units and the majority of the quartz grains are angular to sub-angular with undulose extinction and weak birefringence. Other minerals comprise occasional calcite crystals, occasional plagioclase feldspars and rare orthoclase.

*Basic organic components*

Context 002 contains frequent charcoal components ranging from small flecks up to 10 Um in diameter to large cellular fragments up to 10mm in length. Most of the charcoal is black in PPL, although some is dark brown, indicating that some of the wood has been burnt throughout while a minority of other fragments have been charred. Many of the black charcoal fragments are associated with bright yellow or bright red coatings of the internal cells. There is much disseminated charcoal. There are frequent sand and silt sized charcoal fragments located within the matrix. The majority of the charcoal is decomposed and isotropic although some partially decomposed fragments with high interference colours and cellular structure are identifiable towards the top of the slide.

There are occasional (<10%), well-rounded organic clasts (16μm to 30μm in diameter), possibly representing biological excrement. There are rare (<2%) phytolith fragments within the matrix as well as rare silicified plant remains. The siliceous plant remains preserve some cellular structure but were not identifiable to species level.

*Pedofeatures*

Many of the mineral grains are coated with a thin layer of matrix; this matrix is often dark brown in colour (PPL). Some voids contain indistinct silty clay, dusty material that may be the remnant of ash. Some of the pseudomorphic voids feature orange highly fluorescent organic staining and are indicative of former plant matter. Fecal pellets were identifiable within some of the pseudomorphic voids

### Sample 80

This sample was removed from a buried soil [002] visible in the centre of the ditch overlying natural clay deposits [550]. The boundary between the two units is horizontal and diffuse.

*Microstructure*

Comprises two contexts. The lowermost [550] is a poorly sorted, coarse natural subsoil with a single grained microstructure. Complex packing voids. The uppermost sediment [002] has a complex packing structure comprising a mixture of bridged grain, intergrain and spongy structure. The vughs and voids are randomly oriented and of a spongy nature.

*Matrix*

The lower context is poorly sorted silt containing some quartz and calcite and occasional charcoal fragments. The matrix is yellowish-brown in plane polarised light (PPL). The upper context [002] is a poorly sorted sand embedded in clay. The matrix has a loose poryphoric related distribution and is dominated by sand-sized quartz grains. The matrix also contains some plagioclase feldspar and calcite crystals, although many of the mineral grains are masked by organic material. The matrix is dark reddish/yellowish-brown in plain polarised light (PPL) and very dark reddish-brown in cross polarised light (CPL). The matrix of the upper unit comprises a largely undifferentiated birefringence fabric as it is masked by isotropic organic material. The matrix of the lower unit comprises speckled crystallitic birefringence fabric.

*Basic mineral component and rock fragments*

The basic mineral component and rock fragments comprise approximately 40% of Unit 1 and 60% of Unit 2. Quartz is the dominant mineral component and the majority of the quartz grains are angular to sub-angular with undulose extinction. Other minerals comprise occasional calcite, occasional plagioclase feldspar and rare chlorite.

*Basic organic components*

There are numerous large charcoal fragments within the matrix; one large charcoal fragment measures up to 10mm in width and another up to 6mm. Several other large charcoal fragments measuring between 1mm and 3mm are dispersed throughout the matrix but the condition of these is not sufficiently good to identify species. Most of the charcoal is black in PPL although some is dark brown, indicating that some of the wood has been burnt throughout, while a minority of the other fragments have been charred. Many of the black charcoal fragments are associated with bright yellow or bright red coatings of the internal cells. There is much disseminated charcoal. Frequent sand and silt sized charcoal fragments are located within the matrix. There are seven large cellular charcoal fragments of unidentifiable species. Decomposed cellular organic fragments measuring up to 1000μm are dispersed intermittently throughout the matrix. Fresh and slightly decomposed organic components have very bright fluorescence colours, which decrease in intensity upon decomposition. Partially decomposed fragments with high fluorescence are identifiable throughout Unit 1, although a concentration of these fragments is located near the top of the slide.

*Pedofeatures*

Many of the mineral grains are coated with a thin layer of matrix; often this matrix is dark brown in colour (PPL).

**Sample 82**

This sample was removed from a buried soil [002] identified in the north-east of the site. It consisted of a single dark brown deep organic rich unit, similar in appearance to the buried soil visible throughout the rest of the site.

*Microstructure*

Comprises a single context with complex packing structure comprising a mixture of bridged grain, intergrain and spongy structure. The vughs and voids are randomly oriented and of a spongy nature.

*Matrix*

The lower context is poorly sorted silt containing some quartz and calcite and occasional charcoal fragments. The matrix is yellowish-brown in plane polarised light (PPL). The upper context [002] is a poorly sorted sand embedded in clay. The matrix has a loose poryphoric related distribution and is dominated by sand-sized quartz grains. The matrix also contains some plagioclase feldspar and calcite crystals, although many of the mineral grains are masked by organic material. The matrix is dark reddish/yellowish-brown in plain polarised light (PPL) and very dark reddish-brown in cross polarised light (CPL). The matrix comprises a largely undifferentiated birefringence fabric.

*Basic mineral component and rock fragments*

The basic mineral component and rock fragments comprise approximately 40% of Unit 1 and 60% of Unit 2. Quartz is the dominant mineral component and the majority of the quartz grains are angular to sub-angular with undulose extinction. Other minerals comprise occasional calcite, occasional plagioclase feldspar and rare chlorite.

*Basic organic components*

There are numerous large charcoal fragments within the matrix; one large charcoal fragment measures up to 10mm in width and another up to 6mm. Several other large charcoal fragments measuring between 1mm and 3mm are dispersed throughout the matrix but the condition of these is not sufficiently good to identify species. Most of the charcoal is black in PPL, although some is dark brown indicating that some of the wood has been burnt throughout, while a minority of other fragments have been charred. Many of the black charcoal fragments are associated with bright yellow or bright red coatings of the internal cells. There is much disseminated charcoal. Frequent sand and silt sized charcoal fragments are located within the matrix. There is one large elongated cellular organic fragment of unidentifiable species. Decomposed cellular organic fragments measuring up to 100μm are dispersed intermittently throughout the matrix. Fresh and slightly decomposed organic components have very bright fluorescence colours, which decrease in intensity upon decomposition. Some partially decomposed fragments with high fluorescence are located near the top of the slide.

*Pedofeatures*

Many of the mineral grains are coated with a thin layer of matrix; this matrix is often dark brown in colour (PPL). The soil has been almost entirely reworked and few pedofeatures remain.

# INDEX

Abercorn, Northumbrian ecclesiastical centre 133, 136, 171
   hogback gravestones 134
Aberlady, ecclesiastical settlement, cross fragments 58, 131–3, 137
   Pefferham 166, 169
Abernethy, church 160
Abingdon, Oxfordshire, buckle-plate 55
Aedan, king of Dalriada 129
Aelfred, priest at Durham 144, 146, 148
Alcuin of York 140–1, 167
Amlaib, king of Northumbria 140
Anderson, S 112
animal bone 4–5, 9, 12–13, 33, 37–8, 41, 43–5, 49, 74, 121–2, 126–7, 136, 138–9, 162
   butchery 121–2, 127, 138
   cattle 5, 33, 138
   deer 5
   dog 5
   goat 5
   horse 5
   pig 5, 114, 121–2, 127, 138
   sheep 5, 33, 121–2, 127, 138
'Antiqua Taxatio' or 'Old Extent' 151
Ardwall Isle, Kirkcudbright, Celtic church 137
Aspatria, graves 143
Auchmuthie family 157–8, 166

Bagimond's Roll 151–2
Baldred/Balthere *see* St Baldred/St Balthere
Baldred's Cave 2–4, 159
Balgone, North Berwick, copper alloy vessel fragments 73–4
Balladoole, Isle of Man, bridle & spur fittings 62, 64–5, 143–5
Balnakeil, Sutherland, Viking burial 66
Bamburgh, Northumberland 130, 136
Bara, East Lothian 145, 158
Barhobble, Dumfries & Galloway, church 82
Barrow, GWS 147
Bass Rock *see also* St Baldred/St Balthere 1, 140–2, 145, 149–50, 153, 156, 163–4, 167–8
Beaton, David, Cardinal 154, 156
Beaton, James, Archbishop 156
Bede 91, 130, 133, 136, 138, 160, 167–8
Beowulf 131, 149

de Bernham, David, bishop of St Andrews 150–1, 161
Bernicia 64, 133, 149, 169
Bidford-on-Avon, Warwickshire, Anglo-Saxon mount 55
Biggam, C P 138
Bimson, M 55
bird, bone 121–2, 127, 138
   in diet 127, 138
   solan geese 149–50
Brandon, Suffolk, Anglo-Saxon inkwell 59
Brechin, church, 160
Brough of Deerness, Orkney, chapel, copper alloy vessel fragments 72
Broxmouth, East Lothian, hillfort 4, 129, 148
Building 1, timber oratory 14, 16–17, 21, 49–50, 136–7
Building 2, stone-footed chapel, timber nave 14–16, 39, 49–50, 137, 159, 162
Building 3, stone chapel, chancel 14, 16–17, 38–9, 50–1, 89, 137, 150, 155, 162, 164
   consecration 150–1, 161
Building 4, burial aisle 14, 17–18, 20–1, 24, 31, 50–1, 71, 73, 155, 158, 162–6
   infant burial 20, 50–1, 166
   sandstone slabs/cover slabs 17, 164–5
   silver penny, Edward I 18, 75
burials *see also* graves
   alignment 13, 18, 21, 24, 31, 41, 43, 46, 49, 132, 161
   cist burials 4–6, 8, 19–24, 30–1, 41, 48–9, 112, 129–33, 142, 159, 161–2
   coffin burials 17, 19–25, 31, 41, 48–9, 68, 75–9, 82–3, 112, 142, 161–2
   earth cut 20–1, 31, 41, 45, 48–9, 132, 137, 161
      flexed 19–21, 45, 101, 142
   grave goods *see also* coarse stone, copper alloy, iron & Viking burial 31, 73, 75, 82, 111, 163, 170
   grave markers 31, 132, 136–7
   pillow stones 19–20, 22, 24–5, 31
   Viking *see separate entry*

Camperdown, Angus, socket stone 89
Carlisle Cathedral, Viking metalwork 143
Carnham, ecclesiastical settlement 166
Castledyke, Humberside, cemetery, pin 57
Castle Park, Dunbar 89, 111, 131, 135

# LIVING AND DYING AT AULDHAME, EAST LOTHIAN

The Catstane, Edinburgh, long cist cemetery  132, 169
Chalmers, George  146, 153, 157–8
chapel complex *see also* Buildings 1–4  11, 49, 136
    ditch  2, 8–9, 11, 13–14, 30–5, 37–8, 44, 49–50, 71–3, 78–81, 83–4, 91, 122–3, 126, 129, 131, 136, 138–40, 159, 161–3, 166, 171
    hearth/oven  11, 33, 35–6, 139
    pits/postholes  6, 11, 21, 30, 35, 73, 85, 122, 126, 163
    wall  8, 35, 38, 126
clergy at Auldhame
    Alexander, Patrick  156
    Bassindean, Andrew  153
    Harkars, John  152
    Hay, Archibald  156
    Hay, John  156
    Learmonth, William  156
    Lindsay, William  152–3, 156
    Swinton, David  156
Cliff Hut Site, 1948 excavation  6
cloisonné stud *see copper alloy*
Cnip, Lewis, Viking burial, belt set  62, 143
coarse stone objects  91
    gaming piece  21, 31, 91, 163
    hammerstone  91
    manuport  91
    spindle whorl  7, 39, 89, 92, 163
coastal erosion  5
Cockburnspath, silver hoard  135
coins  18, 74–5, 92, 131
    Edward I  18, 74–5, 92
    William the Conqueror  74–5, 92
Coldingham, East Lothian  130, 156, 166, 168, 179
copper alloy  53–8, 65–7, 70, 91–2, 163
    belt-set  31, 60–4, 66–7, 142–3, 91–2
    brooches  70, 73
    cloisonné stud  53–7, 91
    mounts  70–3
    pins  53, 57, 70–3
    ring buckle  31, 71–3
    vessel fragments  70–3
Coppergate, York, spurs, strap guide  64
Craig, D  86
cropmarks  2–3, 11, 34, 129, 131, 136, 167, 171
cross-incised stones  86–7, 137
Culterham, Cumbria, ecclesiastical settlement  166
Cumwhitton, Cumbria, cemetery  64–6, 143

Dalmeny, West Lothian, Norman church  160
Danelaw  61, 64–5, 134
David I  11, 147–8, 159
David II  152
Denny, Stirlingshire, copper alloy vessel fragments  73–4
dog-whelks *see shells*
Doon Hill, East Lothian  130–1, 171
Dowalton Loch, Dumfries & Galloway, copper alloy vessel  74
Dublin  61–2, 66, 143, 170

Dunbar  50, 130–1, 133, 137, 151–3, 157, 168–9, 171
Duncan II, Charter of 1094  146–8
Dunnichen Moss *see also Nechtansmere*  133
Dunsyre, Lanarkshire  148
Durham *Liber Vitae*  140
dye, dyeing  123, 138, 149, 153, 169

East Linton scabbard mount  56–7
Ecgfrith, king of Northumbria  130, 133, 168–9
Ecgred, bishop of Lindisfarne  168
Echa, anchorite  141
Edgar of Wessex  129
Edinburgh Castle, stone church, bone discs  86, 160
Edzell Church, Lindsay burial aisle  165
Eldbotle, Northumbrian settlement  2, 130–1, 135
Escomb, County Durham, church  160
Ethelfrith, king of Bernicia  129–30
Evison, V I  56

Fernie, E  160
fish, bone  121–2, 138
    in diet  105, 110, 114–16, 163
fishing  118, 123, 127, 138, 158, 163
Fishergate Priory, York, medieval burials  77, 79, 110, 112–13, 115, 119
Flaxengate, Lincoln, strap guide  64
Flixborough, Humberside, pinhead  55
Forman, Andrew, archbishop of St Andrews  154
Fothad, bishop of St Andrews  147–8

Gheghan Rock, settlement  5, 129
glass *see also copper alloy cloisonné stud*  55–60, 71, 73
    inkwell  58–60, 91, 138
Godfreyson, Olaf  116, 140
Gododdin, defeat at Catterick  129
Gordon, Berwickshire, silver hoard  135, 143
graves *see burials*
Greensted, Essex, stave church  160
Guthfrithson, Olaf  170–1

Haddington  148, 151–2
Hallow Hill, Fife, long cist cemetery  132–3
Halton, John, bishop of Carlisle  151
Hamilton, J R C, excavations at Auldhame  6–8, 11, 13, 30, 37, 140
    building  39
    cist  24
Hamwic, cabochon mount  55, 59
Hartlepool  50
Hedderwick  2, 148
Hesket in the Forest, burials  143
The Hirsel, Coldstream, Berwickshire, graveyard  96, 112–19
*Historia de Sancta Cuthberto*  130, 140, 146, 166, 168
*Historia Regum Anglorum*  166, 170
Hoddom, Dumfriesshire, ecclesiastical site  50, 86, 136
hogback tombstones  134

# INDEX

holy relics 144–6, 148–9, 155, 167–8
Hope-Taylor, B 131, 160
Hotham, North Humberside 58
Hownam Law, Roxburghshire 148
human remains
    bone 4–5, 7, 9–13, 35, 41, 72, 93–4, 96–7, 99–106, 110–11, 113–19, 146
    juvenile 18, 20, 22, 29, 31, 45, 47, 49, 51–2, 94, 96, 104–5, 111–16, 166
    neonate/infant 10, 20, 22, 29, 31, 41, 45, 47, 49–51, 94, 105, 111–15, 137, 157–8, 161, 166
Hume of Spott, George 153

Inchcolm & Aberdour, ecclesiastical house & island retreat 167
Inchmarnock 111–17, 137, 146, 149
Inglis, Alexander, archdeacon of St Andrews 153
Inglis, George, of Lochend, Dunbar 153
Inishkea North, County Mayo, Ireland, processing of dog-whelk dye 138
Inveresk 148, 158, 166
Inverkeilor, Angus, socket stone 89
Iona, ecclesiastical site 133, 136, 149, 160–1, 167–8
    & Hinba, island retreat 167
iron 64–8, 73, 75–84, 92, 162–3
    buckles 64–7, 142
    coffin fittings 24–5, 31, 75–9, 81–3, 162
    knives 75, 80–2
    nails 21, 23–5, 75–9, 81–3, 92, 142, 162
    rods 75–6, 79, 81–3, 92
    spearhead 31, 65–6, 68, 142
    spurs 31, 64, 66–7, 142
    strap guide 64–5, 67–8, 142
    tools 75, 79–81, 83, 163
ironworking 85–6, 92, 125, 163
Isle of May, ecclesiastical site 75, 96, 111–17, 127, 141, 146, 149–50, 162–3, 167
    & Kilrenny, island retreat 167

James, Alan 166
Jarrow, Northumbrian monastery 138, 168
Jedburgh Abbey, Roxburghshire 77, 86, 135, 146, 166
Jedworths 166
Johnson South, T 147

Kilmainham, County Dublin 66
Kiloran Bay, Colonsay, burial 61–2, 142–3, 145
Kilrimond, Celtic church 147
Kilspindie Castle, Aberlady 131
Kingston, brooch 55
Kingston Common, North Berwick, long cist cemetery 132, 159
Kirk Hill, East Lothian, enclosure 136
Kirk-town of Auldhame 6
Kneep *see Cnip*
Knowes, East Lothian, long cist cemetery 2, 133, 148

Lamberton, William, bishop of St Andrews 149
Lauder, John, minister of Tyninghame 154, 157–8
Lauder, Robert of Bass 149–50, 153
Lawrie, A C 148
lead 54–5, 72, 92, 162
leather, leatherworking 61–2, 65, 67–8, 71–2, 80, 83, 92, 163
Legatine Council of 1239 150
Leuchars, Fife, Norman church 160
Lindisfarne, ecclesiastical site 130, 134, 136, 140–1, 146–7, 149, 160, 166–70
    & Inner Farne, island retreat 167
Linlithgow Carmelite Friary, copper alloy stud 72, 74
Little Auldhame 154
long-cist cemeteries 133, 159
Lurk Lane, Beverley, inkwell 58–9
Lunt, D A 119

Mail, Shetland, Viking grave 143
Manor Valley, Peeblesshire 148
maps 6, 164
    Adair (1682 & 1736) 6
    Ainslie 6
    Blaeu's Atlas 5–6
    First Edition Ordnance Survey 6, 154, 161
    Forrest (1802) 5–6
    Hamilton's sketch map 7, 11
    Roy's Military Survey 6, 164
    Sharp 5–6
    Thomson 6
Markle, sword 132
Mays, S 113–15
Meal Vennel, Perth, copper alloy vessel 74
Meikle Auldhame 154
Melrose 146, 166–7
Melrose Chronicle 140
metalworking 83, 92, 136, 139, 163
Midross, Loch Lomond, enclosed cemetery 139
Milfield, Northumbrian settlement 130–1
Monifieth, Angus, socket stone 89
Montfode, Ardrossan, cemetery 139
Morham, church, cross fragments 133, 137, 145
Mote of Mark, Kirkcudbrightshire, cross-incised stone 86
Müldner, G & Richards, M 110, 114

Nechtansmere *see also Dunnichen Moss* 133, 160
Newark Bay, Orkney 110
Newbattle Abbey, Midlothian 112–13, 117
Norham, Northumberland 166–8, 170
Norman Conquest 134
Northhampton, iron spurs 64
Northumbria 56, 58, 64, 129–34, 136–41, 144, 146–7, 159–60, 166–8, 170–1

O'Carragain, T 137, 160
'Oldham' village 6, 158, 164
Oswald, king of Northumbria 129, 133, 168

231

Oswiu, king of Northumbria 168
Otterburn, Adam 51, 153–8, 163–6

Parkburn, Dalkeith, long cist cemetery 132
Parliament House, burials 111
Perth, Carmelite Friary 83
Viking graves, objects 70, 74, 86, 143
Piccolimini, Andreas, Pope Pius II 152
pilgrims, pilgrimage 146, 152, 168
Pinder, M 56
place-names 130–1, 133–4, 140, 142, 154, 166, 168
*plaggen* soil 125–6, 139
plant remains 85–6, 106, 114, 121–4, 126
Portmahomack, Ross & Cromarty, monastery 136, 149
pottery 4–5, 7, 38, 53, 68–70, 90–2, 129, 171
    Developed Stamford Ware 70, 92
    Scottish White Gritty Ware 33, 35, 68–70, 129, 162–3
    Yorkshire Type Ware 68, 70
Prestonkirk, parish 2, 140, 151
Proudfoot, E & Aliaga-Kelly, C 130, 132–3, 148

quartz pebbles *see also* grave markers 21, 90–1, 163

radiocarbon dating 11, 14, 72, 109, 111–12
Ragman Roll 152
Ratho, Midlothian, Anglian settlement 130–2
Reformation 147, 154, 156–8, 162, 165–6, 168
Reidhall, Edinburgh 151
Renfrew/Paisley population study 115
Repton, Derbyshire 145
Restennet, Angus, church 160
Roberts, C & Cox, M 111, 114, 116, 119
Rodwell, W 83
Rollason, D 130, 140, 146

St Abb's Head, Anglian monastery *see also Kirk Hill* 168
St Andrews, Fife 112–13, 117, 147–50, 152–6, 160–1
    links with Auldhame 147–50, 152–4, 156, 159, 161
St Baldred/St Balthere 1–2, 4, 6, 116, 130, 133, 140–2, 146, 148–50, 155, 158–9, 161, 163–4, 167–71
    Auldhame & Tyninghame 116, 130, 133, 140–2, 144, 146, 148–52, 166–8, 170–1
    Bass Rock 141–2, 167–8
    relics 144–6, 148–9, 155, 167, 152
St Blane's, Bute, graveyard 161
St Cuthbert 130, 147
    church 160
    pectoral cross 55–6
St Ethernan on the May, pilgrimage 146, 167
St Giles, Edinburgh 72, 163
    copper alloy stud 155
St Helen-on-the-Walls, York 112–13, 115, 117, 119
St Helen's Church, Cockburnspath, silver hoard 135
St Magnus Church, Egilsay 160
St Marnock, Inchmarnock 146
St Mary, Whitekirk, 151

St Michael's, Workington, Cumbria, belt set 62
St Olaf's Churchyard, Whiteness, Shetland, axe 143
St Ronan's, Iona 77, 83
St Serf's Isle, Lochleven 167
Sancton, Lincolnshire, pin 55
Sarre brooch, Kent 56
Scar, Sanday, Orkney, Viking boat burial 62
Schevez, John, of Greenspott 153
Schevez, William, archbishop of St Andrews 153
Scoughall Estate 2, 147–50, 153, 156–8, 168
*scriptorium* 138, 169
Seacliff 1, 4, 141, 145, 149, 152, 157–8
    cist burials 5
    roundhouses 129
shells 4, 6, 13–14, 21, 25, 121, 123
    dog-whelks 14, 123, 138, 149
    periwinkles 33, 123, 136
Siege of Edinburgh, AD638–753 129–30
silver *see also* copper alloy cloisonné stud, coins 70–1, 74–5, 92, 135
Sligo, G 2, 4, 159
socket stones 14, 17, 86, 88–9, 137
Southampton, inkwell 59
South Newbold, Yorkshire, pin 57–8
Sprouston, Roxburghshire, Anglian settlement 131, 136
Stephanus, Eddius, *Life of Wilfred* 130–1
stone *see also* coarse stone objects 86–9
    cross-incised stones *see separate entry*
    socket stones *see separate entry*
Sutton Hoo, *millefiori*, scabbard mounts, sword 55–7, 132
Symeon of Durham *Historia Dunelmensis Ecclesiae, History of the Kings of England & Historia de Sancto Cuthberto* 140, 146, 166, 168

textiles, textile working 61–2, 64, 67–8, 71–3, 92, 138, 163
Thirlings, Anglian settlement 131
Thomas, AC 133
Thornybank, Midlothian, long cist cemetery 111, 132
Thwing, Yorkshire, *Grubenhaus*, pin 58
Tigbrethingham, ecclesiastical settlement 166
Tostock, Suffolk, buckle 56
Towton, Yorkshire, battle site 96, 110
Trumwine, bishop 133
Tyninghame, ecclesiastical site *see also St Baldred/St Balthere* 2, 116, 130–1, 133, 140–2, 144–8, 150–4, 156–8, 166–71
    cross fragments 133, 137, 140
    hogback gravestones 140
    parish union with Auldhame & Whitekirk 145–6, 157
Tyre, Levantine coast, processing of dog-whelk dye 138

Viking, burial 1, 19, 26, 45, 50, 60–8, 75, 82, 91, 111, 129, 134, 142–5, 166, 170–1
    raids 116, 134, 143–4, 146, 149, 168

Waldron, T 111, 115, 119
Westness, Rousay, Orkney, Viking cemetery 66
Wetwang, Yorkshire, Iron Age cemetery 110

# INDEX

Wetweather Cave, Geodha Smoo, Durness, Sutherland 138
Wharram Percy, Yorkshire, medieval burials 110–15, 118
Whissonset, Norfolk, pinhead 55
Whitby Abbey, Yorkshire 50
Whitekirk, ecclesiastical site *see also St Baldred/St Balthere* 2, 6, 131, 146, 148
   parish union with Tyninghame 145–6, 157
   timber hall 131
   votive images 152

Whithorn, ecclesiastical site, grave goods, quartz pebbles 61, 72, 77–8, 82–3, 91, 136, 139, 160
Wilfred, Bishop of York 130
Wright, LE & Yoder, CJ 112

Yeavering, ecclesiastical site 130–1, 136–7, 159–60
York 143
   miscellaneous objects 58, 62, 64–5, 68, 77, 79, 143
   timber church 136

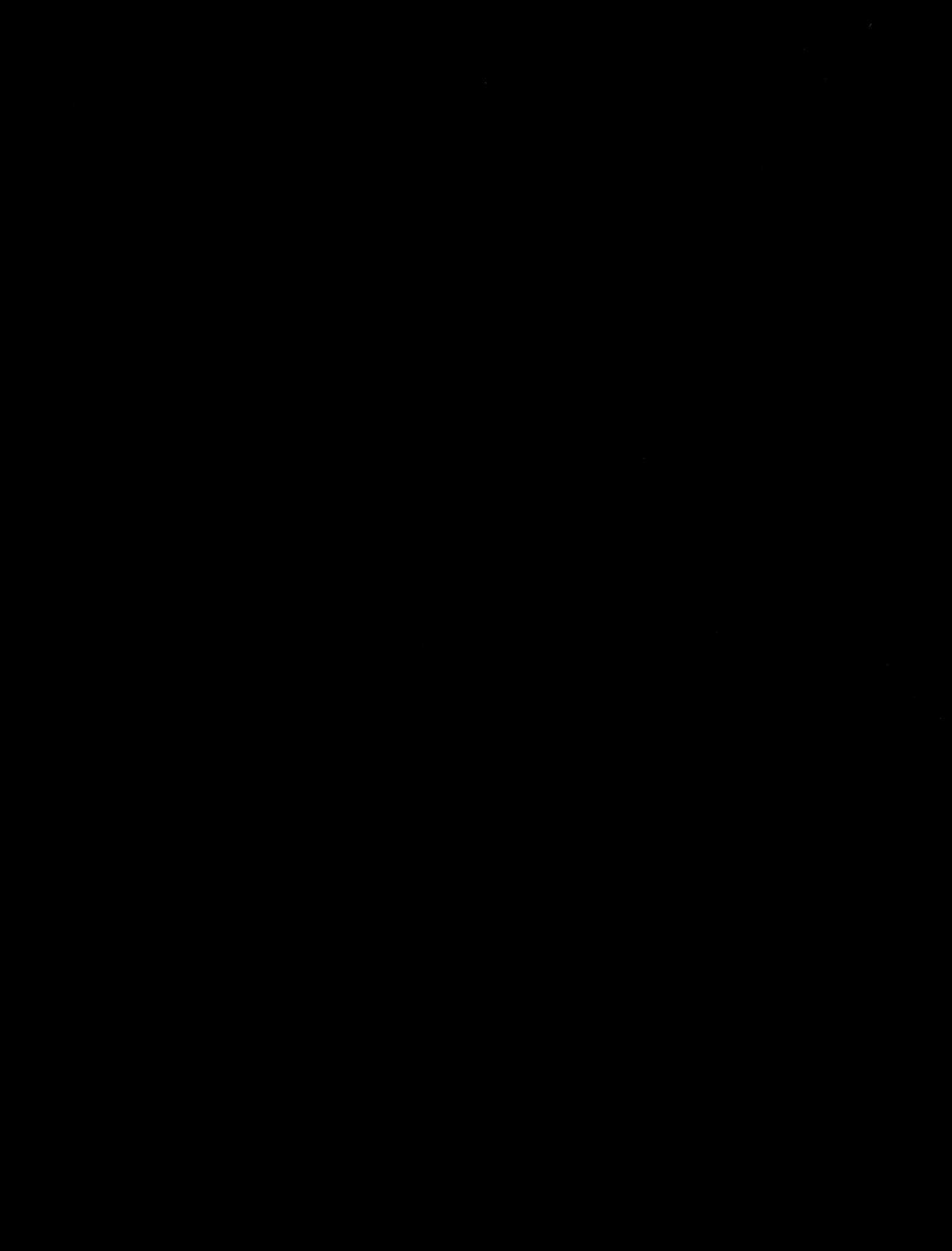